POSUKA DEMIZU

Wow, an anime version was announced! I can't wait for 2019!

By the way, when are you reading this book?

Of course there are those who are reading this right when it comes out, but perhaps there are those reading this after the anime has started airing.
Are there people reading after the anime has finished?
If you're from the future, let me know what you think!

By the way, 2019 is when Krone was born. I'm looking forward to reaching all the characters' birthdays slowly as we progress into the future.

KAIU SHIRAI

Writer Shirai's personal highlights for *The Promised Neverland* fanatics, part 6!

1. Gillian's patches (the way they're drawn is amazing!)

2. The demon monkey's reactions (they're fun)

3. Emma's right hand on the cover and the left hand under the cover (the location!!)

Please enjoy this volume!

(Did you find where the "umeboshi in the shelter" is in volume 7? It's not just in chapter 58, but also in the bonus pages for volume 7!)

Posuka Demizu debuted as a manga artist with the 2013 *CoroCoro* series *Oreca Monster Bouken Retsuden*. A collection of illustrations, *The Art of Posuka Demizu,* was released in 2016 by PIE International.

Kaiu Shirai debuted in 2015 with *Ashley Gate no Yukue* on the *Shonen Jump+* website. Shirai first worked with Posuka Demizu on the two-shot *Poppy no Negai*, which was released in February 2016.

THE PROMISED NEVERLAND

VOLUME 9
SHONEN JUMP Manga Edition

STORY BY KAIU SHIRAI
ART BY POSUKA DEMIZU

Translation/Satsuki Yamashita
Touch-Up Art & Lettering/Mark McMurray
Design/Julian [JR] Robinson
Editor/Alexis Kirsch

YAKUSOKU NO NEVERLAND © 2016 by Kaiu Shirai, Posuka Demizu
All rights reserved.
First published in Japan in 2016 by SHUEISHA Inc., Tokyo.
English translation rights arranged by SHUEISHA Inc.

Printed in Italy

Published by VIZ Media, LLC
P.O. Box 77010
San Francisco, CA 94107

10 9 8 7 6 5 4
First printing, April 2019
Fourth printing, June 2021

PARENTAL ADVISORY
THE PROMISED NEVERLAND is rated T+
and is recommended for ages 16 and up.
This volume contains fantasy violence and
adult themes.

THE PROMISED NEVERLAND

9

The Battle Begins

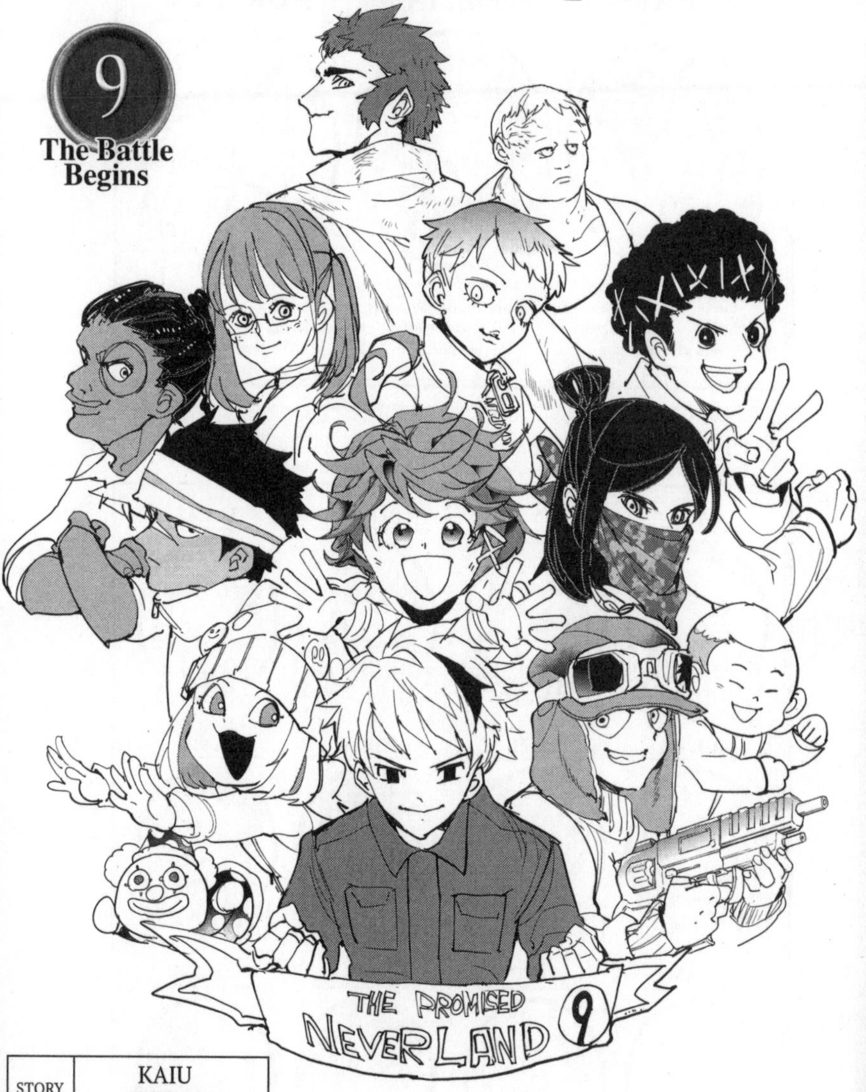
THE PROMISED
NEVERLAND 9

STORY	KAIU SHIRAI
ART	POSUKA DEMIZU

The Children of Grace Field House
They aim to free all of the children who are trapped in Grace Field House within two years.

CHARACTERS

RAY

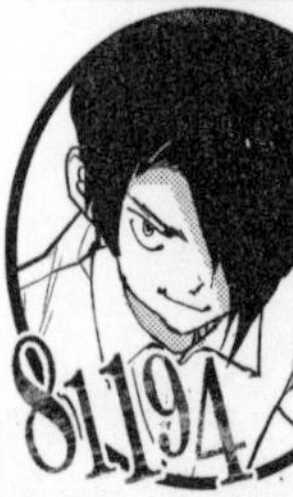
81194

The only one among the Grace Field House children who can match wits with Norman.

EMMA

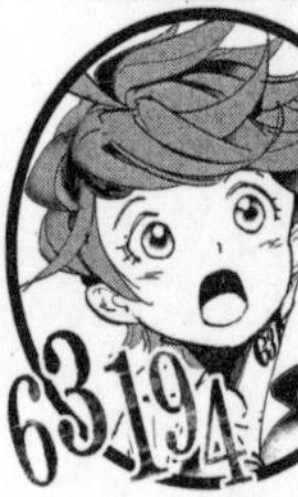
63194

An enthusiastic and optimistic girl with superb athletic and learning abilities.

NORMAN

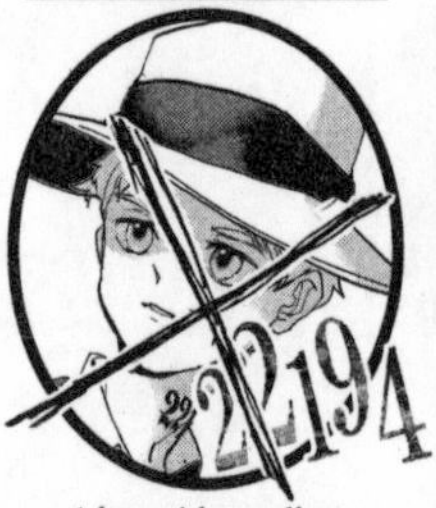
22194

A boy with excellent analytical and decision-making capabilities. He was the smartest child at Grace Field House.

The People of Goldy Pond
They plan to annihilate the demons of Goldy Pond, who hunt children for fun.

ZACK

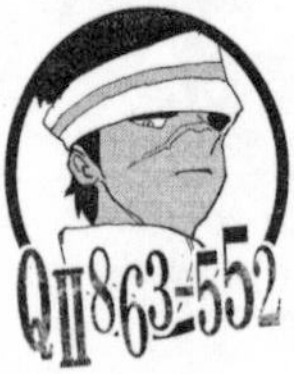
QII863-552

SONYA

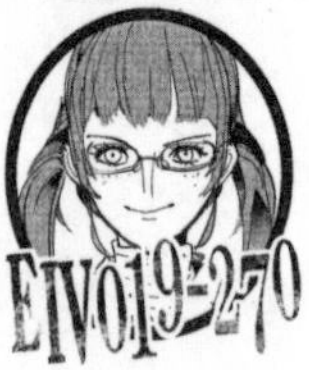
EIV019-270

OLIVER

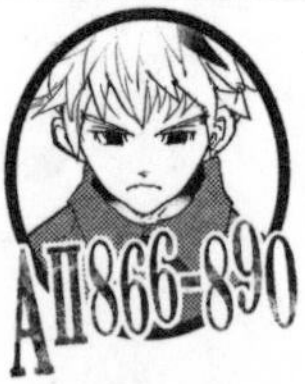
AII866-890

LUCAS

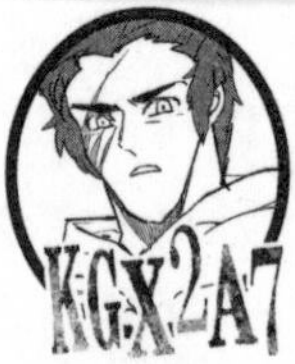
KGX2A7

VIOLET

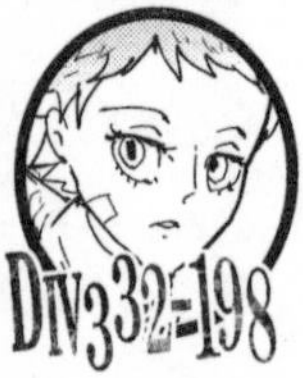
DIV332-198

NIGEL

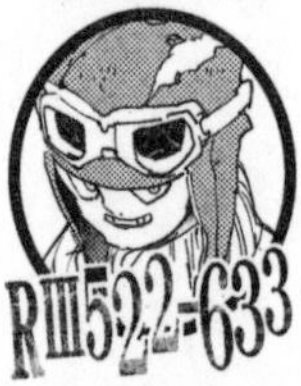
RIII522-633

PAULA

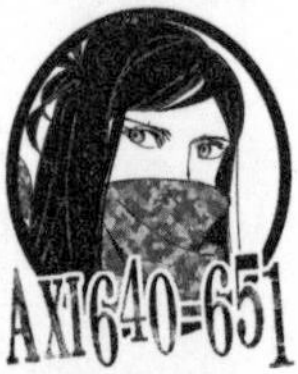
AXI640-651

SANDY

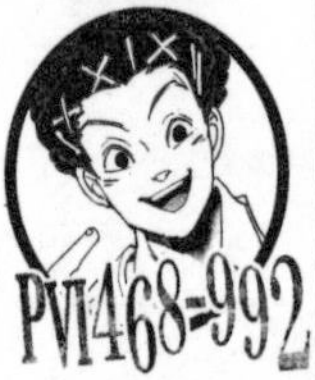
PVI468-992

ADAM

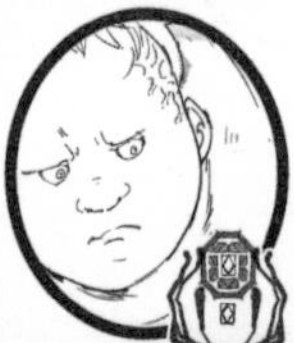

THEO

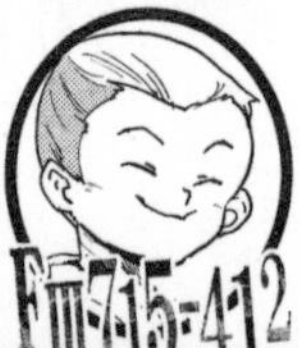
FIII715-412

PEPE

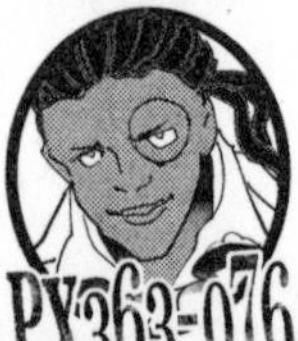
PX363-076

GILLIAN

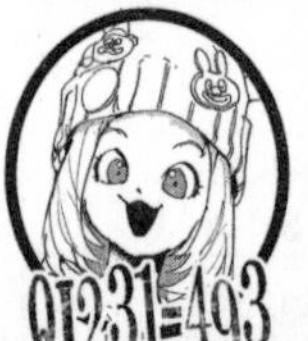
QI231-493

???

WILLIAM MINERVA

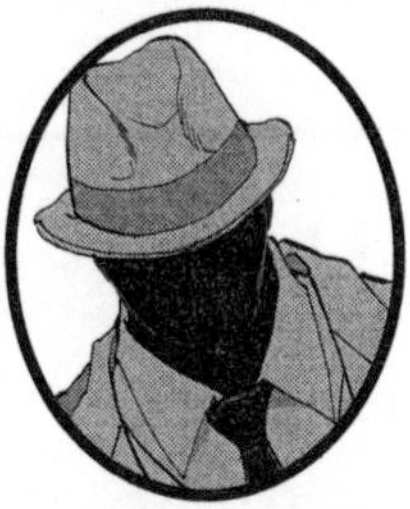

A mysterious figure who leaves various items that seem to help the children.

Mysterious Man at B06-32

GEEZER

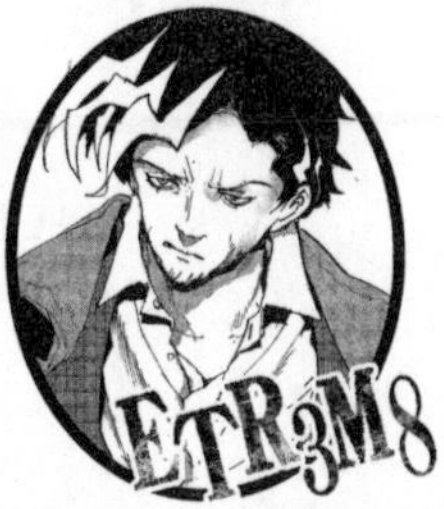
ETR3M8

A survivor of the runaways who escaped the top-class farm Glory Bell. His real name is unknown.

The Demons of Goldy Pond

GRAND DUKE LEUVIS

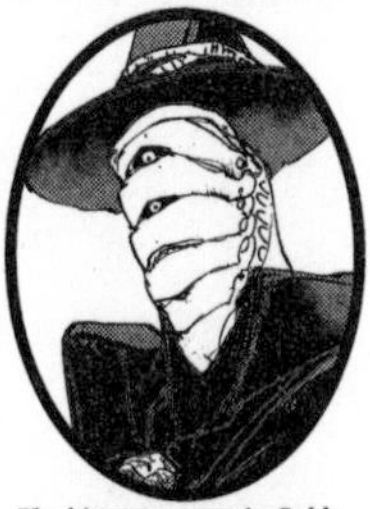

The biggest enemy in Goldy Pond. He desires a serious life-or-death battle against the humans.

LORD BAYON

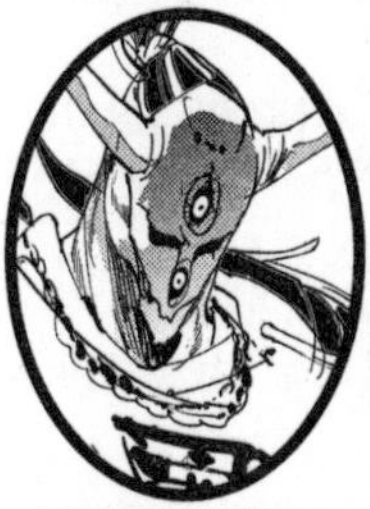

An aristocratic demon who hosts the secret hunt within Goldy Pond.

The Adult of Grace Field House

ISABELLA

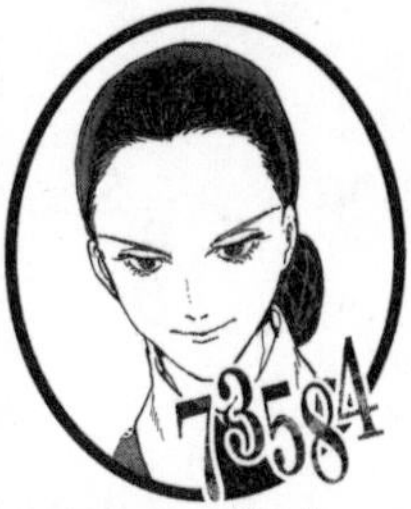
73584

A competent handler who raised Emma and the other children.

The Story So Far

Emma is living happily at Grace Field House with her foster siblings. One day, she realizes that they are being bred as food for demons and decides to escape with everyone except for the younger children under the age of four. They arrive at point B06-32, a location indicated by a pen thought to be left by a supposed collaborator named Minerva. But a mysterious man is already there, and using him as a guide, Emma and Ray head to a new location called Goldy Pond. But Emma is kidnapped and taken inside Goldy Pond, where she discovers that demons hunt humans. The humans are uniting to fight back and kill the demons, and among them is Lucas, someone from Glory Bell who escaped with the geezer many years ago.

THE PROMISED NEVERLAND 9

The Battle Begins

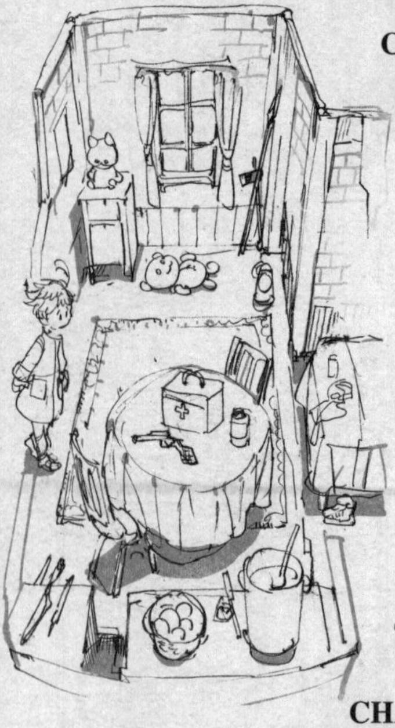

CHAPTER 71: REAL INTENTIONS

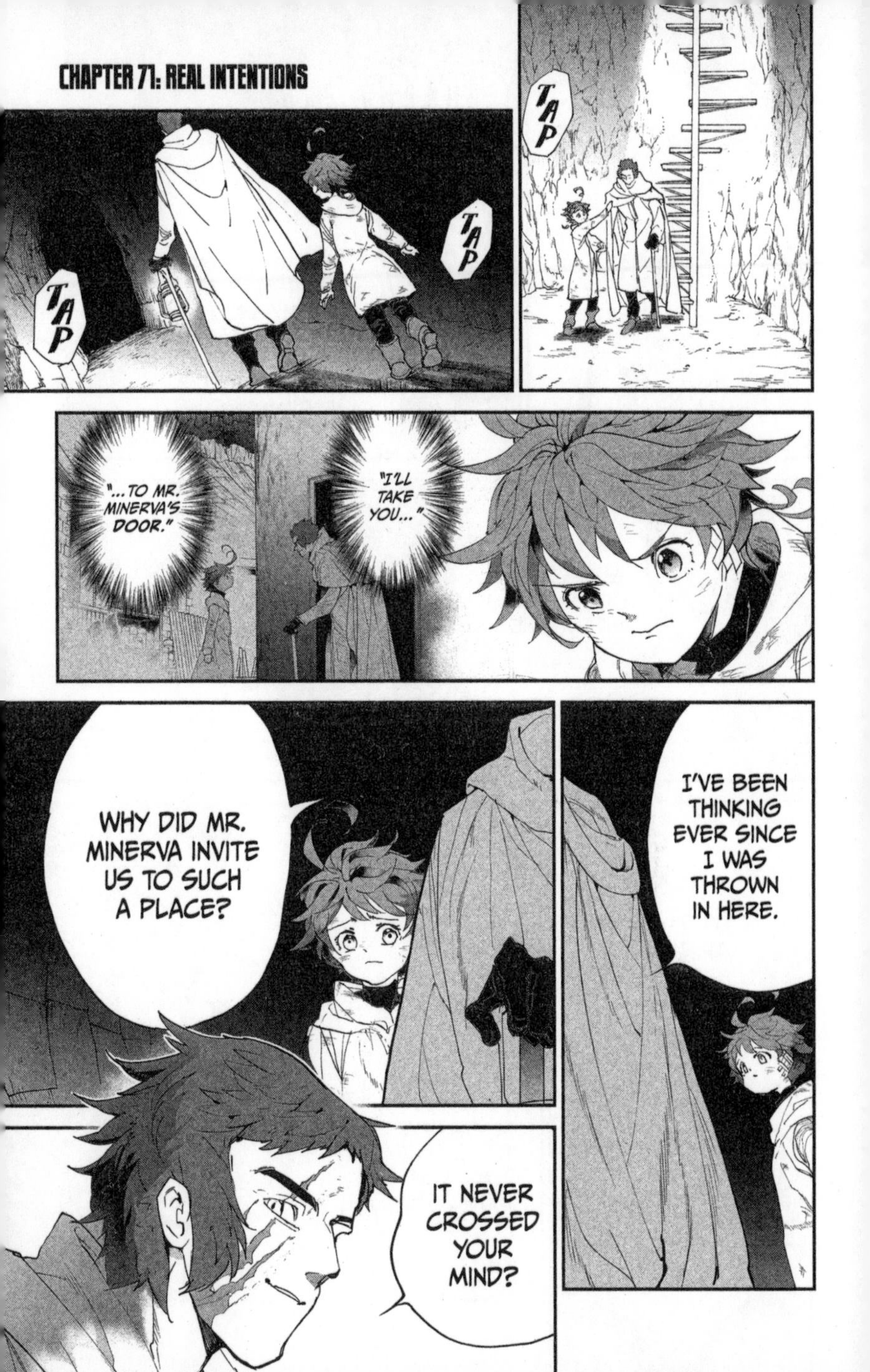
TAP
TAP
TAP
"I'LL TAKE YOU..."
"...TO MR. MINERVA'S DOOR."
I'VE BEEN THINKING EVER SINCE I WAS THROWN IN HERE.
WHY DID MR. MINERVA INVITE US TO SUCH A PLACE?
IT NEVER CROSSED YOUR MIND?

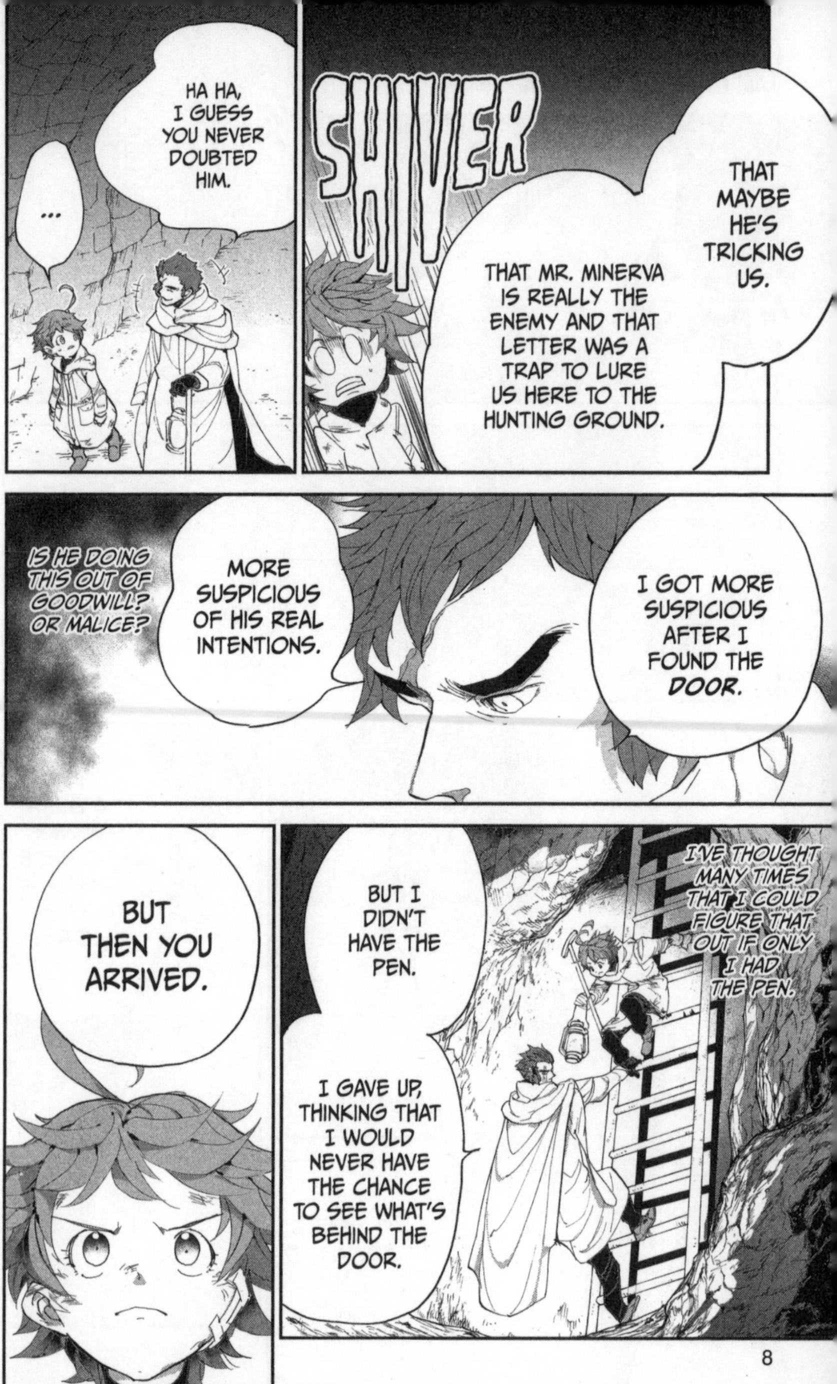
THAT MAYBE HE'S TRICKING US.
SHIVER
THAT MR. MINERVA IS REALLY THE ENEMY AND THAT LETTER WAS A TRAP TO LURE US HERE TO THE HUNTING GROUND.
HA HA, I GUESS YOU NEVER DOUBTED HIM.
...
I GOT MORE SUSPICIOUS AFTER I FOUND THE *DOOR*.
MORE SUSPICIOUS OF HIS REAL INTENTIONS.
IS HE DOING THIS OUT OF GOODWILL? OR MALICE?
I'VE THOUGHT MANY TIMES THAT I COULD FIGURE THAT OUT IF ONLY I HAD THE PEN.
BUT I DIDN'T HAVE THE PEN.
I GAVE UP, THINKING THAT I WOULD NEVER HAVE THE CHANCE TO SEE WHAT'S BEHIND THE DOOR.
BUT THEN YOU ARRIVED.

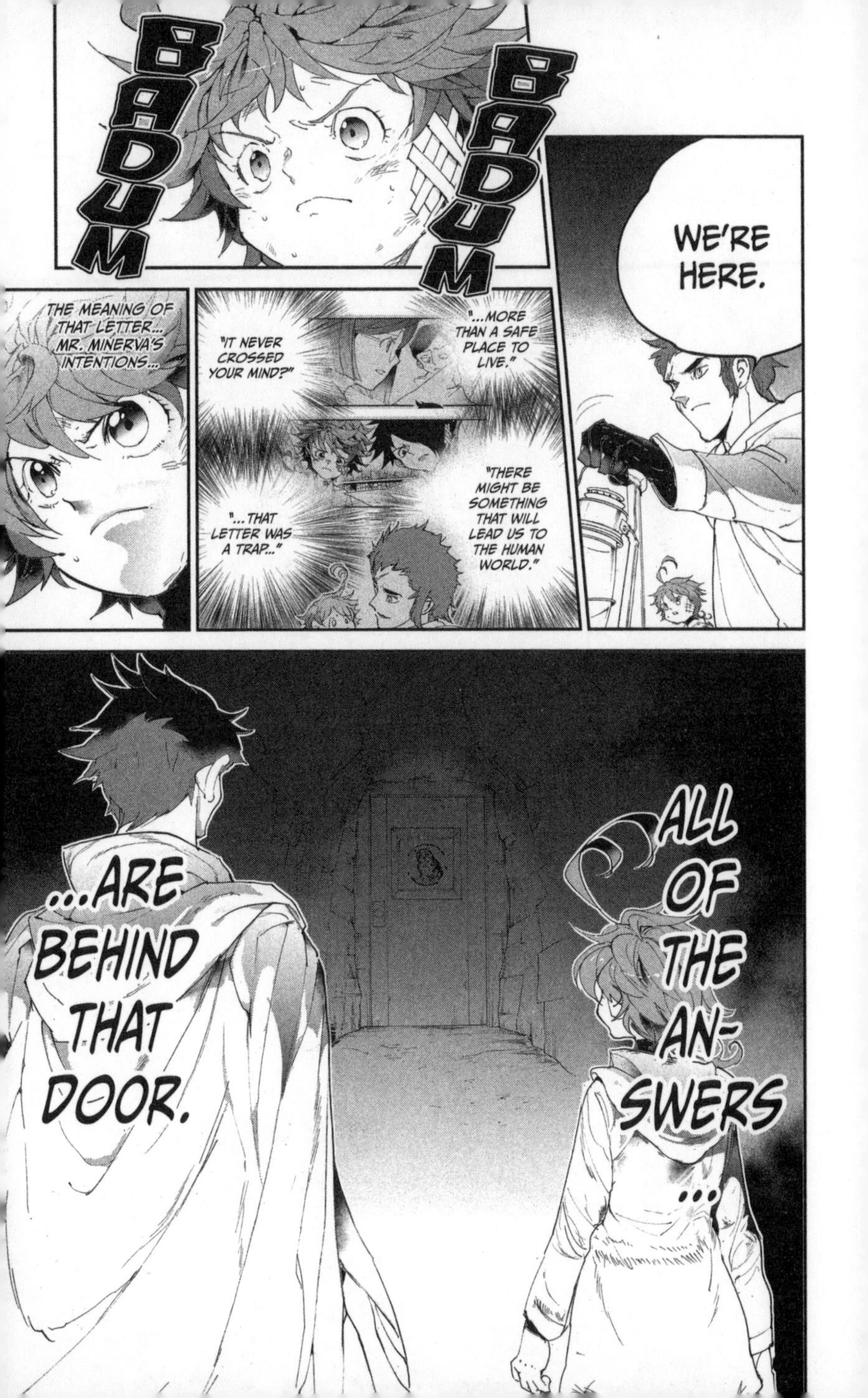
WE'RE HERE.
BADUM
BADUM
"...MORE THAN A SAFE PLACE TO LIVE."
"IT NEVER CROSSED YOUR MIND?"
"THERE MIGHT BE SOMETHING THAT WILL LEAD US TO THE HUMAN WORLD."
"...THAT LETTER WAS A TRAP..."
THE MEANING OF THAT LETTER... MR. MINERVA'S INTENTIONS...
ALL OF THE AN-SWERS...
...ARE BEHIND THAT DOOR.

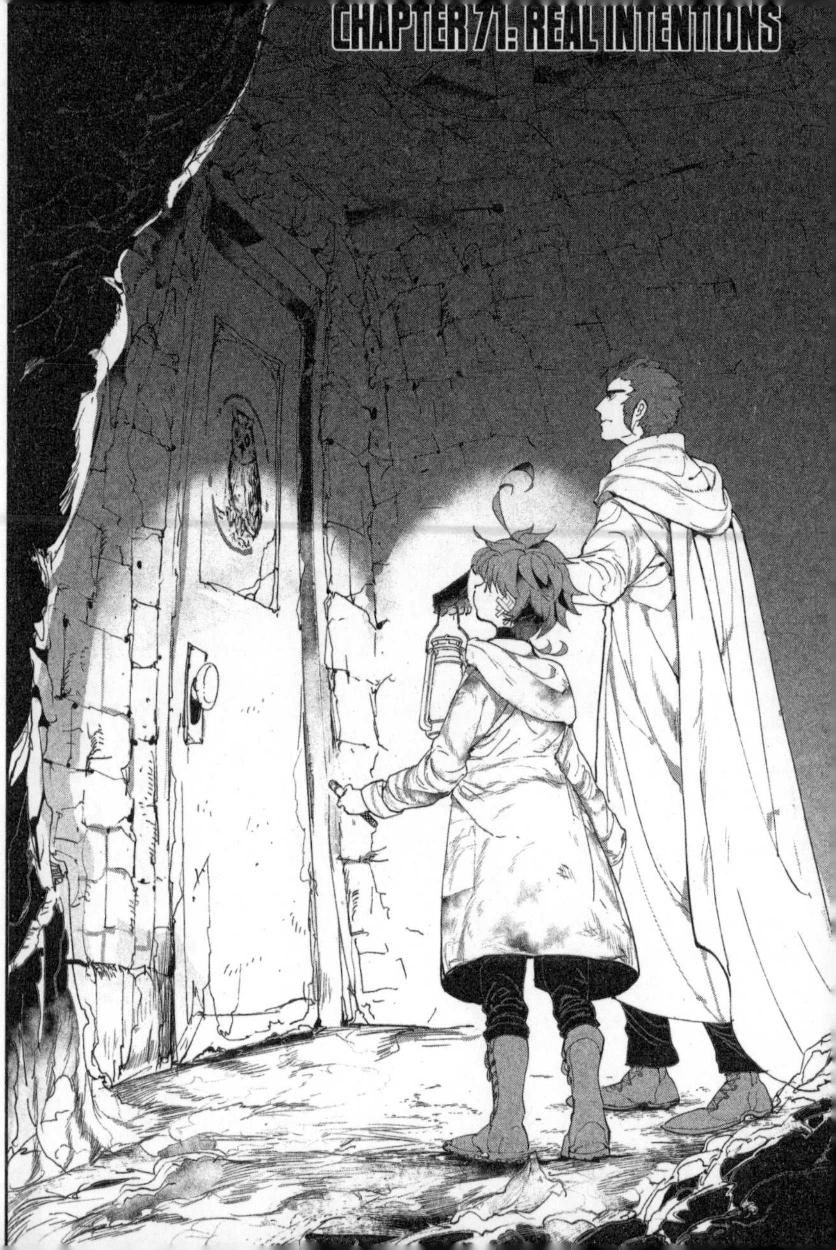
CHAPTER 71: REAL INTENTIONS

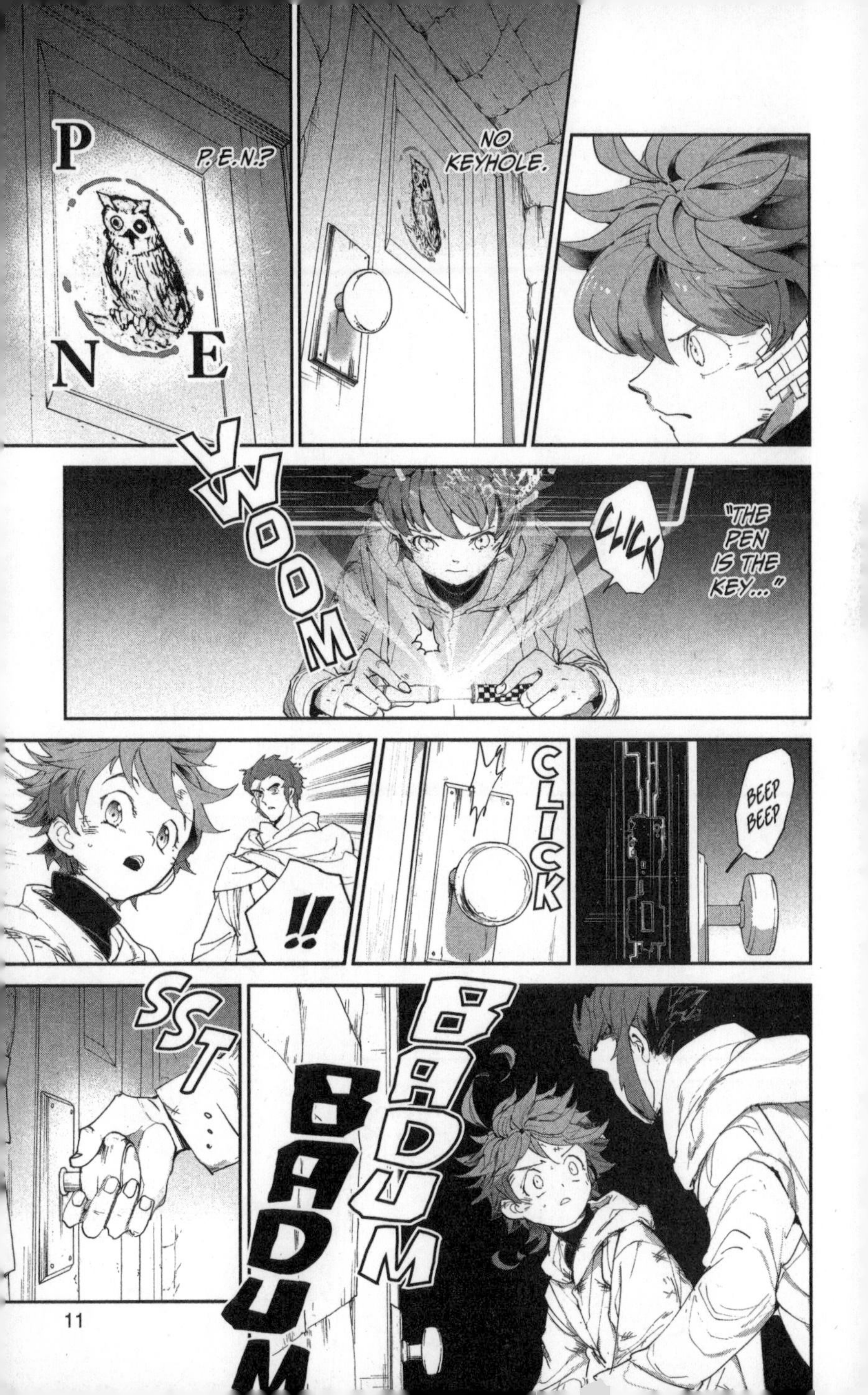
NO KEYHOLE.
P.E.N.?
P
N
E
"THE PEN IS THE KEY..."
CLICK
VWOOM
BEEP BEEP
CLICK
!!
BADUM
BADUM
SST

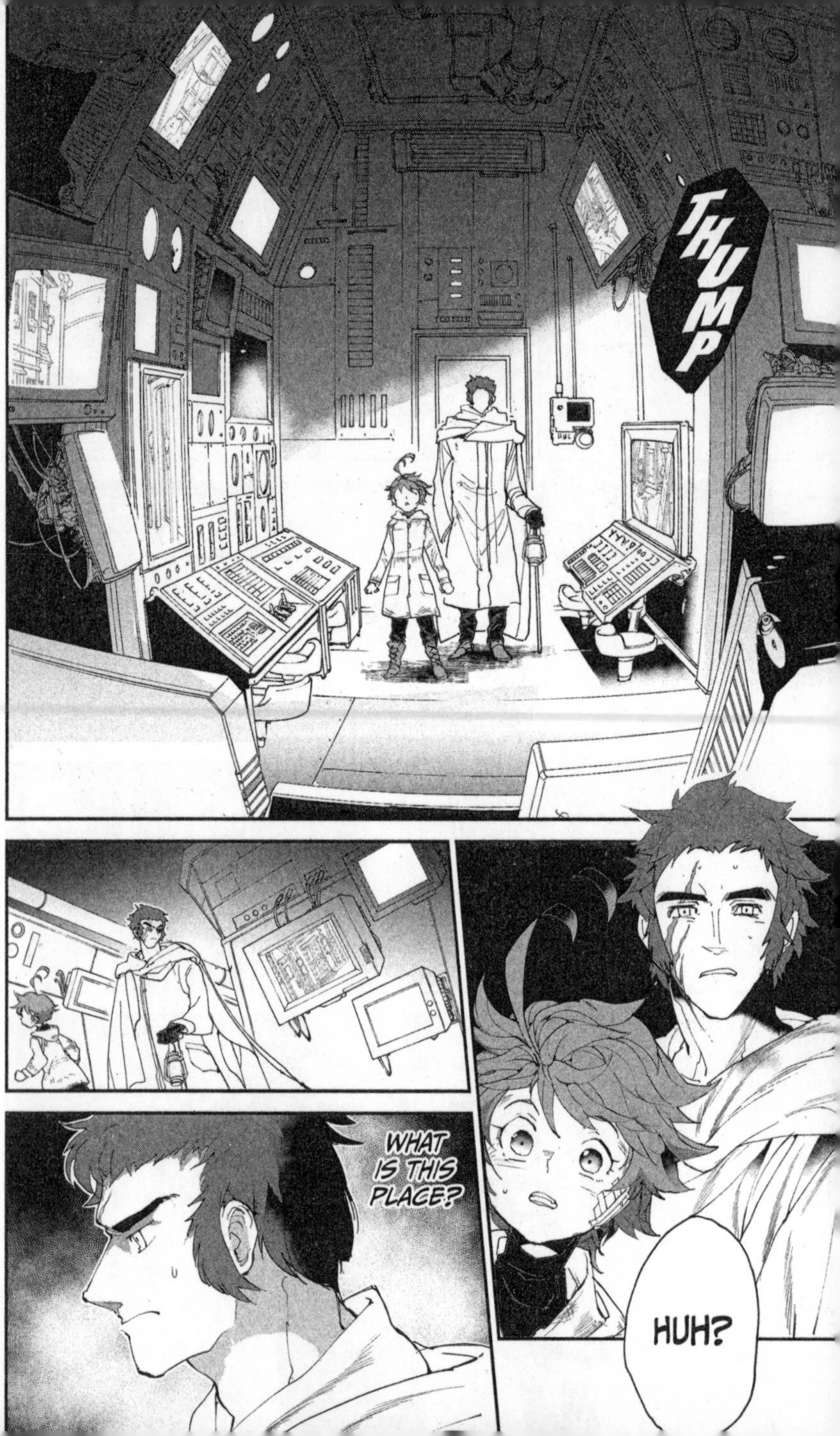
THUMP
HUH?
WHAT IS THIS PLACE?

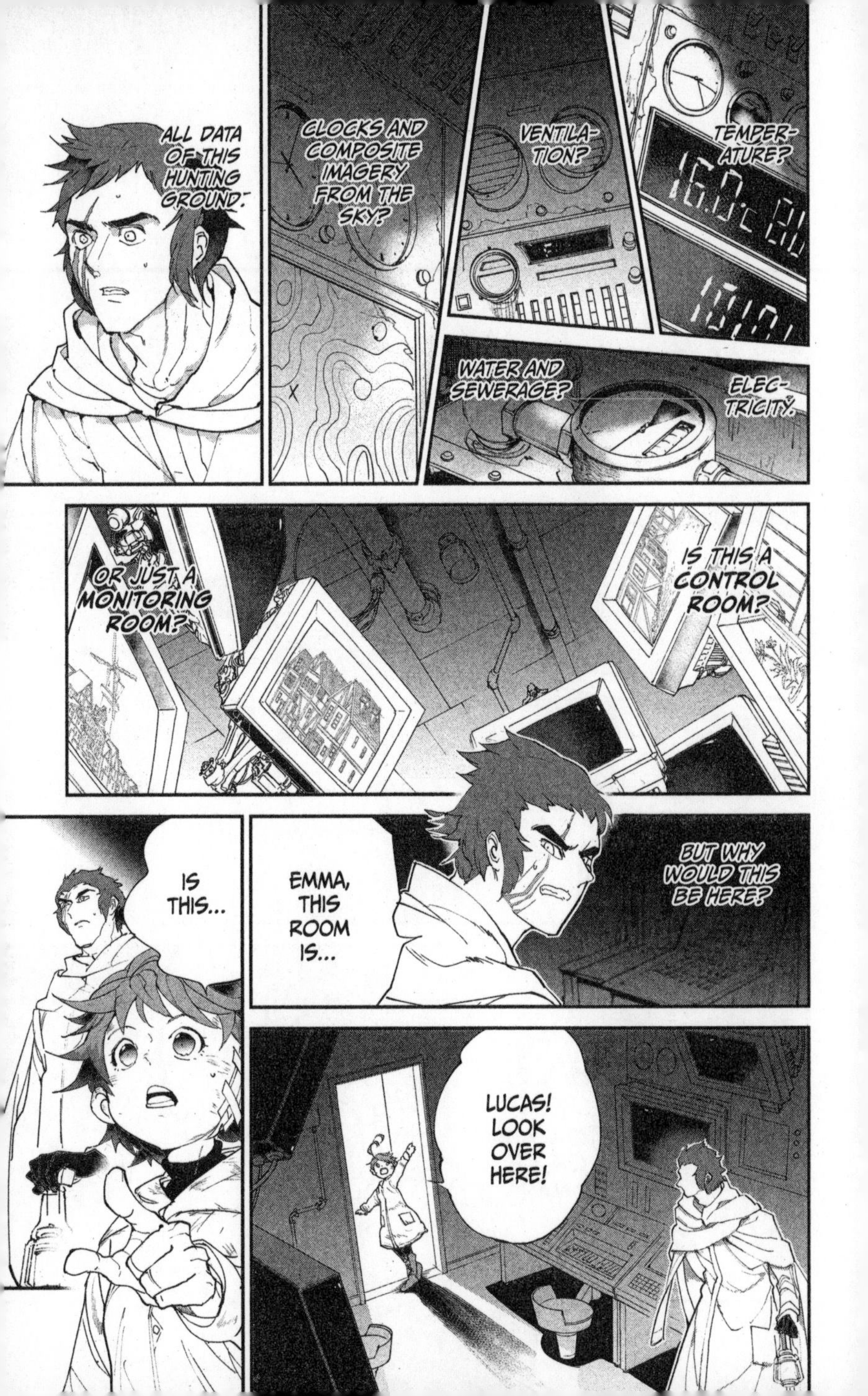
TEMPERATURE?
VENTILATION?
ELECTRICITY.
WATER AND SEWERAGE?
CLOCKS AND COMPOSITE IMAGERY FROM THE SKY?
ALL DATA OF THIS HUNTING GROUND.
IS THIS A CONTROL ROOM?
OR JUST A MONITORING ROOM?
BUT WHY WOULD THIS BE HERE?
EMMA, THIS ROOM IS...
LUCAS! LOOK OVER HERE!
IS THIS...

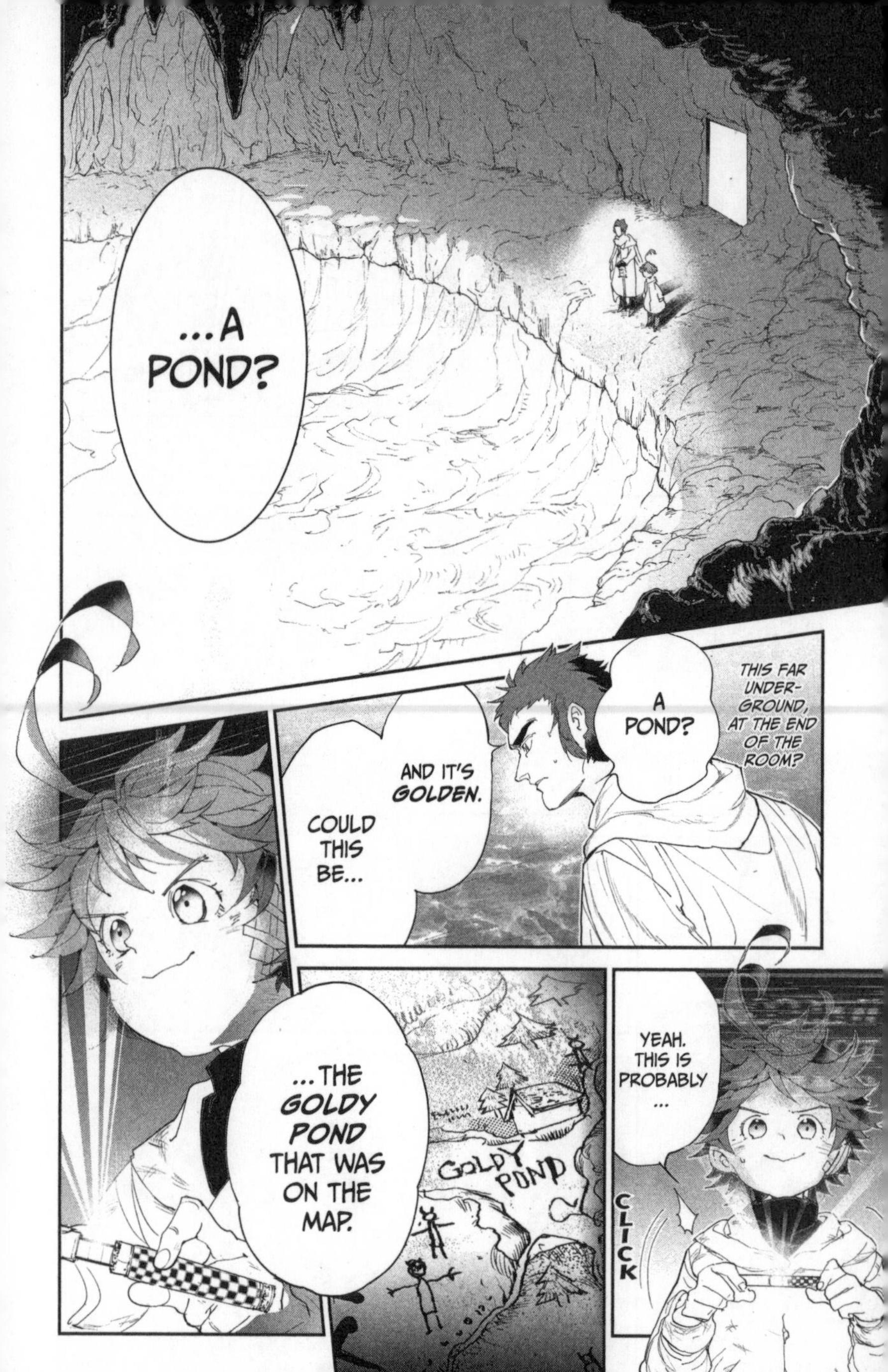
...A POND?
THIS FAR UNDER-GROUND, AT THE END OF THE ROOM?
A POND?
AND IT'S *GOLDEN*.
COULD THIS BE...
YEAH. THIS IS PROBABLY ...
CLICK
GOLDY POND
...THE *GOLDY POND* THAT WAS ON THE MAP.

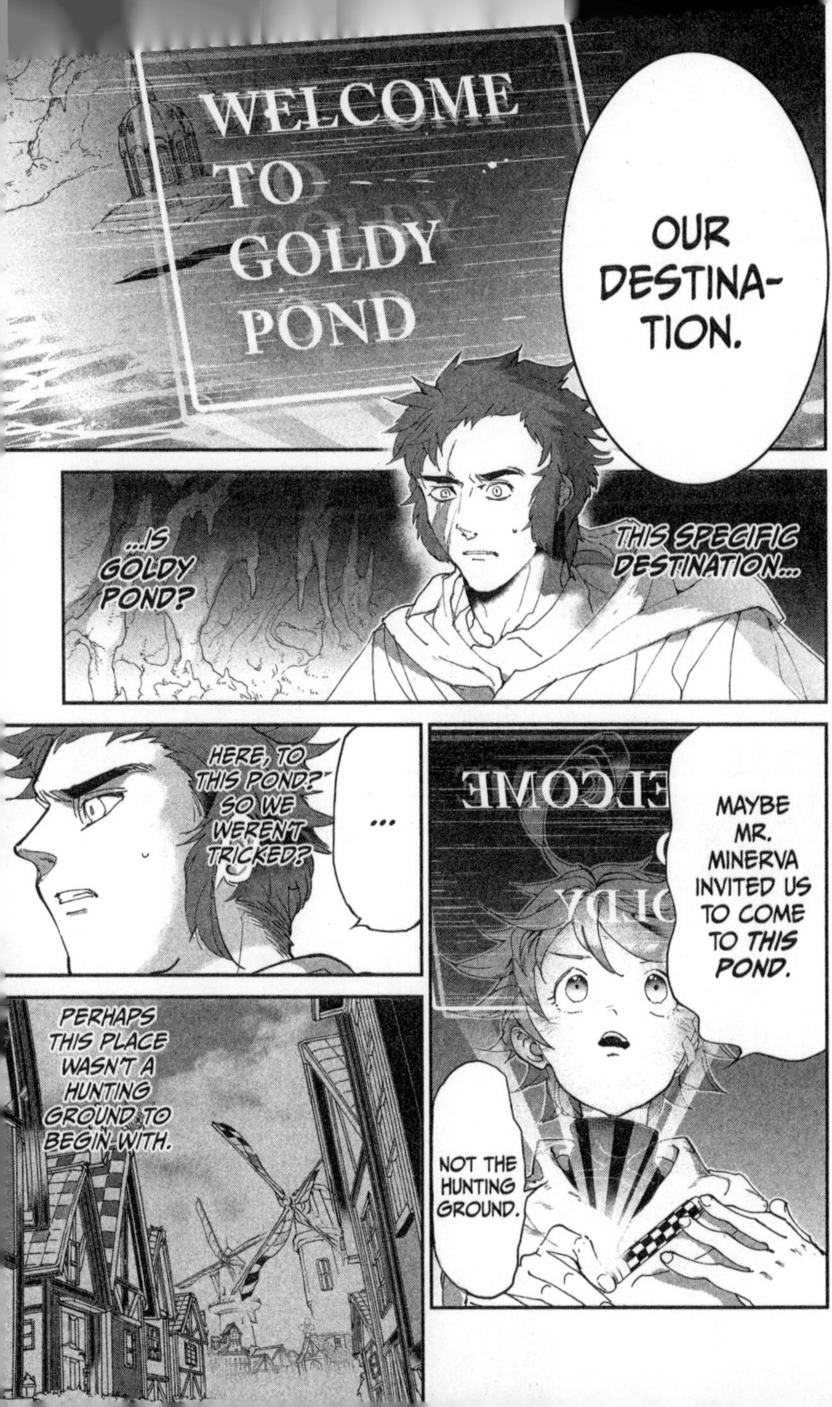
OUR DESTINATION.
WELCOME TO GOLDY POND
THIS SPECIFIC DESTINATION...
...IS GOLDY POND?
MAYBE MR. MINERVA INVITED US TO COME TO *THIS* POND.
NOT THE HUNTING GROUND.
...
HERE, TO THIS POND? SO WE WEREN'T TRICKED?
PERHAPS THIS PLACE WASN'T A HUNTING GROUND TO BEGIN WITH.

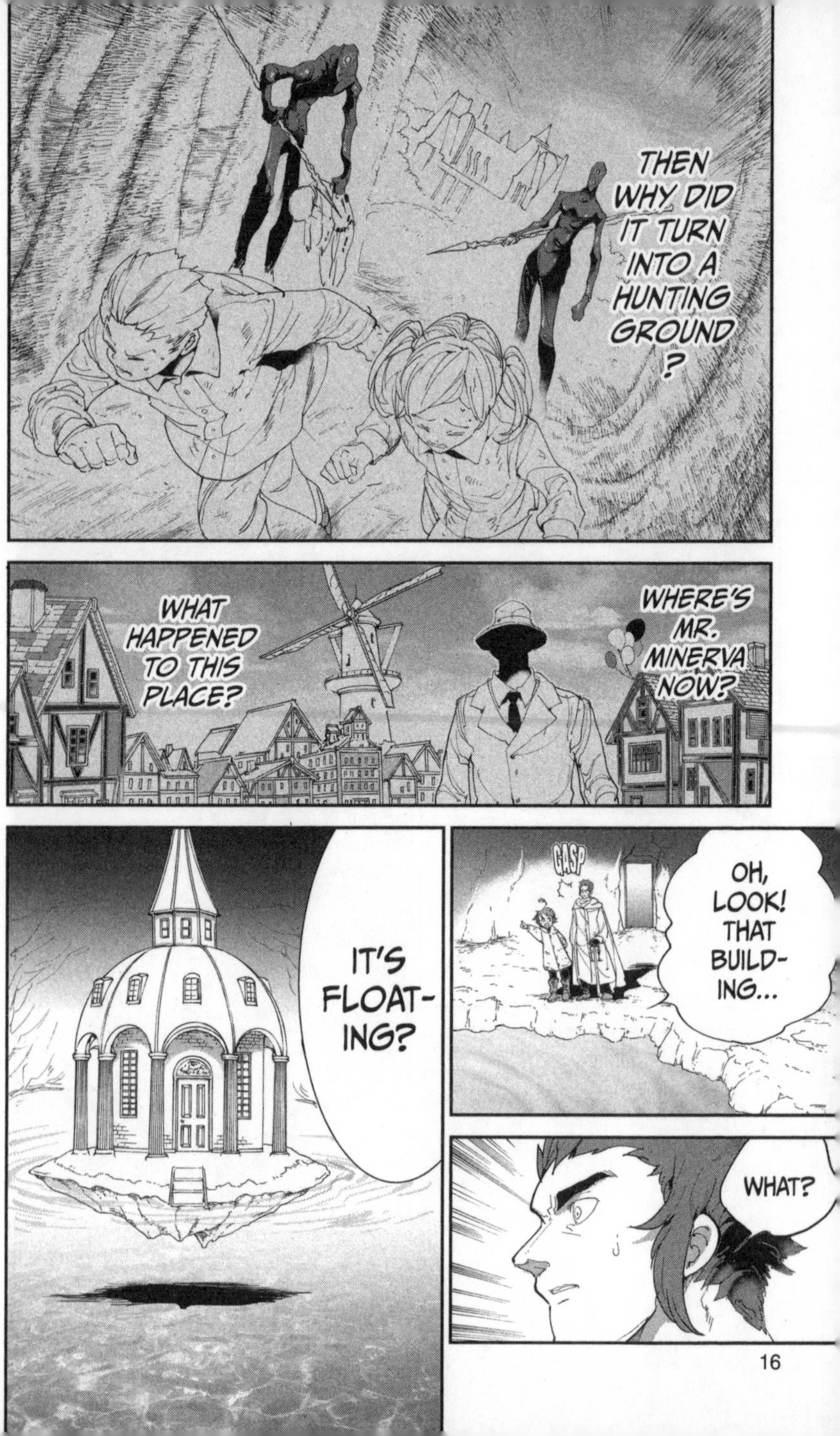
THEN WHY DID IT TURN INTO A HUNTING GROUND?
WHERE'S MR. MINERVA NOW?
WHAT HAPPENED TO THIS PLACE?
GASP
OH, LOOK! THAT BUILD-ING...
WHAT?
IT'S FLOAT-ING?

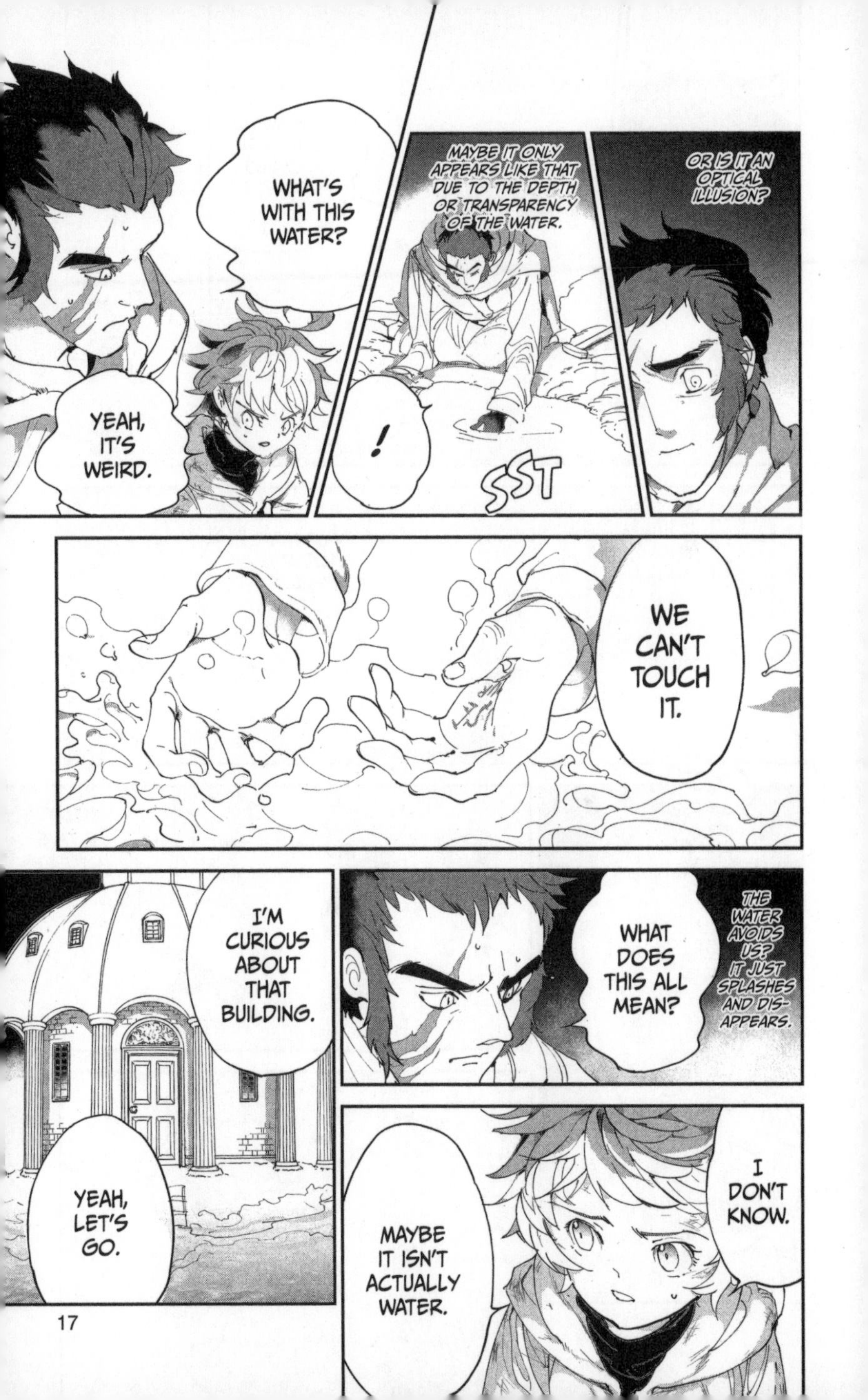
OR IS IT AN OPTICAL ILLUSION?
MAYBE IT ONLY APPEARS LIKE THAT DUE TO THE DEPTH OR TRANSPARENCY OF THE WATER.
!
SST
WHAT'S WITH THIS WATER?
YEAH, IT'S WEIRD.
WE CAN'T TOUCH IT.
THE WATER AVOIDS US? IT JUST SPLASHES AND DIS-APPEARS.
WHAT DOES THIS ALL MEAN?
I DON'T KNOW.
MAYBE IT ISN'T ACTUALLY WATER.
I'M CURIOUS ABOUT THAT BUILDING.
YEAH, LET'S GO.

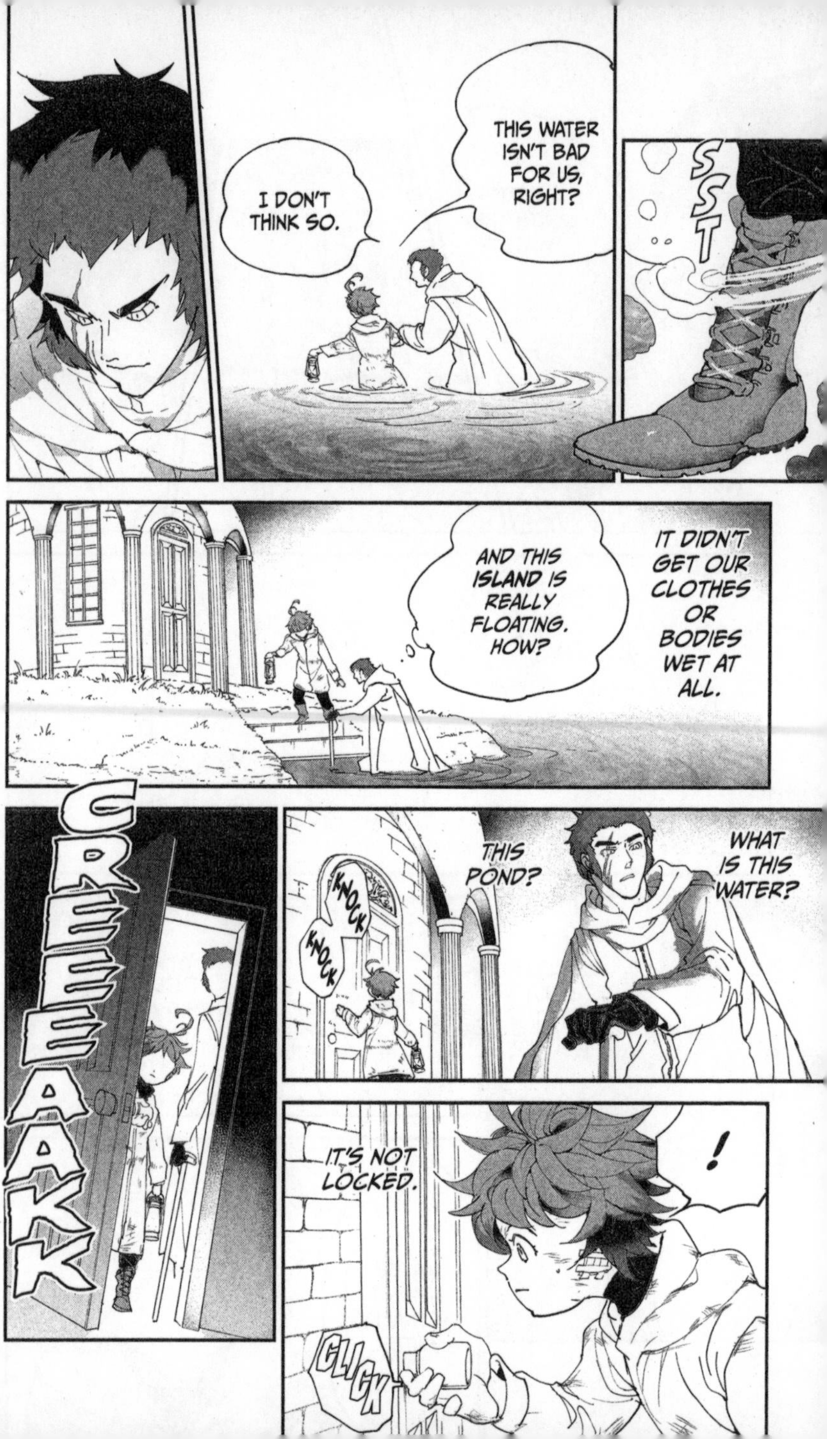
SST
THIS WATER ISN'T BAD FOR US, RIGHT?
I DON'T THINK SO.
IT DIDN'T GET OUR CLOTHES OR BODIES WET AT ALL.
AND THIS ISLAND IS REALLY FLOATING. HOW?
WHAT IS THIS WATER?
THIS POND?
KNOCK
KNOCK
!
IT'S NOT LOCKED.
CLICK
CREEEAKK

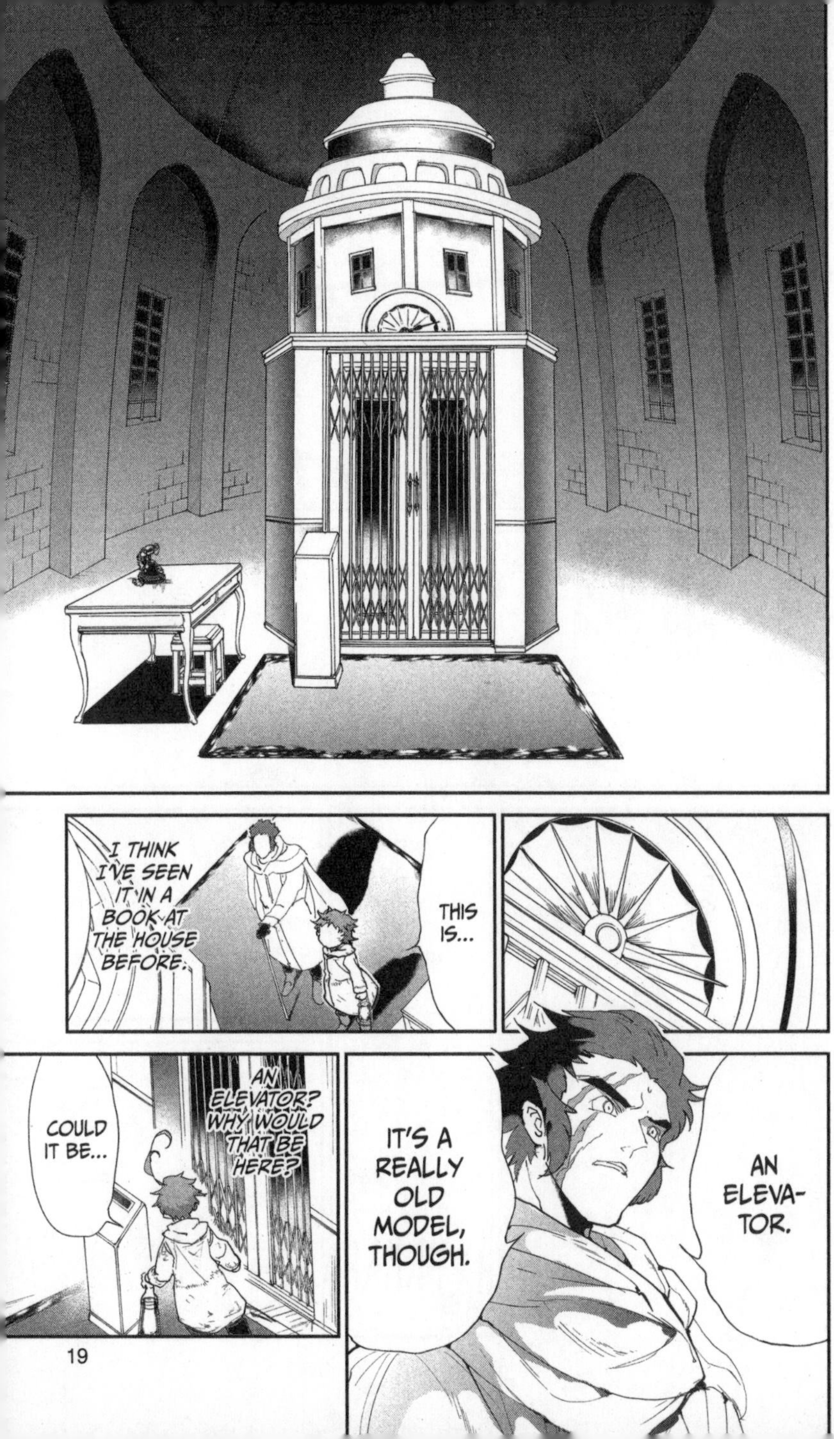
THIS IS...
I THINK I'VE SEEN IT IN A BOOK AT THE HOUSE BEFORE.
AN ELEVATOR.
IT'S A REALLY OLD MODEL, THOUGH.
AN ELEVATOR? WHY WOULD THAT BE HERE?
COULD IT BE...

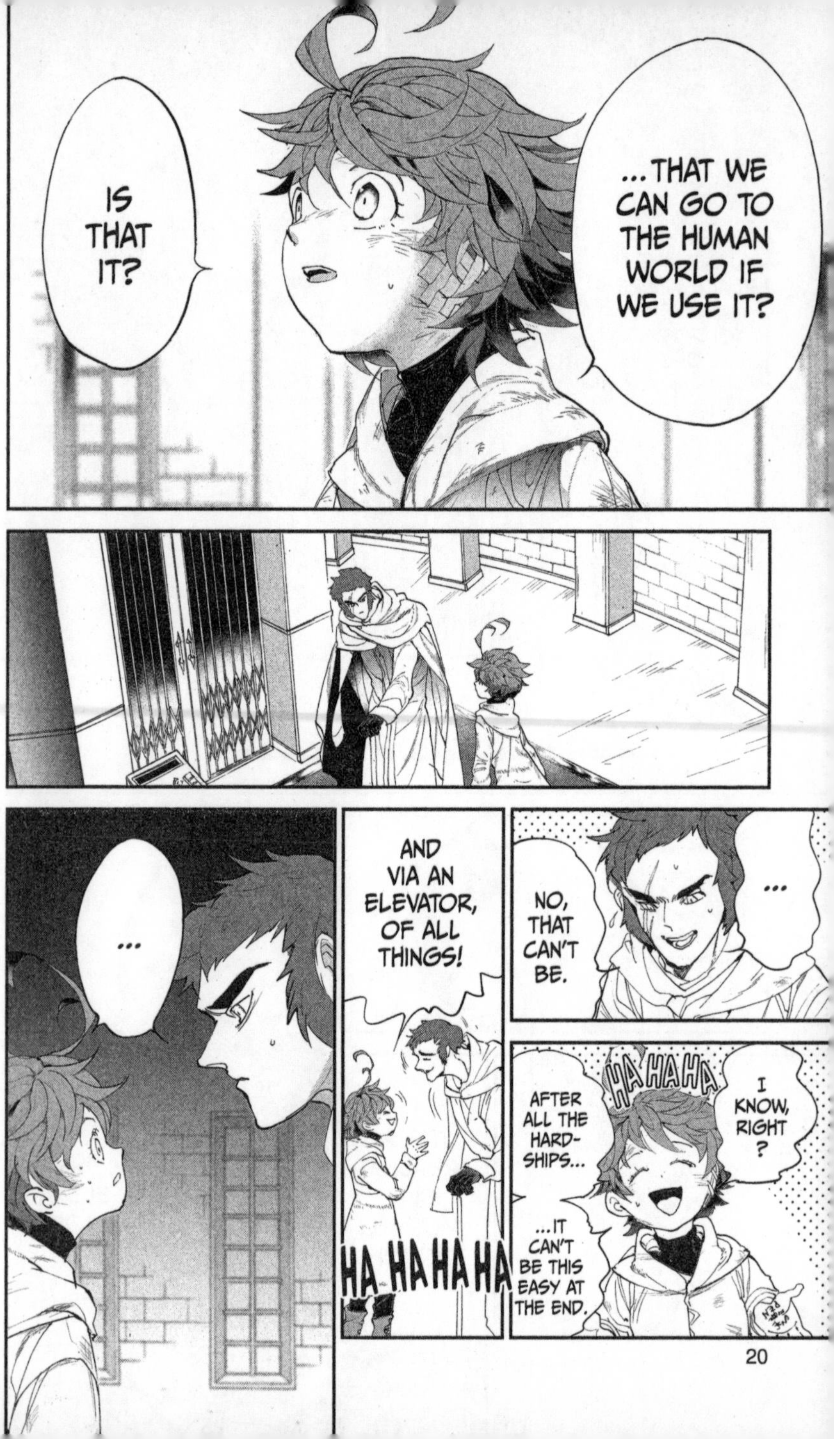
IS THAT IT?
...THAT WE CAN GO TO THE HUMAN WORLD IF WE USE IT?
...
NO, THAT CAN'T BE.
I KNOW, RIGHT?
HAHAHA
AFTER ALL THE HARDSHIPS...
...IT CAN'T BE THIS EASY AT THE END.
AND VIA AN ELEVATOR, OF ALL THINGS!
HA HAHAHA
...

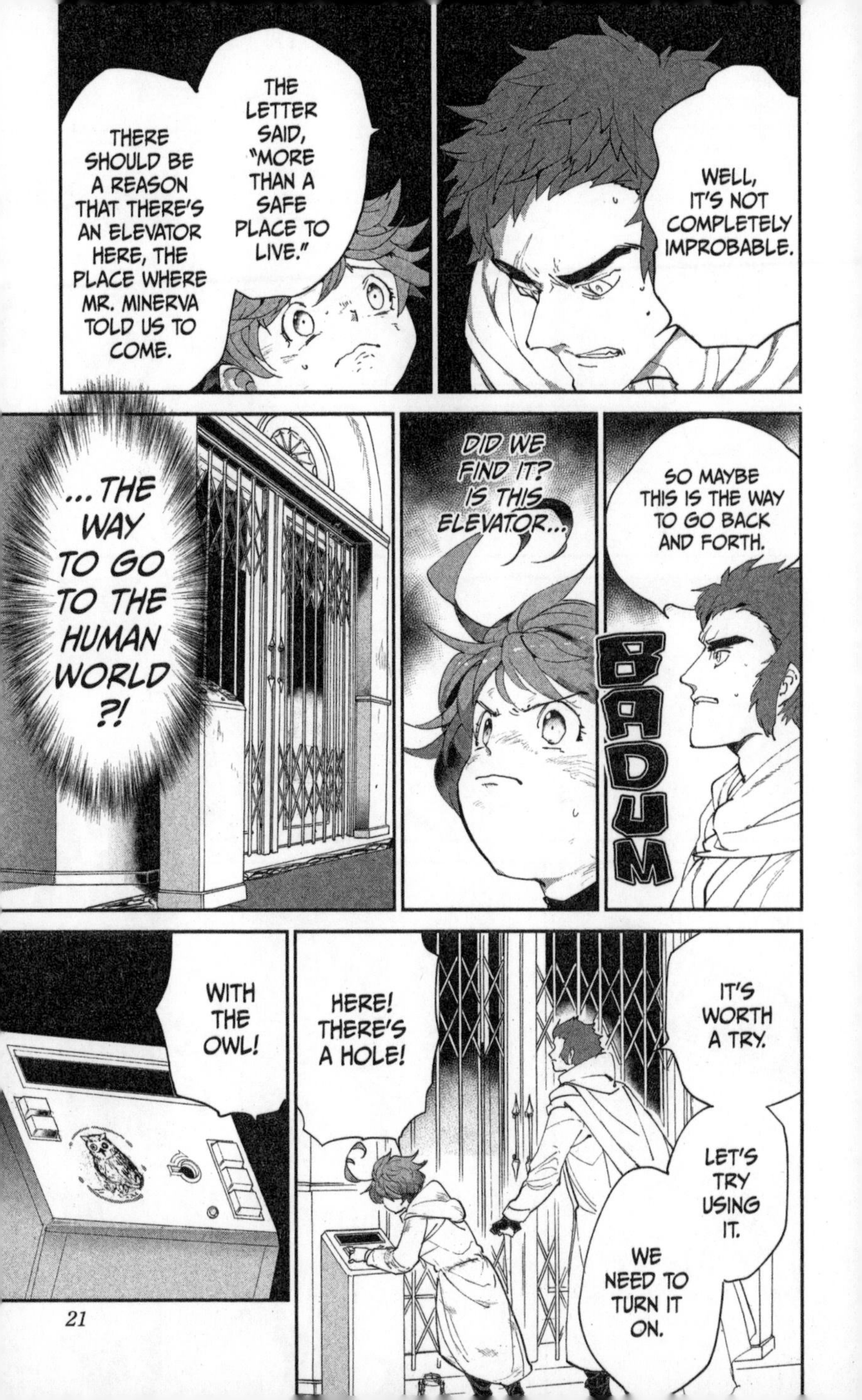
WELL, IT'S NOT COMPLETELY IMPROBABLE.
THE LETTER SAID, "MORE THAN A SAFE PLACE TO LIVE."
THERE SHOULD BE A REASON THAT THERE'S AN ELEVATOR HERE, THE PLACE WHERE MR. MINERVA TOLD US TO COME.
SO MAYBE THIS IS THE WAY TO GO BACK AND FORTH.
BADUM
DID WE FIND IT? IS THIS ELEVATOR...
...THE WAY TO GO TO THE HUMAN WORLD?!
IT'S WORTH A TRY.
LET'S TRY USING IT.
WE NEED TO TURN IT ON.
HERE! THERE'S A HOLE!
WITH THE OWL!

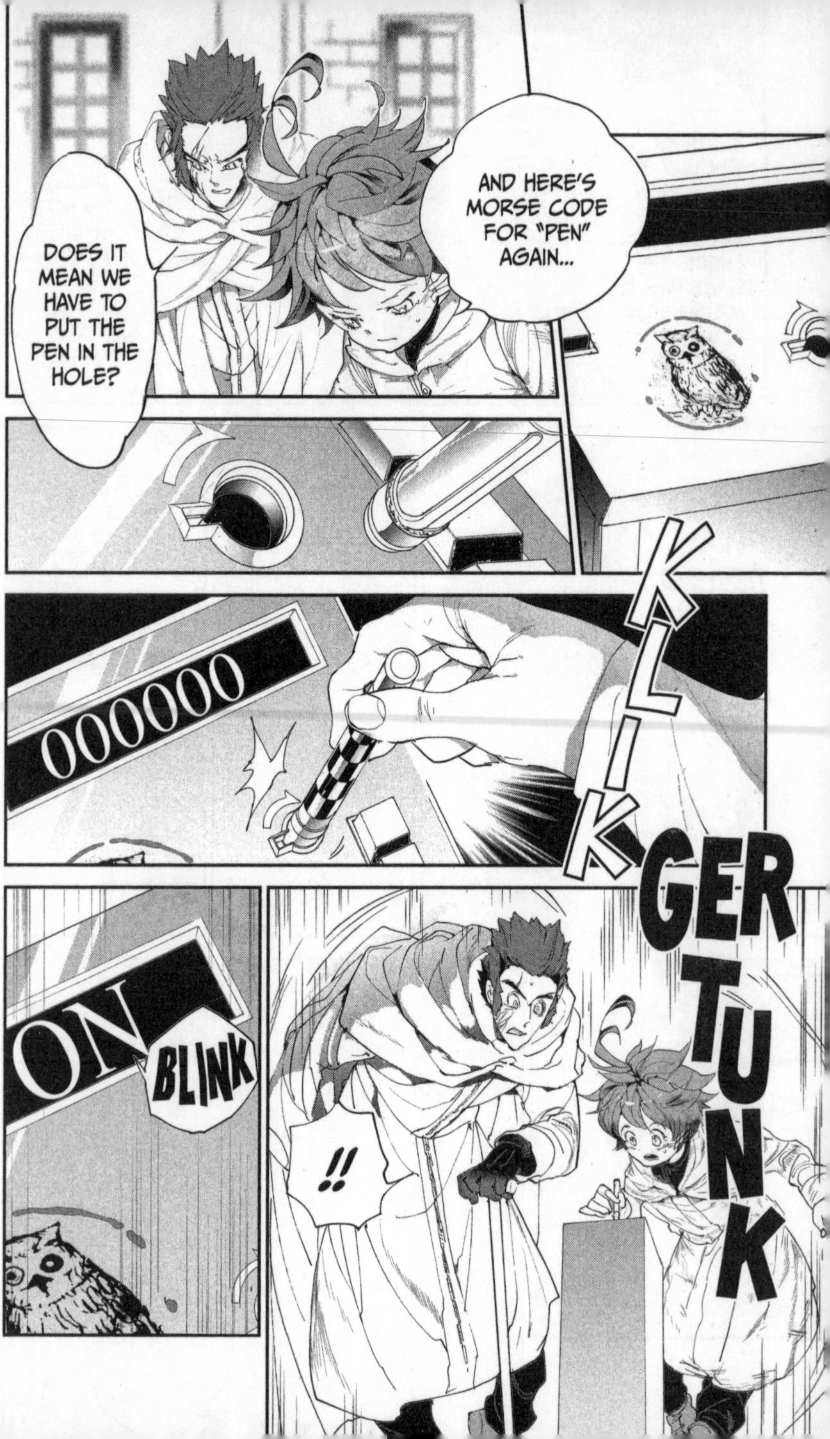
AND HERE'S MORSE CODE FOR "PEN" AGAIN...
DOES IT MEAN WE HAVE TO PUT THE PEN IN THE HOLE?
KLLIK
000000
GERTUNK
!!
ON
BLINK

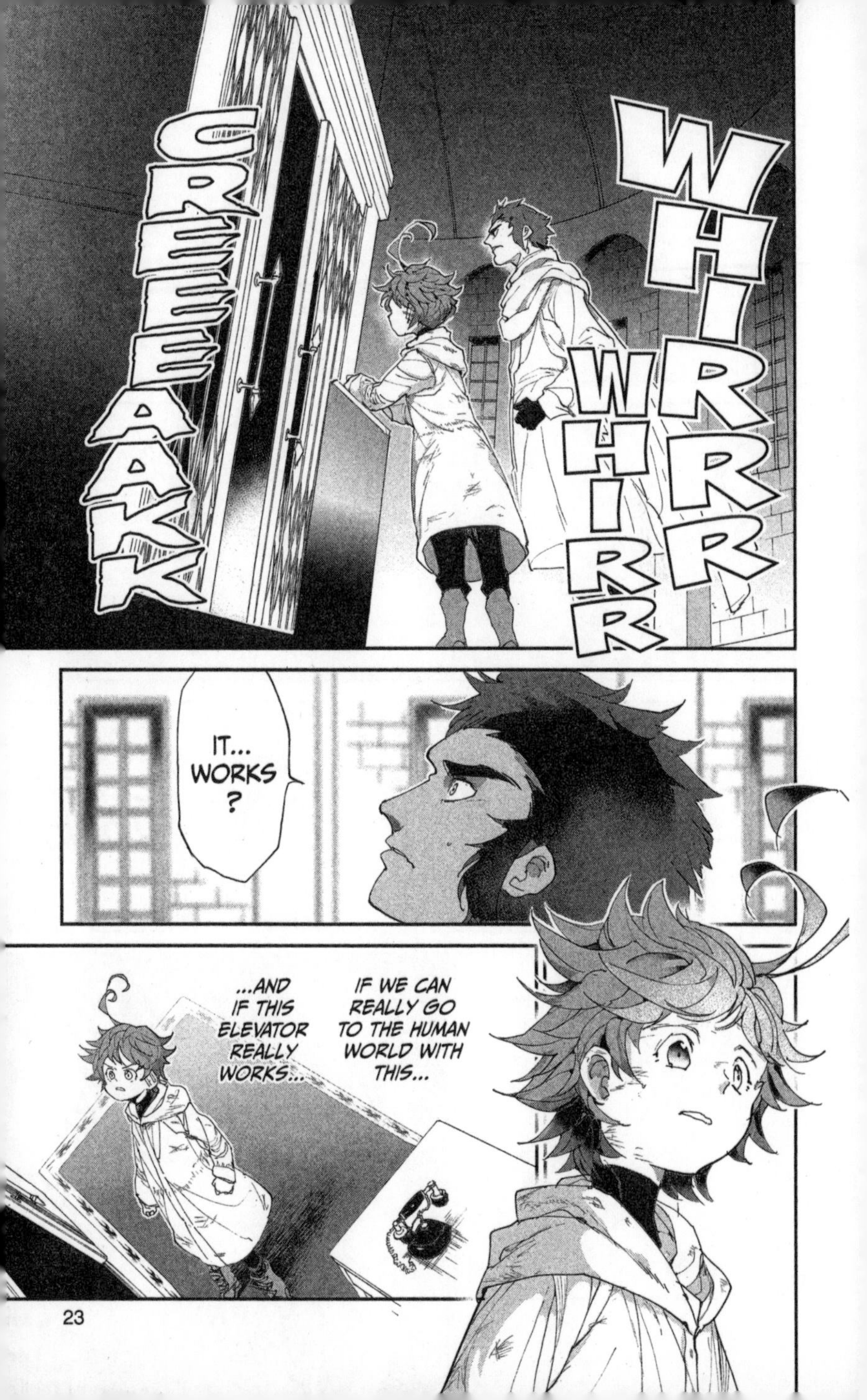
WHIRRR
WHIRRR
CREEEAAKK
IT... WORKS?
IF WE CAN REALLY GO TO THE HUMAN WORLD WITH THIS...
...AND IF THIS ELEVATOR REALLY WORKS...

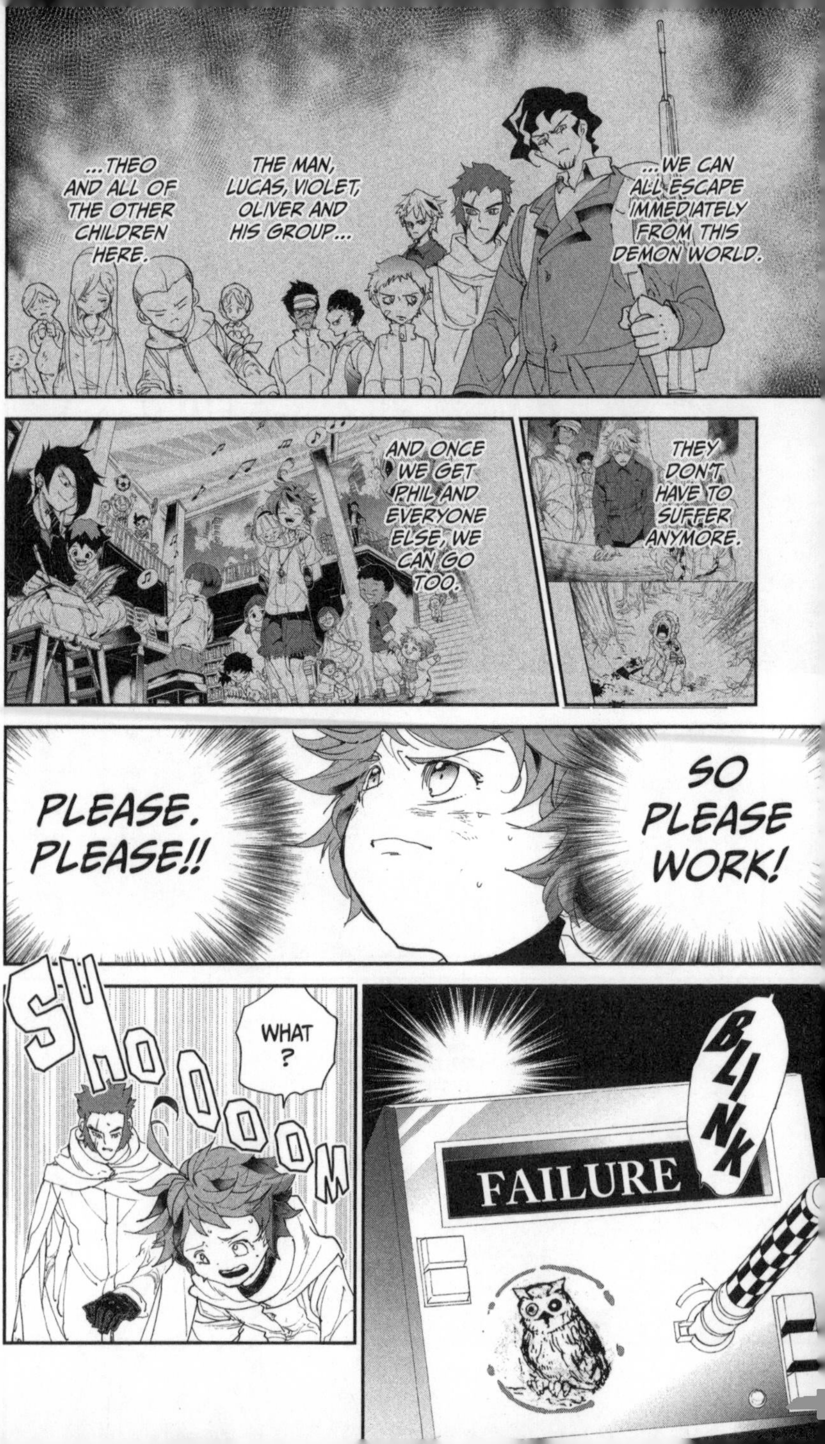
...WE CAN ALL ESCAPE IMMEDIATELY FROM THIS DEMON WORLD.
THE MAN, LUCAS, VIOLET, OLIVER AND HIS GROUP...
...THEO AND ALL OF THE OTHER CHILDREN HERE.
THEY DON'T HAVE TO SUFFER ANYMORE.
AND ONCE WE GET PHIL AND EVERYONE ELSE, WE CAN GO TOO.
SO PLEASE WORK!
PLEASE. PLEASE!!
BLINK
FAILURE
SHOOOOOM
WHAT?

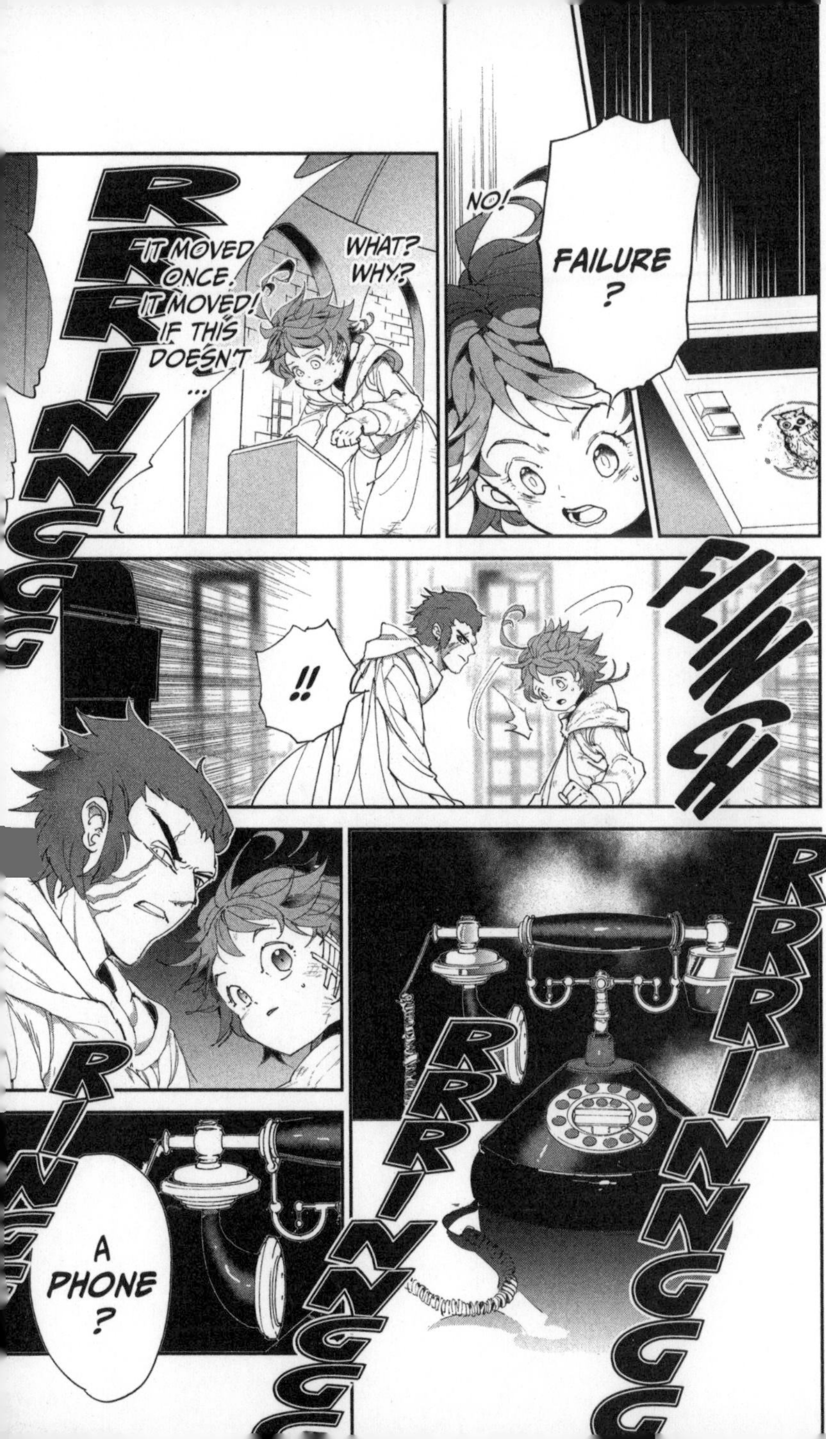
FAILURE ?
NO!
WHAT? WHY?
IT MOVED ONCE. IT MOVED! IF THIS DOESN'T ...
RRRINNGGG
FLINCH
!!
RRRINNGGG
RRRINNGGG
RINGG
A PHONE ?

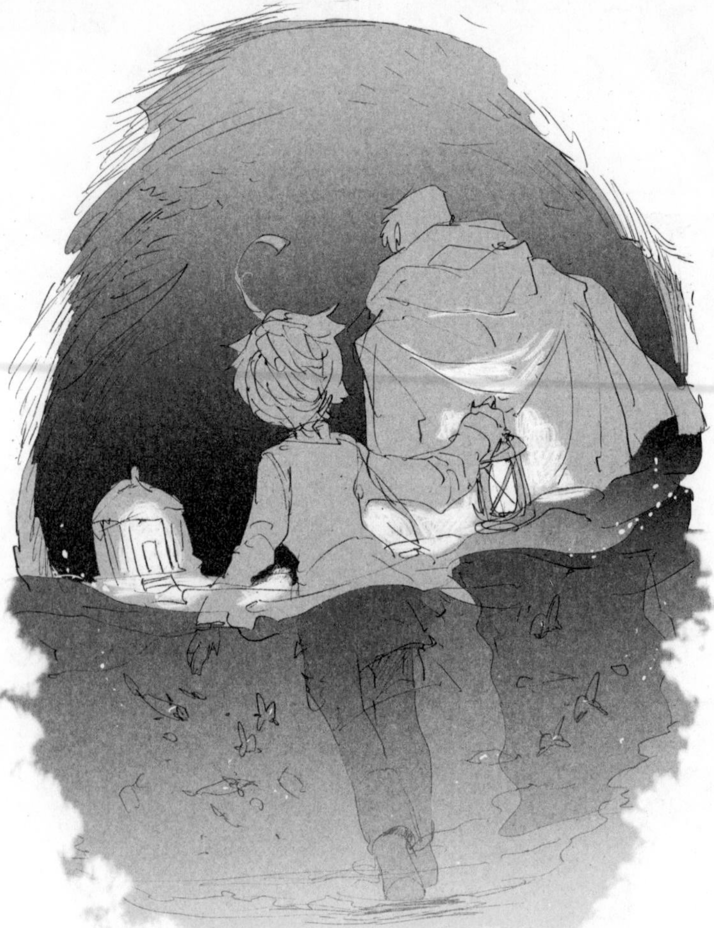

GOLDY POND

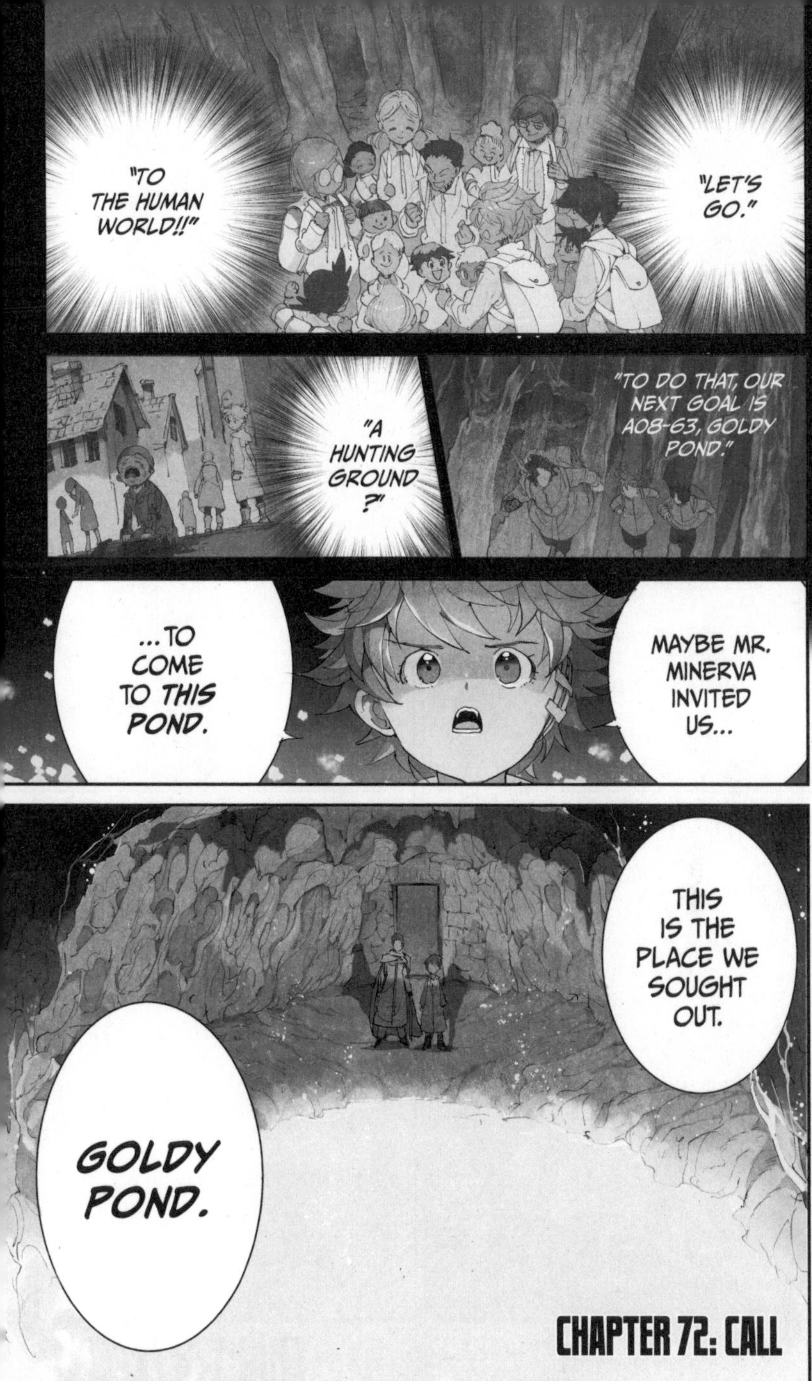
"LET'S GO."
"TO THE HUMAN WORLD!!"
"TO DO THAT, OUR NEXT GOAL IS A08-63, GOLDY POND."
"A HUNTING GROUND?"
MAYBE MR. MINERVA INVITED US...
...TO COME TO THIS POND.
THIS IS THE PLACE WE SOUGHT OUT.
GOLDY POND.
CHAPTER 72: CALL

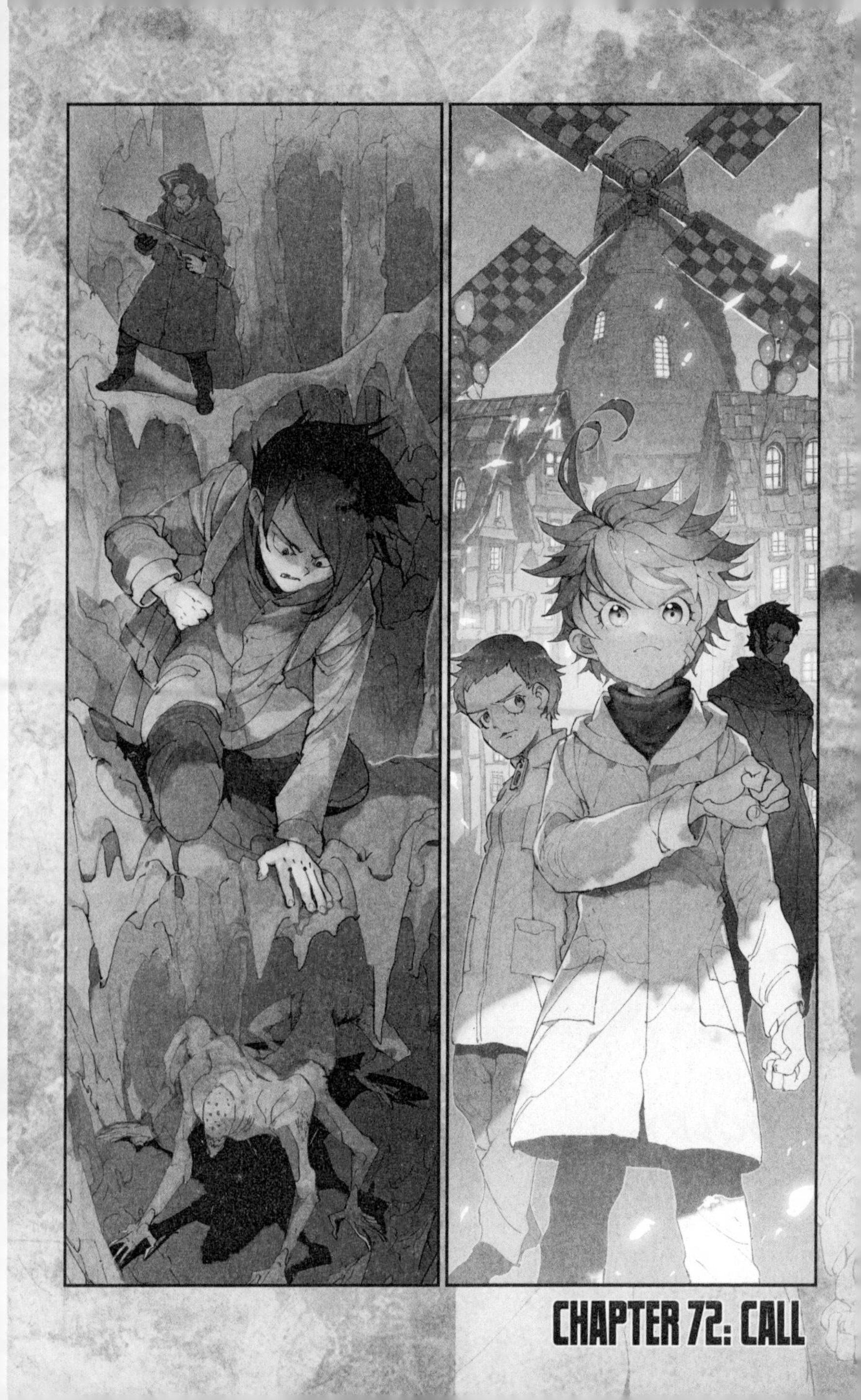

CHAPTER 72: CALL

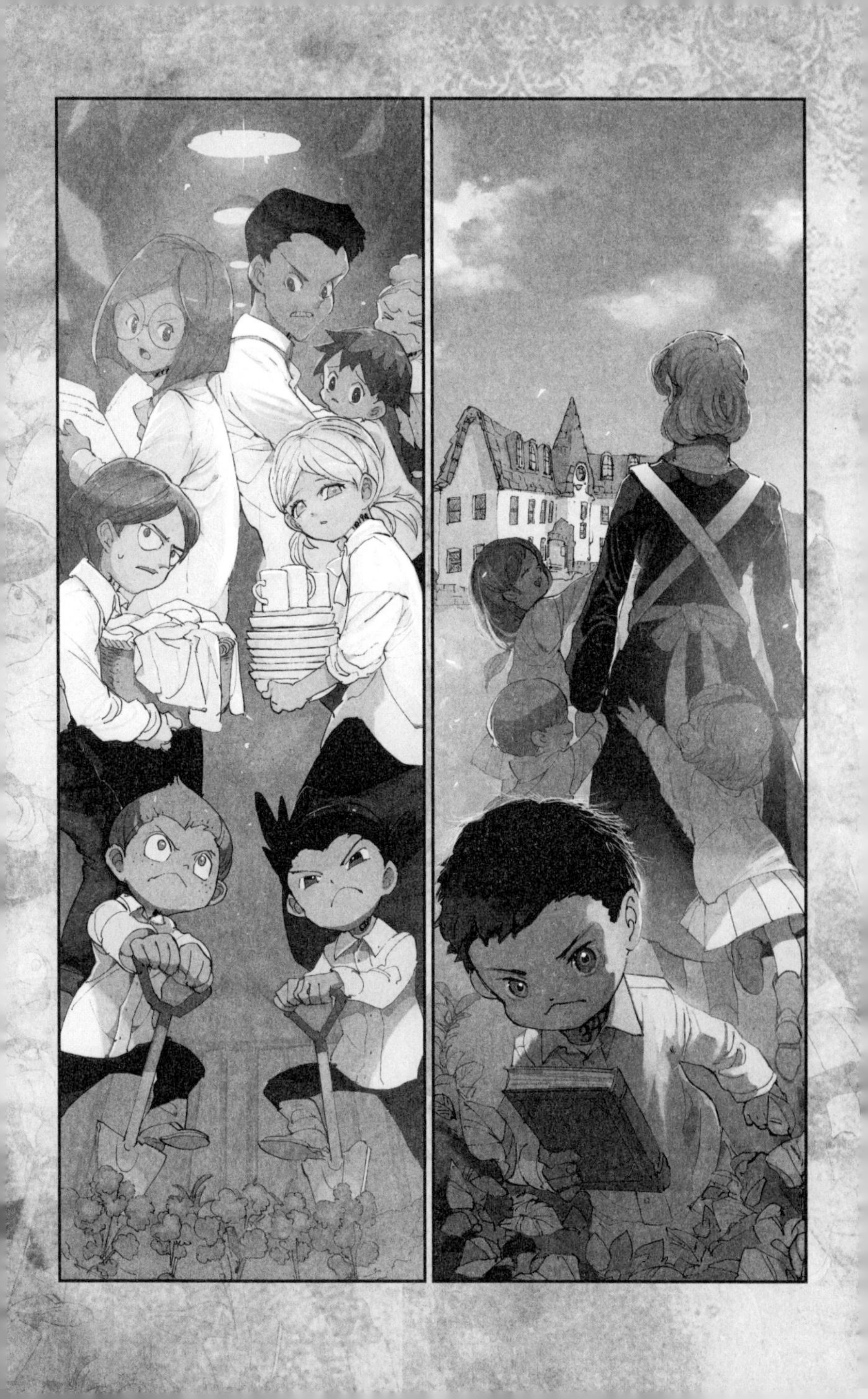

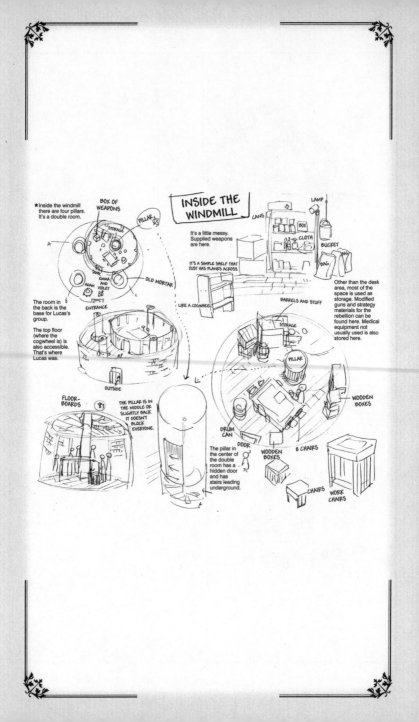

INSIDE THE WINDMILL
★Inside the windmill there are four pillars. It's a double room.
BOX OF WEAPONS
STORAGE
PILLAR
A
DOOR
EMMA AND VIOLET
ADAM
OLD MORTAR
The room in the back is the base for Lucas's group.
The top floor (where the cogwheel is) is also accessible. That's where Lucas was.
ENTRANCE
OUTSIDE
It's a little messy. Supplied weapons are here.
IT'S A SIMPLE SHELF THAT JUST HAS PLANKS ACROSS.
LIKE A COGWHEEL
CANS
LAMP
BOX
CLOTH
BUCKET
BAG
BAG
Other than the desk area, most of the space is used as storage. Modified guns and strategy materials for the rebellion can be found here. Medical equipment not usually used is also stored here.
BARRELS AND STUFF
STORAGE
PILLAR
WOODEN BOXES
FLOOR-BOARDS
THE PILLAR IS IN THE MIDDLE OR SLIGHTLY BACK. IT DOESN'T BLOCK EVERYONE.
DRUM CAN
DOOR
The pillar in the center of the double room has a hidden door and has stairs leading underground.
WOODEN BOXES
8 CHAIRS
CHAIRS
WORK CHAIRS

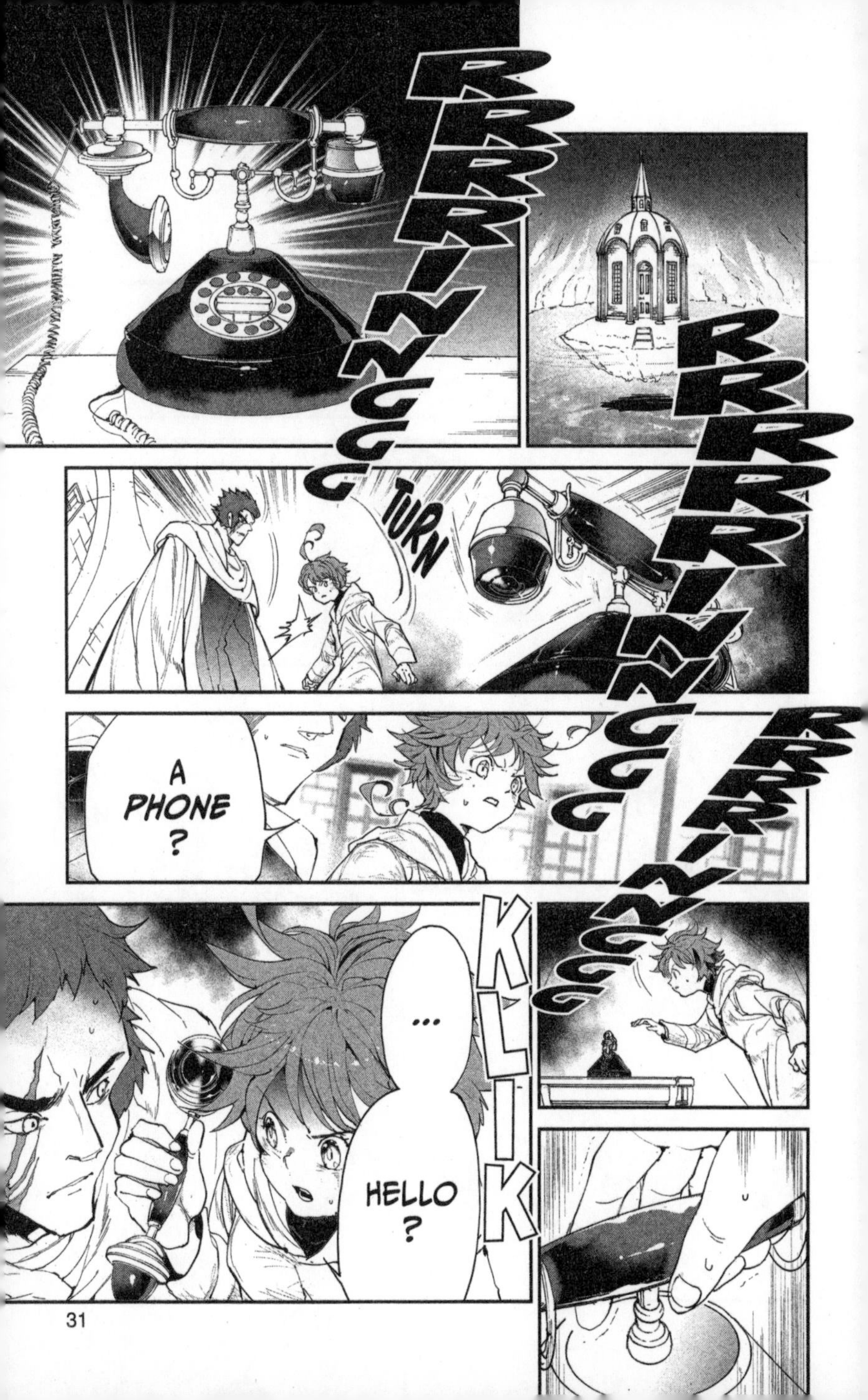
RRRRRINNGGG
RRRRRRRINNGGG
TURN
RRRRINNGGG
A PHONE?
KLIK
...
HELLO?

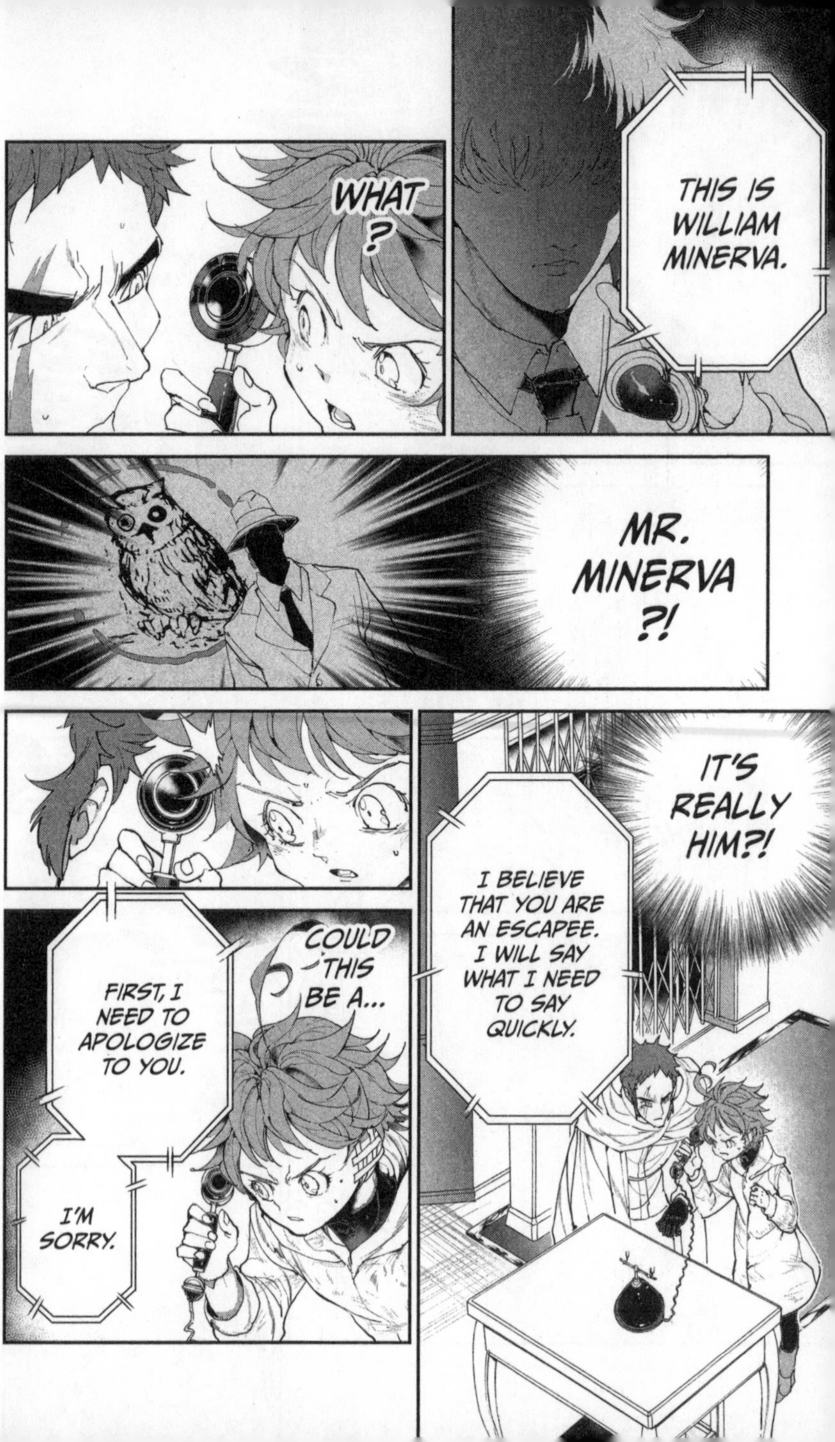

THIS IS WILLIAM MINERVA.
WHAT ?
MR. MINERVA ?!
IT'S REALLY HIM?!
I BELIEVE THAT YOU ARE AN ESCAPEE. I WILL SAY WHAT I NEED TO SAY QUICKLY.
COULD THIS BE A...
FIRST, I NEED TO APOLOGIZE TO YOU.
I'M SORRY.

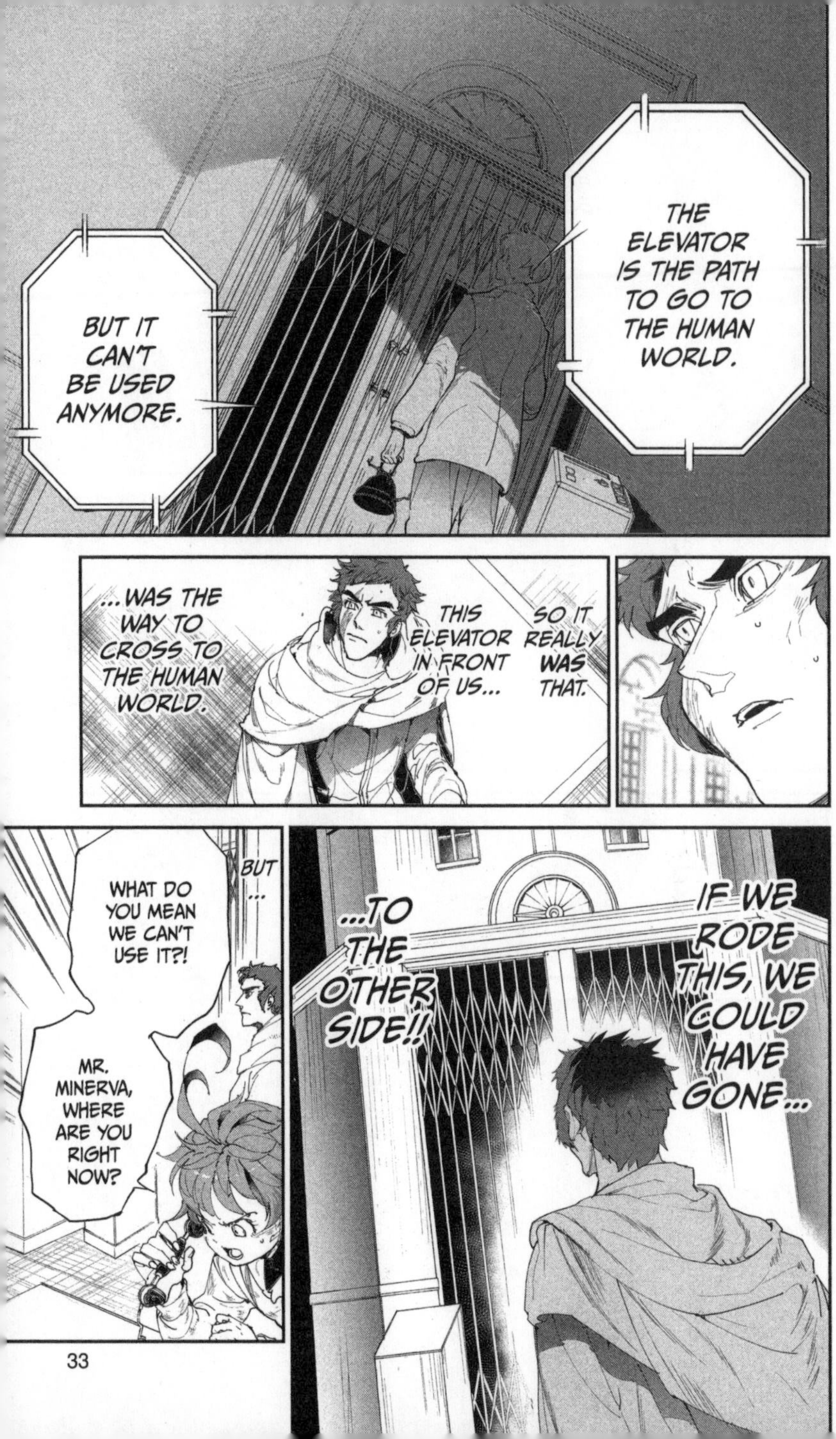
THE ELEVATOR IS THE PATH TO GO TO THE HUMAN WORLD.
BUT IT CAN'T BE USED ANYMORE.
SO IT REALLY WAS THAT.
THIS ELEVATOR IN FRONT OF US...
...WAS THE WAY TO CROSS TO THE HUMAN WORLD.
IF WE RODE THIS, WE COULD HAVE GONE...
...TO THE OTHER SIDE!!
BUT...
WHAT DO YOU MEAN WE CAN'T USE IT?!
MR. MINERVA, WHERE ARE YOU RIGHT NOW?

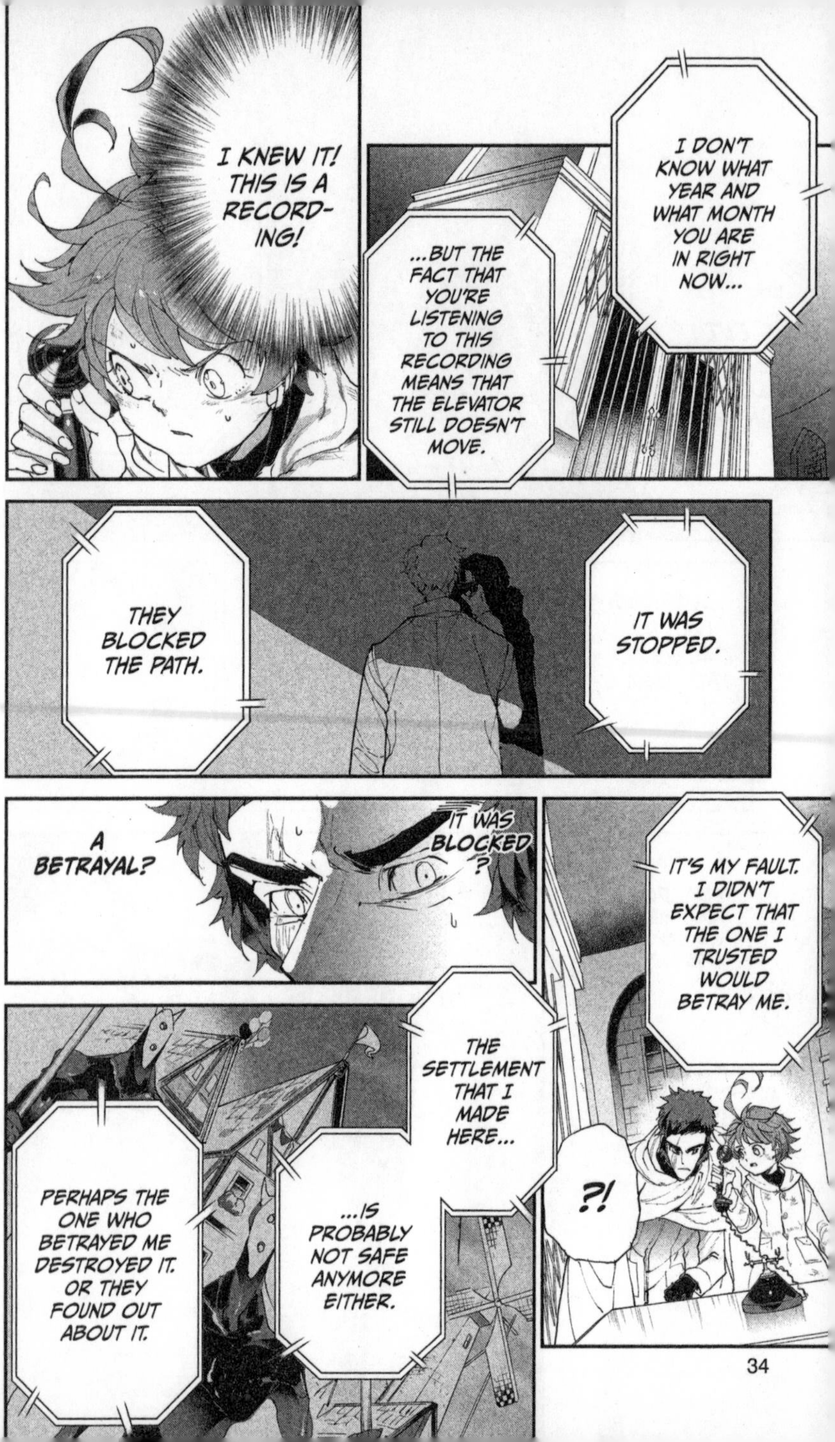
I DON'T KNOW WHAT YEAR AND WHAT MONTH YOU ARE IN RIGHT NOW...
...BUT THE FACT THAT YOU'RE LISTENING TO THIS RECORDING MEANS THAT THE ELEVATOR STILL DOESN'T MOVE.
I KNEW IT! THIS IS A RECORD-ING!
IT WAS STOPPED.
THEY BLOCKED THE PATH.
IT'S MY FAULT. I DIDN'T EXPECT THAT THE ONE I TRUSTED WOULD BETRAY ME.
?!
IT WAS BLOCKED?
A BETRAYAL?
THE SETTLEMENT THAT I MADE HERE...
...IS PROBABLY NOT SAFE ANYMORE EITHER.
PERHAPS THE ONE WHO BETRAYED ME DESTROYED IT. OR THEY FOUND OUT ABOUT IT.

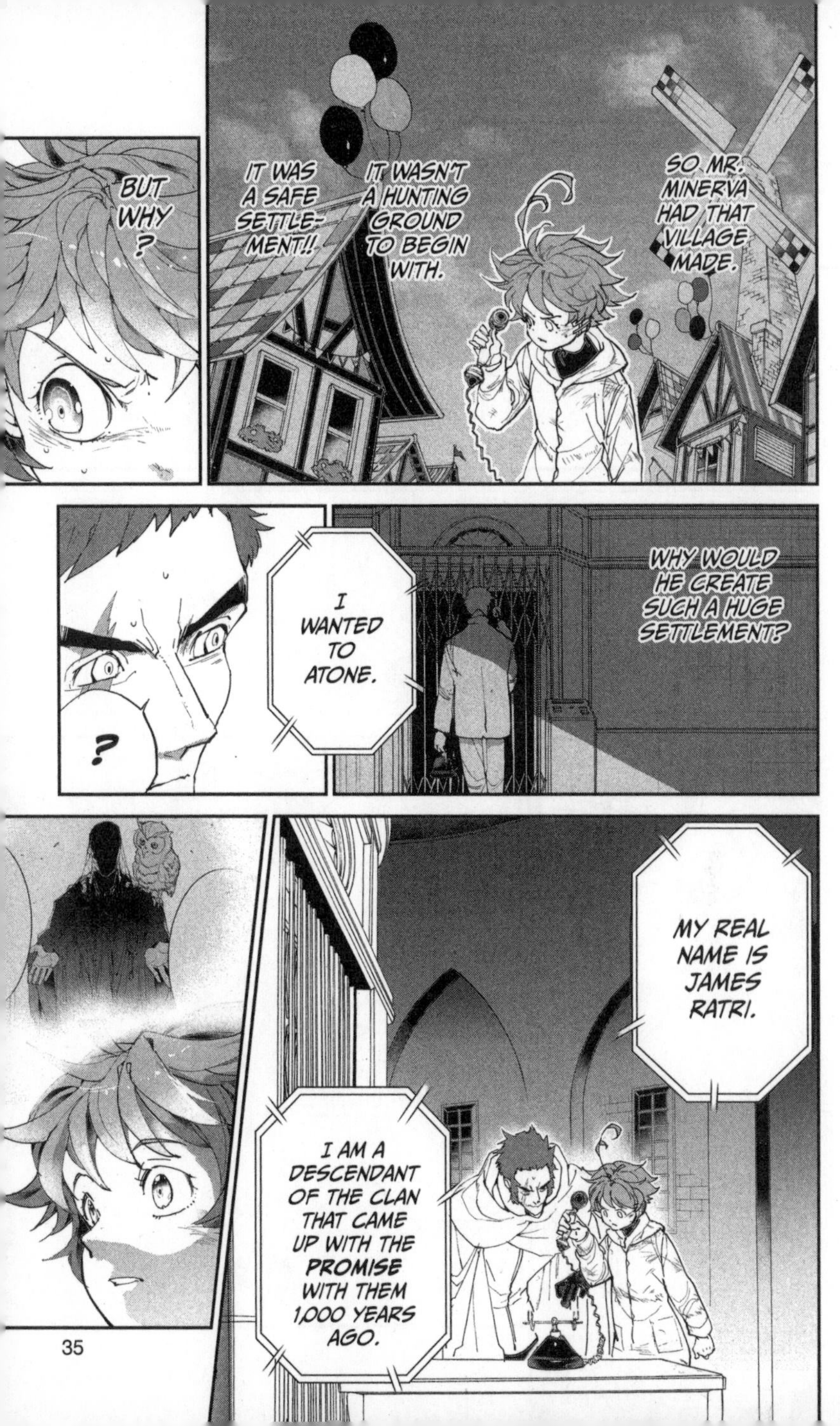
SO MR. MINERVA HAD THAT VILLAGE MADE.
IT WASN'T A HUNTING GROUND TO BEGIN WITH.
IT WAS A SAFE SETTLEMENT!!
BUT WHY?
WHY WOULD HE CREATE SUCH A HUGE SETTLEMENT?
I WANTED TO ATONE.
?
MY REAL NAME IS JAMES RATRI.
I AM A DESCENDANT OF THE CLAN THAT CAME UP WITH THE PROMISE WITH THEM 1,000 YEARS AGO.

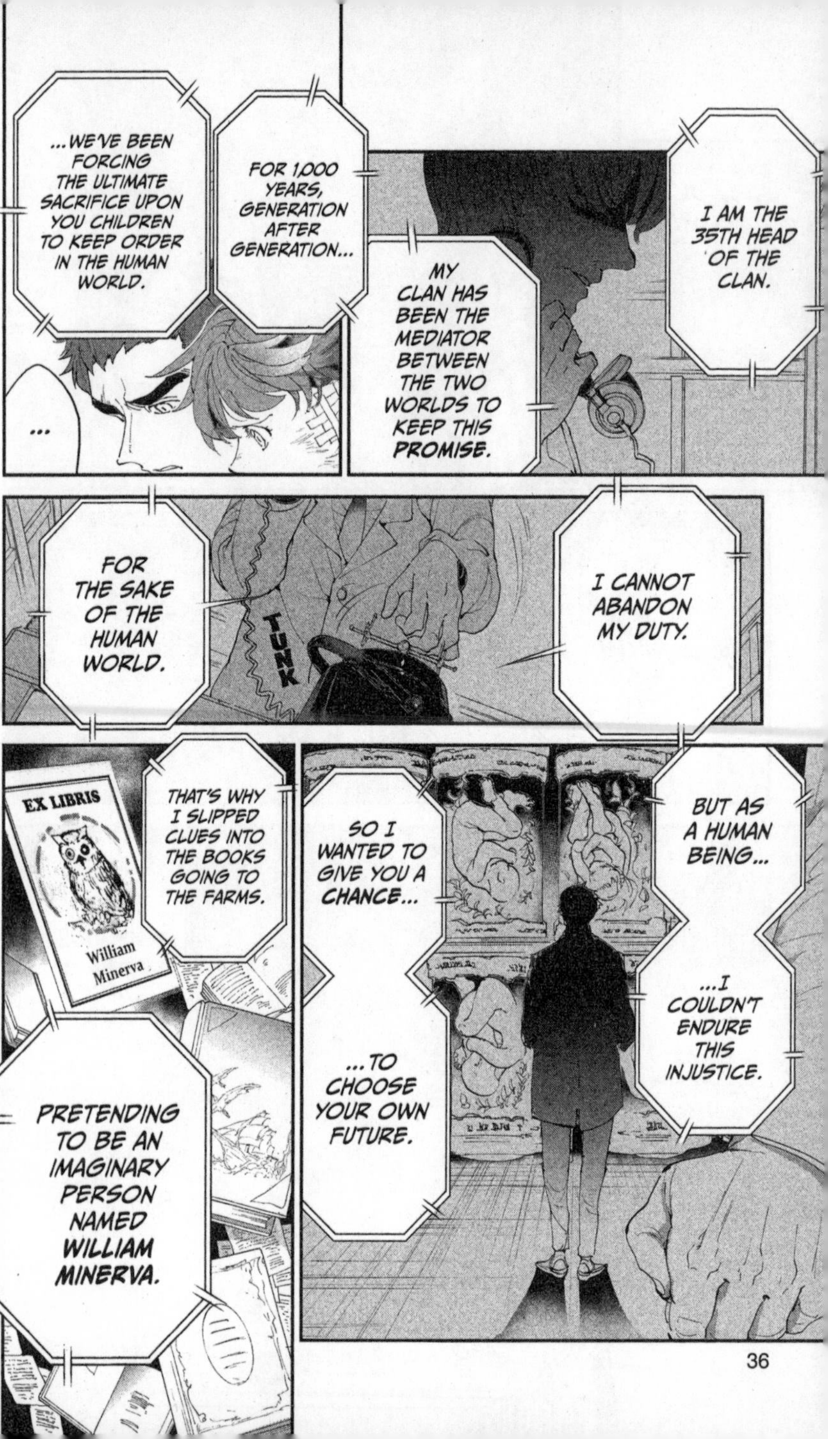
I AM THE 35TH HEAD OF THE CLAN.
MY CLAN HAS BEEN THE MEDIATOR BETWEEN THE TWO WORLDS TO KEEP THIS PROMISE.
FOR 1,000 YEARS, GENERATION AFTER GENERATION...
...WE'VE BEEN FORCING THE ULTIMATE SACRIFICE UPON YOU CHILDREN TO KEEP ORDER IN THE HUMAN WORLD.
...
I CANNOT ABANDON MY DUTY.
TUNK
FOR THE SAKE OF THE HUMAN WORLD.
BUT AS A HUMAN BEING...
...I COULDN'T ENDURE THIS INJUSTICE.
SO I WANTED TO GIVE YOU A CHANCE...
...TO CHOOSE YOUR OWN FUTURE.
THAT'S WHY I SLIPPED CLUES INTO THE BOOKS GOING TO THE FARMS.
EX LIBRIS
William Minerva
PRETENDING TO BE AN IMAGINARY PERSON NAMED WILLIAM MINERVA.

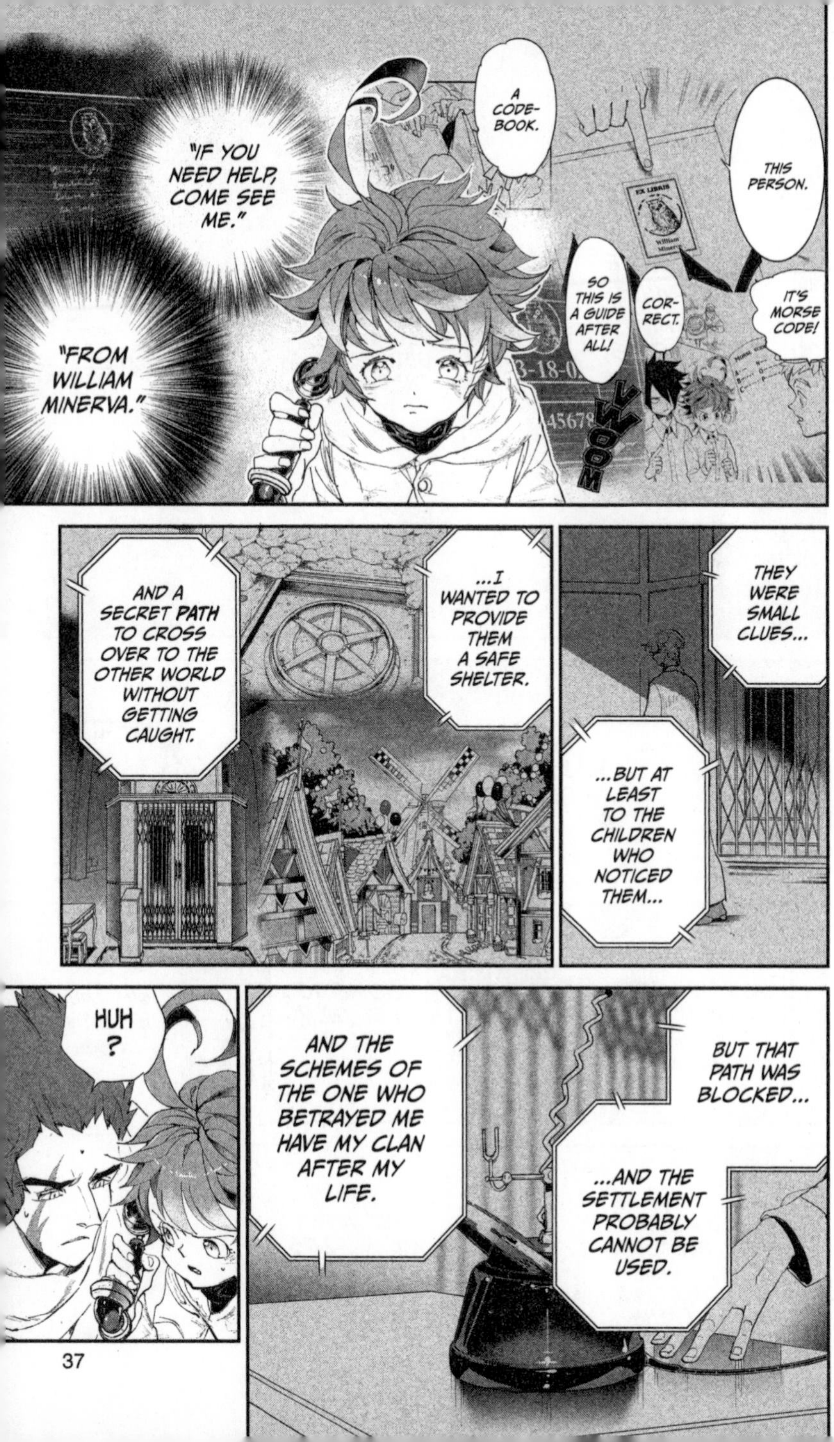
THIS PERSON.
IT'S MORSE CODE!
COR-RECT.
SO THIS IS A GUIDE AFTER ALL!
A CODE-BOOK.
VWOOM
"IF YOU NEED HELP, COME SEE ME."
"FROM WILLIAM MINERVA."
THEY WERE SMALL CLUES...
...BUT AT LEAST TO THE CHILDREN WHO NOTICED THEM...
...I WANTED TO PROVIDE THEM A SAFE SHELTER.
AND A SECRET PATH TO CROSS OVER TO THE OTHER WORLD WITHOUT GETTING CAUGHT.
BUT THAT PATH WAS BLOCKED...
...AND THE SETTLEMENT PROBABLY CANNOT BE USED.
AND THE SCHEMES OF THE ONE WHO BETRAYED ME HAVE MY CLAN AFTER MY LIFE.
HUH?

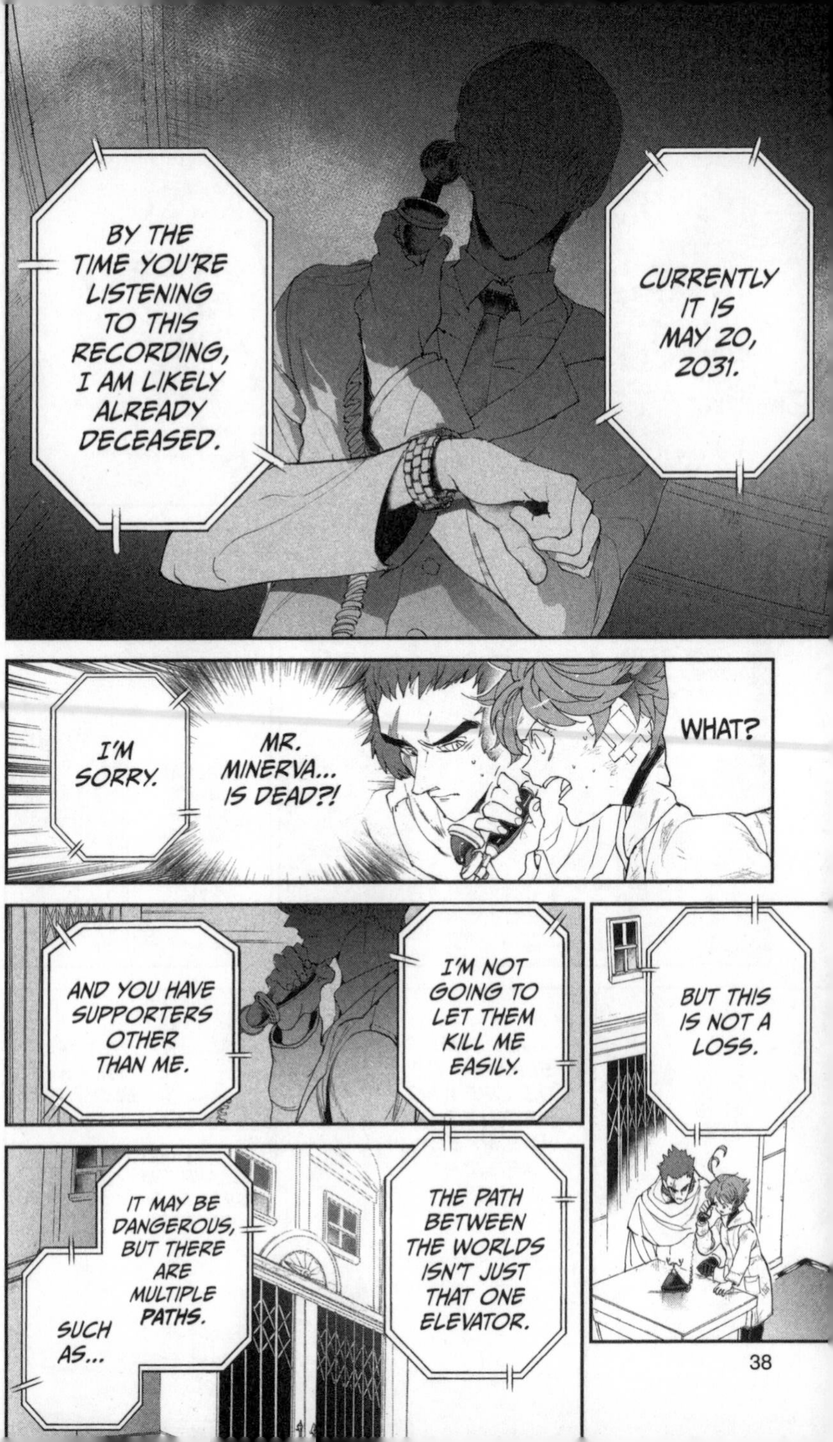
CURRENTLY IT IS MAY 20, 2031.
BY THE TIME YOU'RE LISTENING TO THIS RECORDING, I AM LIKELY ALREADY DECEASED.
WHAT?
MR. MINERVA... IS DEAD?!
I'M SORRY.
BUT THIS IS NOT A LOSS.
I'M NOT GOING TO LET THEM KILL ME EASILY.
AND YOU HAVE SUPPORTERS OTHER THAN ME.
THE PATH BETWEEN THE WORLDS ISN'T JUST THAT ONE ELEVATOR.
IT MAY BE DANGEROUS, BUT THERE ARE MULTIPLE PATHS.
SUCH AS...

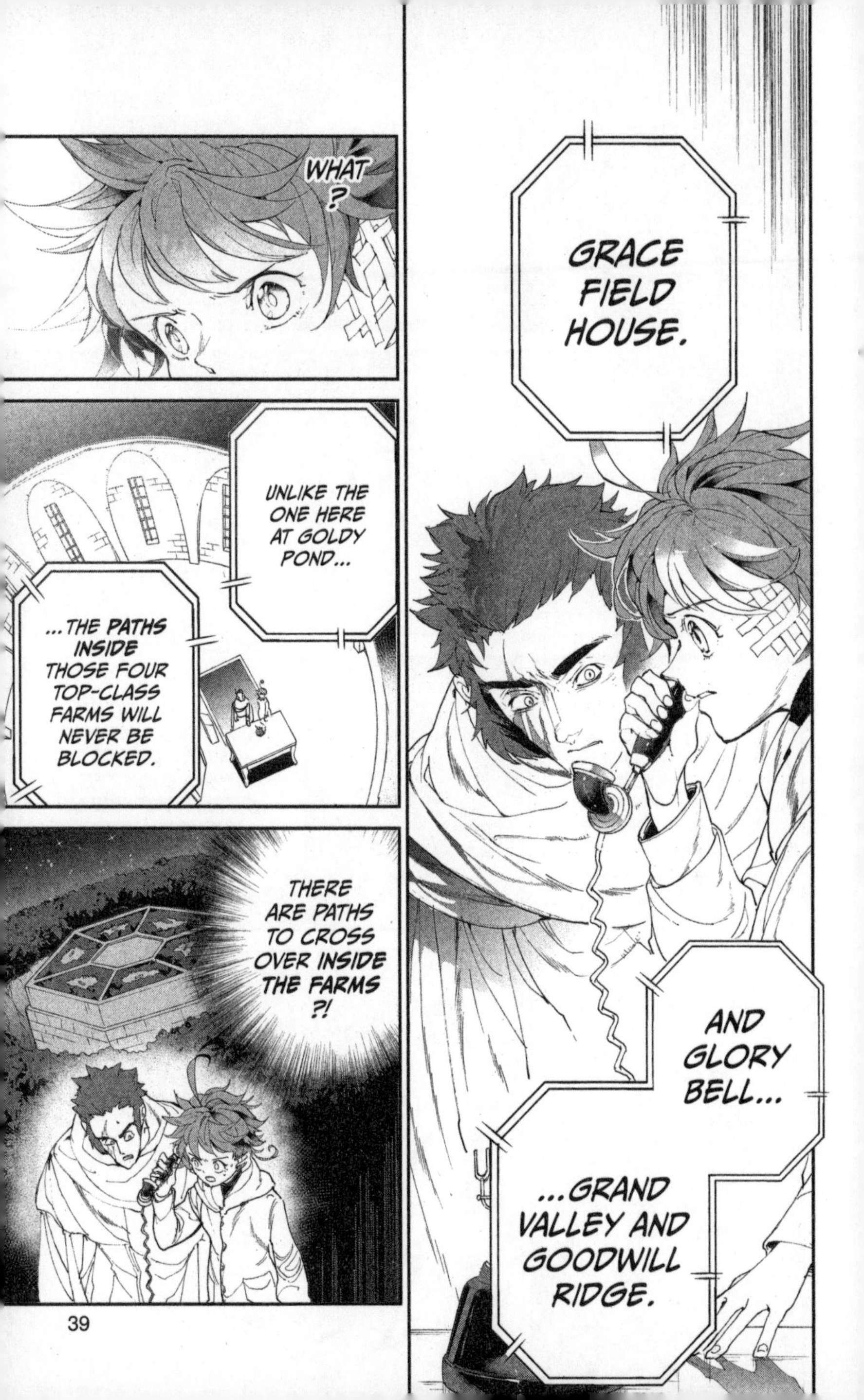
GRACE FIELD HOUSE.
AND GLORY BELL...
...GRAND VALLEY AND GOODWILL RIDGE.
WHAT?
UNLIKE THE ONE HERE AT GOLDY POND...
...THE PATHS INSIDE THOSE FOUR TOP-CLASS FARMS WILL NEVER BE BLOCKED.
THERE ARE PATHS TO CROSS OVER INSIDE THE FARMS?!

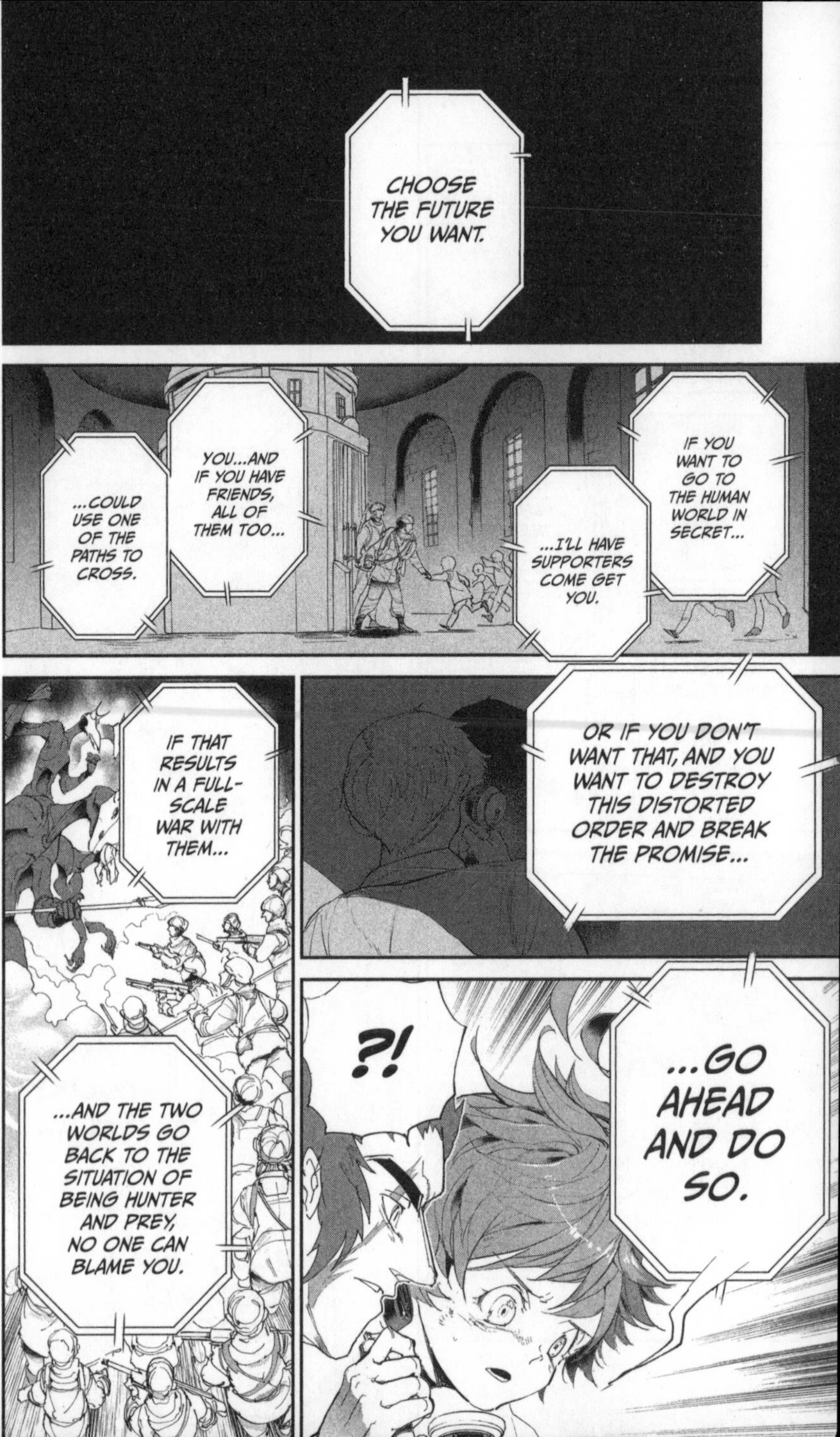
CHOOSE THE FUTURE YOU WANT.
IF YOU WANT TO GO TO THE HUMAN WORLD IN SECRET...
...I'LL HAVE SUPPORTERS COME GET YOU.
YOU...AND IF YOU HAVE FRIENDS, ALL OF THEM TOO...
...COULD USE ONE OF THE PATHS TO CROSS.
OR IF YOU DON'T WANT THAT, AND YOU WANT TO DESTROY THIS DISTORTED ORDER AND BREAK THE PROMISE...
...GO AHEAD AND DO SO.
?!
IF THAT RESULTS IN A FULL-SCALE WAR WITH THEM...
...AND THE TWO WORLDS GO BACK TO THE SITUATION OF BEING HUNTER AND PREY, NO ONE CAN BLAME YOU.

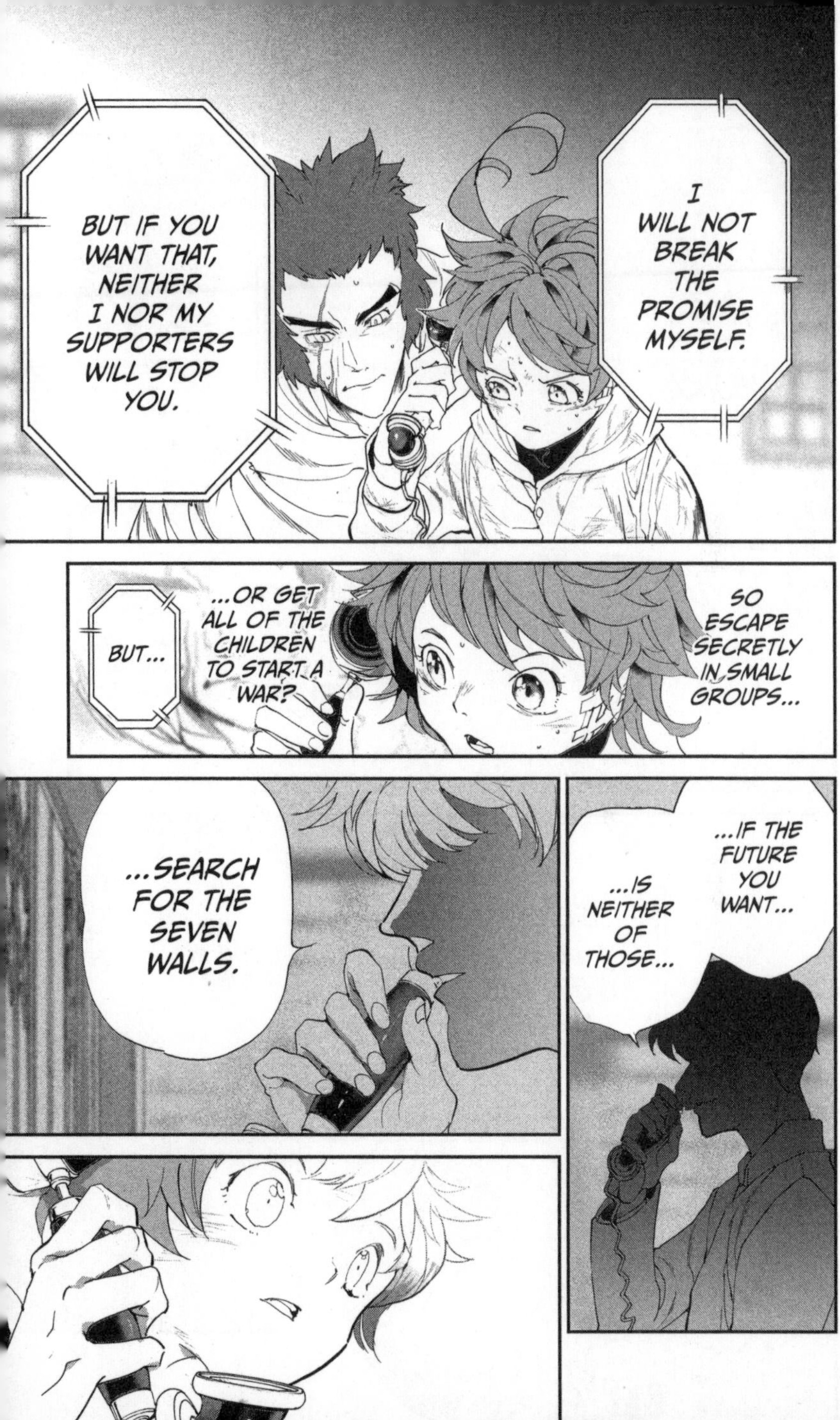
I WILL NOT BREAK THE PROMISE MYSELF.
BUT IF YOU WANT THAT, NEITHER I NOR MY SUPPORTERS WILL STOP YOU.
SO ESCAPE SECRETLY IN SMALL GROUPS...
...OR GET ALL OF THE CHILDREN TO START A WAR?
BUT...
...IF THE FUTURE YOU WANT...
...IS NEITHER OF THOSE...
...SEARCH FOR THE SEVEN WALLS.

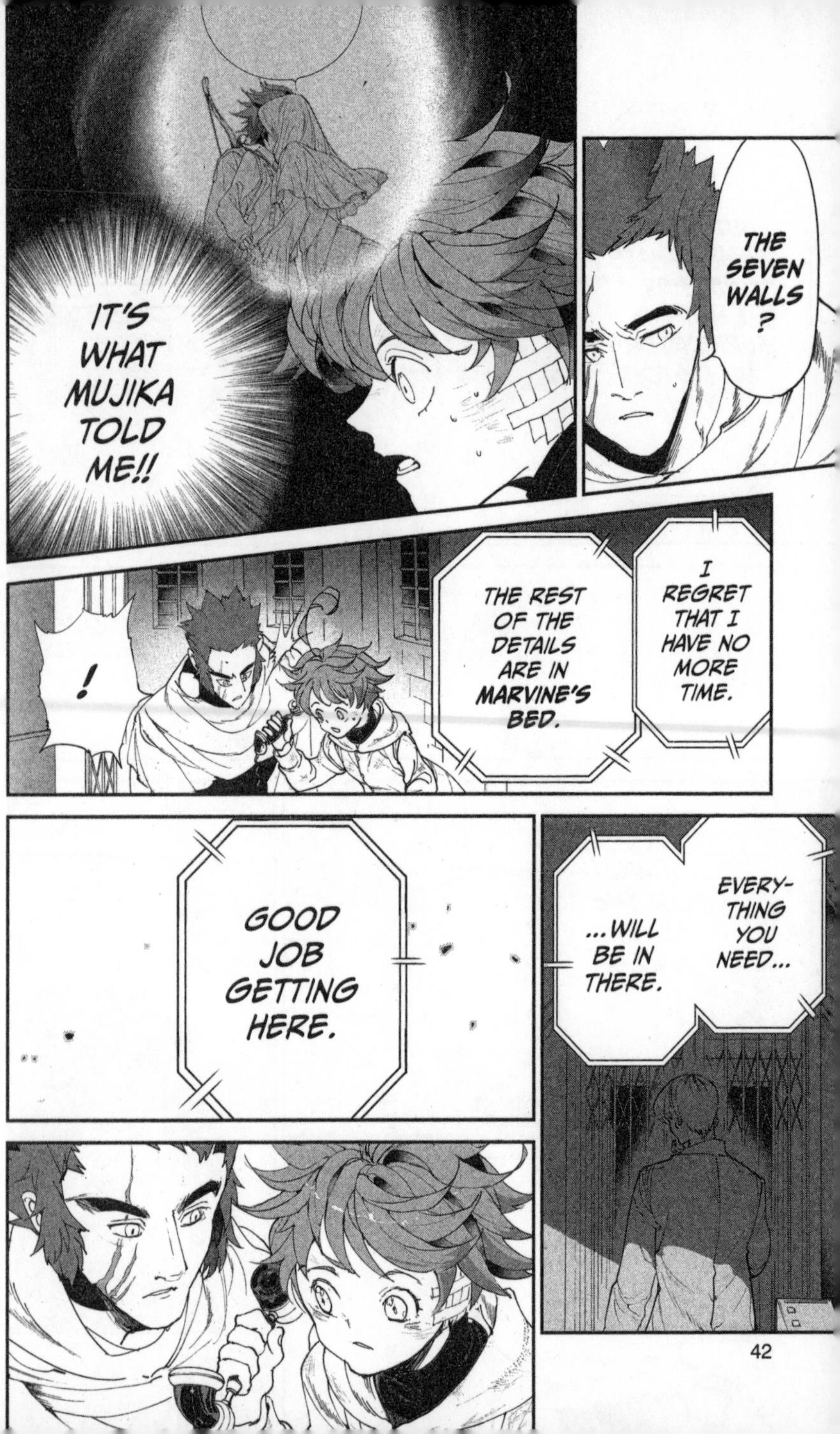
THE SEVEN WALLS?
IT'S WHAT MUJIKA TOLD ME!!
I REGRET THAT I HAVE NO MORE TIME.
THE REST OF THE DETAILS ARE IN MARVINE'S BED.
!
EVERYTHING YOU NEED...
...WILL BE IN THERE.
GOOD JOB GETTING HERE.

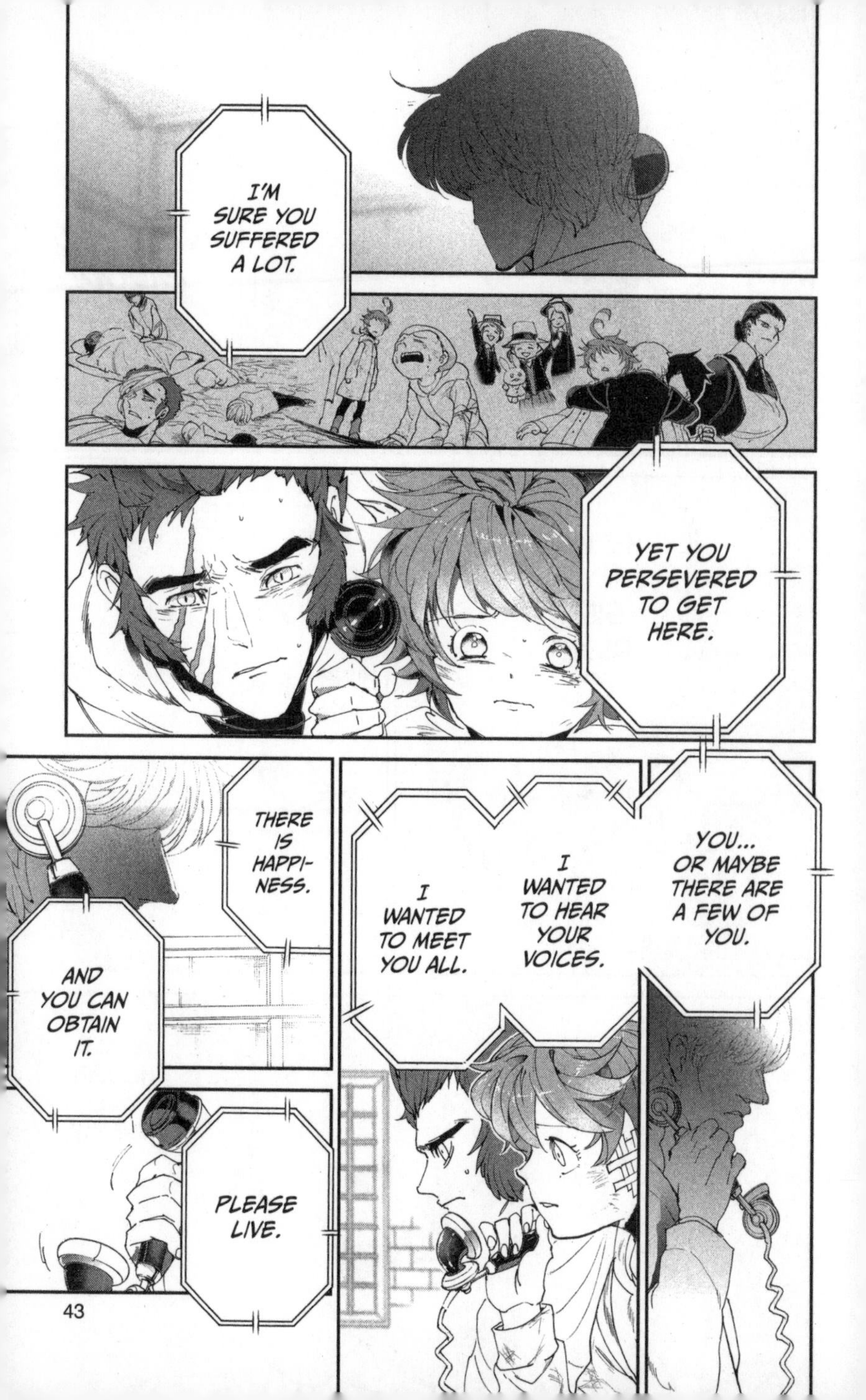
I'M SURE YOU SUFFERED A LOT.
YET YOU PERSEVERED TO GET HERE.
YOU... OR MAYBE THERE ARE A FEW OF YOU.
I WANTED TO HEAR YOUR VOICES.
I WANTED TO MEET YOU ALL.
THERE IS HAPPINESS.
AND YOU CAN OBTAIN IT.
PLEASE LIVE.

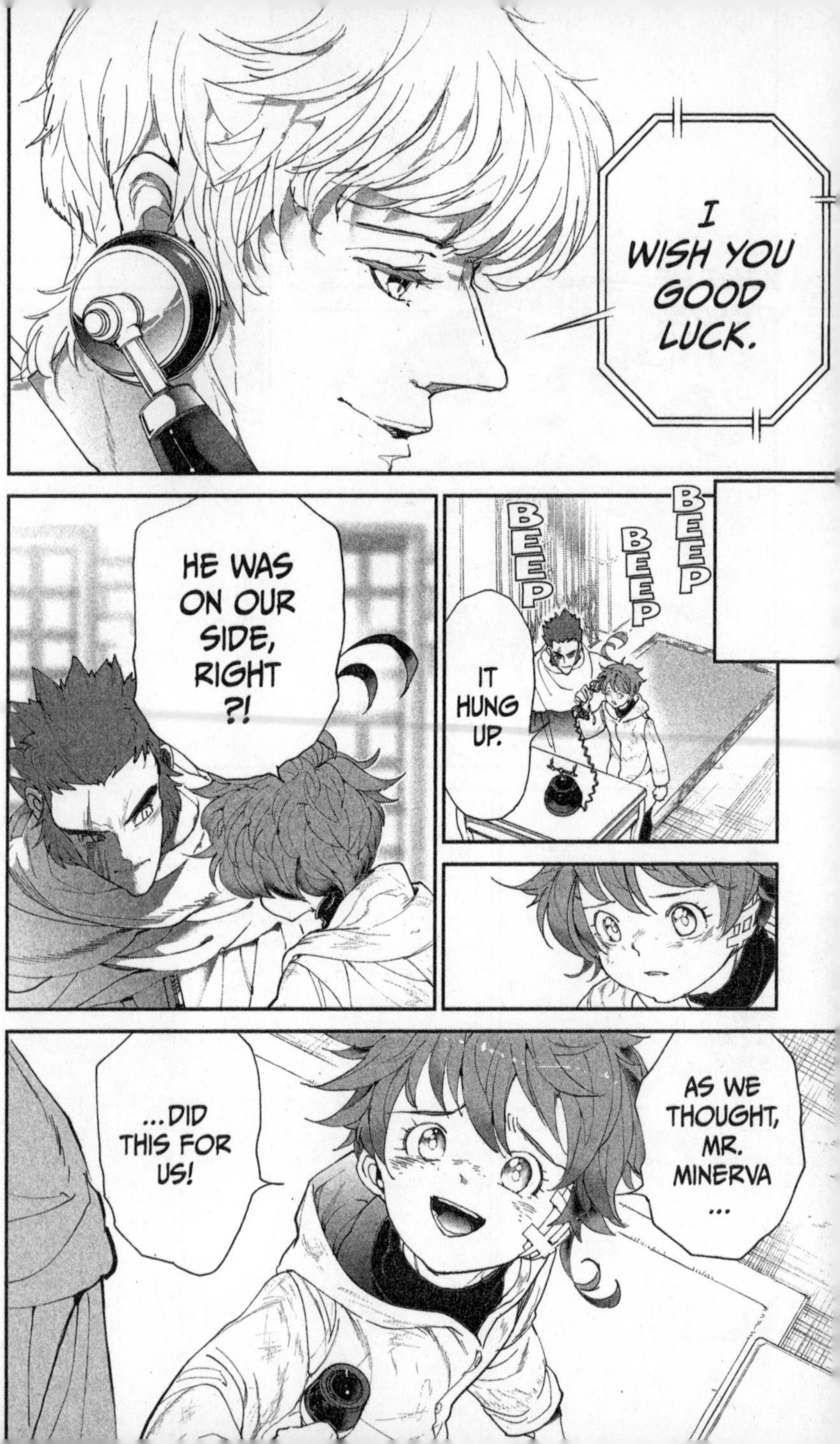
I WISH YOU GOOD LUCK.
BEEP
BEEP
BEEP
IT HUNG UP.
HE WAS ON OUR SIDE, RIGHT?!
AS WE THOUGHT, MR. MINERVA...
...DID THIS FOR US!

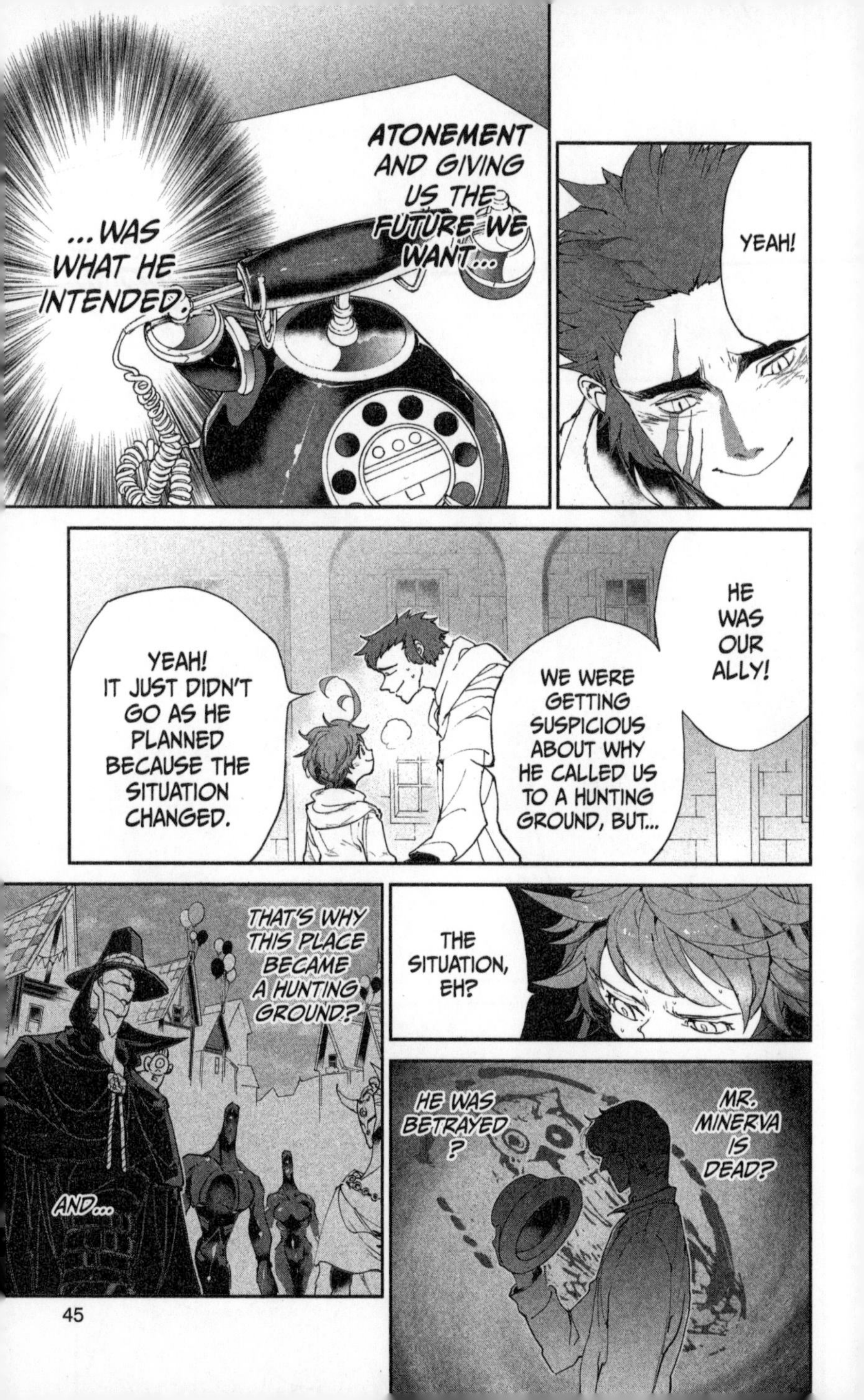
YEAH!
ATONEMENT AND GIVING US THE FUTURE WE WANT...
...WAS WHAT HE INTENDED.
HE WAS OUR ALLY!
WE WERE GETTING SUSPICIOUS ABOUT WHY HE CALLED US TO A HUNTING GROUND, BUT...
YEAH! IT JUST DIDN'T GO AS HE PLANNED BECAUSE THE SITUATION CHANGED.
THE SITUATION, EH?
MR. MINERVA IS DEAD?
HE WAS BETRAYED?
THAT'S WHY THIS PLACE BECAME A HUNTING GROUND?
AND...

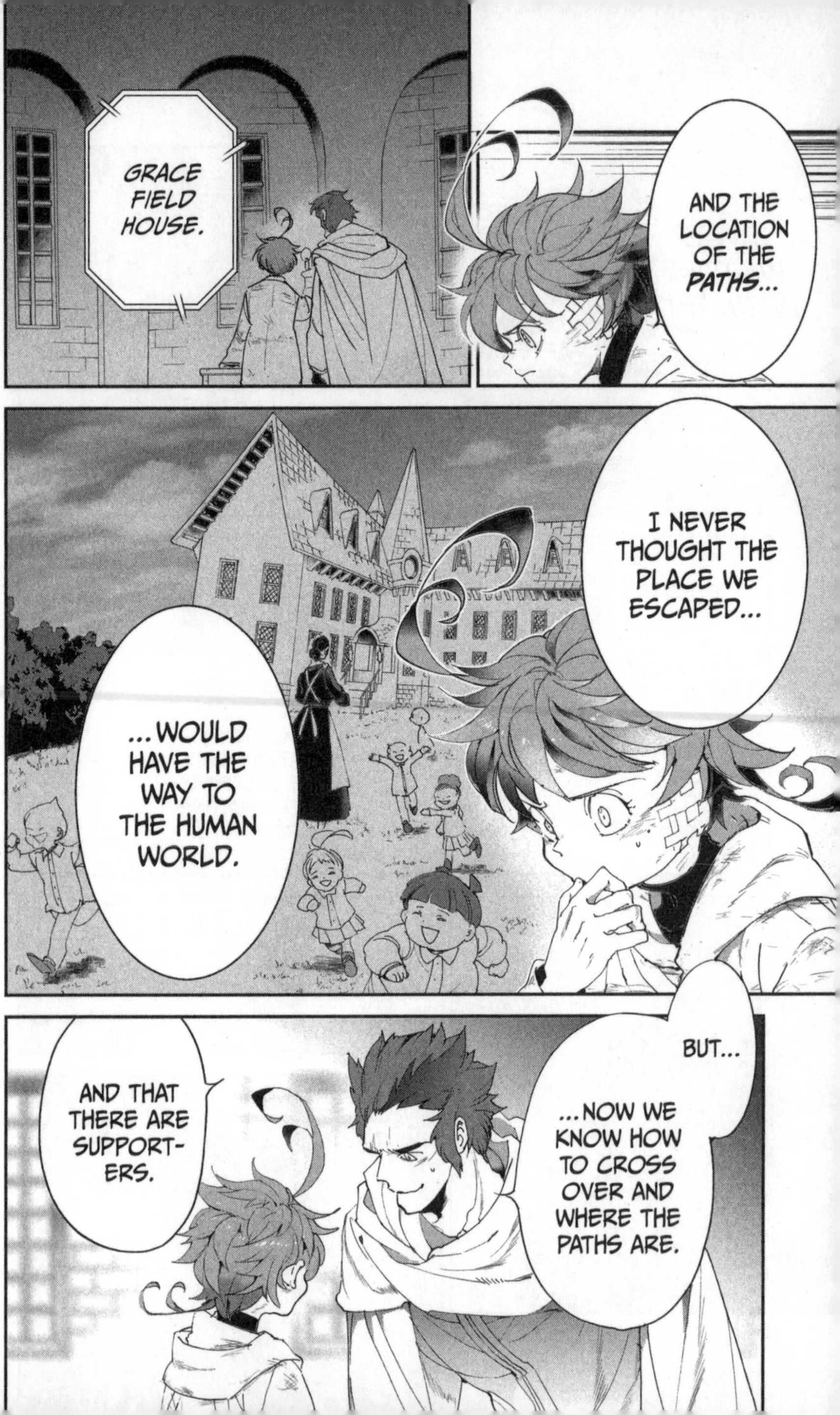
AND THE LOCATION OF THE PATHS...
GRACE FIELD HOUSE.
I NEVER THOUGHT THE PLACE WE ESCAPED...
...WOULD HAVE THE WAY TO THE HUMAN WORLD.
BUT...
...NOW WE KNOW HOW TO CROSS OVER AND WHERE THE PATHS ARE.
AND THAT THERE ARE SUPPORT-ERS.

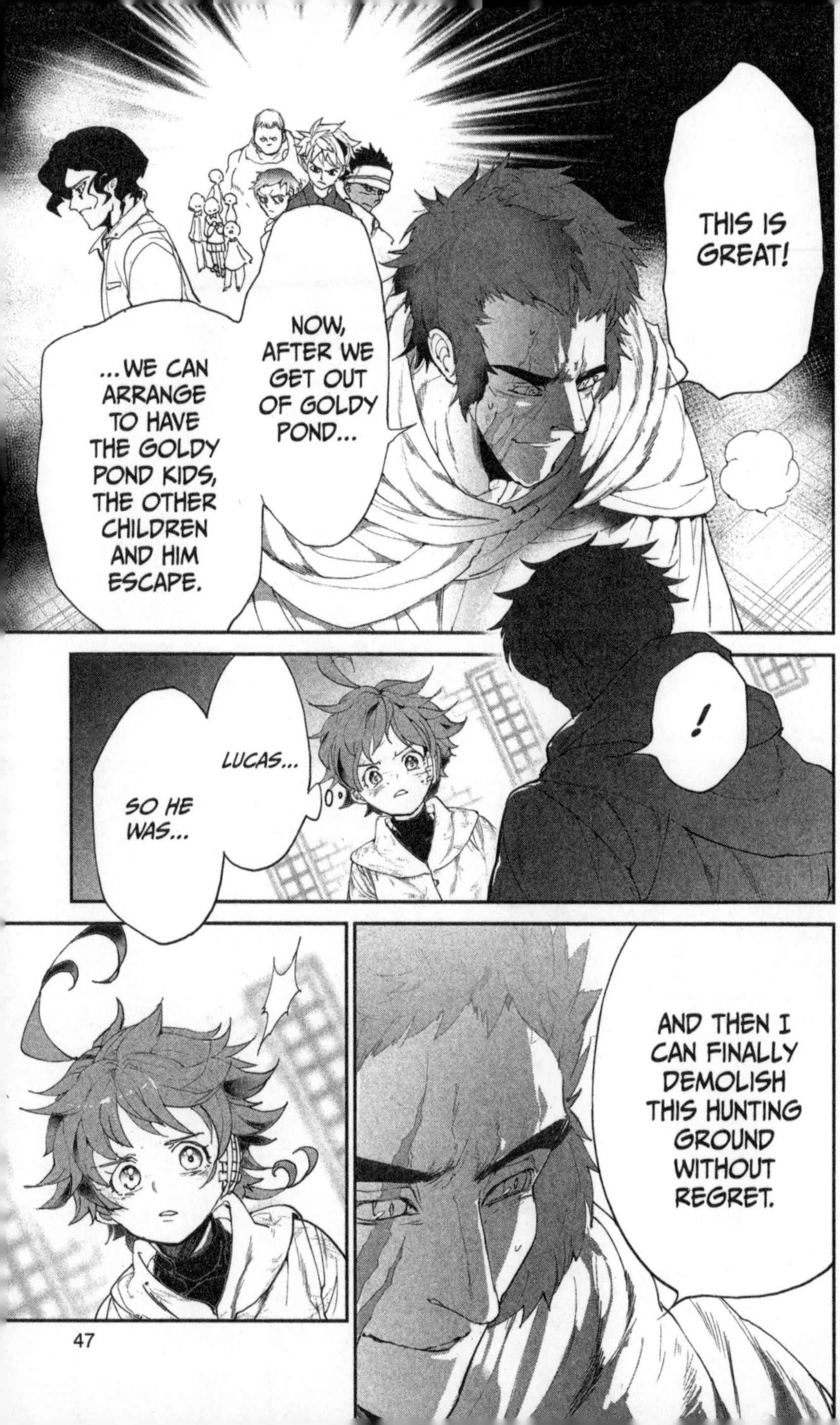
THIS IS GREAT!
NOW, AFTER WE GET OUT OF GOLDY POND...
...WE CAN ARRANGE TO HAVE THE GOLDY POND KIDS, THE OTHER CHILDREN AND HIM ESCAPE.
!
LUCAS...
SO HE WAS...
AND THEN I CAN FINALLY DEMOLISH THIS HUNTING GROUND WITHOUT REGRET.

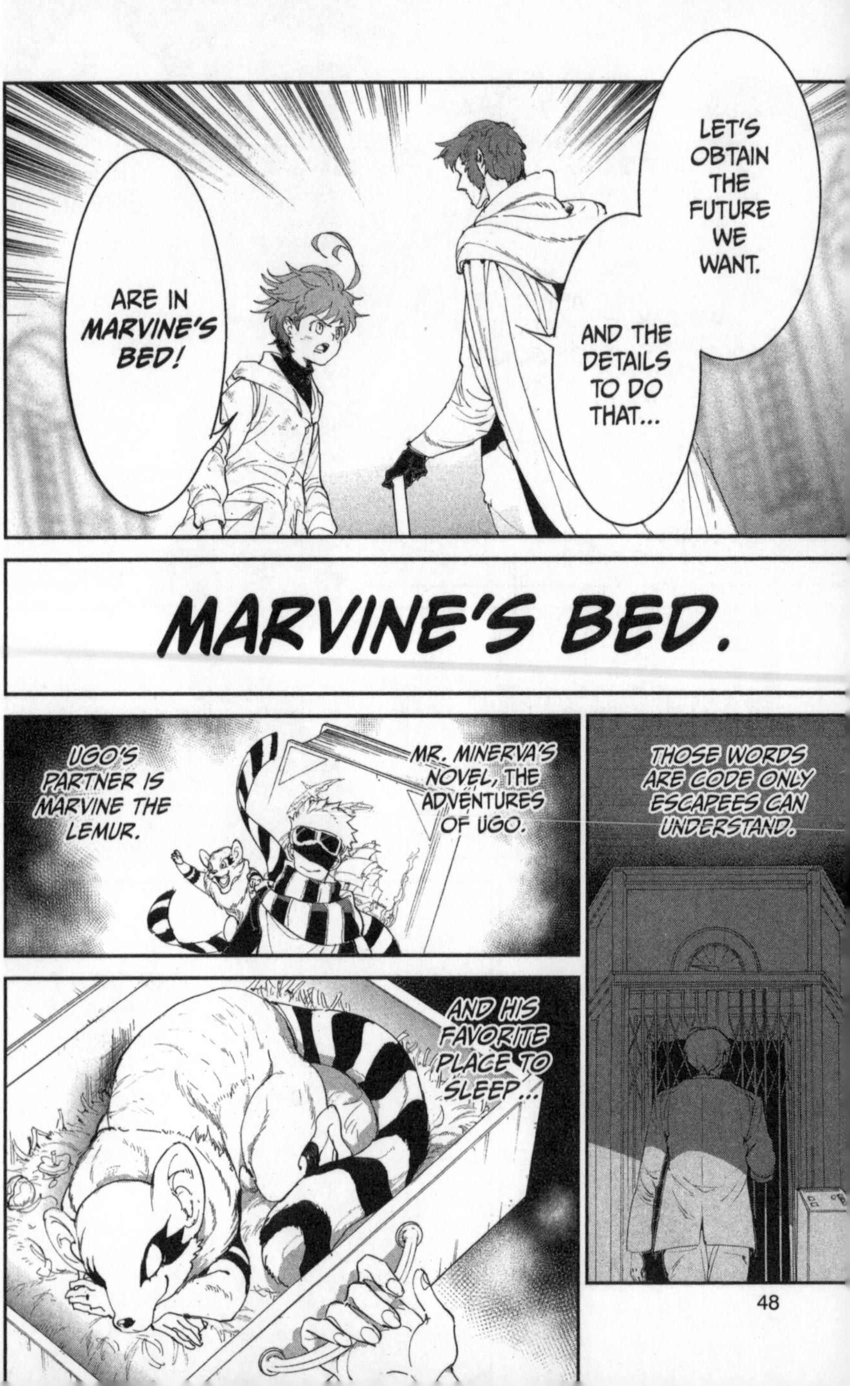
LET'S OBTAIN THE FUTURE WE WANT.
AND THE DETAILS TO DO THAT...
ARE IN MARVINE'S BED!
MARVINE'S BED.
THOSE WORDS ARE CODE ONLY ESCAPEES CAN UNDERSTAND.
MR. MINERVA'S NOVEL, THE ADVENTURES OF UGO.
UGO'S PARTNER IS MARVINE THE LEMUR.
AND HIS FAVORITE PLACE TO SLEEP...

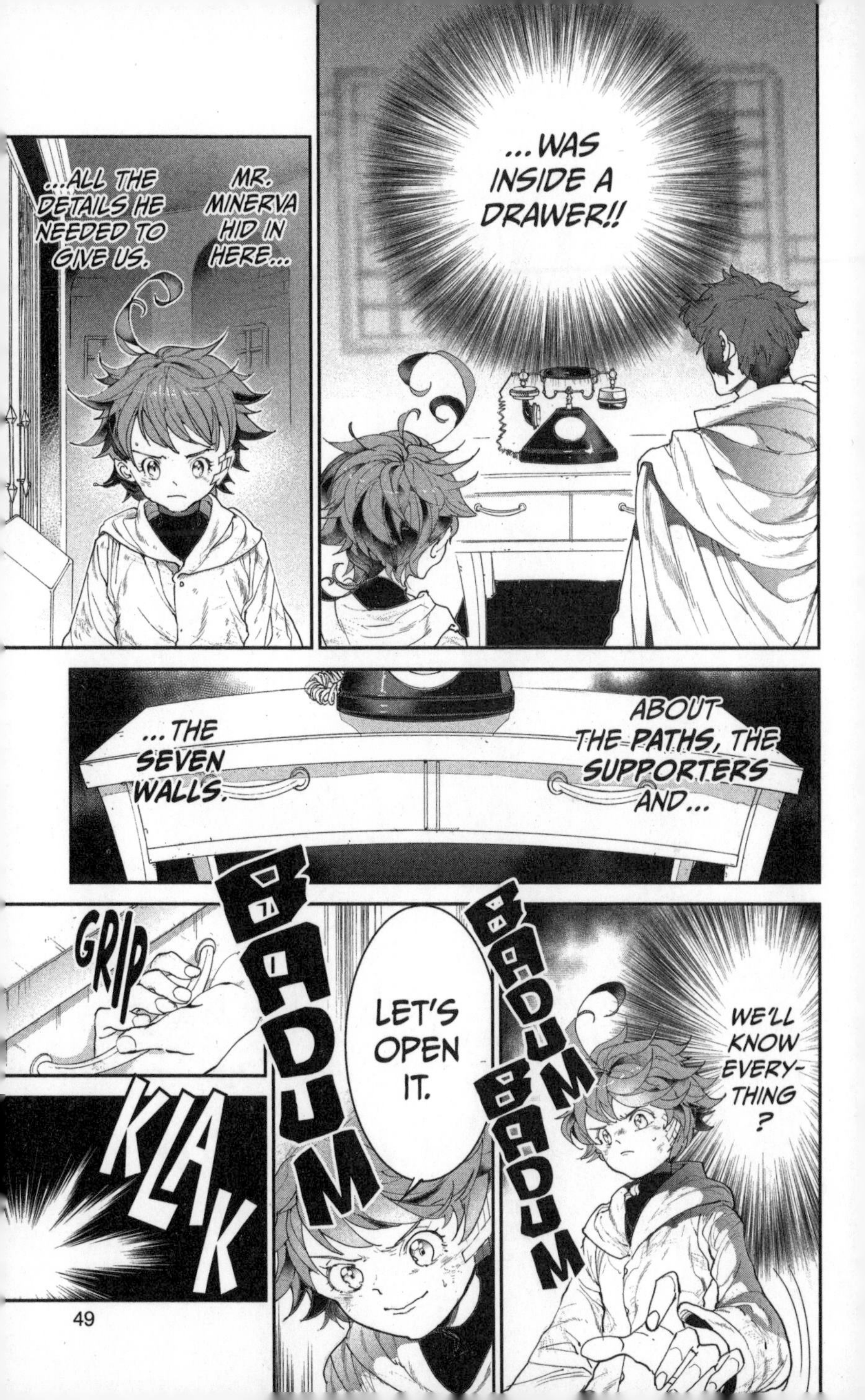
...WAS INSIDE A DRAWER!!
MR. MINERVA HID IN HERE...
...ALL THE DETAILS HE NEEDED TO GIVE US.
ABOUT THE PATHS, THE SUPPORTERS AND...
...THE SEVEN WALLS.
WE'LL KNOW EVERYTHING?
BADUM BADUM BADUM
LET'S OPEN IT.
BADUM
GRIP
KLAK

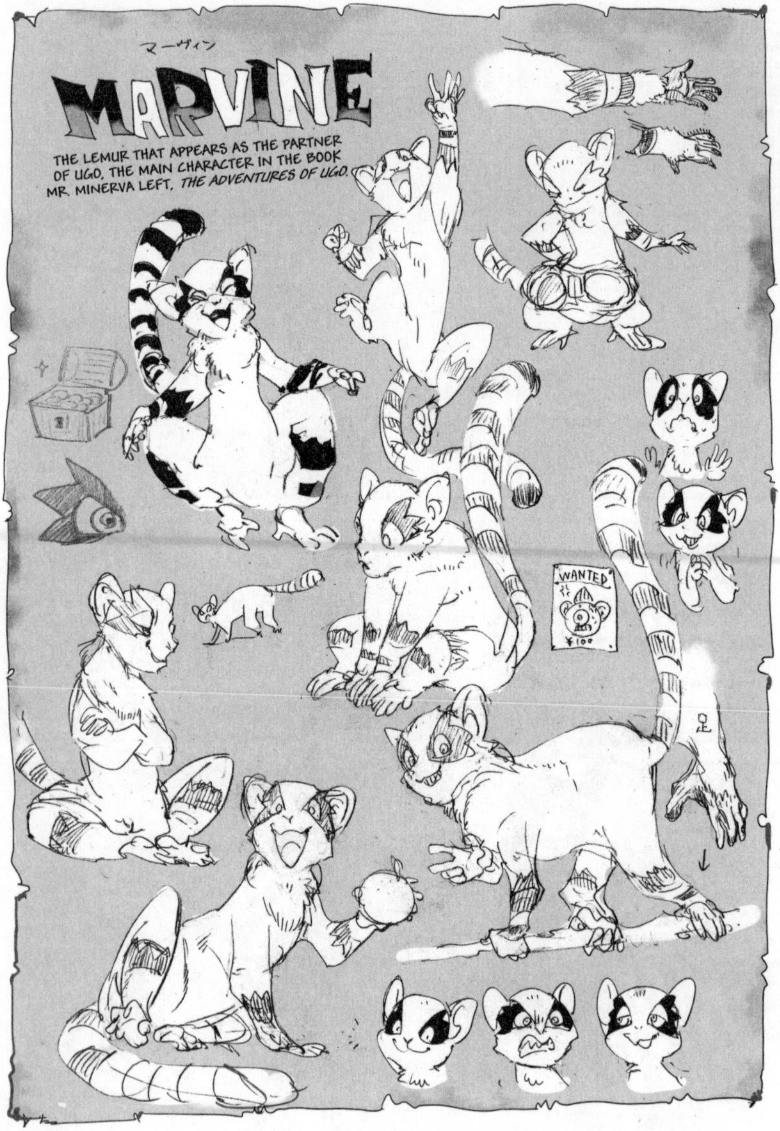
マーヴィン
MARVINE
THE LEMUR THAT APPEARS AS THE PARTNER OF UGO, THE MAIN CHARACTER IN THE BOOK MR. MINERVA LEFT, THE ADVENTURES OF UGO.
WANTED
¥100

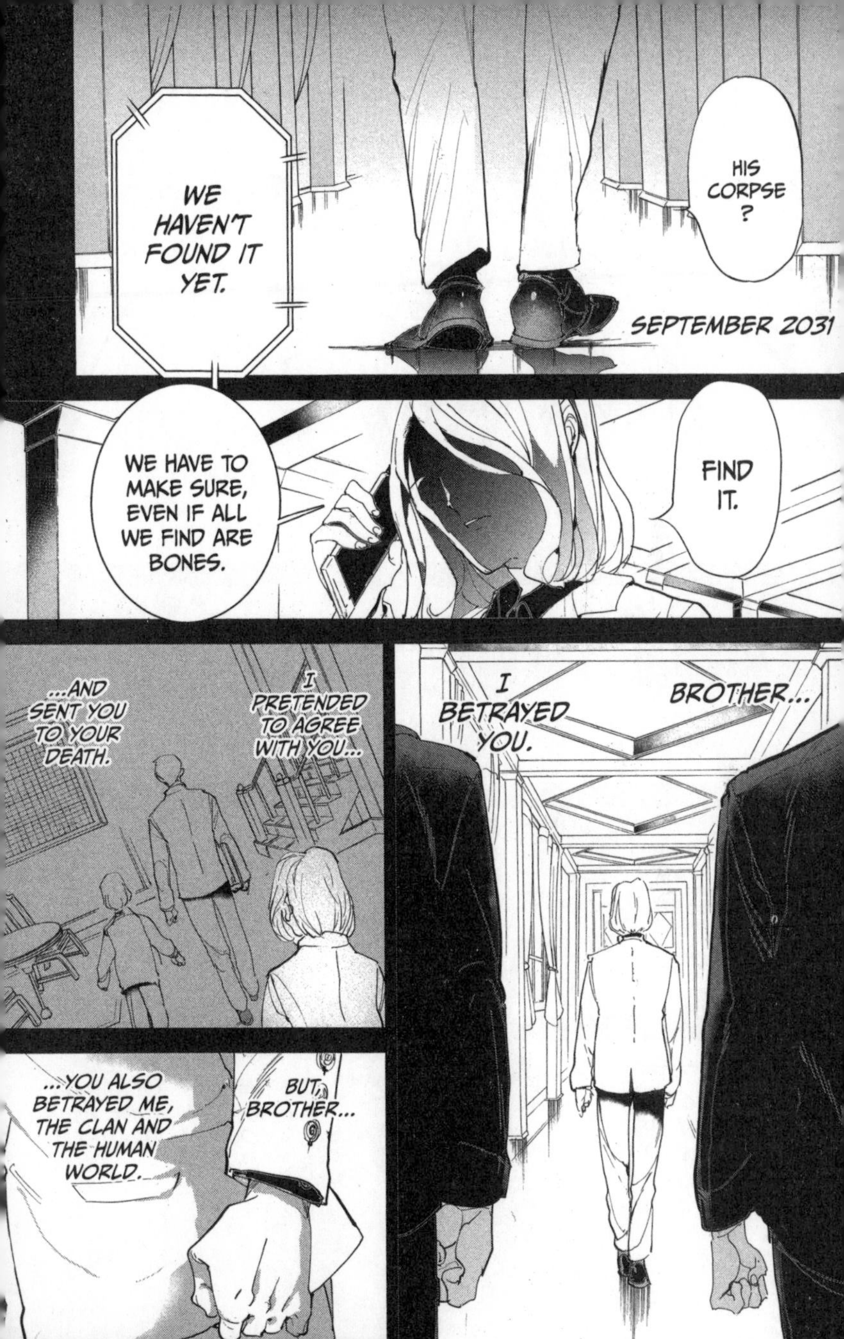
HIS CORPSE?
WE HAVEN'T FOUND IT YET.
SEPTEMBER 2031
FIND IT.
WE HAVE TO MAKE SURE, EVEN IF ALL WE FIND ARE BONES.
BROTHER...
I BETRAYED YOU.
I PRETENDED TO AGREE WITH YOU...
...AND SENT YOU TO YOUR DEATH.
BUT, BROTHER...
...YOU ALSO BETRAYED ME, THE CLAN AND THE HUMAN WORLD.

CHAPTER 73: RALLYING UP

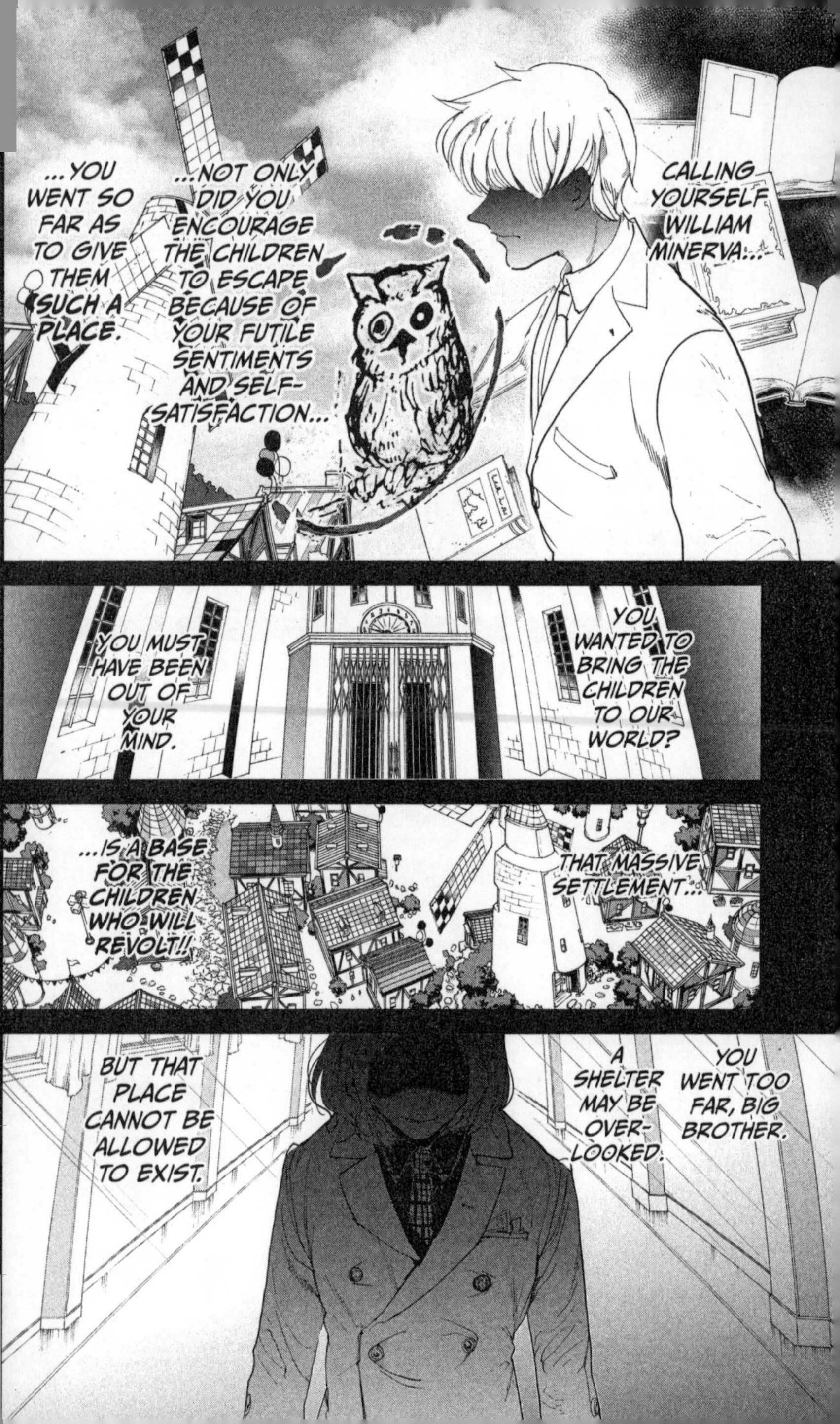
CALLING YOURSELF WILLIAM MINERVA...
...NOT ONLY DID YOU ENCOURAGE THE CHILDREN TO ESCAPE BECAUSE OF YOUR FUTILE SENTIMENTS AND SELF-SATISFACTION...
...YOU WENT SO FAR AS TO GIVE THEM SUCH A PLACE.
YOU WANTED TO BRING THE CHILDREN TO OUR WORLD?
YOU MUST HAVE BEEN OUT OF YOUR MIND.
THAT MASSIVE SETTLEMENT...
...IS A BASE FOR THE CHILDREN WHO WILL REVOLT!!
YOU WENT TOO FAR, BIG BROTHER.
A SHELTER MAY BE OVER-LOOKED.
BUT THAT PLACE CANNOT BE ALLOWED TO EXIST.

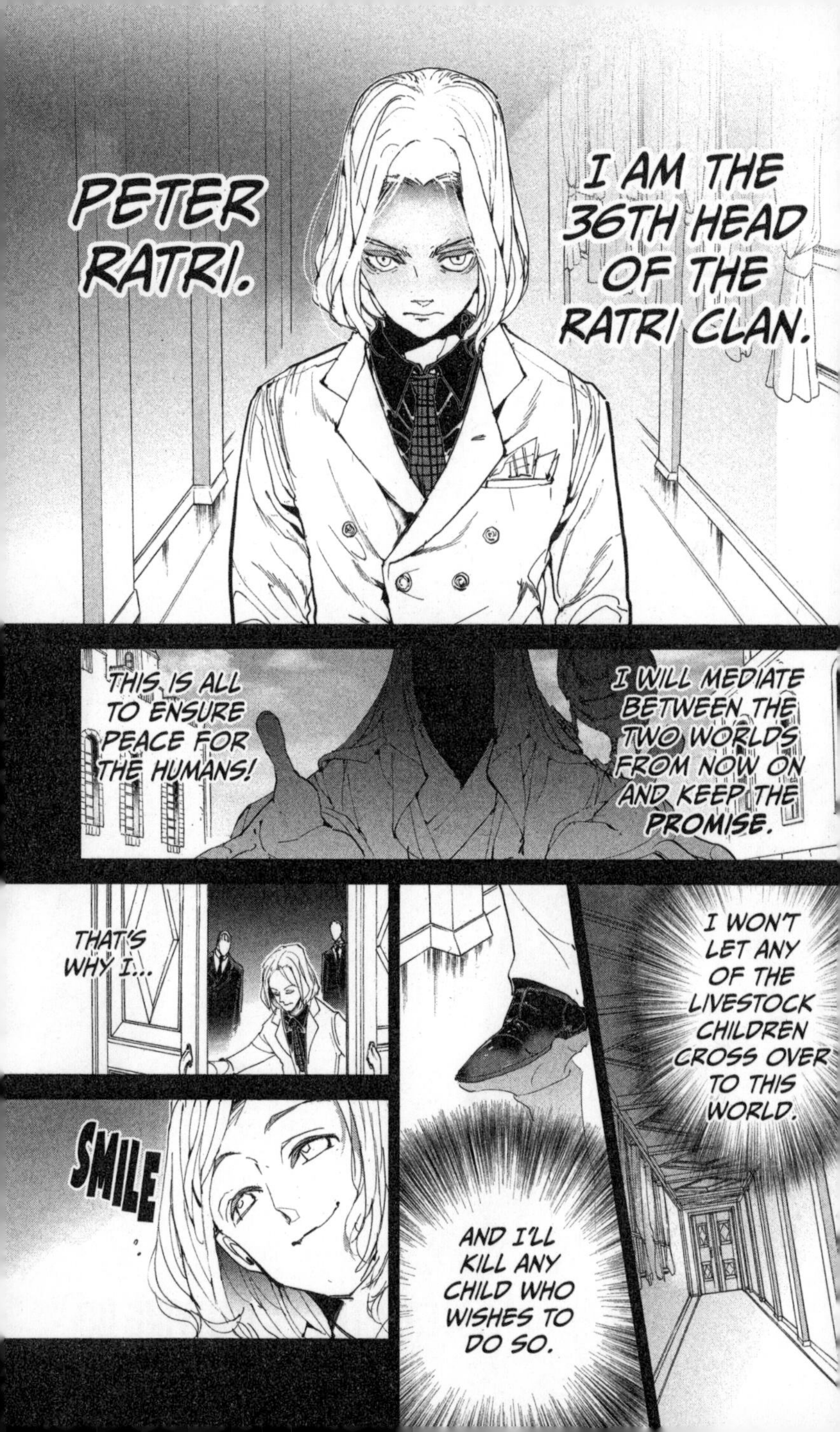
I AM THE 36TH HEAD OF THE RATRI CLAN.
PETER RATRI.
I WILL MEDIATE BETWEEN THE TWO WORLDS FROM NOW ON AND KEEP THE PROMISE.
THIS IS ALL TO ENSURE PEACE FOR THE HUMANS!
I WON'T LET ANY OF THE LIVESTOCK CHILDREN CROSS OVER TO THIS WORLD.
AND I'LL KILL ANY CHILD WHO WISHES TO DO SO.
THAT'S WHY I...
SMILE

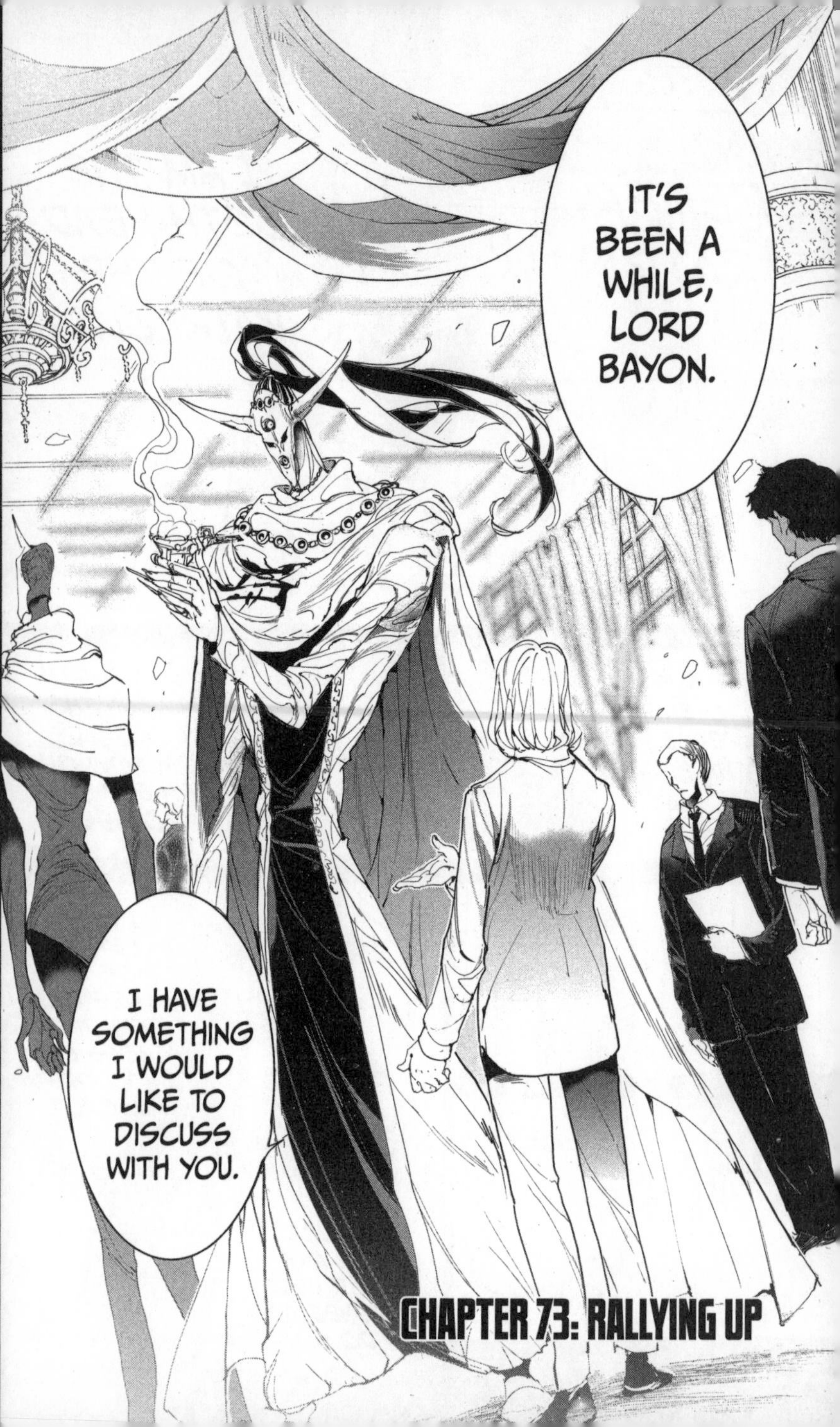
IT'S BEEN A WHILE, LORD BAYON.
I HAVE SOMETHING I WOULD LIKE TO DISCUSS WITH YOU.
CHAPTER 73: RALLYING UP

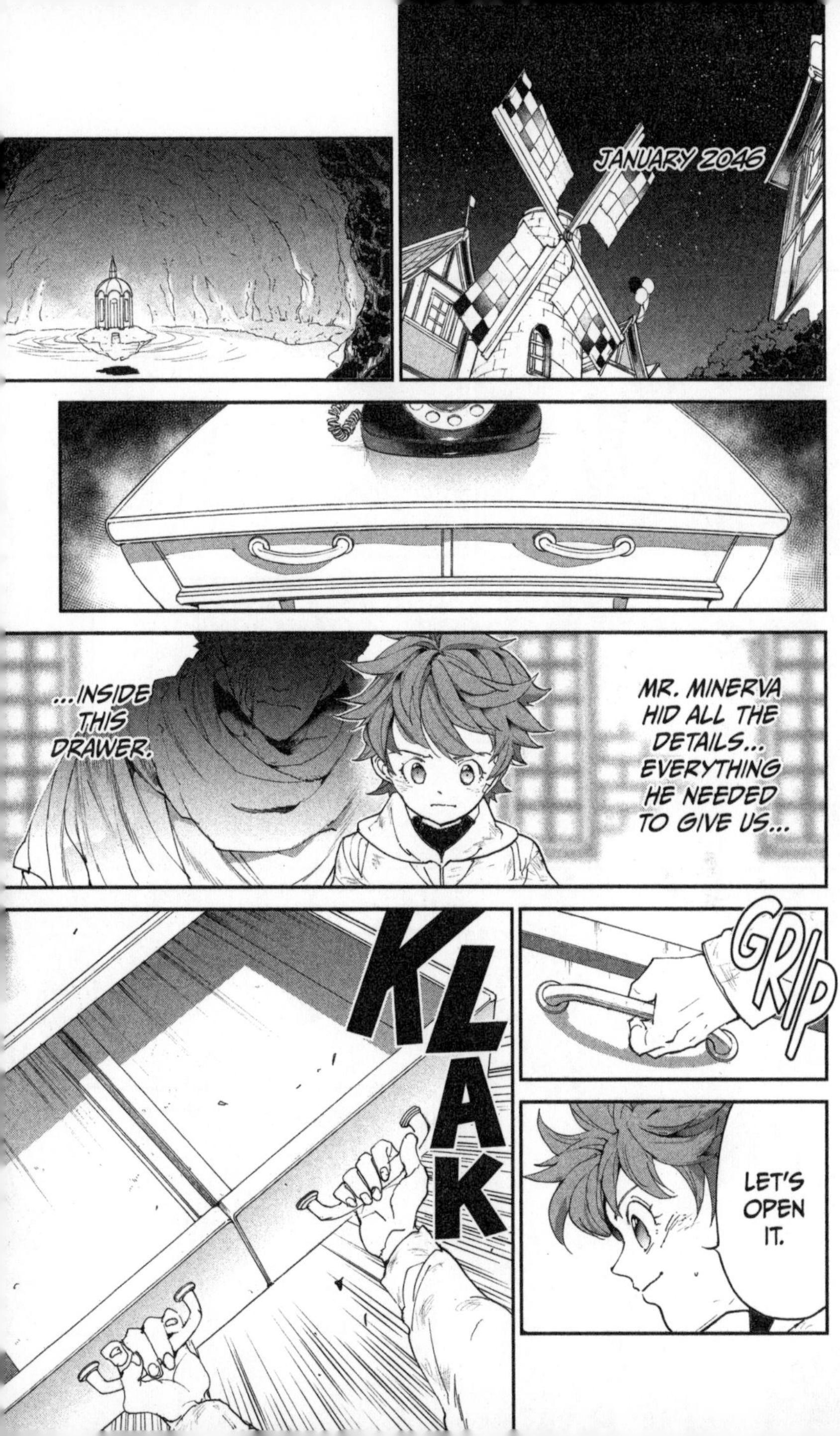
JANUARY 2046
MR. MINERVA HID ALL THE DETAILS... EVERYTHING HE NEEDED TO GIVE US...
...INSIDE THIS DRAWER.
GRIP
LET'S OPEN IT.
KLAK

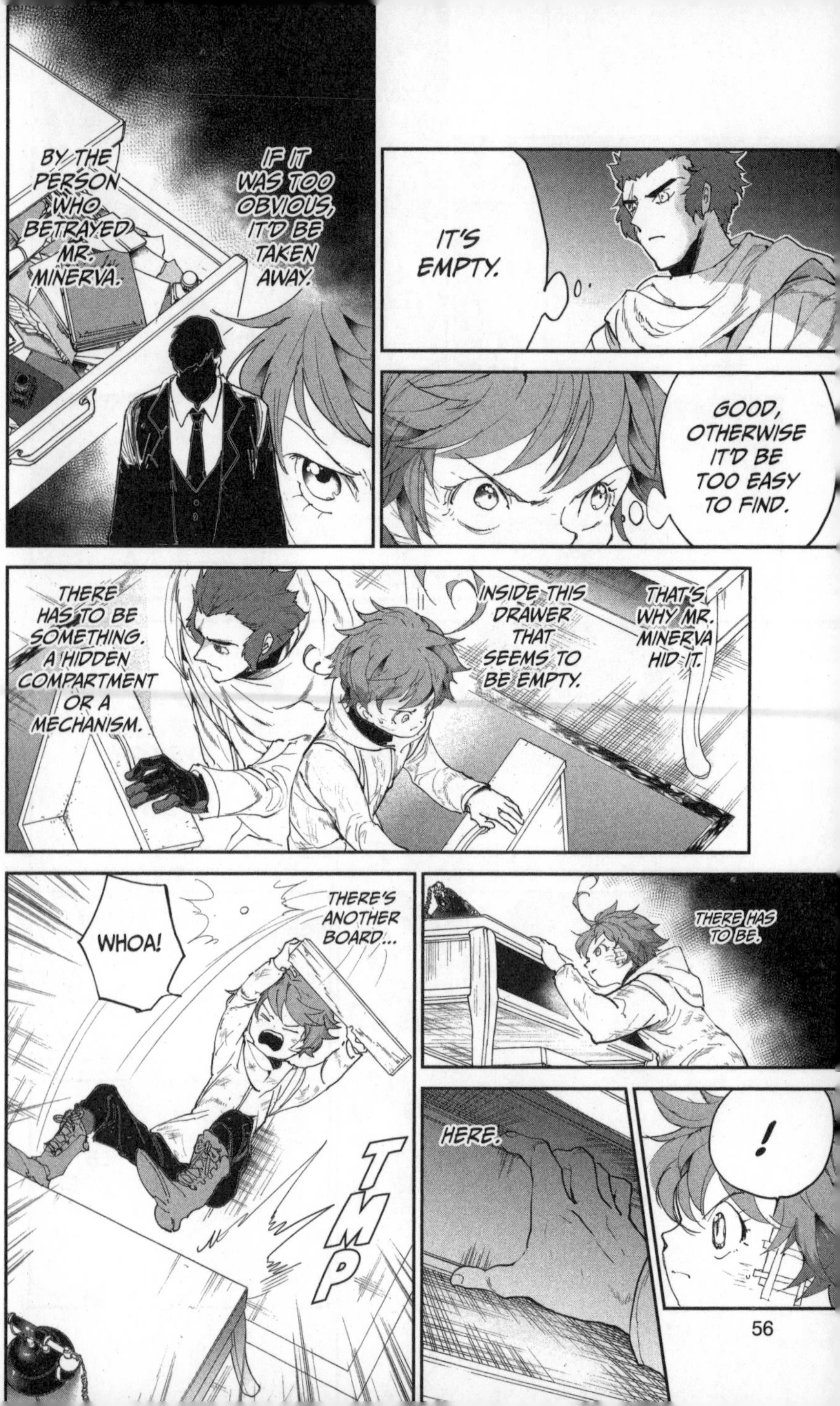
IT'S EMPTY.
GOOD, OTHERWISE IT'D BE TOO EASY TO FIND.
IF IT WAS TOO OBVIOUS, IT'D BE TAKEN AWAY.
BY THE PERSON WHO BETRAYED MR. MINERVA.
THAT'S WHY MR. MINERVA HID IT.
INSIDE THIS DRAWER THAT SEEMS TO BE EMPTY.
THERE HAS TO BE SOMETHING. A HIDDEN COMPARTMENT OR A MECHANISM.
THERE HAS TO BE.
!
HERE.
THERE'S ANOTHER BOARD...
WHOA!
TMP

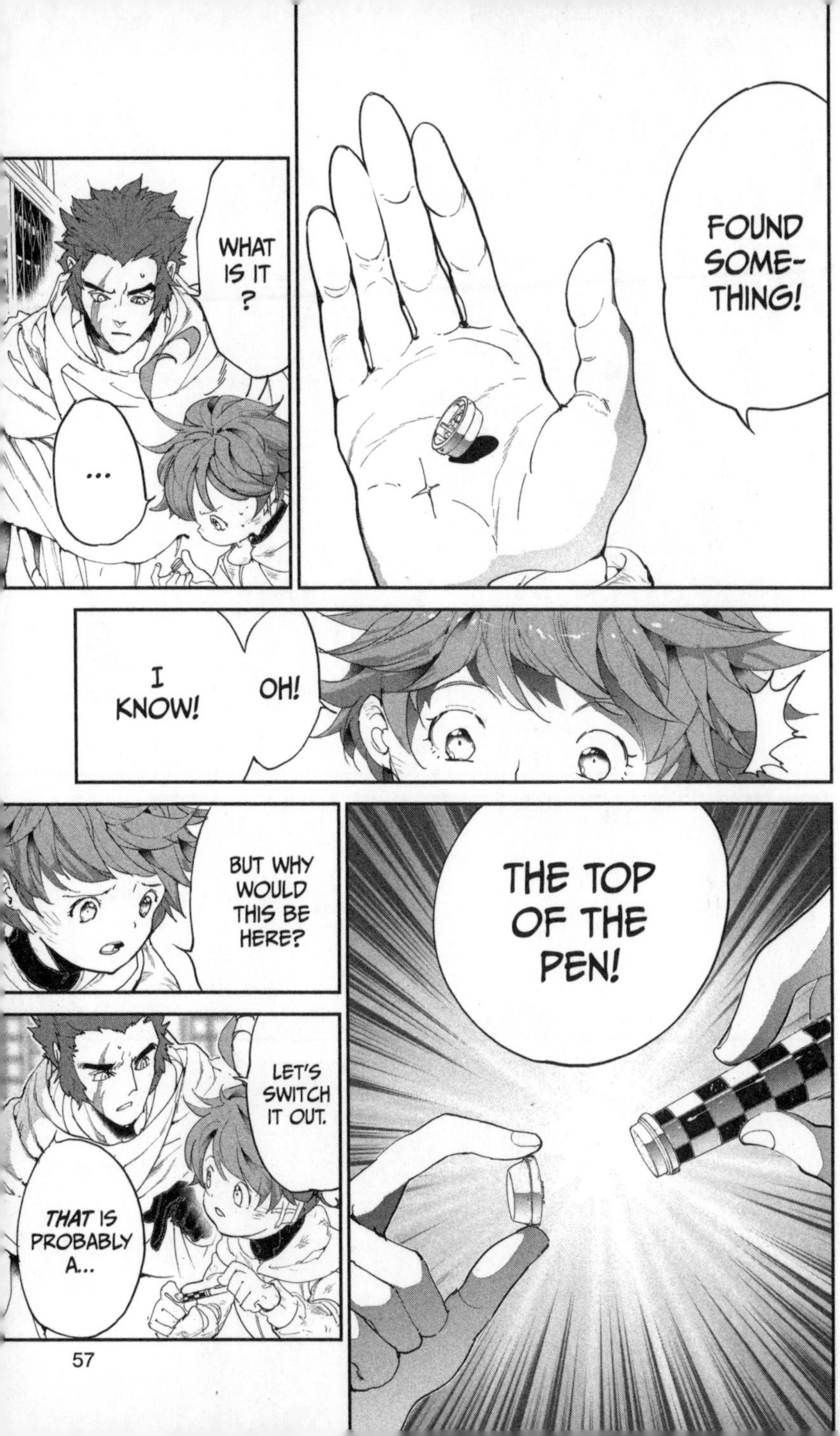
FOUND SOMETHING!
WHAT IS IT?
...
OH!
I KNOW!
THE TOP OF THE PEN!
BUT WHY WOULD THIS BE HERE?
LET'S SWITCH IT OUT.
THAT IS PROBABLY A...

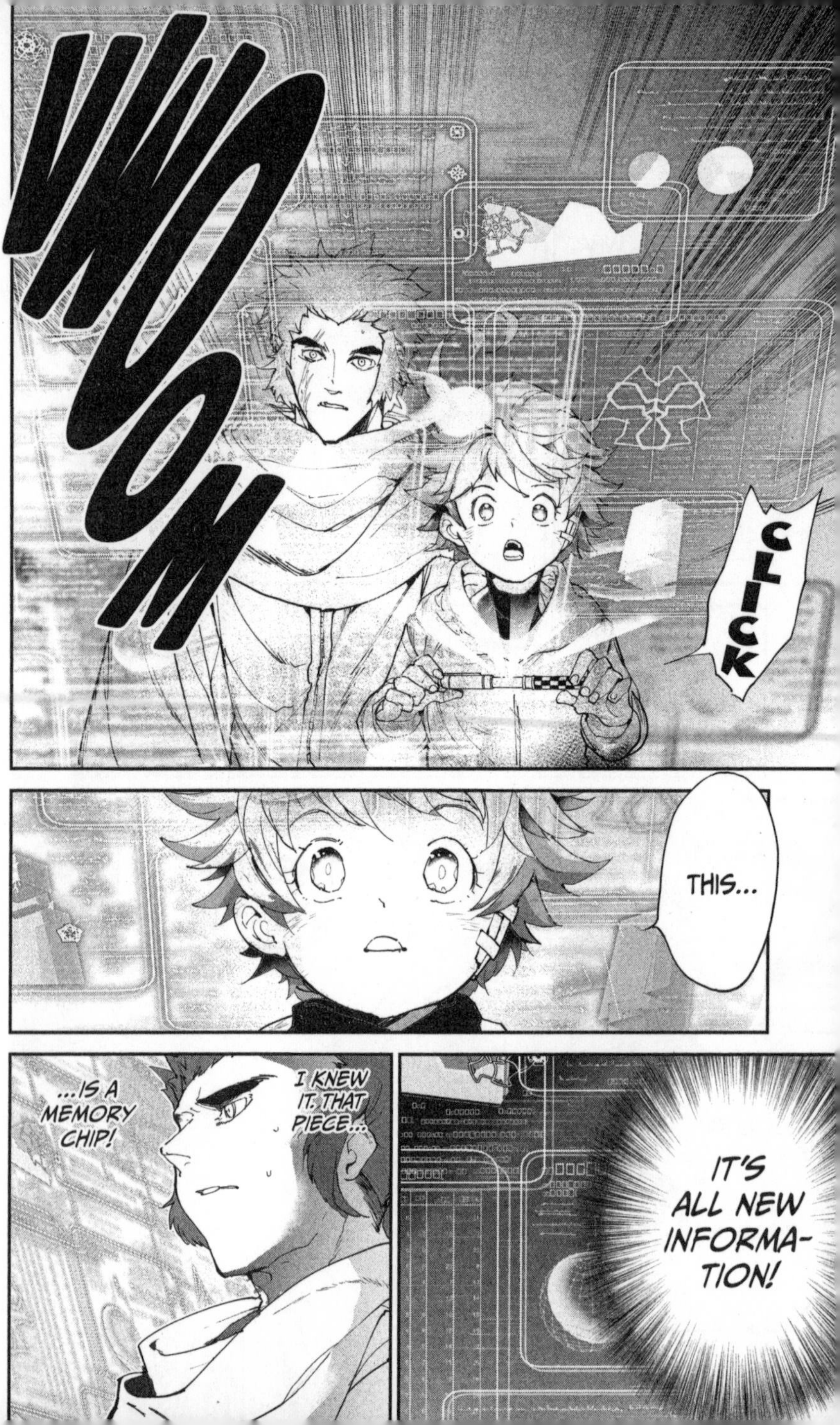
WHOOSH
CLICK
THIS...
IT'S ALL NEW INFORMATION!
I KNEW IT, THAT PIECE...
...IS A MEMORY CHIP!

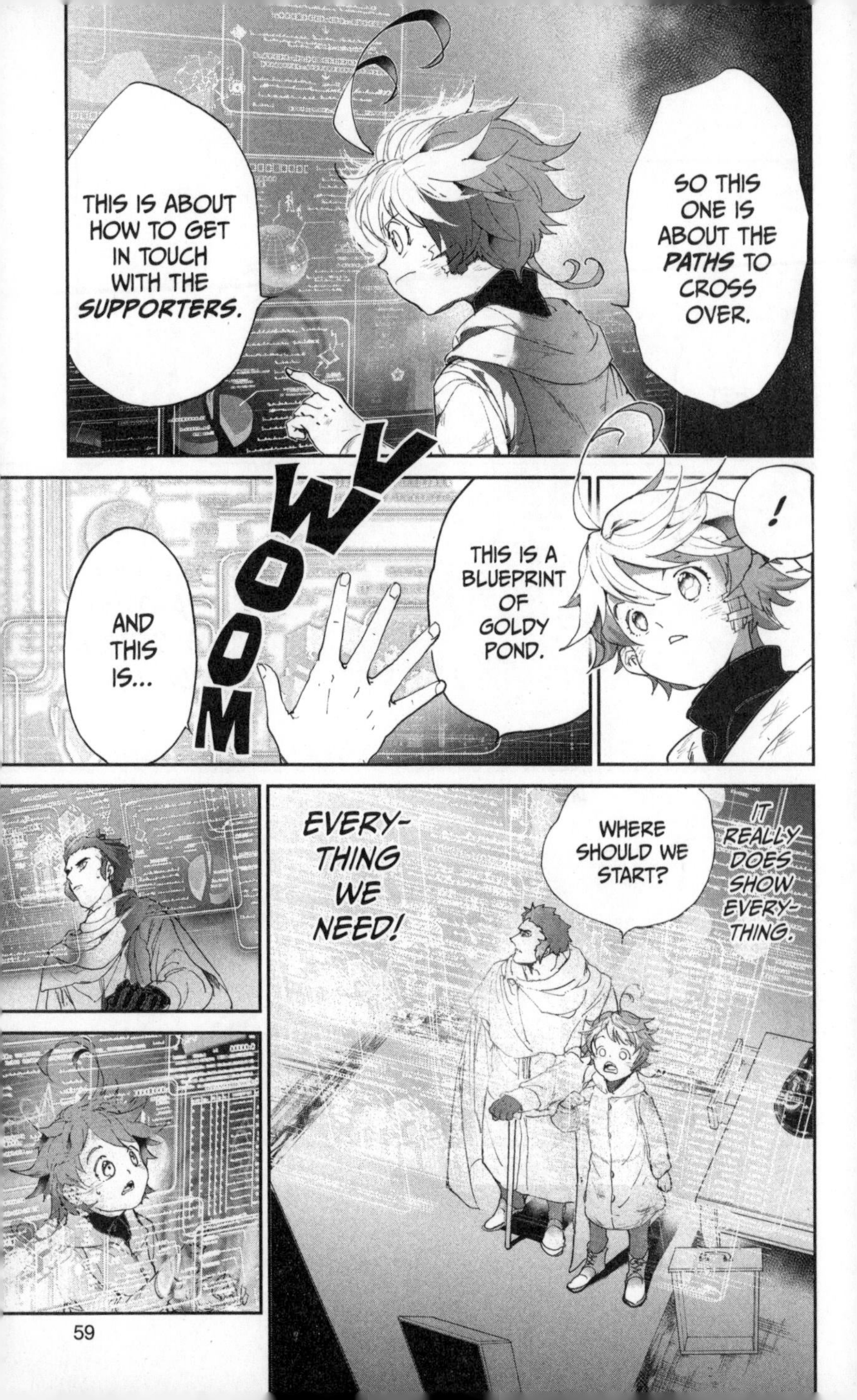
SO THIS ONE IS ABOUT THE *PATHS* TO CROSS OVER.
THIS IS ABOUT HOW TO GET IN TOUCH WITH THE *SUPPORTERS*.
!
THIS IS A BLUEPRINT OF GOLDY POND.
WOOM
AND THIS IS...
IT REALLY DOES SHOW EVERY-THING.
WHERE SHOULD WE START?
EVERY-THING WE NEED!

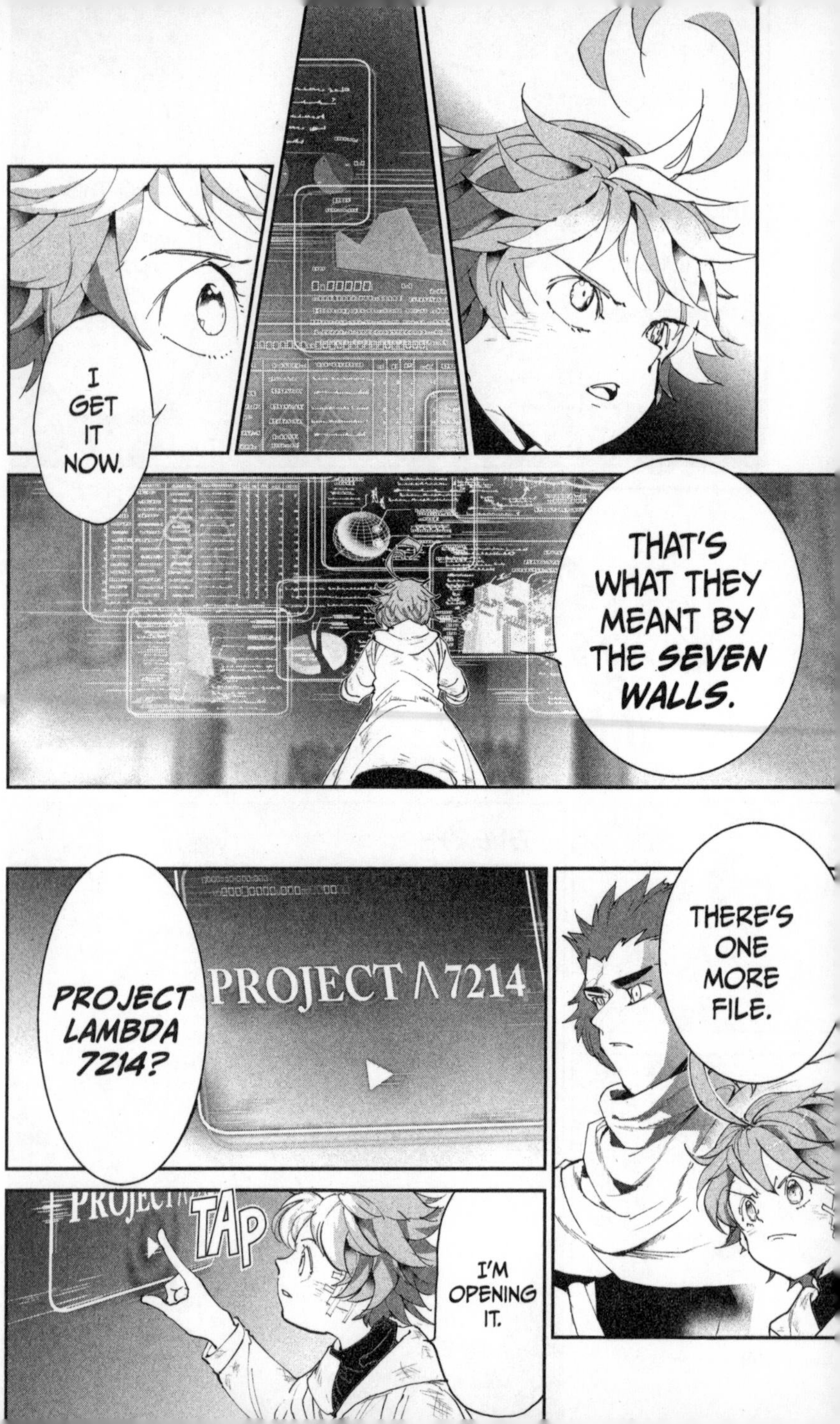
I GET IT NOW.
THAT'S WHAT THEY MEANT BY THE *SEVEN WALLS*.
THERE'S ONE MORE FILE.
PROJECT Λ7214
PROJECT LAMBDA 7214?
TAP
I'M OPENING IT.

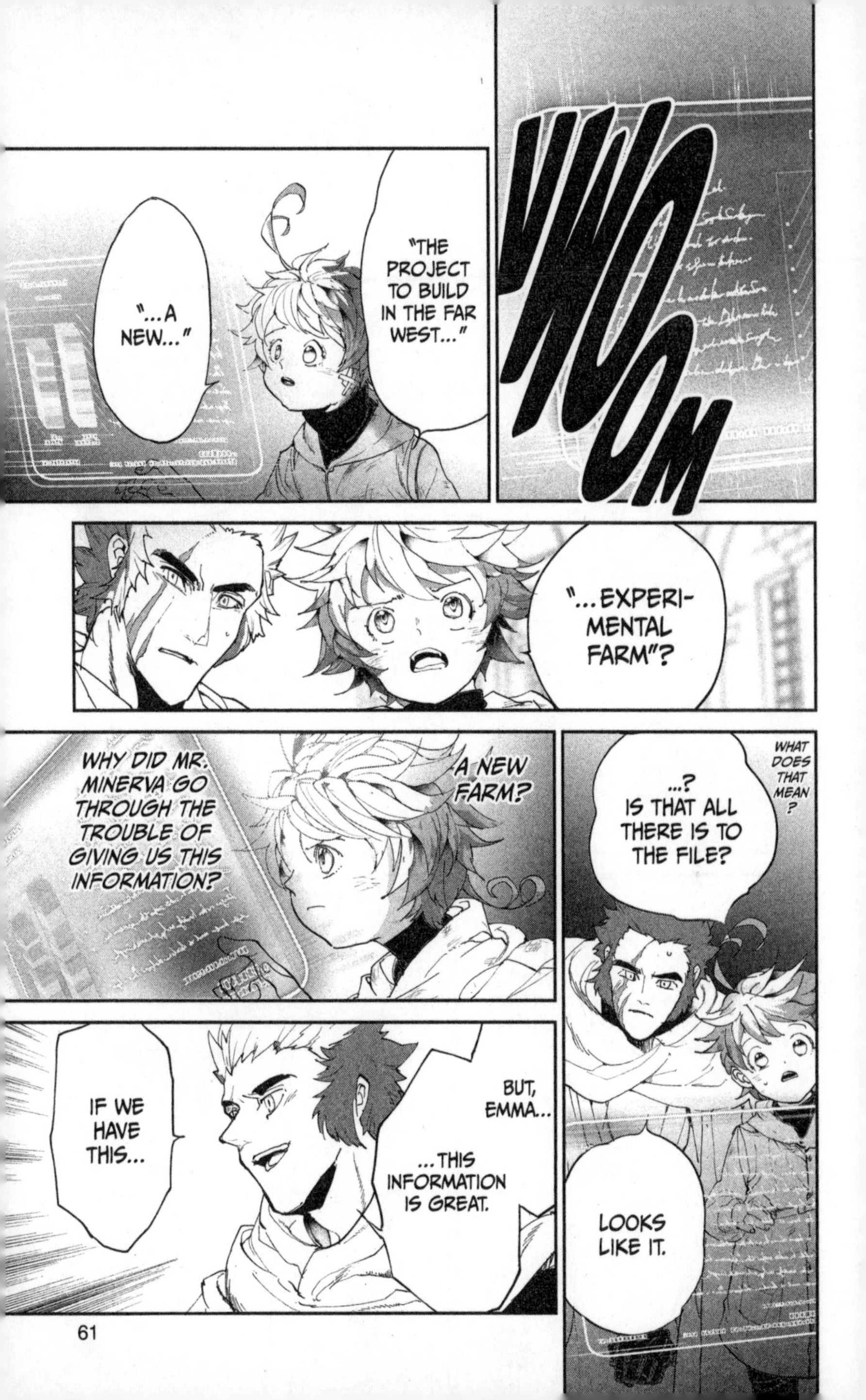
WHOOM
"THE PROJECT TO BUILD IN THE FAR WEST..."
"...A NEW..."
"...EXPERIMENTAL FARM"?
WHAT DOES THAT MEAN?
...? IS THAT ALL THERE IS TO THE FILE?
LOOKS LIKE IT.
A NEW FARM?
WHY DID MR. MINERVA GO THROUGH THE TROUBLE OF GIVING US THIS INFORMATION?
BUT, EMMA...
...THIS INFORMATION IS GREAT.
IF WE HAVE THIS...

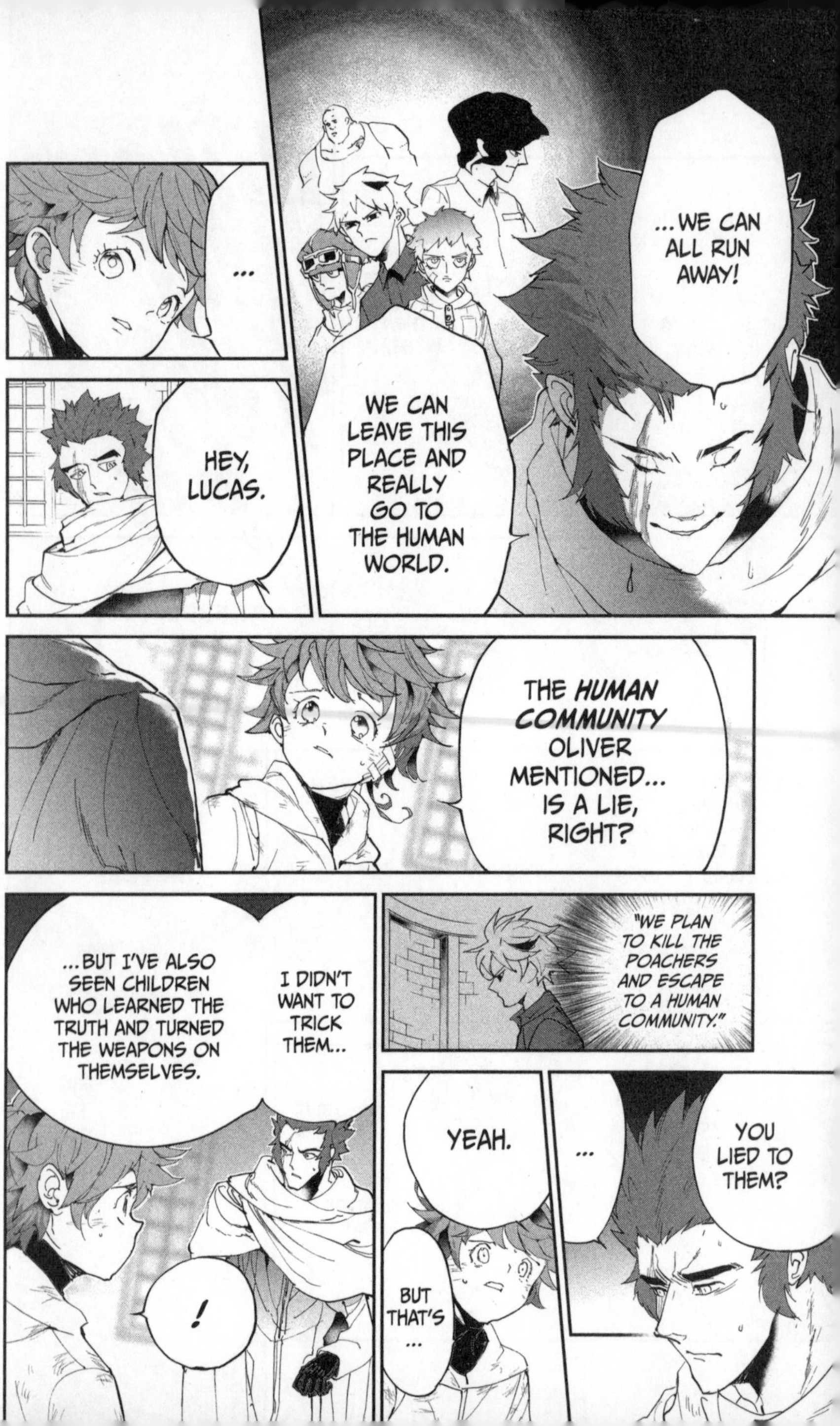
...WE CAN ALL RUN AWAY!
WE CAN LEAVE THIS PLACE AND REALLY GO TO THE HUMAN WORLD.
...
HEY, LUCAS.
THE *HUMAN COMMUNITY* OLIVER MENTIONED... IS A LIE, RIGHT?
"WE PLAN TO KILL THE POACHERS AND ESCAPE TO A HUMAN COMMUNITY."
YOU LIED TO THEM?
...
YEAH.
BUT THAT'S ...
I DIDN'T WANT TO TRICK THEM...
...BUT I'VE ALSO SEEN CHILDREN WHO LEARNED THE TRUTH AND TURNED THE WEAPONS ON THEMSELVES.
!

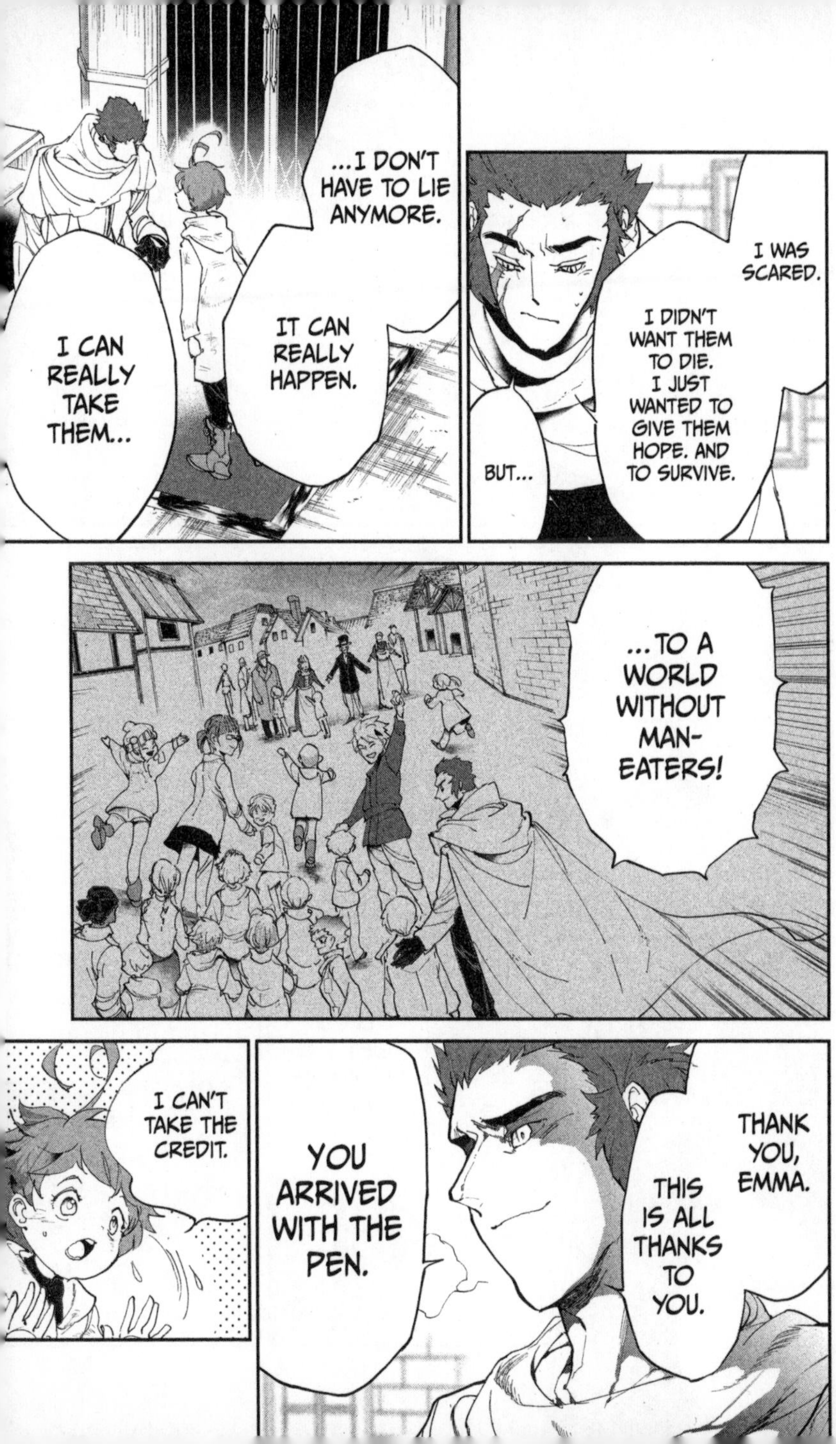
I WAS SCARED.
I DIDN'T WANT THEM TO DIE. I JUST WANTED TO GIVE THEM HOPE. AND TO SURVIVE.
BUT...
...I DON'T HAVE TO LIE ANYMORE.
IT CAN REALLY HAPPEN.
I CAN REALLY TAKE THEM...
...TO A WORLD WITHOUT MAN-EATERS!
THANK YOU, EMMA.
THIS IS ALL THANKS TO YOU.
YOU ARRIVED WITH THE PEN.
I CAN'T TAKE THE CREDIT.

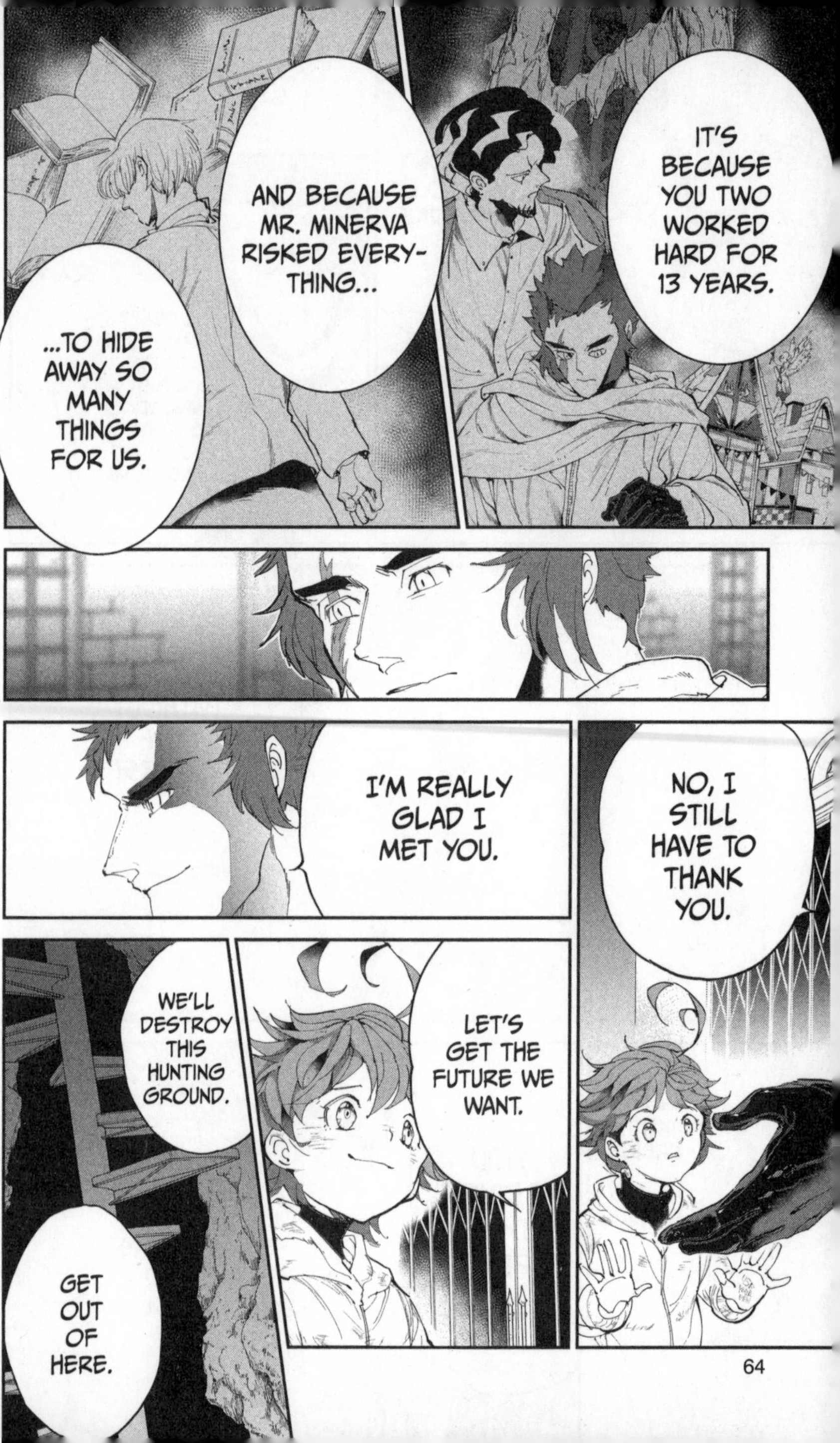
IT'S BECAUSE YOU TWO WORKED HARD FOR 13 YEARS.
AND BECAUSE MR. MINERVA RISKED EVERY-THING...
...TO HIDE AWAY SO MANY THINGS FOR US.
NO, I STILL HAVE TO THANK YOU.
I'M REALLY GLAD I MET YOU.
LET'S GET THE FUTURE WE WANT.
WE'LL DESTROY THIS HUNTING GROUND.
GET OUT OF HERE.

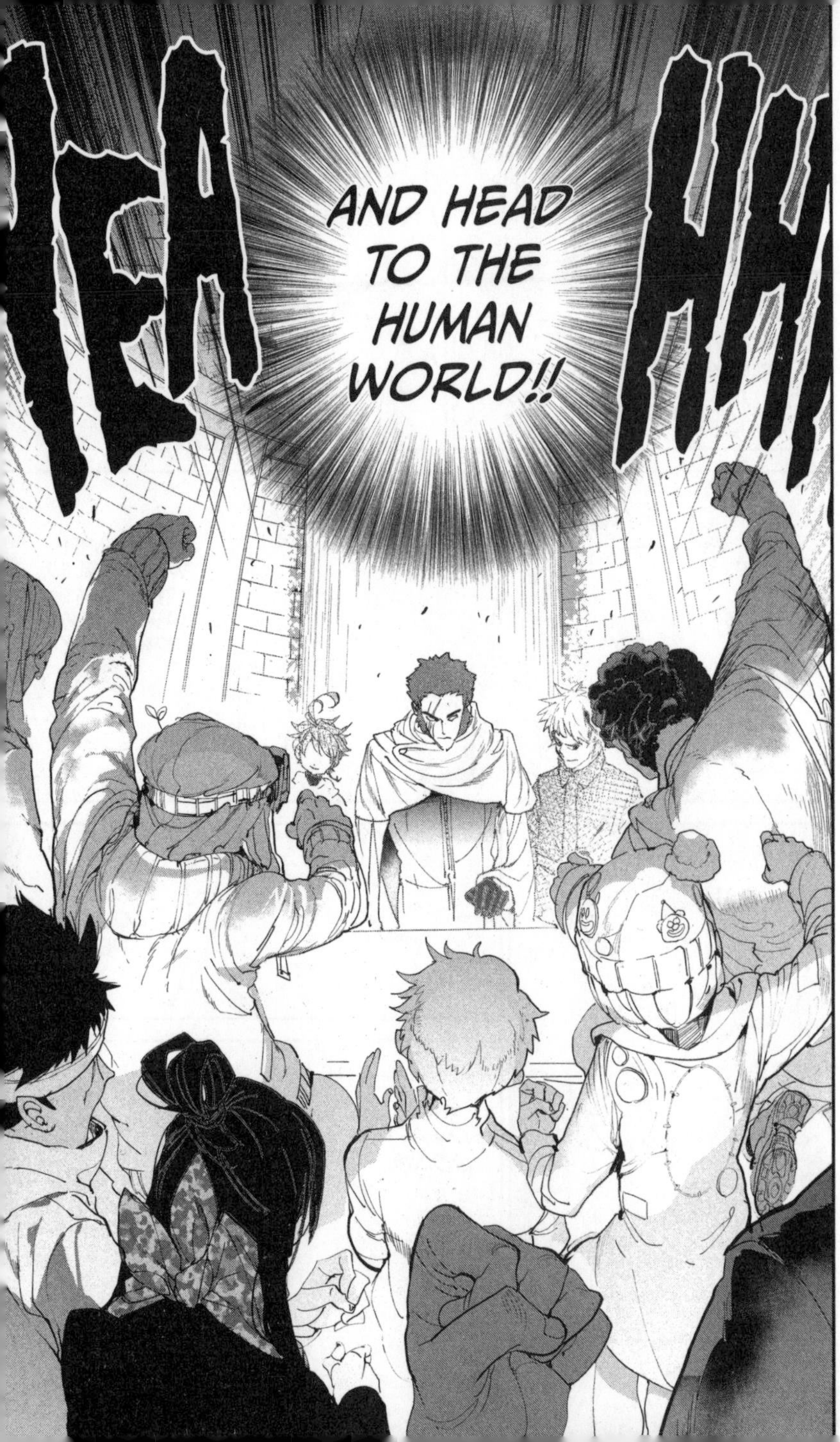
AND HEAD TO THE HUMAN WORLD!!

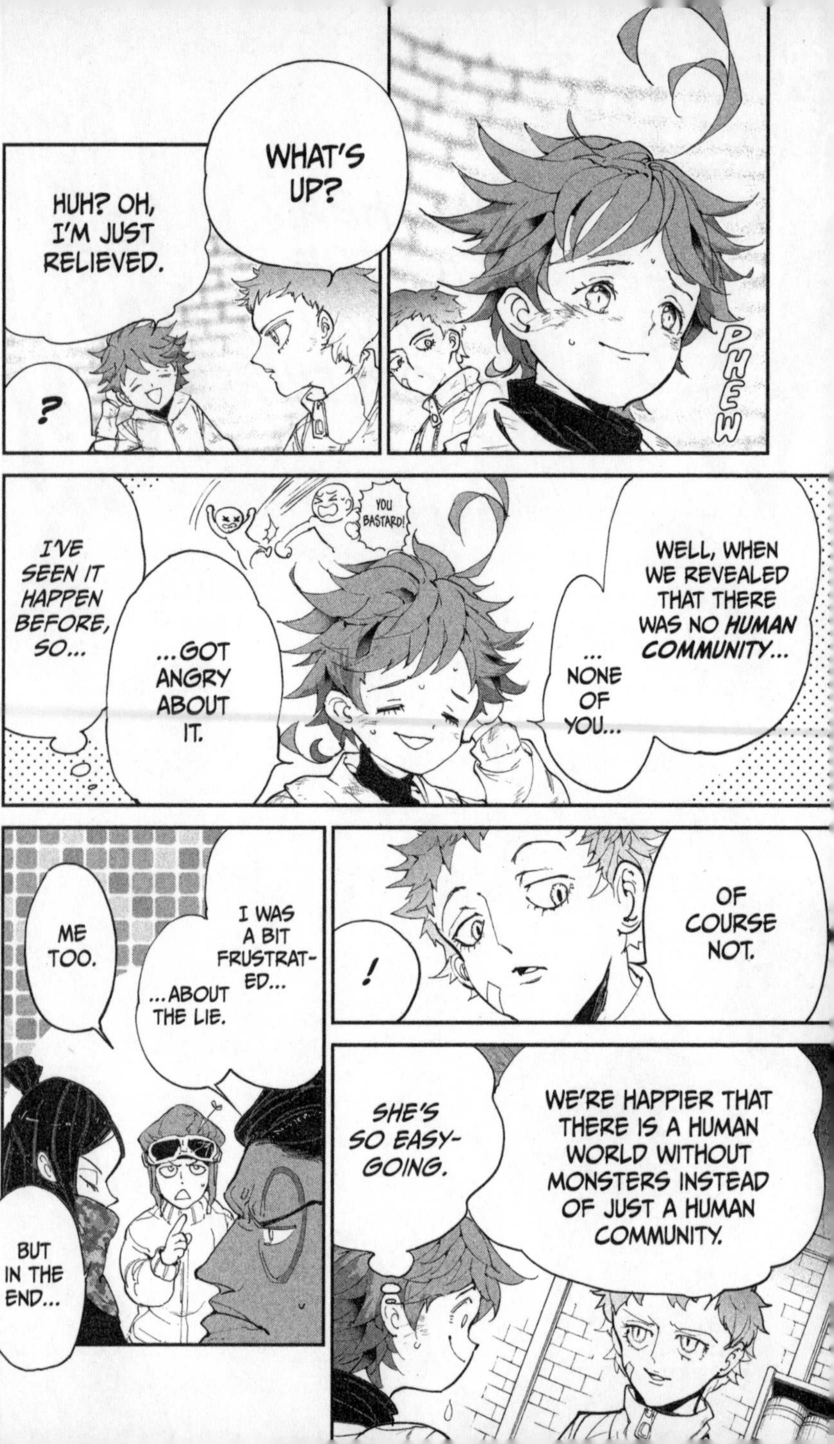
PHEW
WHAT'S UP?
HUH? OH, I'M JUST RELIEVED.
?
WELL, WHEN WE REVEALED THAT THERE WAS NO *HUMAN COMMUNITY*...
...NONE OF YOU...
YOU BASTARD!
...GOT ANGRY ABOUT IT.
I'VE SEEN IT HAPPEN BEFORE, SO...
OF COURSE NOT.
!
WE'RE HAPPIER THAT THERE IS A HUMAN WORLD WITHOUT MONSTERS INSTEAD OF JUST A HUMAN COMMUNITY.
SHE'S SO EASY-GOING.
I WAS A BIT FRUSTRATED...
...ABOUT THE LIE.
ME TOO.
BUT IN THE END...

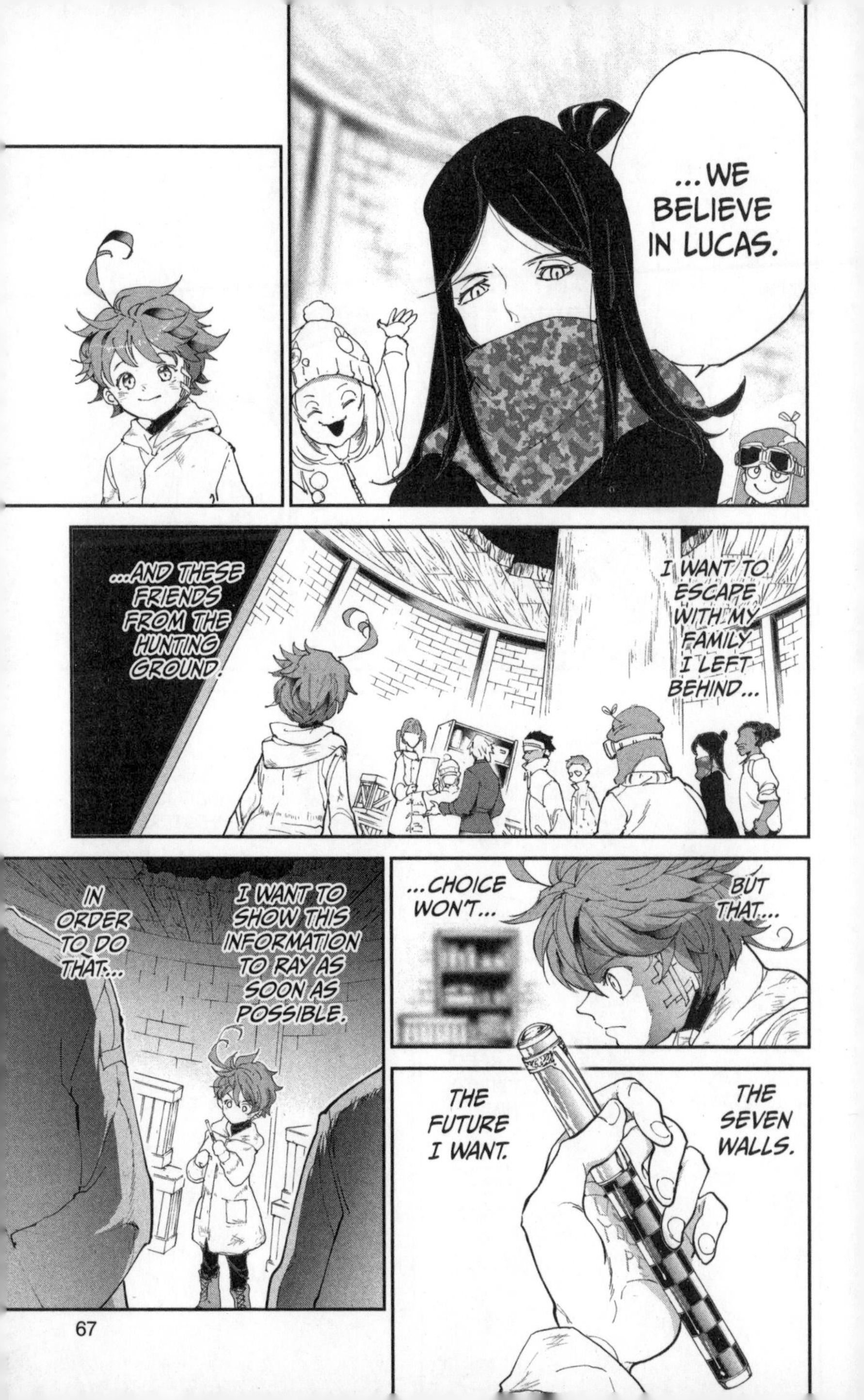
...WE BELIEVE IN LUCAS.
I WANT TO ESCAPE WITH MY FAMILY I LEFT BEHIND...
...AND THESE FRIENDS FROM THE HUNTING GROUND.
BUT THAT...
...CHOICE WON'T...
THE SEVEN WALLS.
THE FUTURE I WANT.
I WANT TO SHOW THIS INFORMATION TO RAY AS SOON AS POSSIBLE.
IN ORDER TO DO THAT...

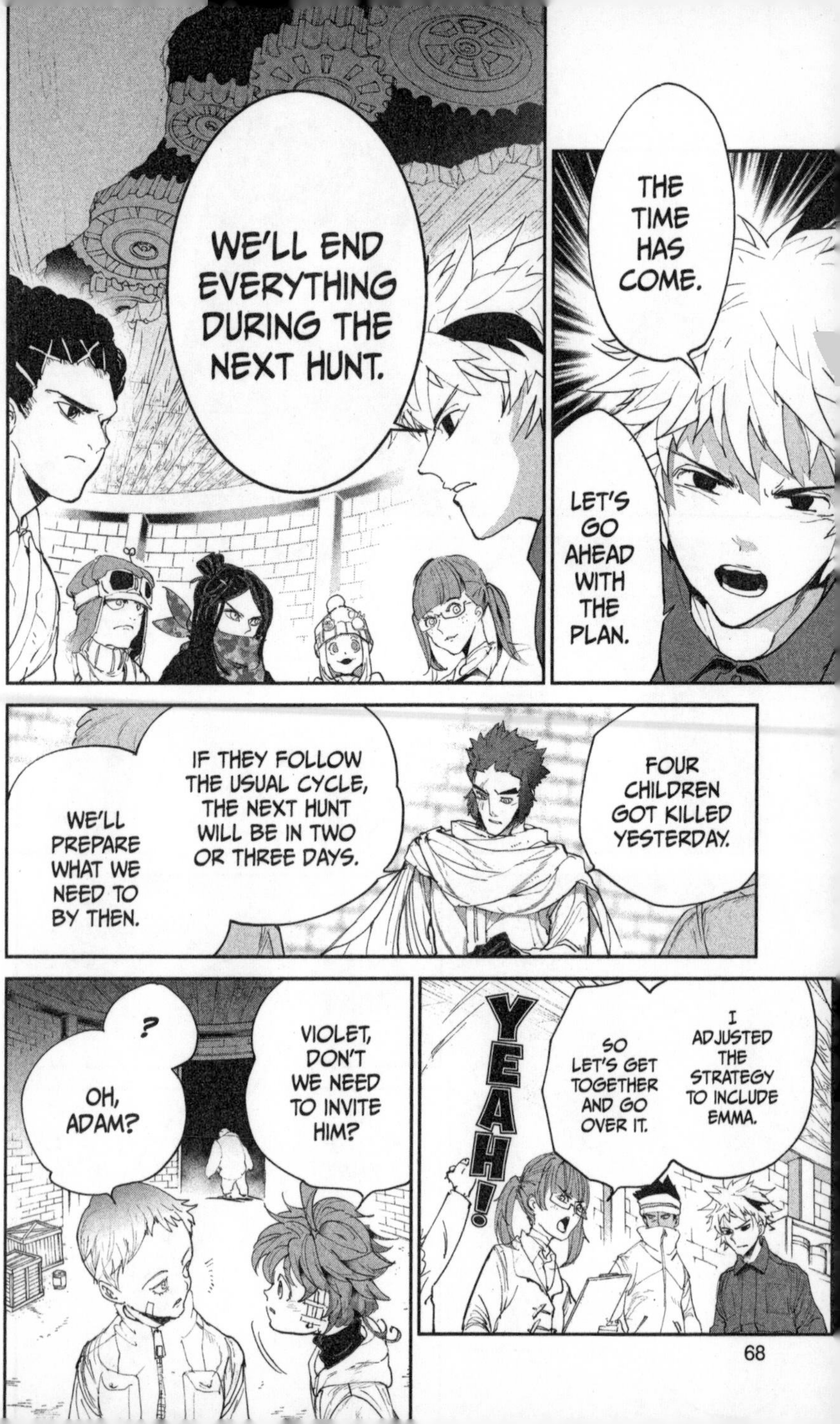
THE TIME HAS COME.
LET'S GO AHEAD WITH THE PLAN.
WE'LL END EVERYTHING DURING THE NEXT HUNT.
FOUR CHILDREN GOT KILLED YESTERDAY.
IF THEY FOLLOW THE USUAL CYCLE, THE NEXT HUNT WILL BE IN TWO OR THREE DAYS.
WE'LL PREPARE WHAT WE NEED TO BY THEN.
I ADJUSTED THE STRATEGY TO INCLUDE EMMA.
SO LET'S GET TOGETHER AND GO OVER IT.
YEAH!
VIOLET, DON'T WE NEED TO INVITE HIM?
?
OH, ADAM?

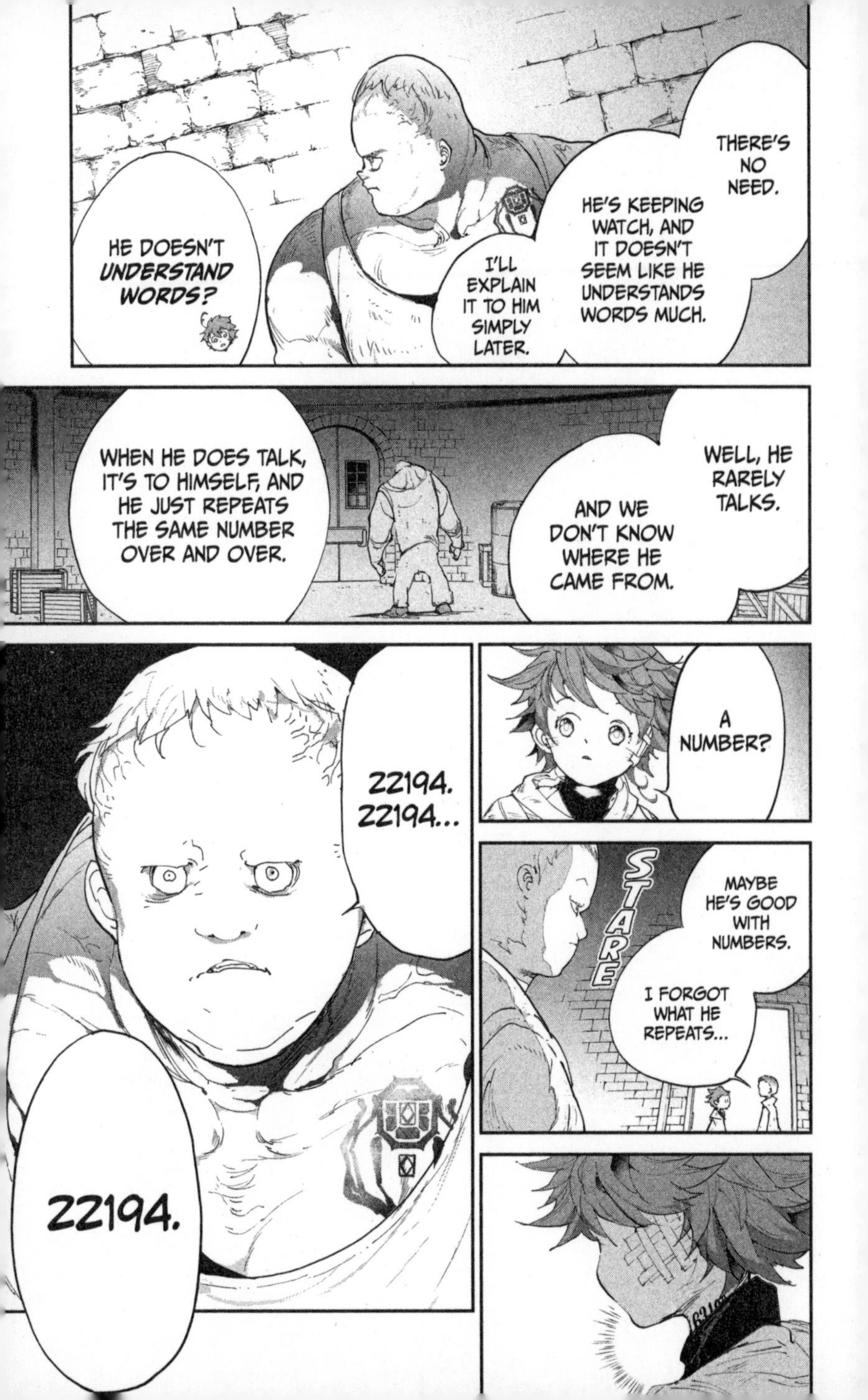
THERE'S NO NEED.
HE'S KEEPING WATCH, AND IT DOESN'T SEEM LIKE HE UNDERSTANDS WORDS MUCH.
I'LL EXPLAIN IT TO HIM SIMPLY LATER.
HE DOESN'T *UNDERSTAND WORDS?*
WELL, HE RARELY TALKS.
AND WE DON'T KNOW WHERE HE CAME FROM.
WHEN HE DOES TALK, IT'S TO HIMSELF, AND HE JUST REPEATS THE SAME NUMBER OVER AND OVER.
A NUMBER?
STARE
MAYBE HE'S GOOD WITH NUMBERS.
I FORGOT WHAT HE REPEATS...
22194. 22194...
22194.

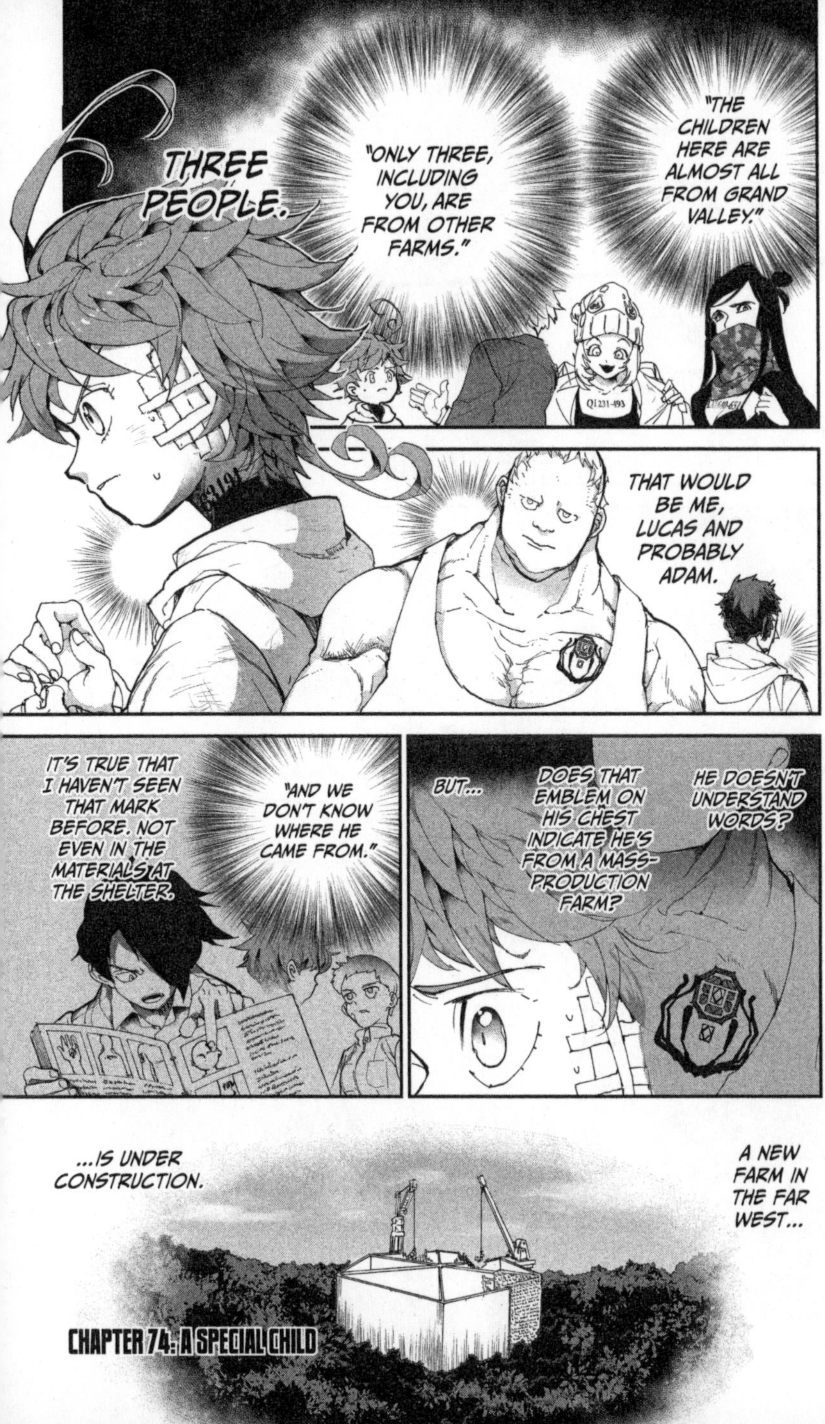
"THE CHILDREN HERE ARE ALMOST ALL FROM GRAND VALLEY."
"ONLY THREE, INCLUDING YOU, ARE FROM OTHER FARMS."
THREE PEOPLE.
Q1231-493
THAT WOULD BE ME, LUCAS AND PROBABLY ADAM.
HE DOESN'T UNDERSTAND WORDS?
DOES THAT EMBLEM ON HIS CHEST INDICATE HE'S FROM A MASS-PRODUCTION FARM?
BUT...
"AND WE DON'T KNOW WHERE HE CAME FROM."
IT'S TRUE THAT I HAVEN'T SEEN THAT MARK BEFORE. NOT EVEN IN THE MATERIALS AT THE SHELTER.
A NEW FARM IN THE FAR WEST...
...IS UNDER CONSTRUCTION.
CHAPTER 74: A SPECIAL CHILD

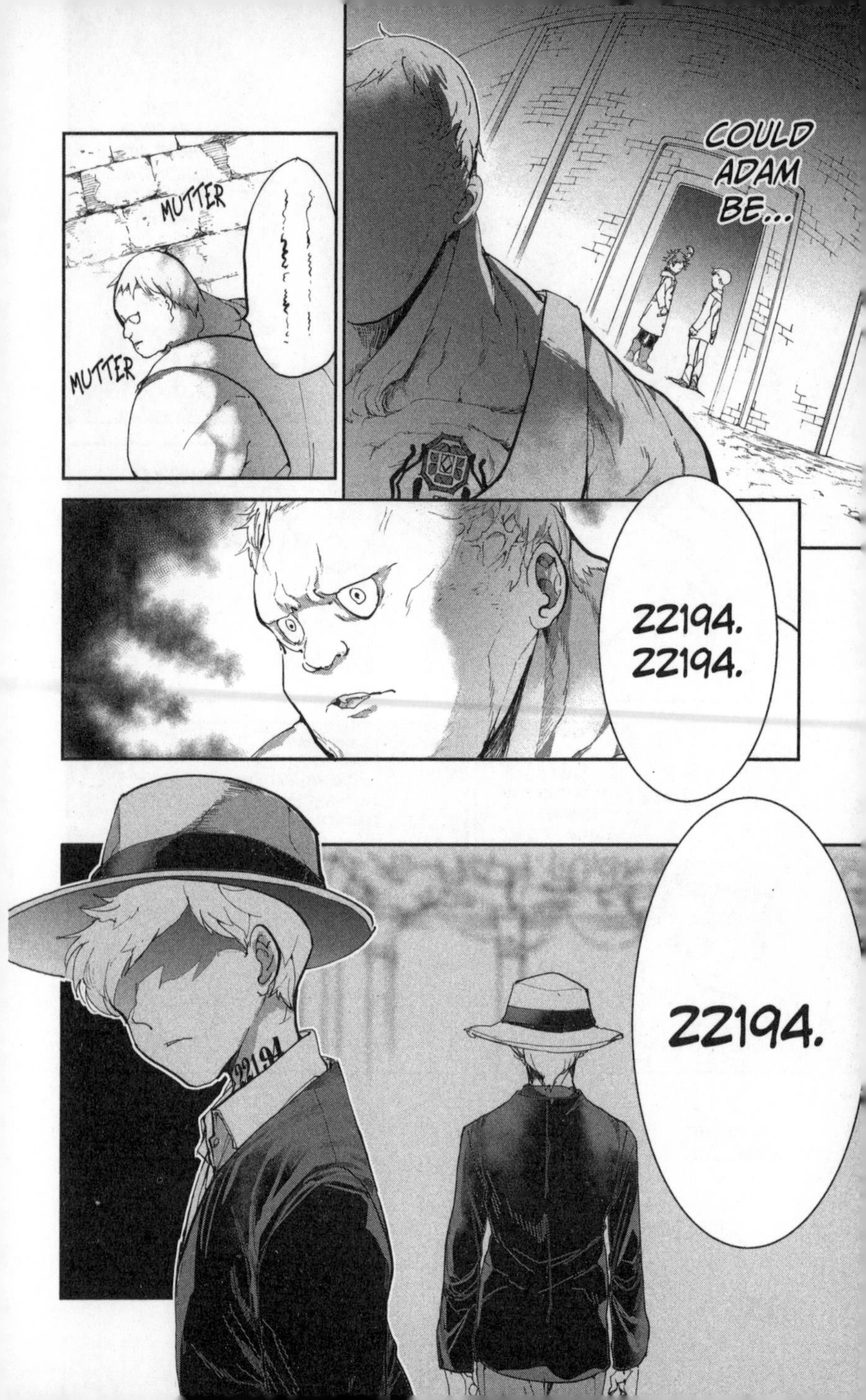
COULD ADAM BE...
MUTTER
MUTTER
22194. 22194.
22194.
22194

CHAPTER 74: A SPECIAL CHILD

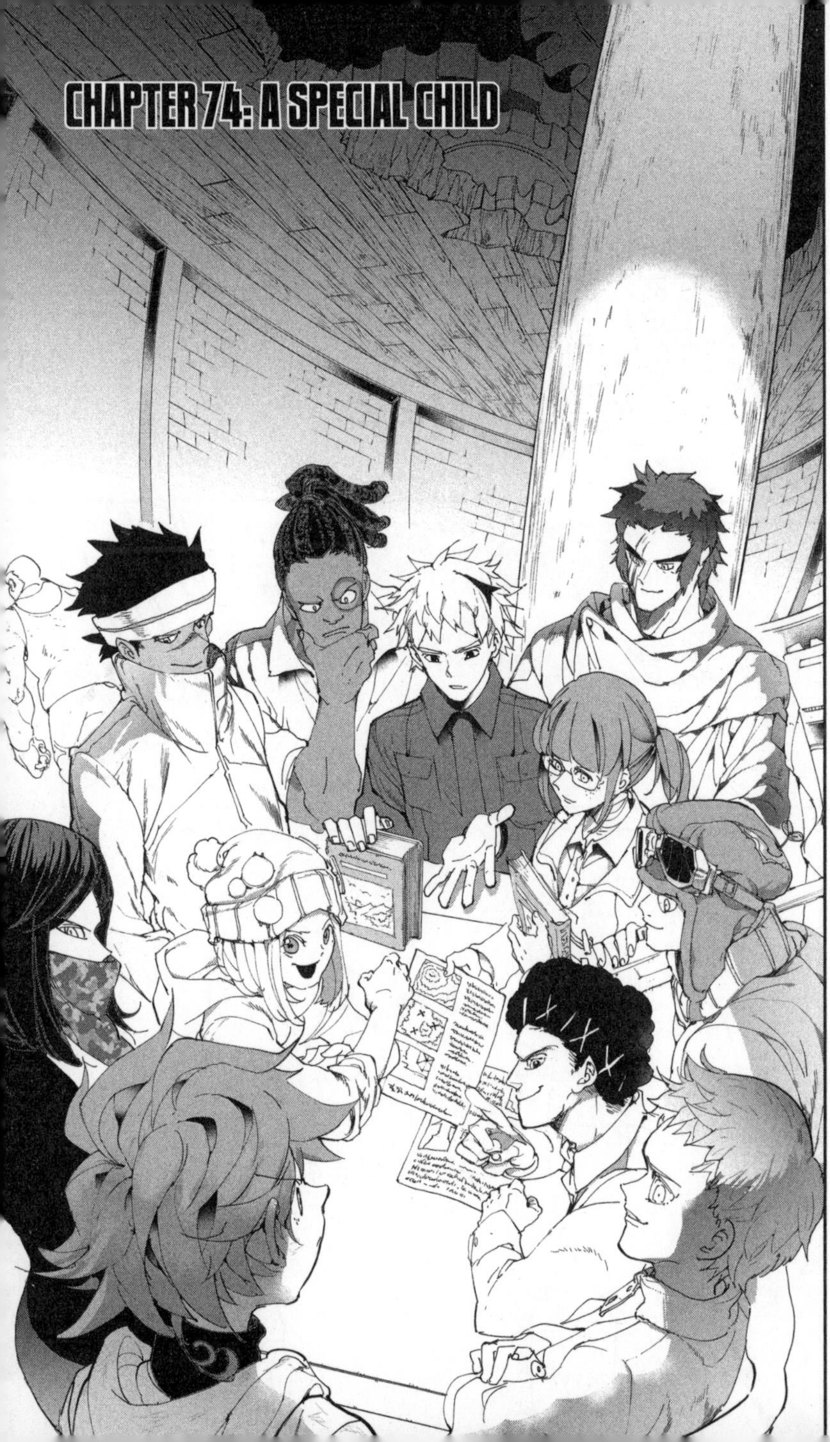

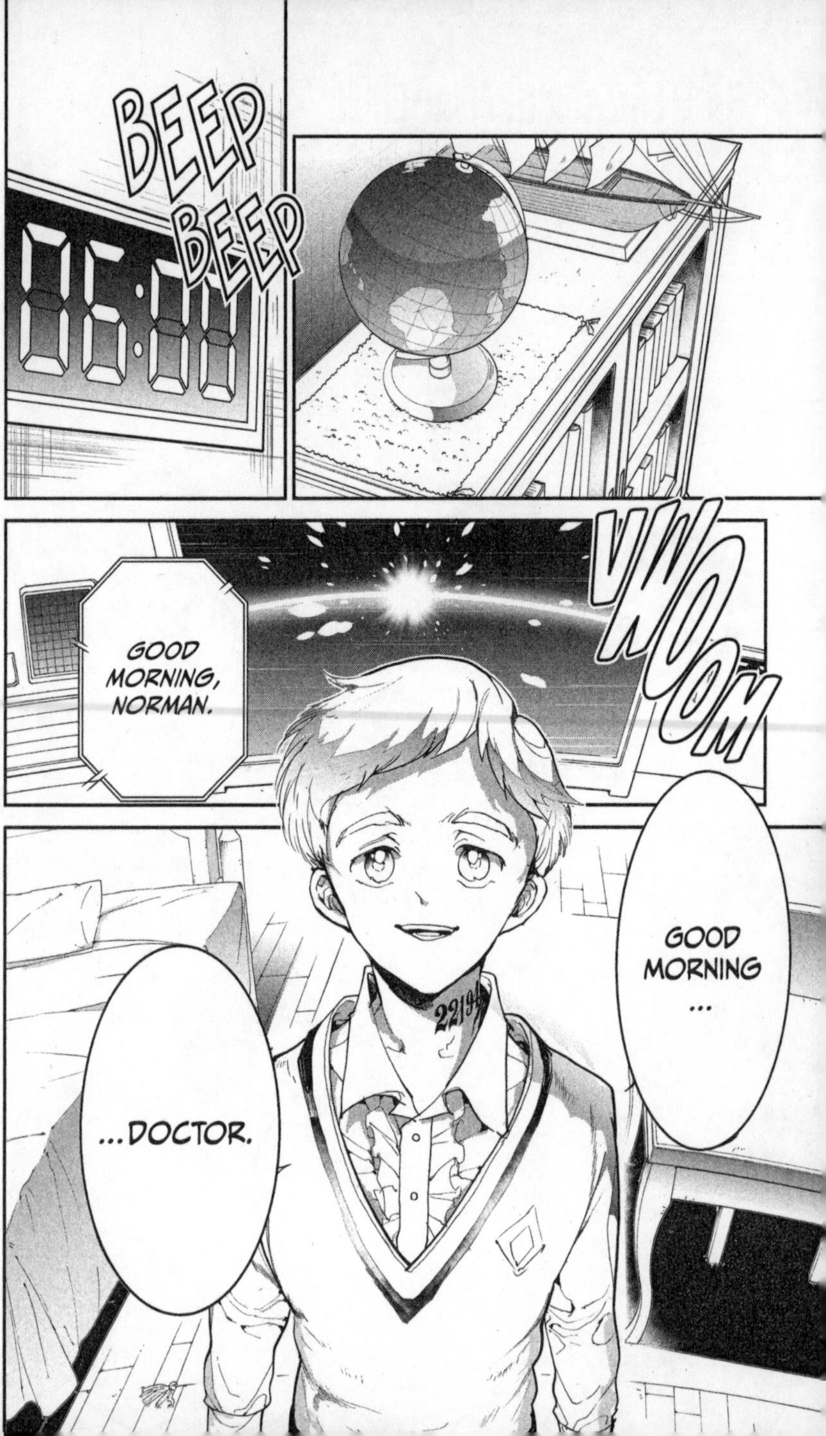

BEEP BEEP
06:00
WHOOM
GOOD MORNING, NORMAN.
GOOD MORNING ...
...DOCTOR.

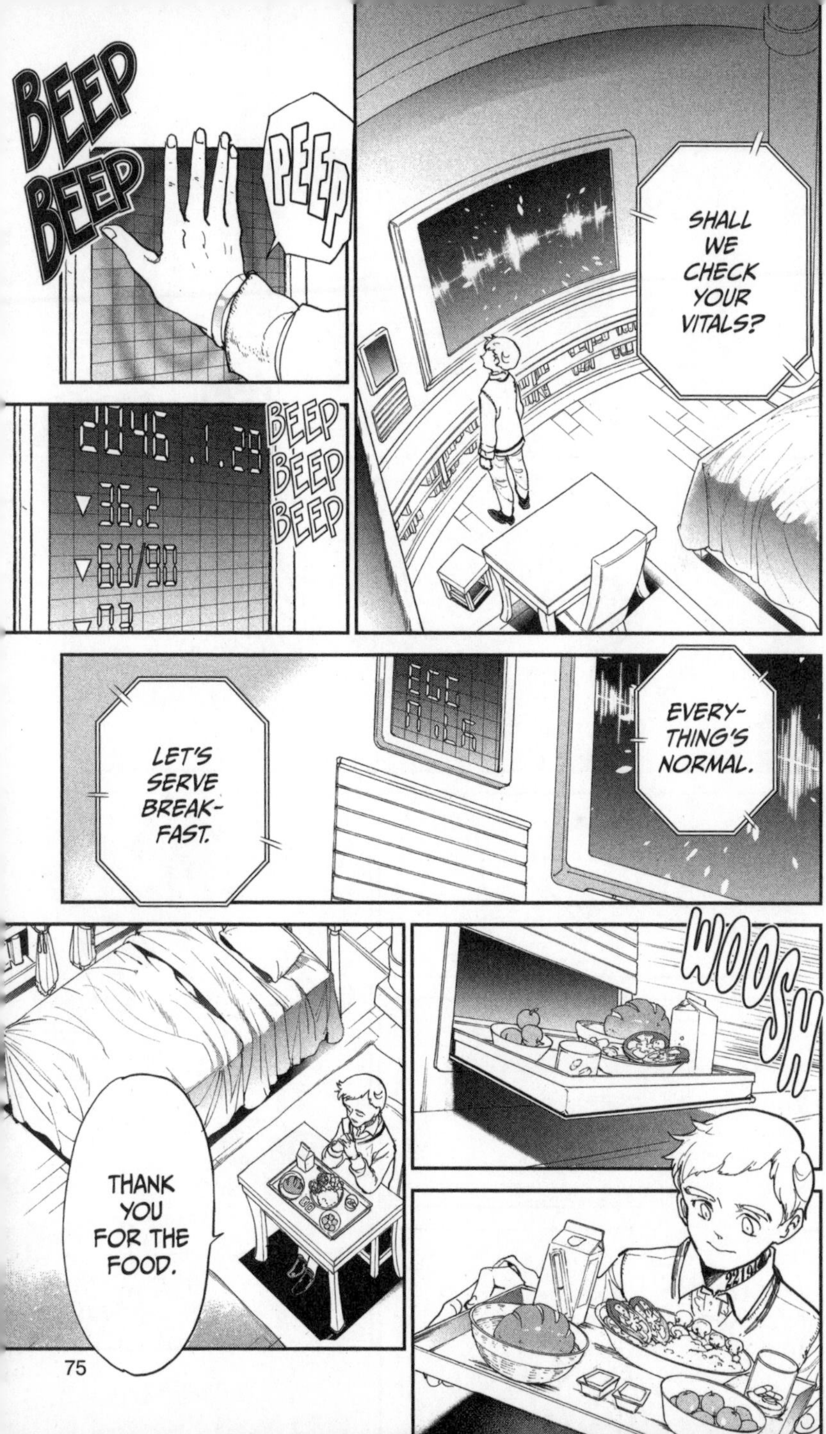
SHALL WE CHECK YOUR VITALS?
BEEP BEEP
PEEP
2046 .1.29
▼36.2
▼60/90
BEEP BEEP BEEP
EVERY-THING'S NORMAL.
LET'S SERVE BREAK-FAST.
WOOSH
THANK YOU FOR THE FOOD.

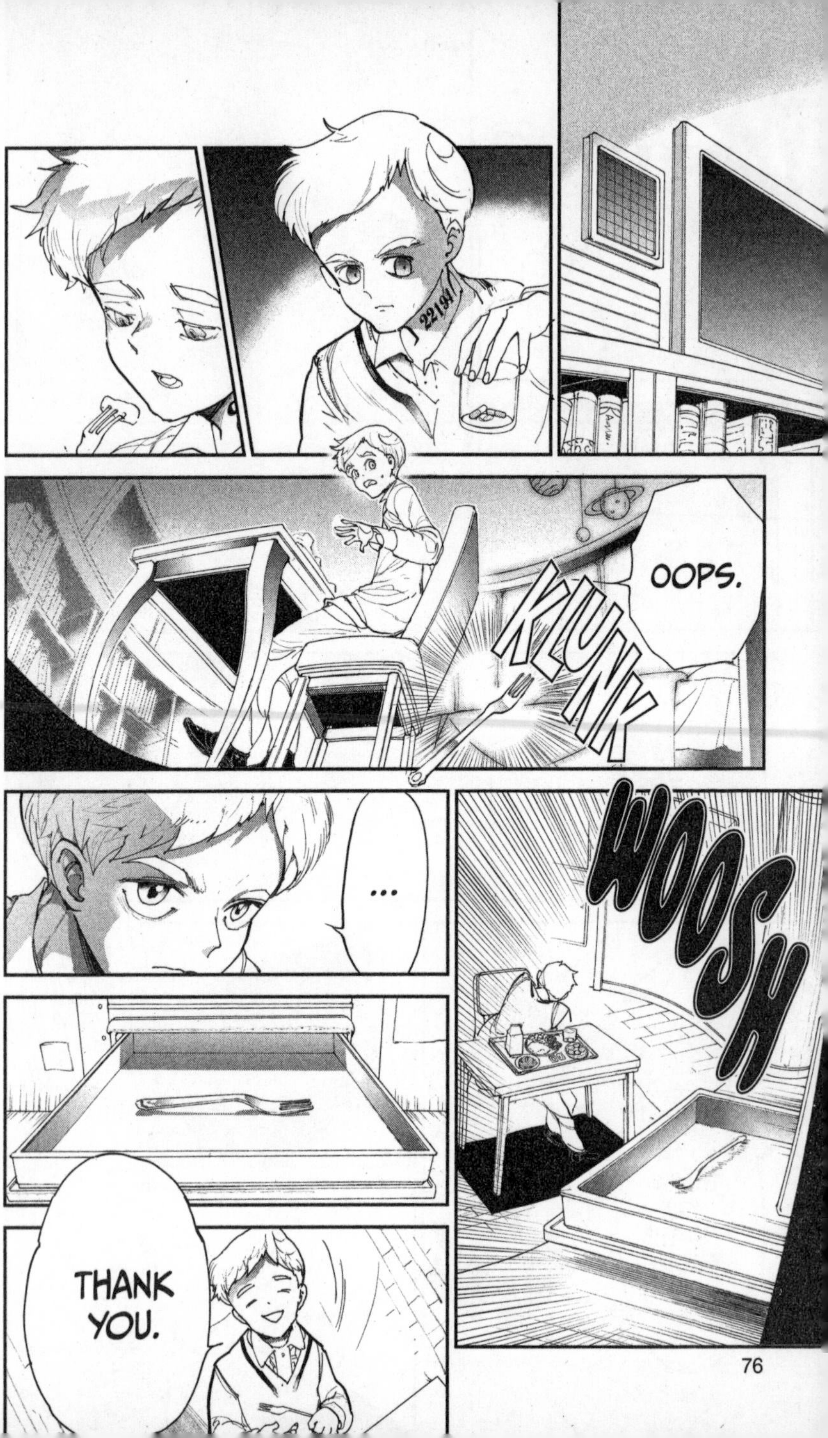
22194
OOPS.
KLUNK
WOOSH
...
THANK YOU.

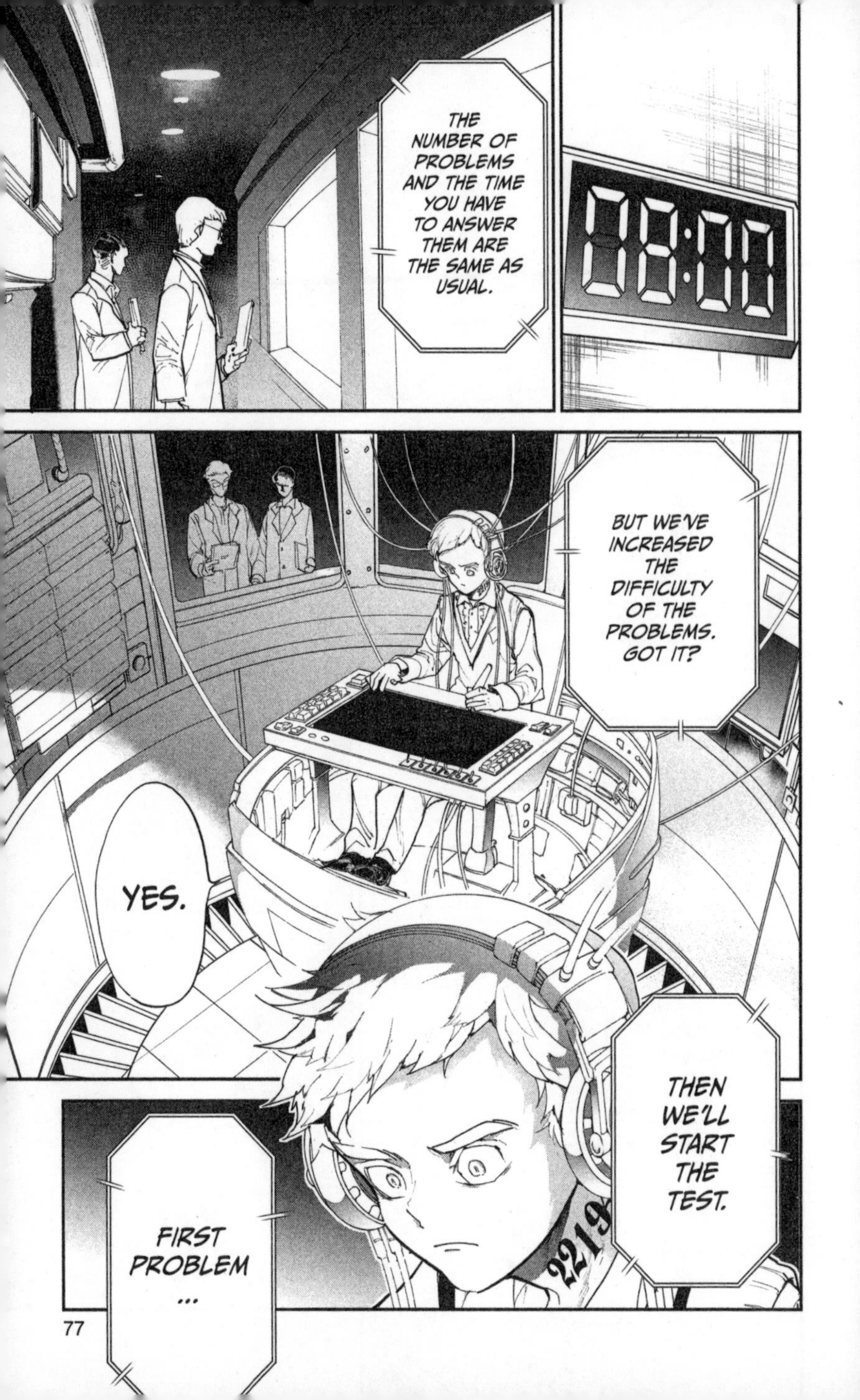
THE NUMBER OF PROBLEMS AND THE TIME YOU HAVE TO ANSWER THEM ARE THE SAME AS USUAL.
BUT WE'VE INCREASED THE DIFFICULTY OF THE PROBLEMS. GOT IT?
YES.
THEN WE'LL START THE TEST.
FIRST PROBLEM ...

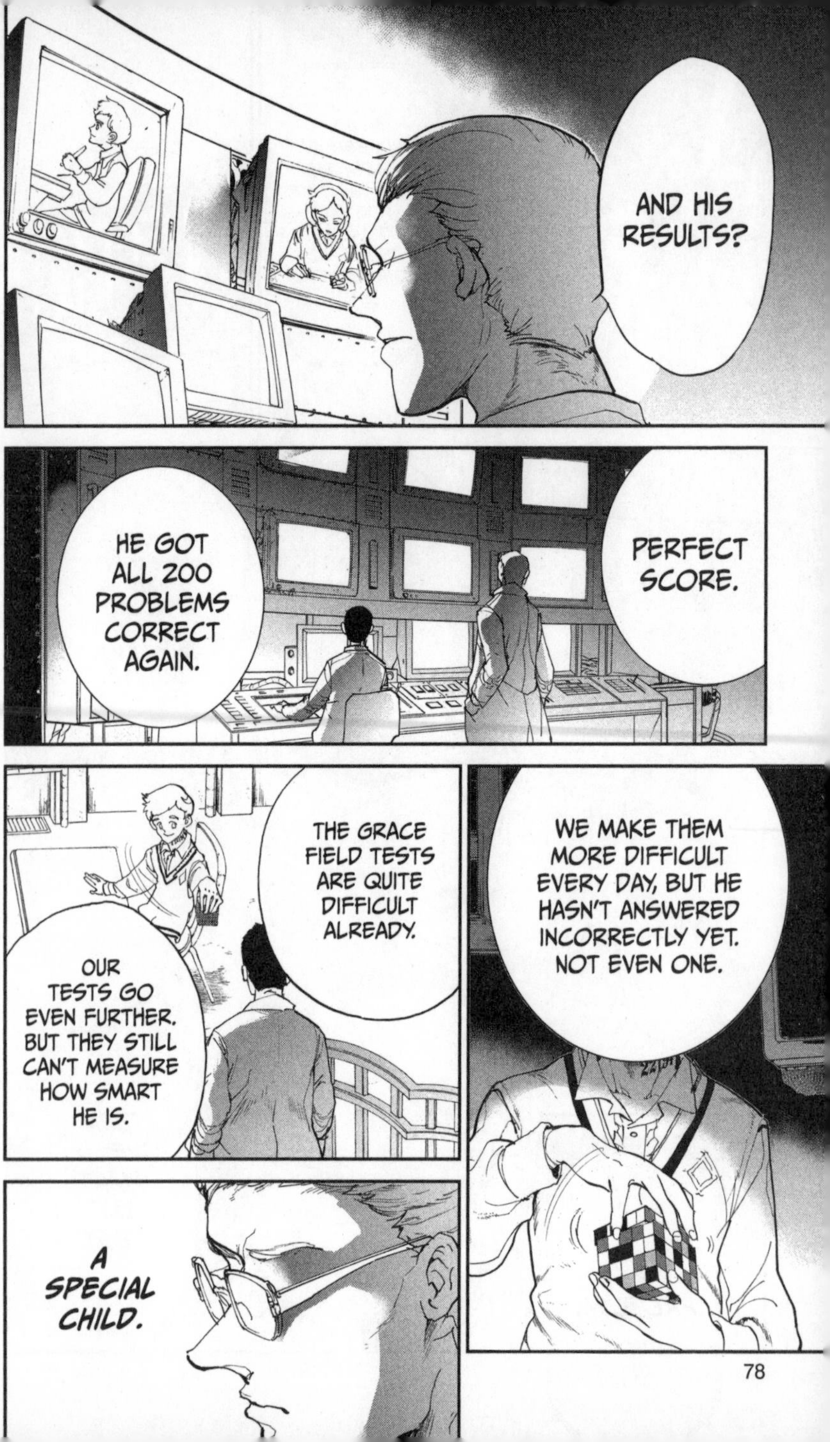
AND HIS RESULTS?
PERFECT SCORE.
HE GOT ALL 200 PROBLEMS CORRECT AGAIN.
WE MAKE THEM MORE DIFFICULT EVERY DAY, BUT HE HASN'T ANSWERED INCORRECTLY YET. NOT EVEN ONE.
THE GRACE FIELD TESTS ARE QUITE DIFFICULT ALREADY.
OUR TESTS GO EVEN FURTHER. BUT THEY STILL CAN'T MEASURE HOW SMART HE IS.
A SPECIAL CHILD.

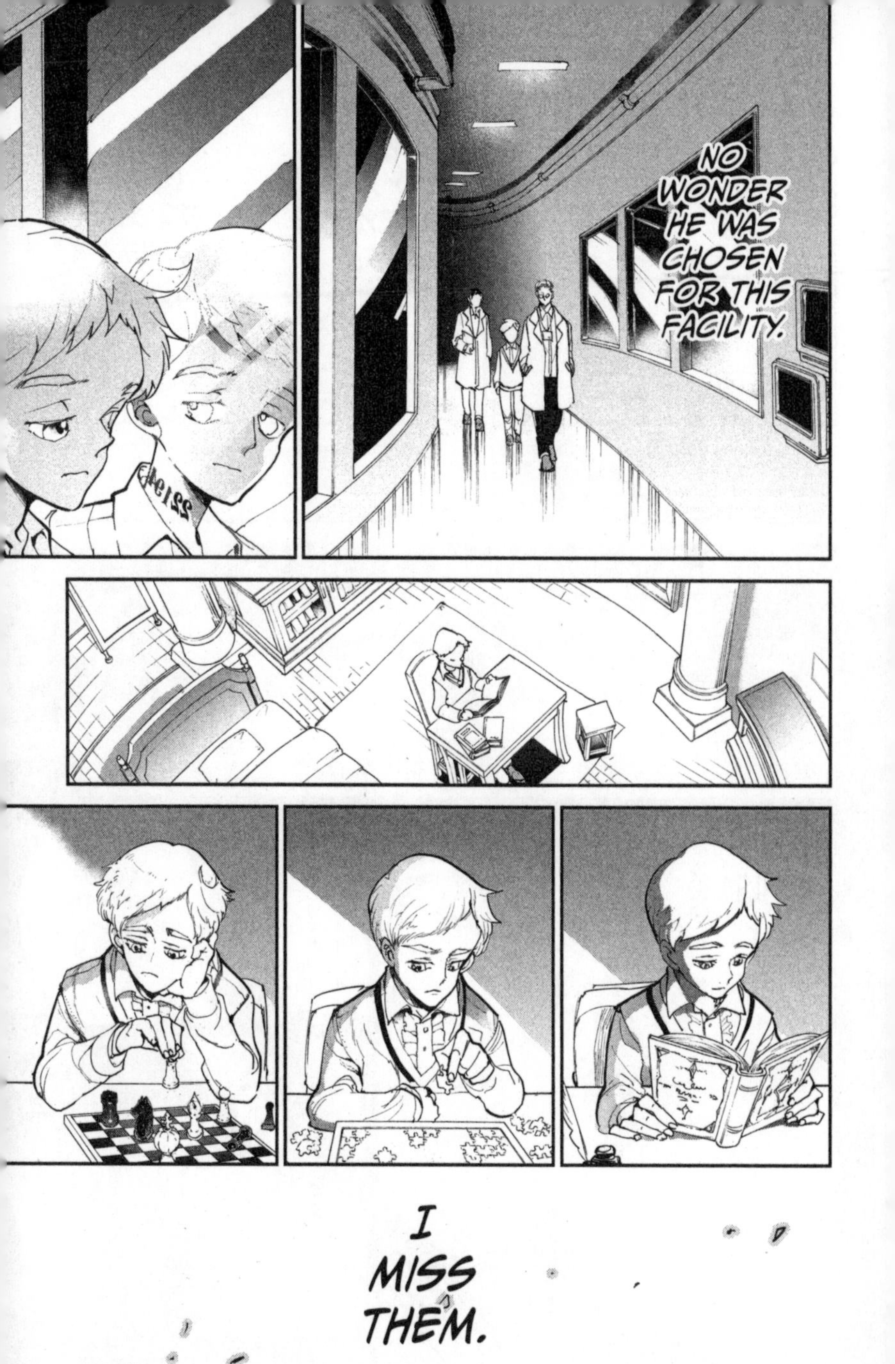
NO WONDER HE WAS CHOSEN FOR THIS FACILITY.
I MISS THEM.

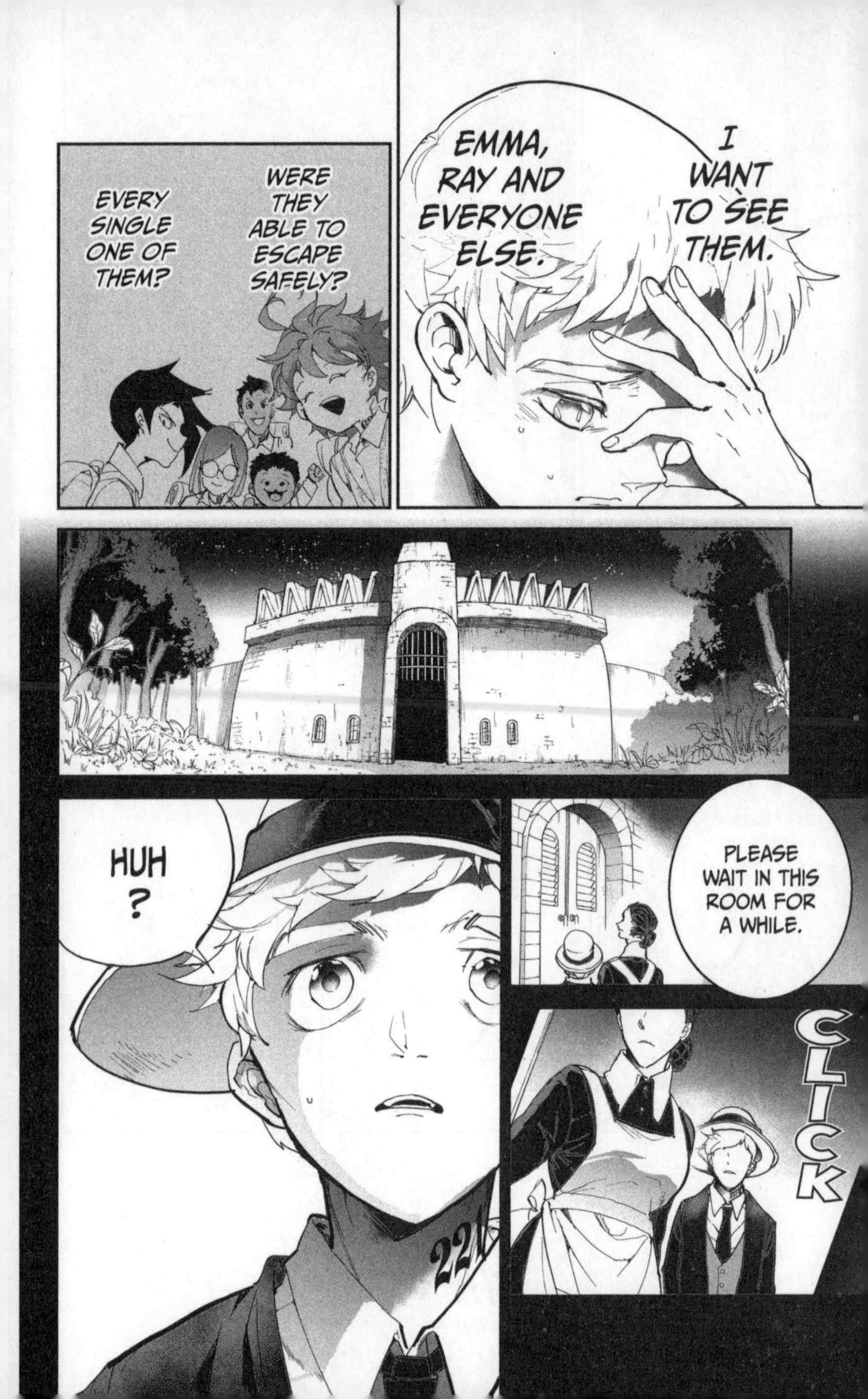
EMMA, RAY AND EVERYONE ELSE.
I WANT TO SEE THEM.
WERE THEY ABLE TO ESCAPE SAFELY?
EVERY SINGLE ONE OF THEM?
PLEASE WAIT IN THIS ROOM FOR A WHILE.
CLICK
HUH ?
22

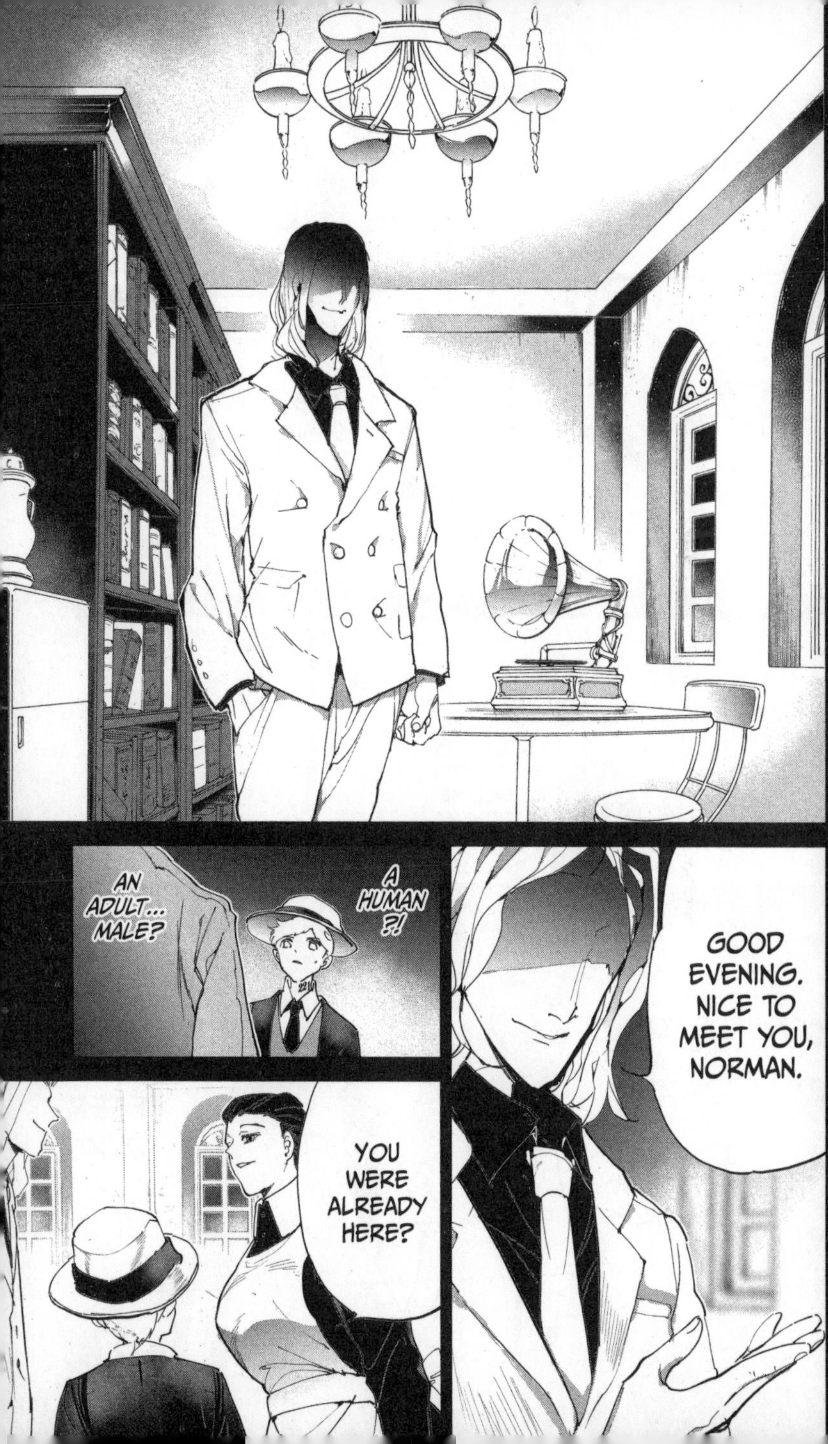
GOOD EVENING. NICE TO MEET YOU, NORMAN.
A HUMAN?!
AN ADULT... MALE?
YOU WERE ALREADY HERE?

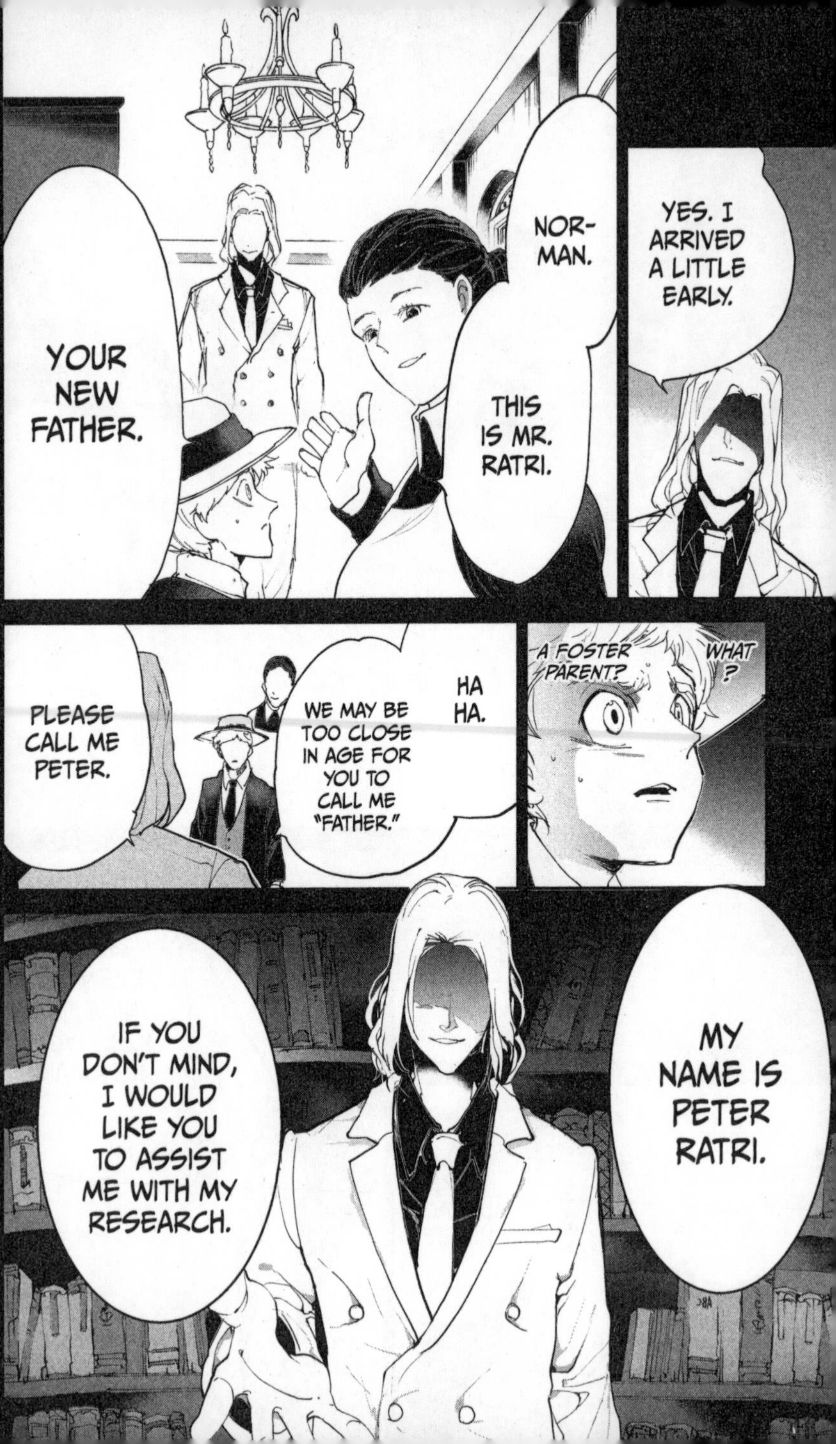
YES. I ARRIVED A LITTLE EARLY.
NOR-MAN.
THIS IS MR. RATRI.
YOUR NEW FATHER.
WHAT?
A FOSTER PARENT?
HA HA.
WE MAY BE TOO CLOSE IN AGE FOR YOU TO CALL ME "FATHER."
PLEASE CALL ME PETER.
MY NAME IS PETER RATRI.
IF YOU DON'T MIND, I WOULD LIKE YOU TO ASSIST ME WITH MY RESEARCH.

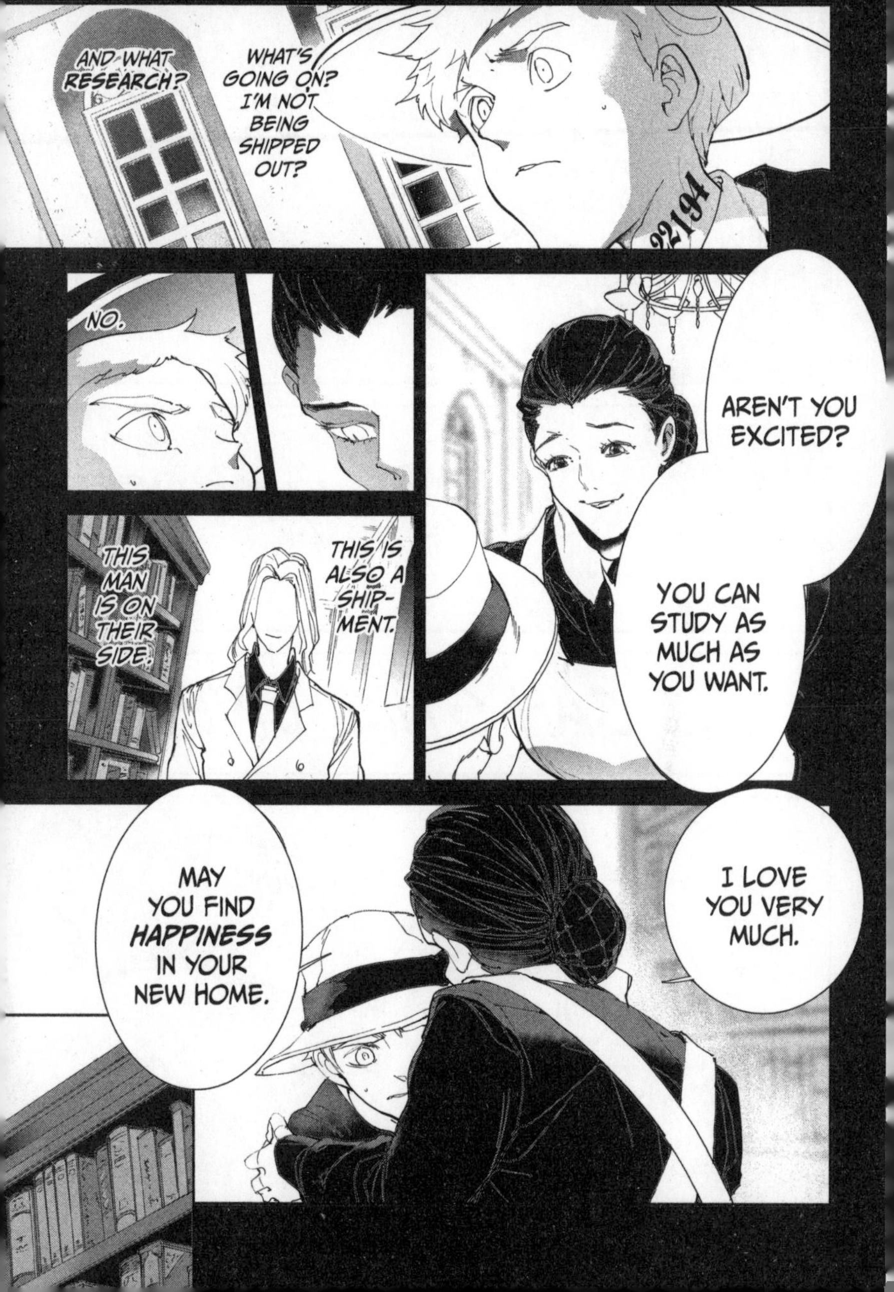
WHAT'S GOING ON? I'M NOT BEING SHIPPED OUT?
AND WHAT RESEARCH?
AREN'T YOU EXCITED?
YOU CAN STUDY AS MUCH AS YOU WANT.
NO.
THIS IS ALSO A SHIPMENT.
THIS MAN IS ON THEIR SIDE.
I LOVE YOU VERY MUCH.
MAY YOU FIND **HAPPINESS** IN YOUR NEW HOME.

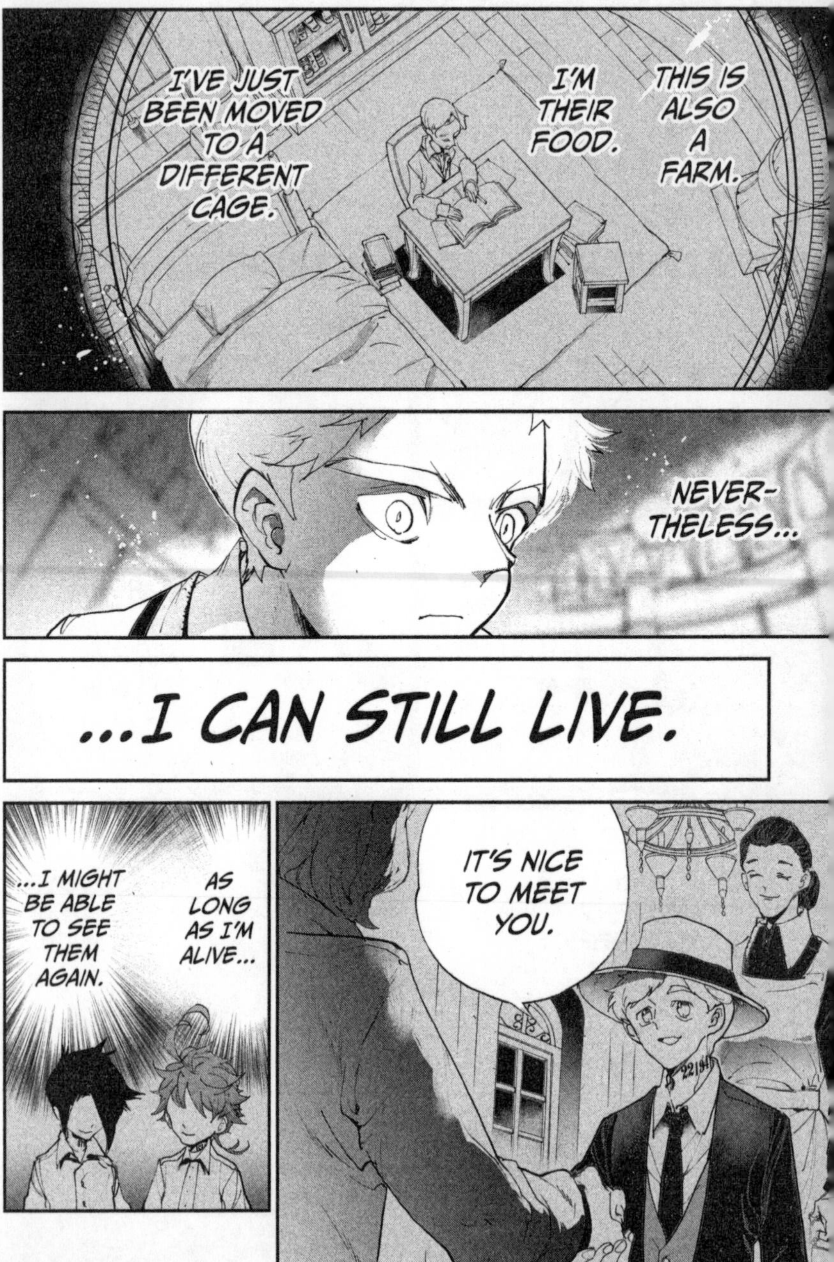
THIS IS ALSO A FARM.
I'M THEIR FOOD.
I'VE JUST BEEN MOVED TO A DIFFERENT CAGE.
NEVER-THELESS...
...I CAN STILL LIVE.
IT'S NICE TO MEET YOU.
AS LONG AS I'M ALIVE...
...I MIGHT BE ABLE TO SEE THEM AGAIN.

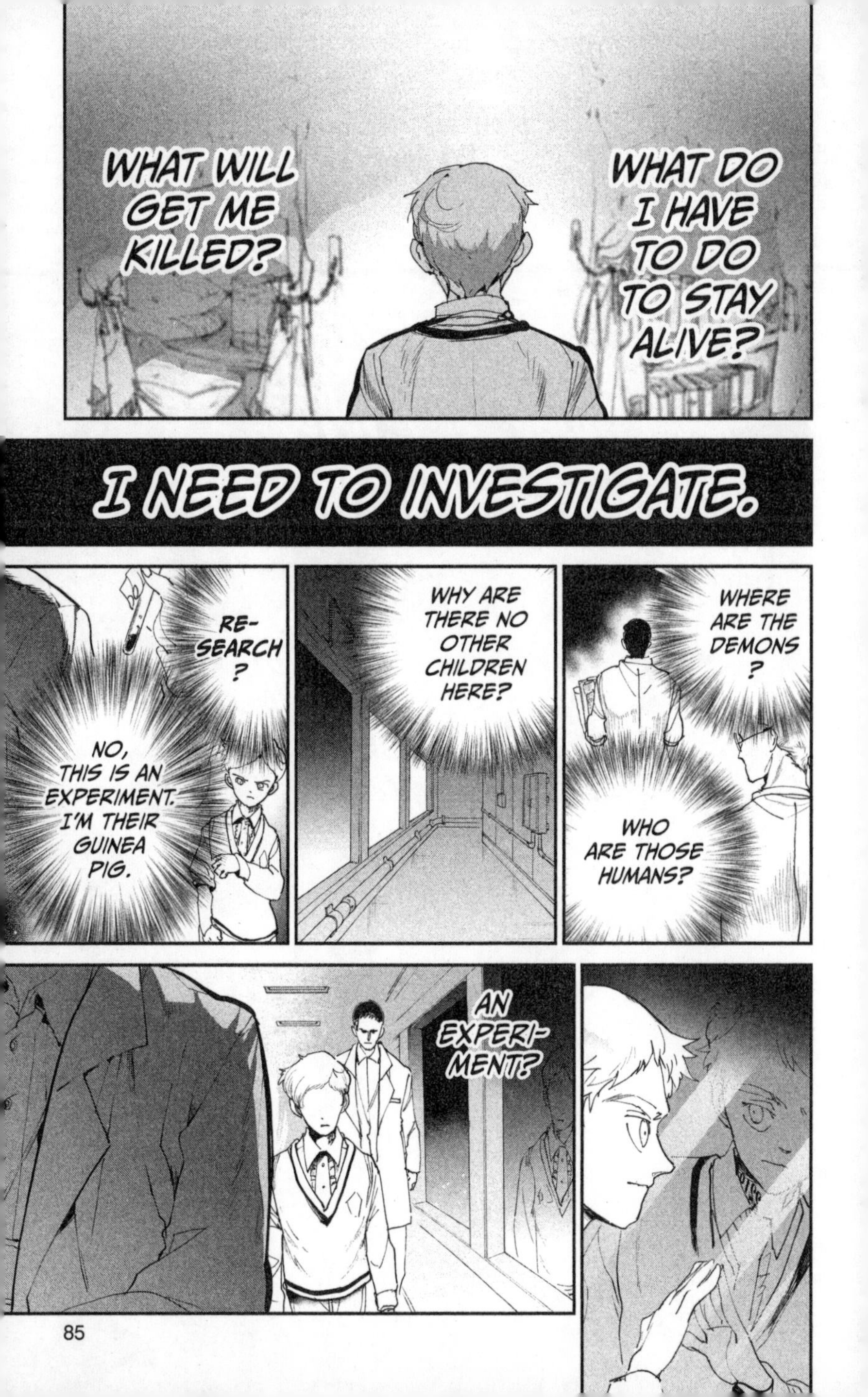
WHAT DO I HAVE TO DO TO STAY ALIVE?
WHAT WILL GET ME KILLED?
I NEED TO INVESTIGATE.
WHERE ARE THE DEMONS?
WHO ARE THOSE HUMANS?
WHY ARE THERE NO OTHER CHILDREN HERE?
RE-SEARCH?
NO, THIS IS AN EXPERIMENT. I'M THEIR GUINEA PIG.
AN EXPERI-MENT?

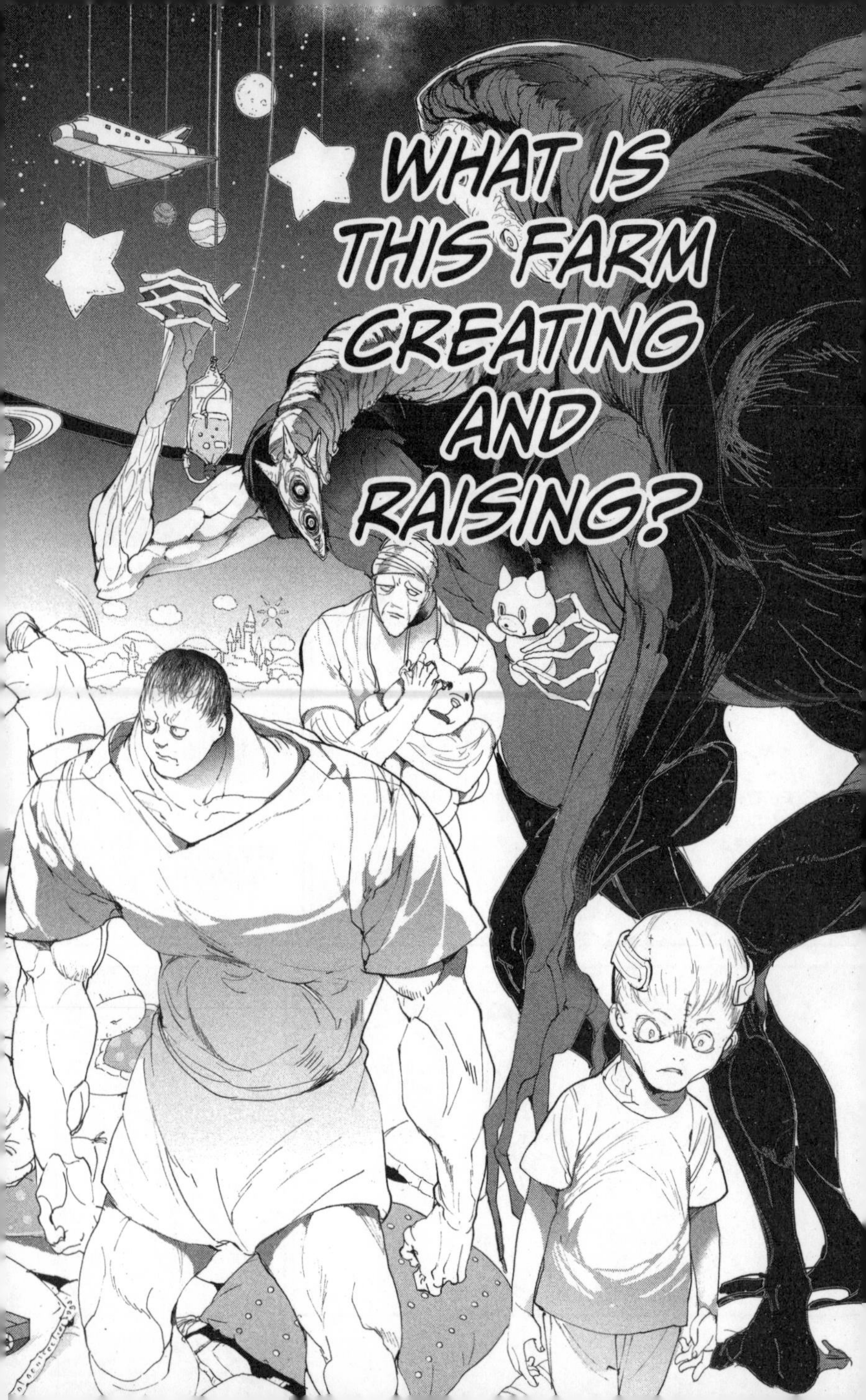
WHAT IS THIS FARM CREATING AND RAISING?

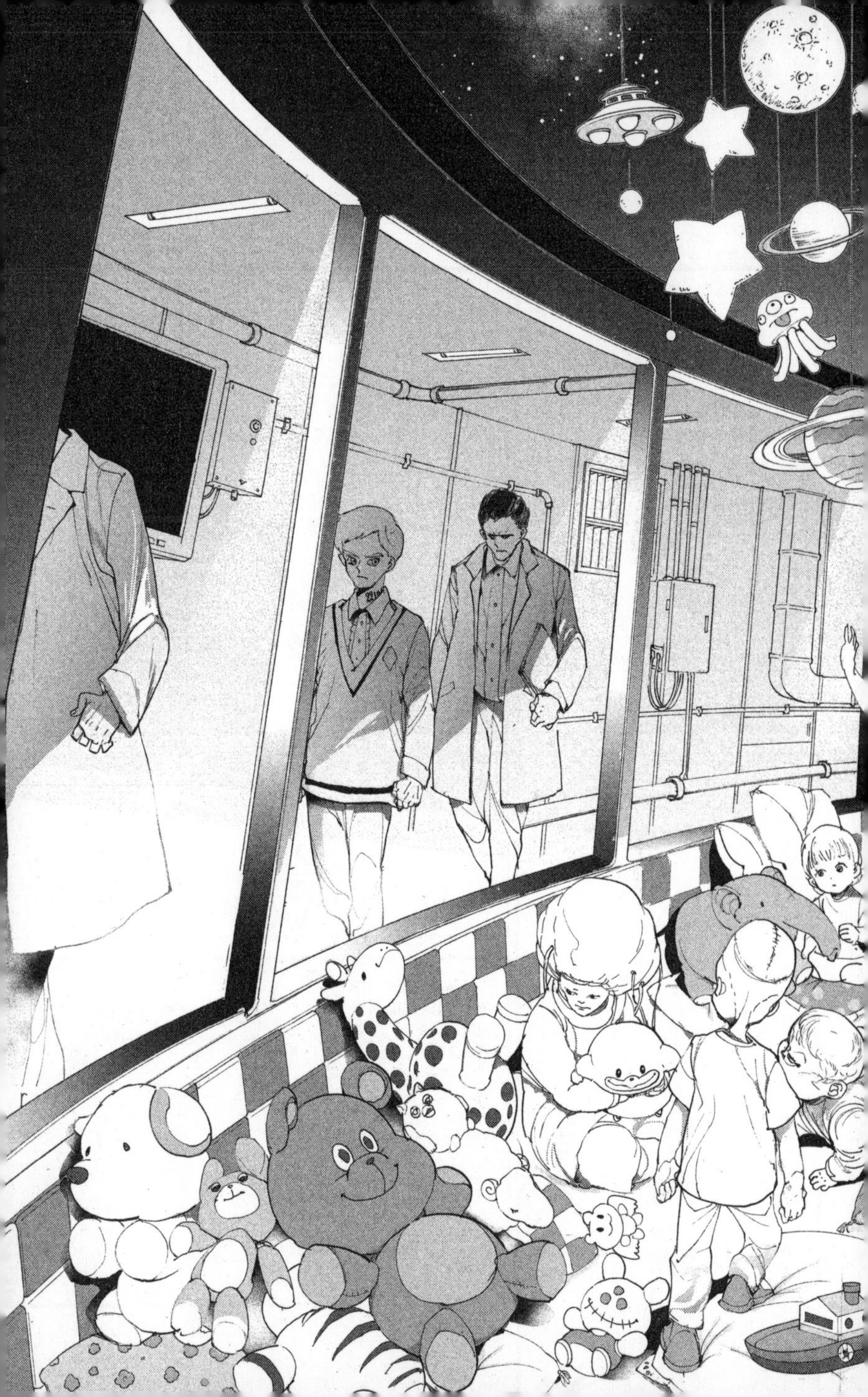

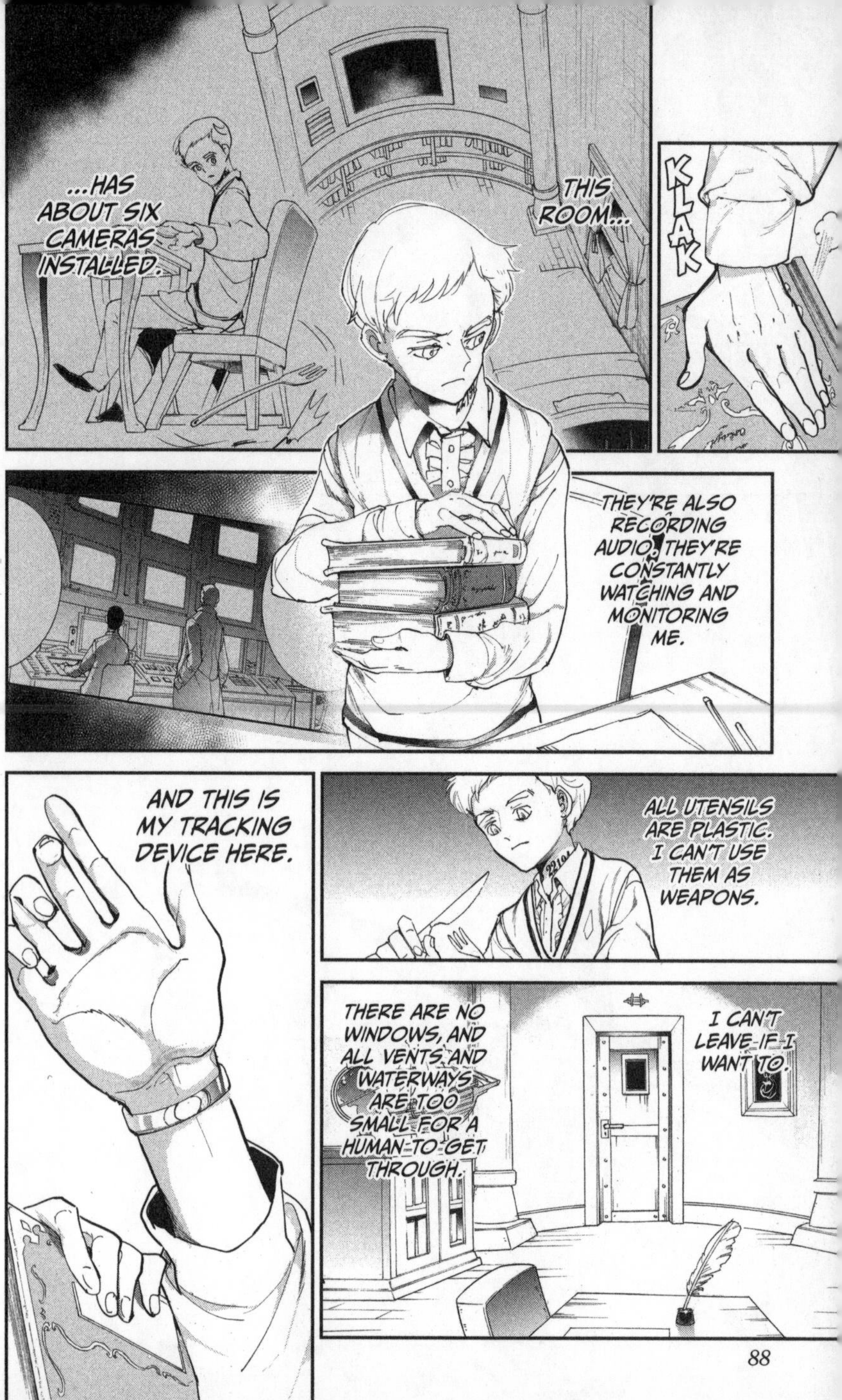
KLAK
THIS ROOM...
...HAS ABOUT SIX CAMERAS INSTALLED.
THEY'RE ALSO RECORDING AUDIO. THEY'RE CONSTANTLY WATCHING AND MONITORING ME.
ALL UTENSILS ARE PLASTIC. I CAN'T USE THEM AS WEAPONS.
I CAN'T LEAVE IF I WANT TO.
THERE ARE NO WINDOWS, AND ALL VENTS AND WATERWAYS ARE TOO SMALL FOR A HUMAN TO GET THROUGH.
AND THIS IS MY TRACKING DEVICE HERE.

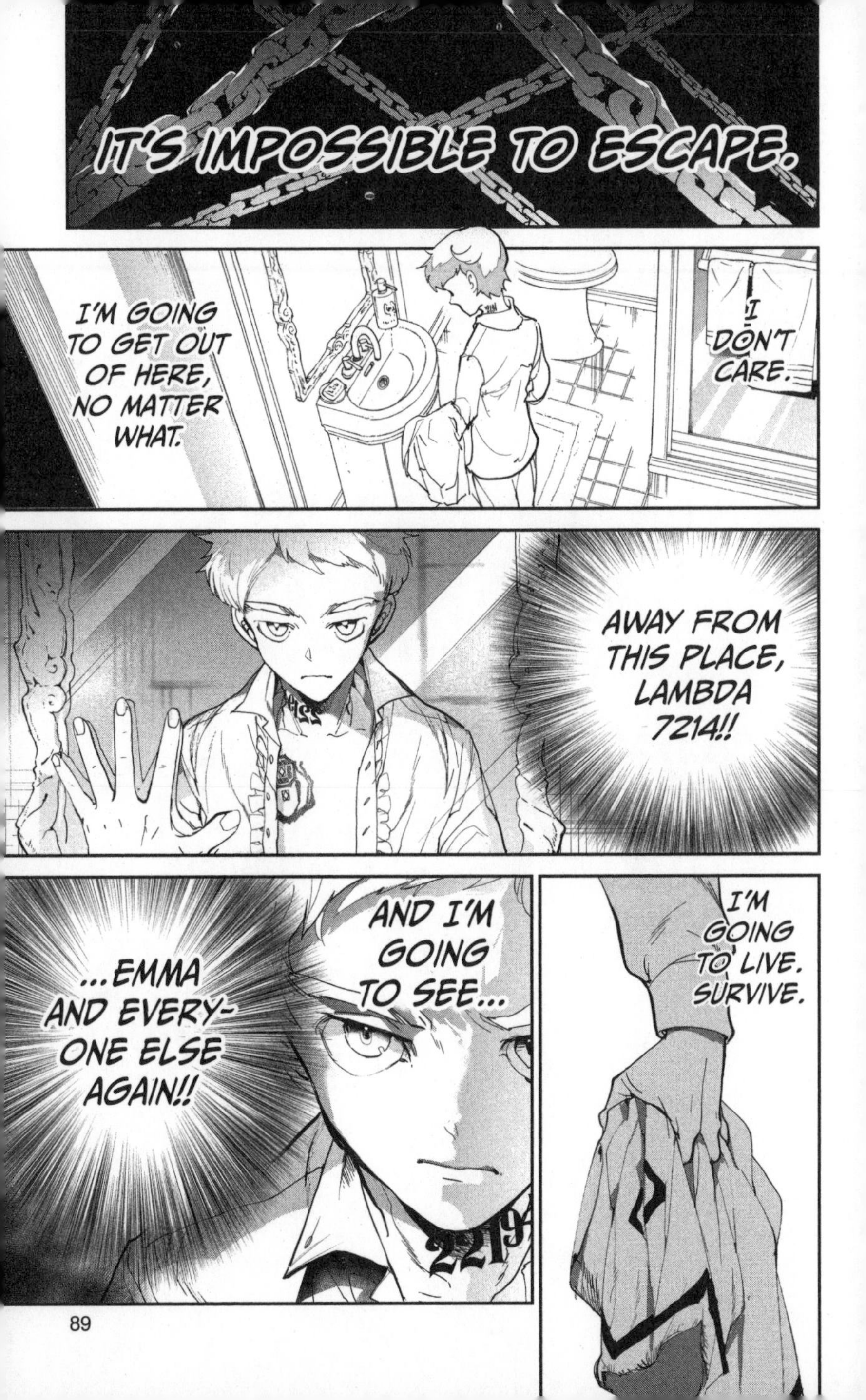
IT'S IMPOSSIBLE TO ESCAPE.
I DON'T CARE.
I'M GOING TO GET OUT OF HERE, NO MATTER WHAT.
AWAY FROM THIS PLACE, LAMBDA 7214!!
I'M GOING TO LIVE. SURVIVE.
AND I'M GOING TO SEE...
...EMMA AND EVERY-ONE ELSE AGAIN!!

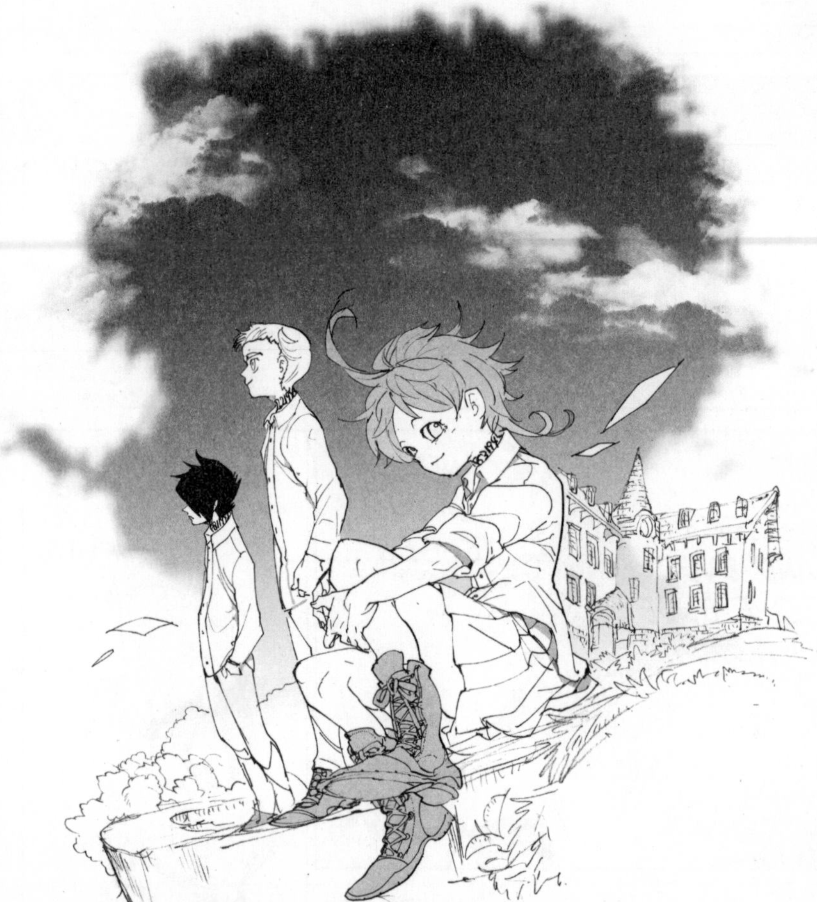

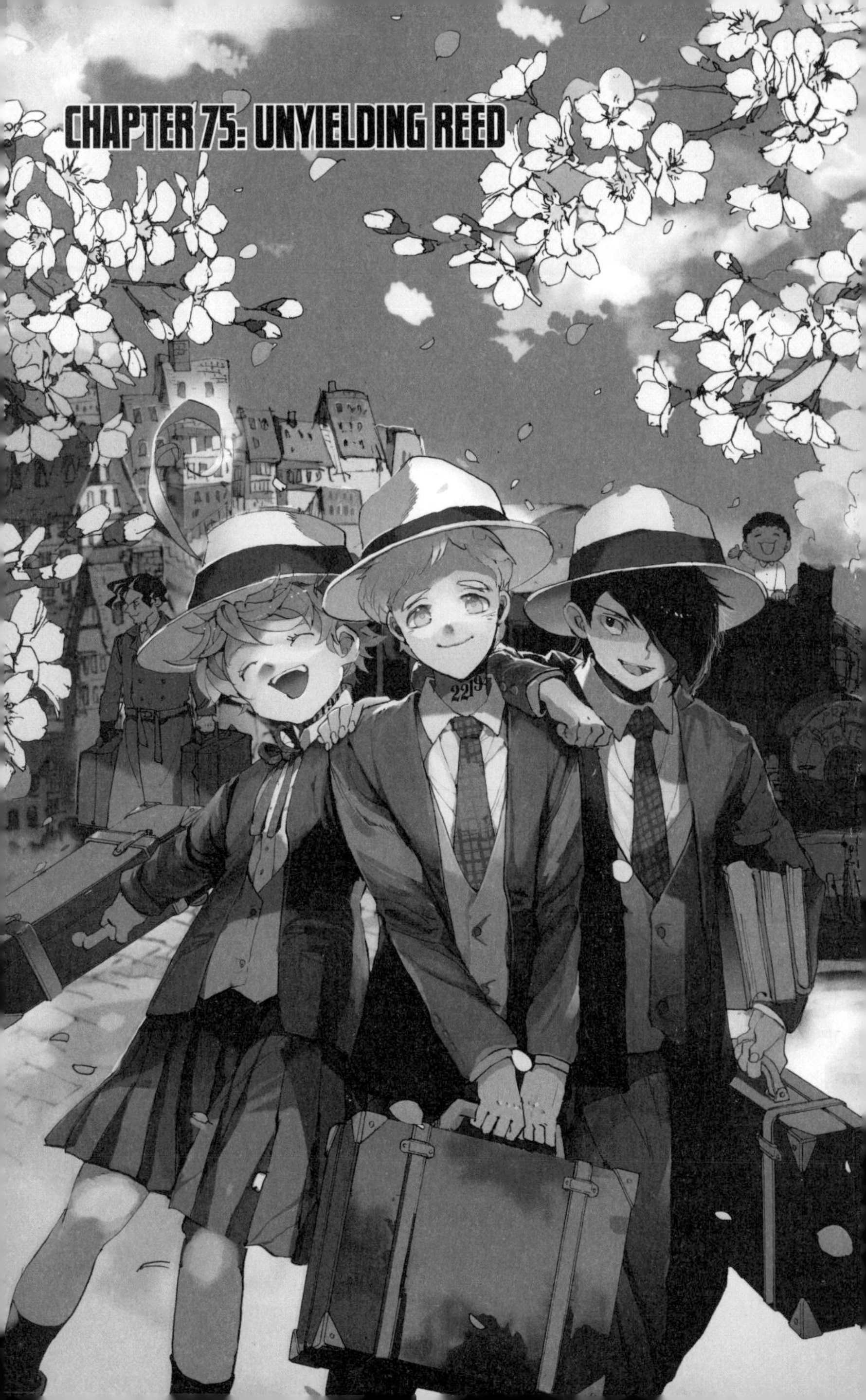
CHAPTER 75: UNYIELDING REED
22194

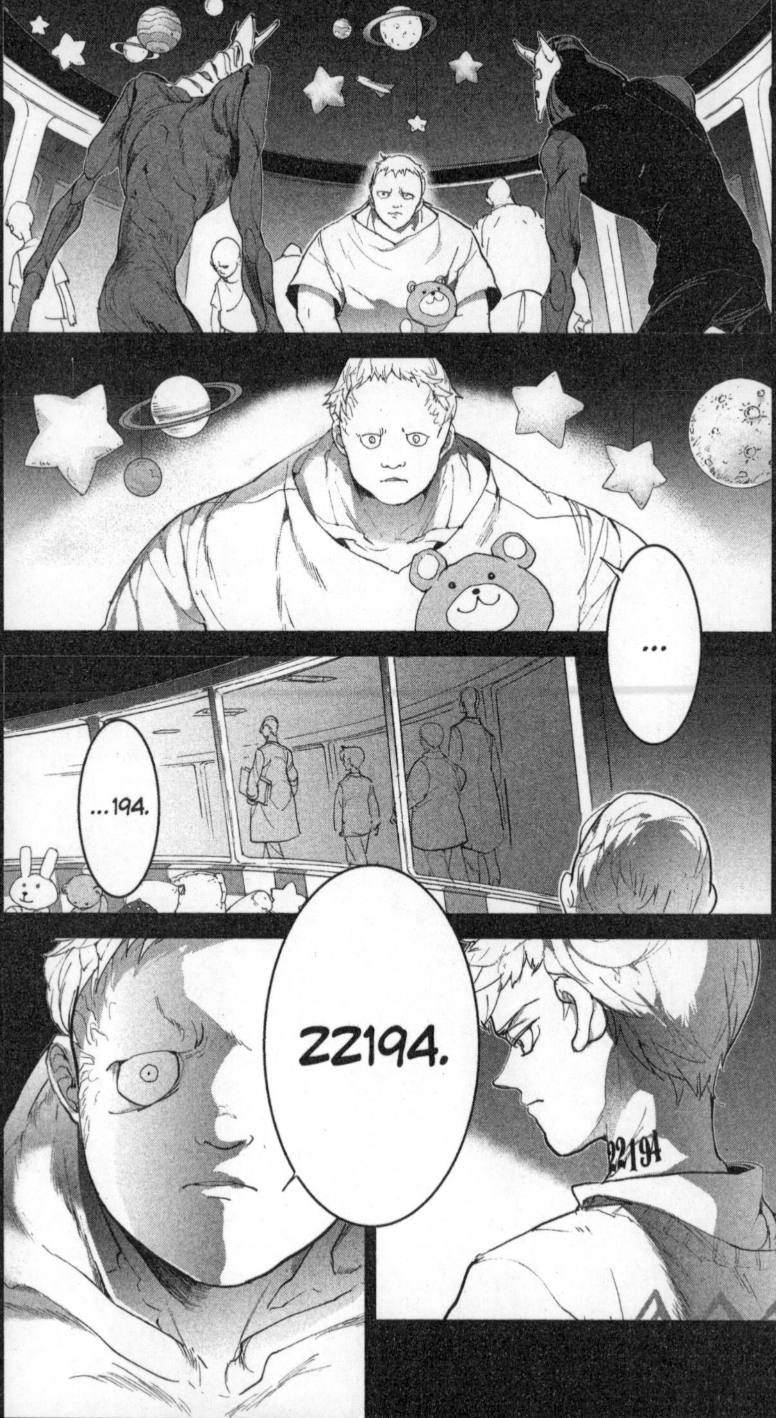
...
...194.
22194.
22194

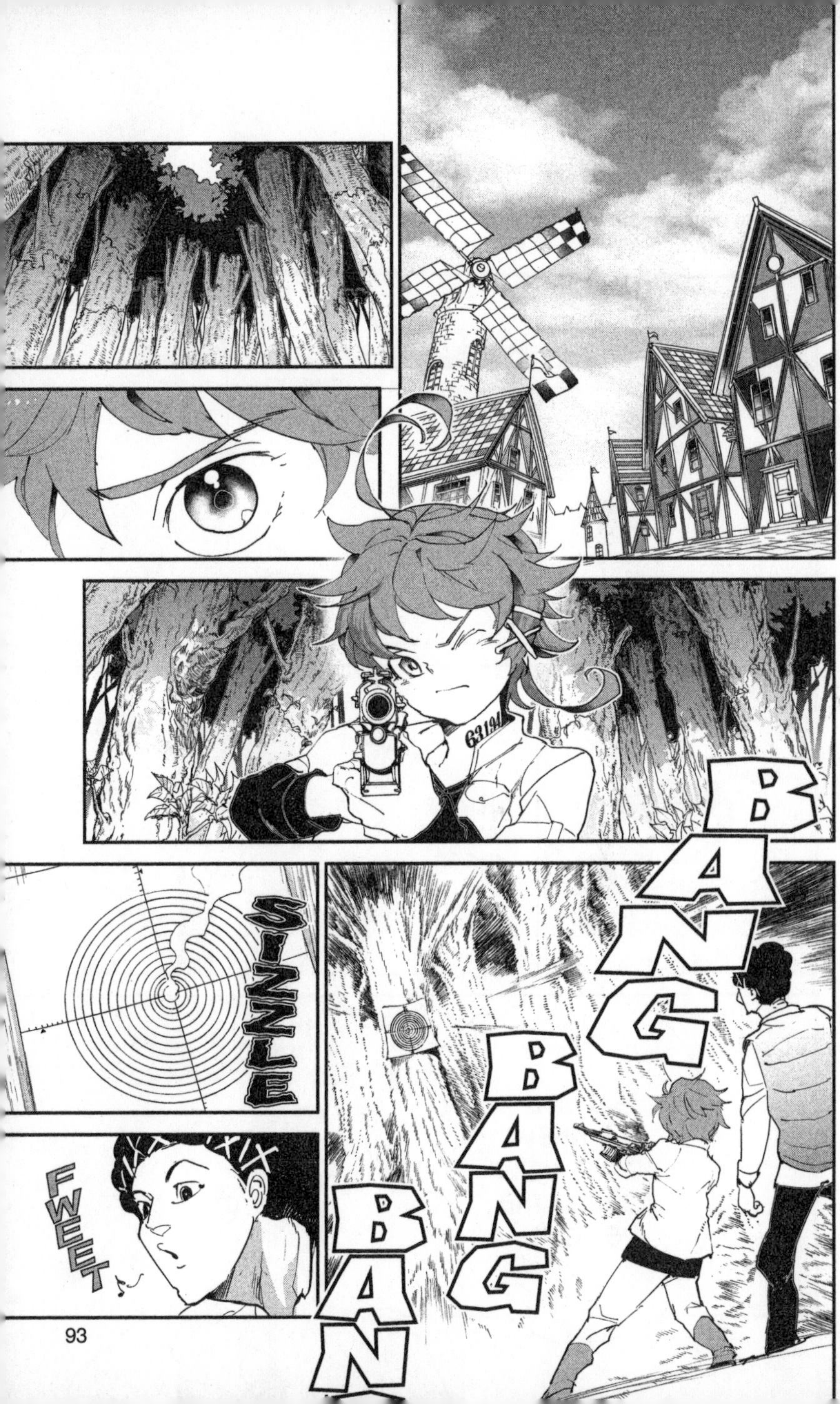
BANG
BANG
BAN
SIZZLE
FWEET

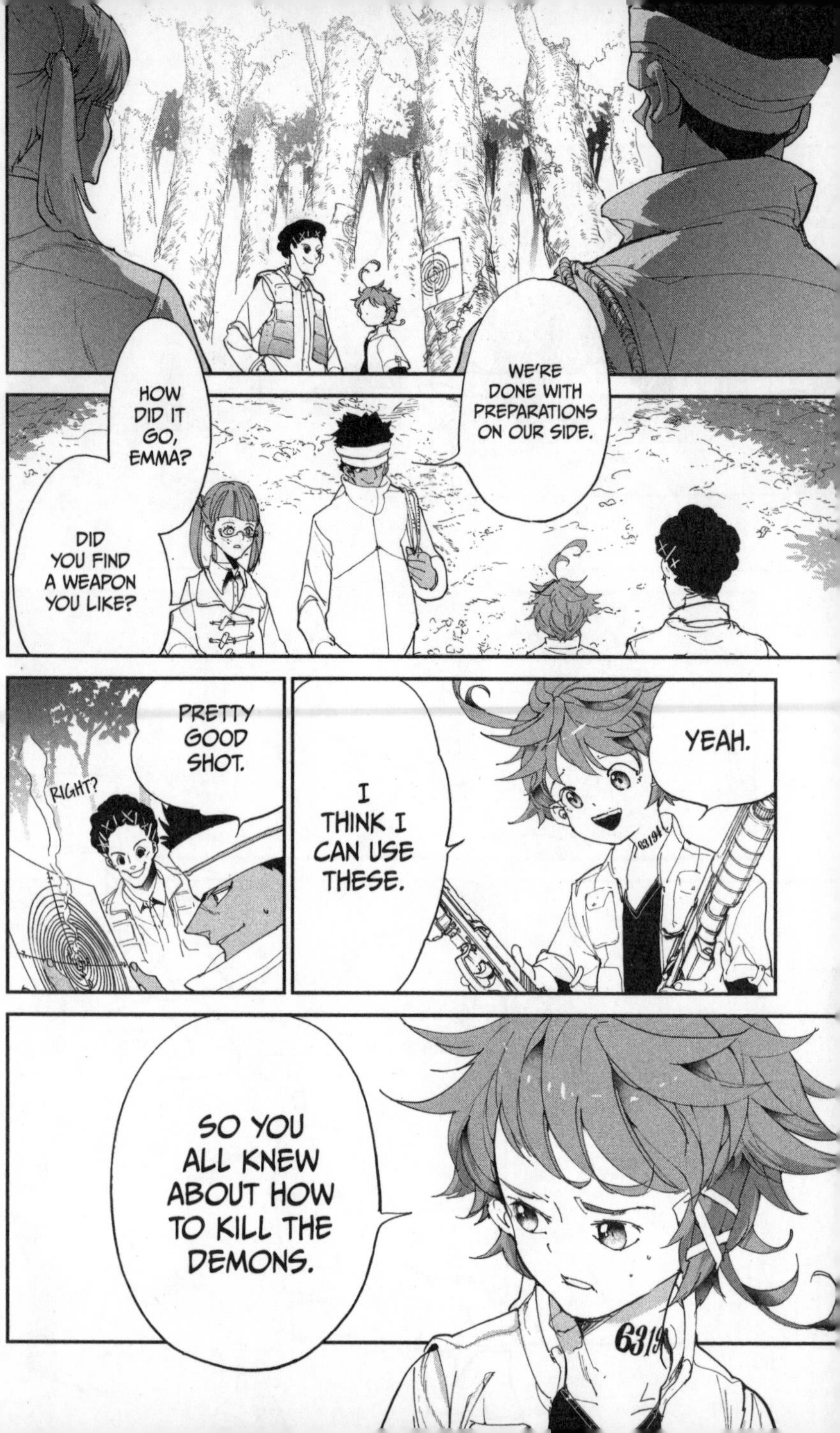
WE'RE DONE WITH PREPARATIONS ON OUR SIDE.
HOW DID IT GO, EMMA?
DID YOU FIND A WEAPON YOU LIKE?
YEAH.
I THINK I CAN USE THESE.
PRETTY GOOD SHOT.
RIGHT?
SO YOU ALL KNEW ABOUT HOW TO KILL THE DEMONS.

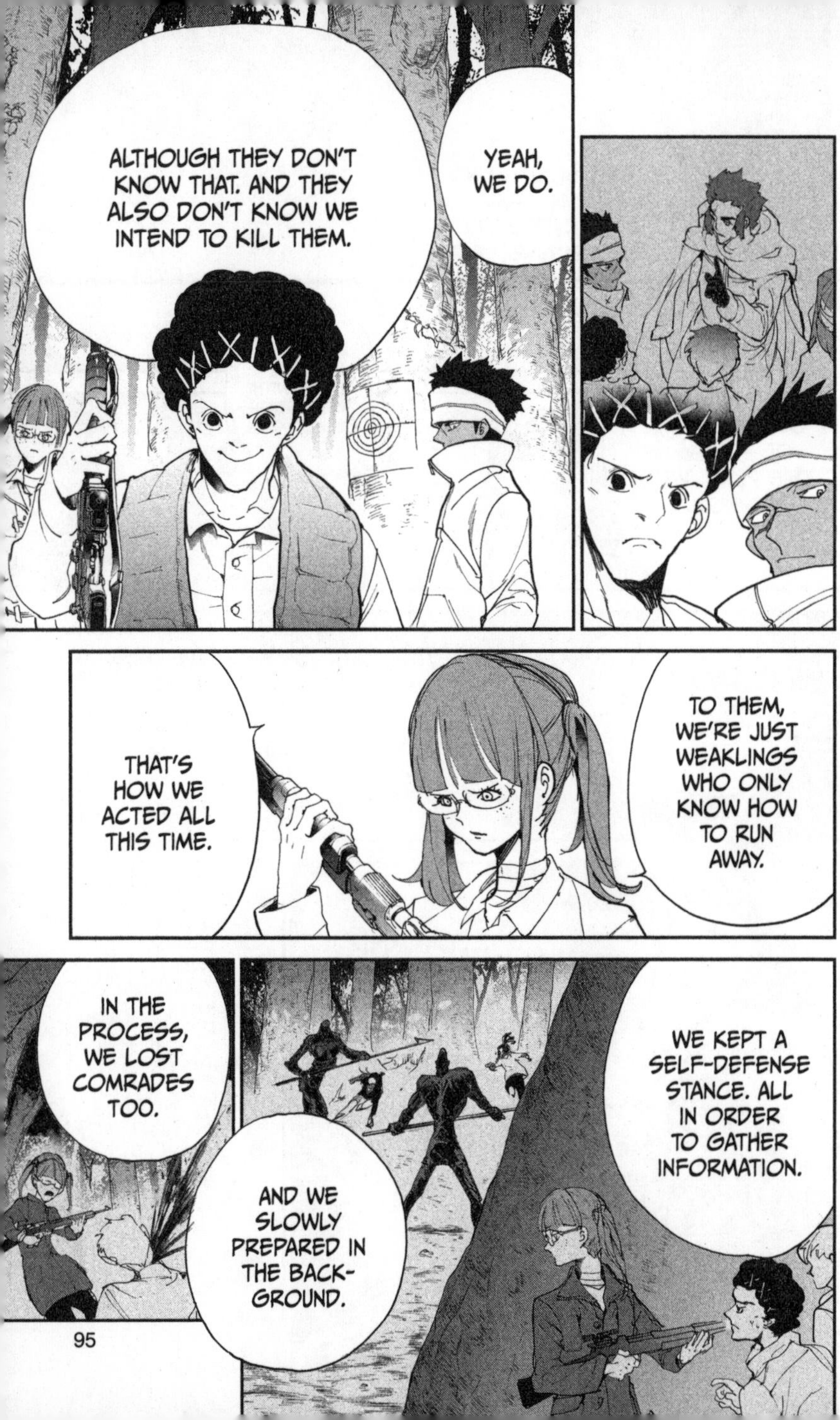
YEAH, WE DO.
ALTHOUGH THEY DON'T KNOW THAT. AND THEY ALSO DON'T KNOW WE INTEND TO KILL THEM.
TO THEM, WE'RE JUST WEAKLINGS WHO ONLY KNOW HOW TO RUN AWAY.
THAT'S HOW WE ACTED ALL THIS TIME.
WE KEPT A SELF-DEFENSE STANCE. ALL IN ORDER TO GATHER INFORMATION.
AND WE SLOWLY PREPARED IN THE BACK-GROUND.
IN THE PROCESS, WE LOST COMRADES TOO.

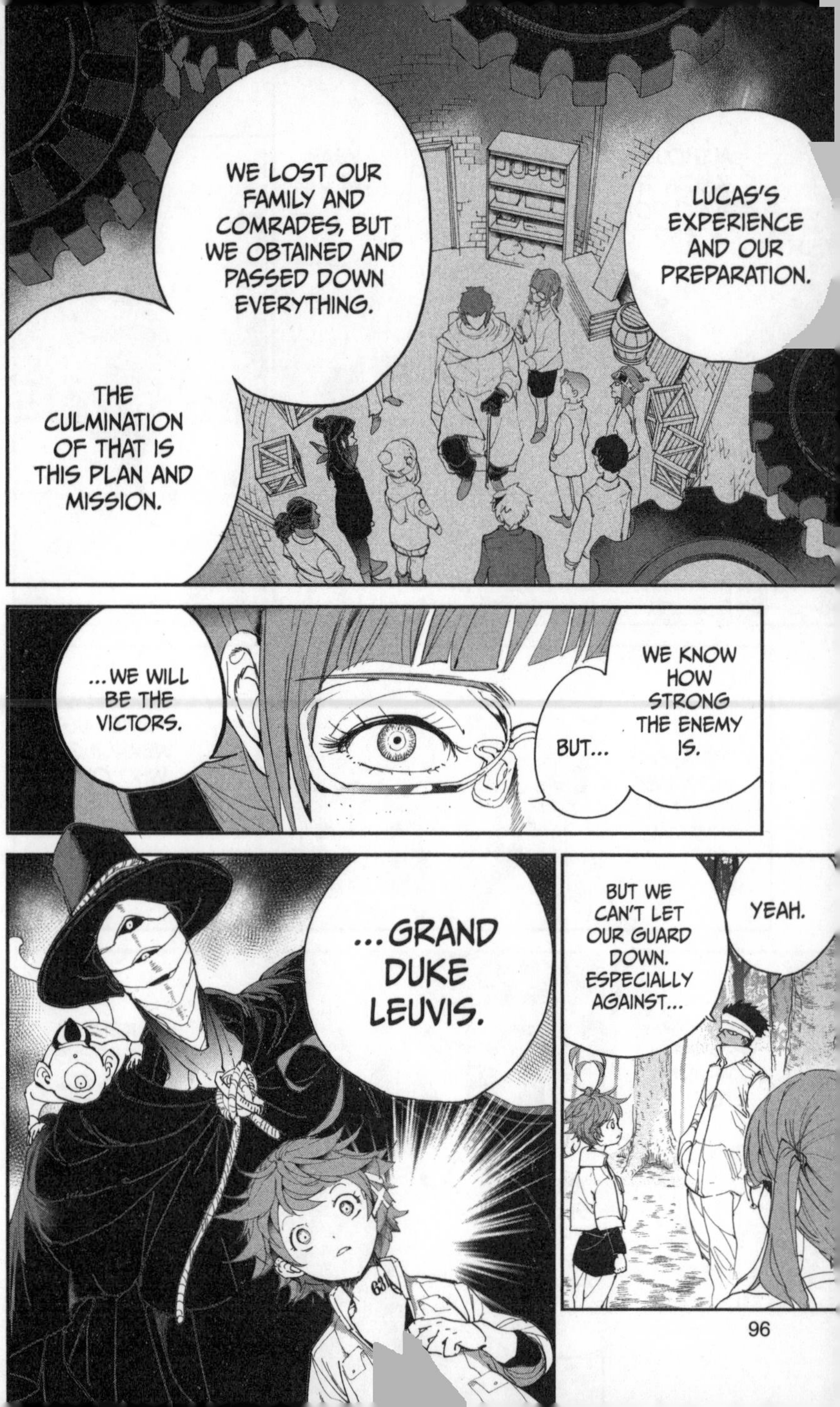
LUCAS'S EXPERIENCE AND OUR PREPARATION.
WE LOST OUR FAMILY AND COMRADES, BUT WE OBTAINED AND PASSED DOWN EVERYTHING.
THE CULMINATION OF THAT IS THIS PLAN AND MISSION.
WE KNOW HOW STRONG THE ENEMY IS.
BUT...
...WE WILL BE THE VICTORS.
YEAH.
BUT WE CAN'T LET OUR GUARD DOWN. ESPECIALLY AGAINST...
...GRAND DUKE LEUVIS.

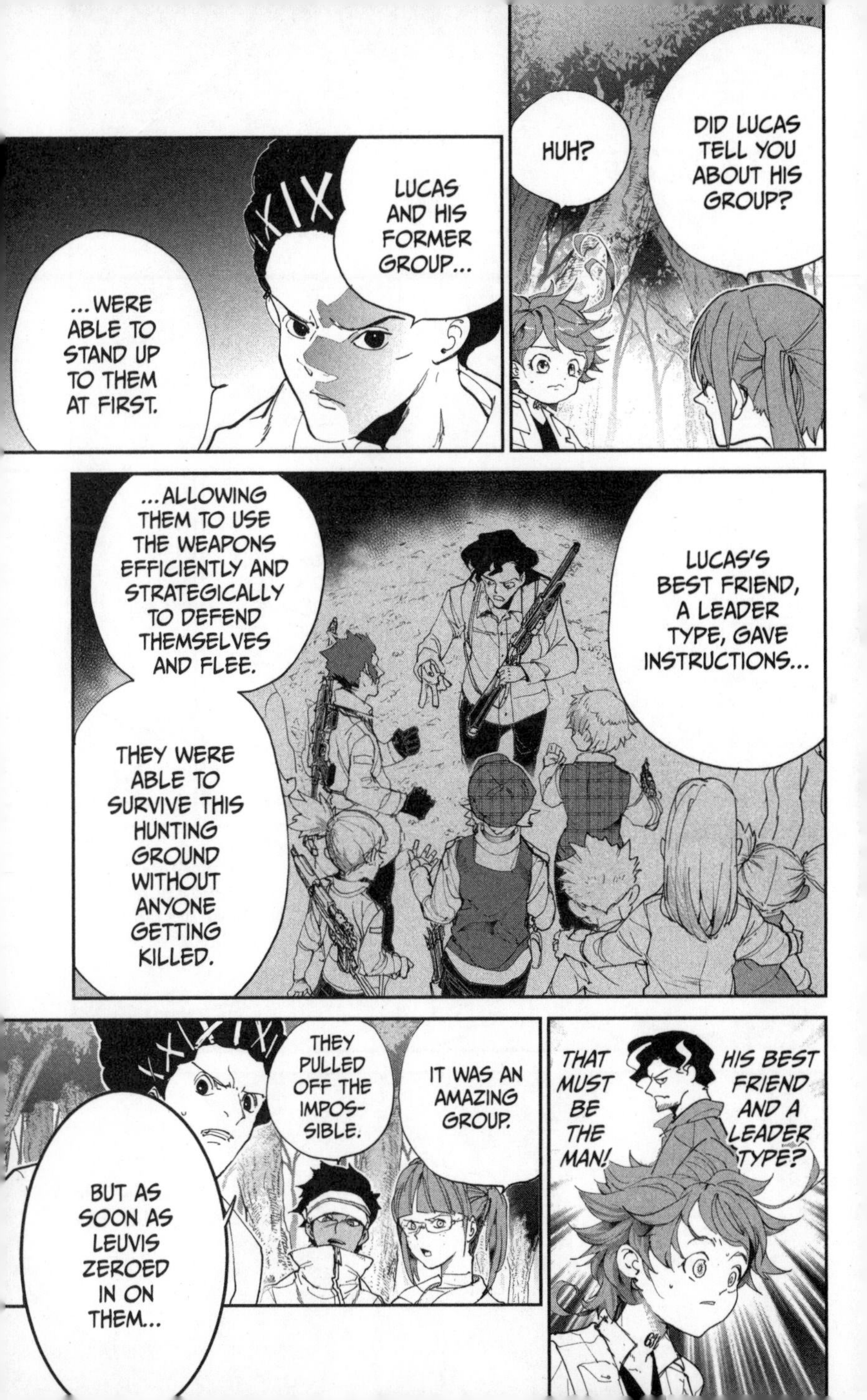
DID LUCAS TELL YOU ABOUT HIS GROUP?
HUH?
LUCAS AND HIS FORMER GROUP...
...WERE ABLE TO STAND UP TO THEM AT FIRST.
LUCAS'S BEST FRIEND, A LEADER TYPE, GAVE INSTRUCTIONS...
...ALLOWING THEM TO USE THE WEAPONS EFFICIENTLY AND STRATEGICALLY TO DEFEND THEMSELVES AND FLEE.
THEY WERE ABLE TO SURVIVE THIS HUNTING GROUND WITHOUT ANYONE GETTING KILLED.
HIS BEST FRIEND AND A LEADER TYPE?
THAT MUST BE THE MAN!
IT WAS AN AMAZING GROUP.
THEY PULLED OFF THE IMPOS-SIBLE.
BUT AS SOON AS LEUVIS ZEROED IN ON THEM...

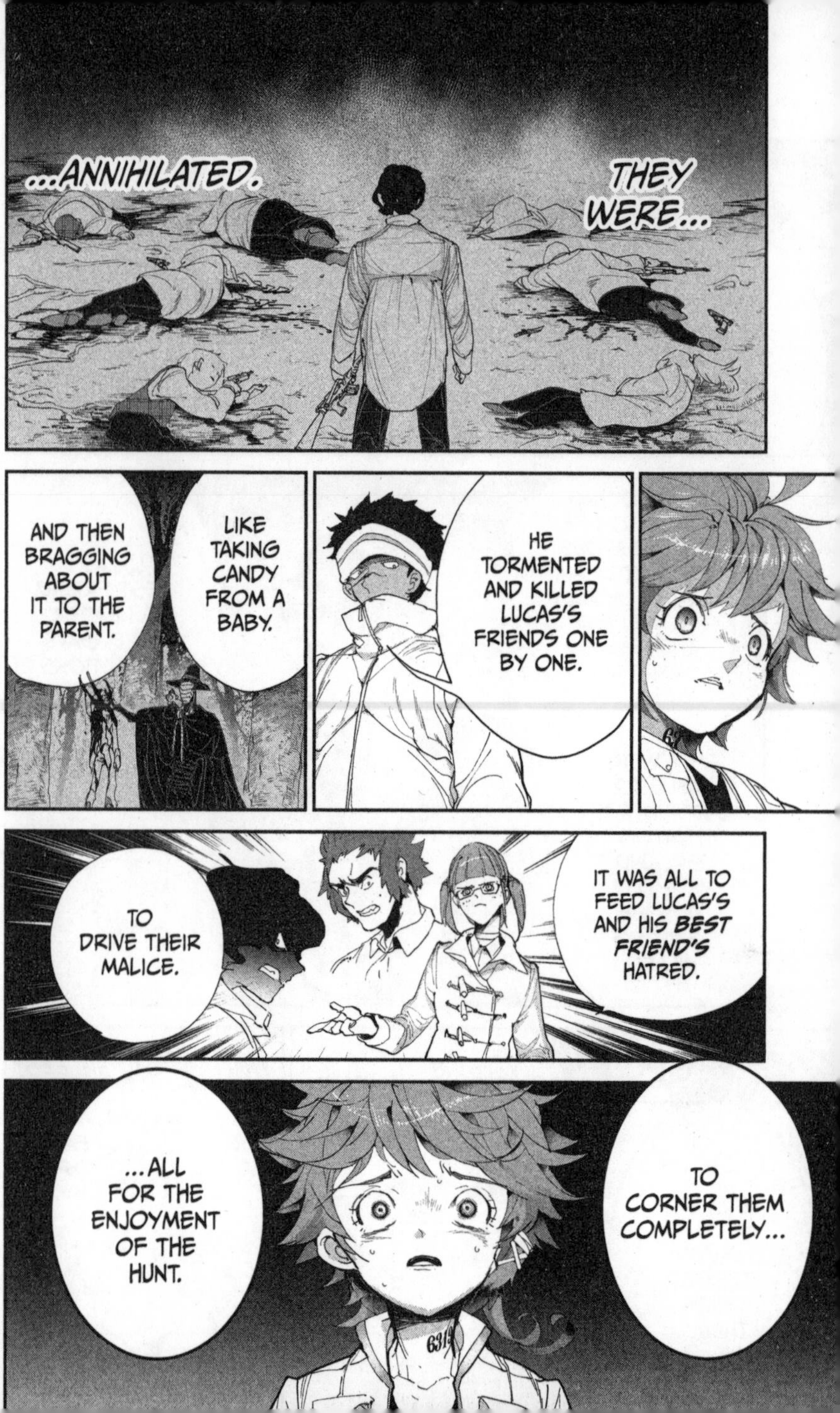
THEY WERE...
...ANNIHILATED.
HE TORMENTED AND KILLED LUCAS'S FRIENDS ONE BY ONE.
LIKE TAKING CANDY FROM A BABY.
AND THEN BRAGGING ABOUT IT TO THE PARENT.
IT WAS ALL TO FEED LUCAS'S AND HIS *BEST FRIEND'S* HATRED.
TO DRIVE THEIR MALICE.
TO CORNER THEM COMPLETELY...
...ALL FOR THE ENJOYMENT OF THE HUNT.

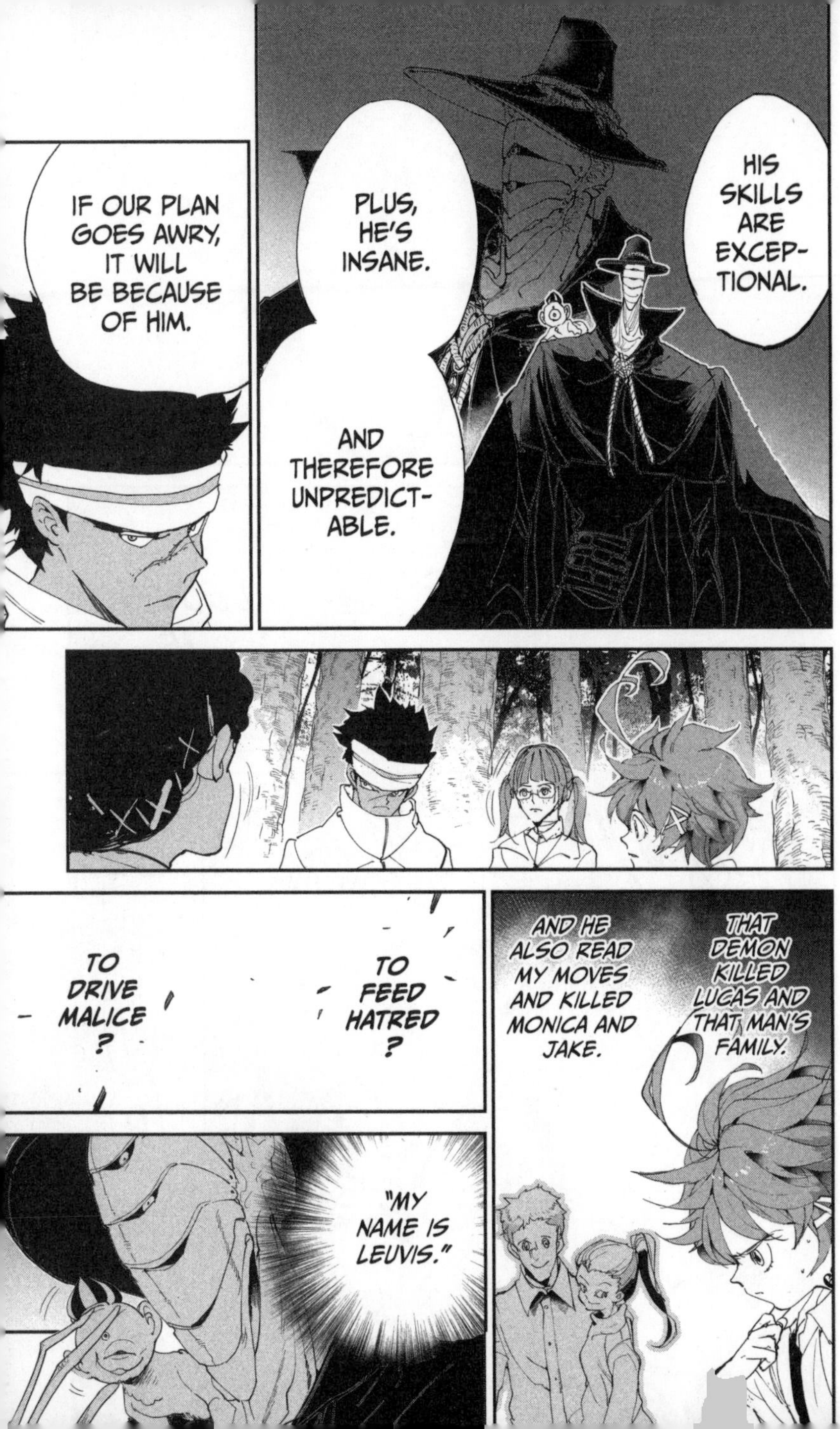
HIS SKILLS ARE EXCEP-TIONAL.
PLUS, HE'S INSANE.
AND THEREFORE UNPREDICT-ABLE.
IF OUR PLAN GOES AWRY, IT WILL BE BECAUSE OF HIM.
THAT DEMON KILLED LUCAS AND THAT MAN'S FAMILY.
AND HE ALSO READ MY MOVES AND KILLED MONICA AND JAKE.
TO FEED HATRED?
TO DRIVE MALICE?
"MY NAME IS LEUVIS."

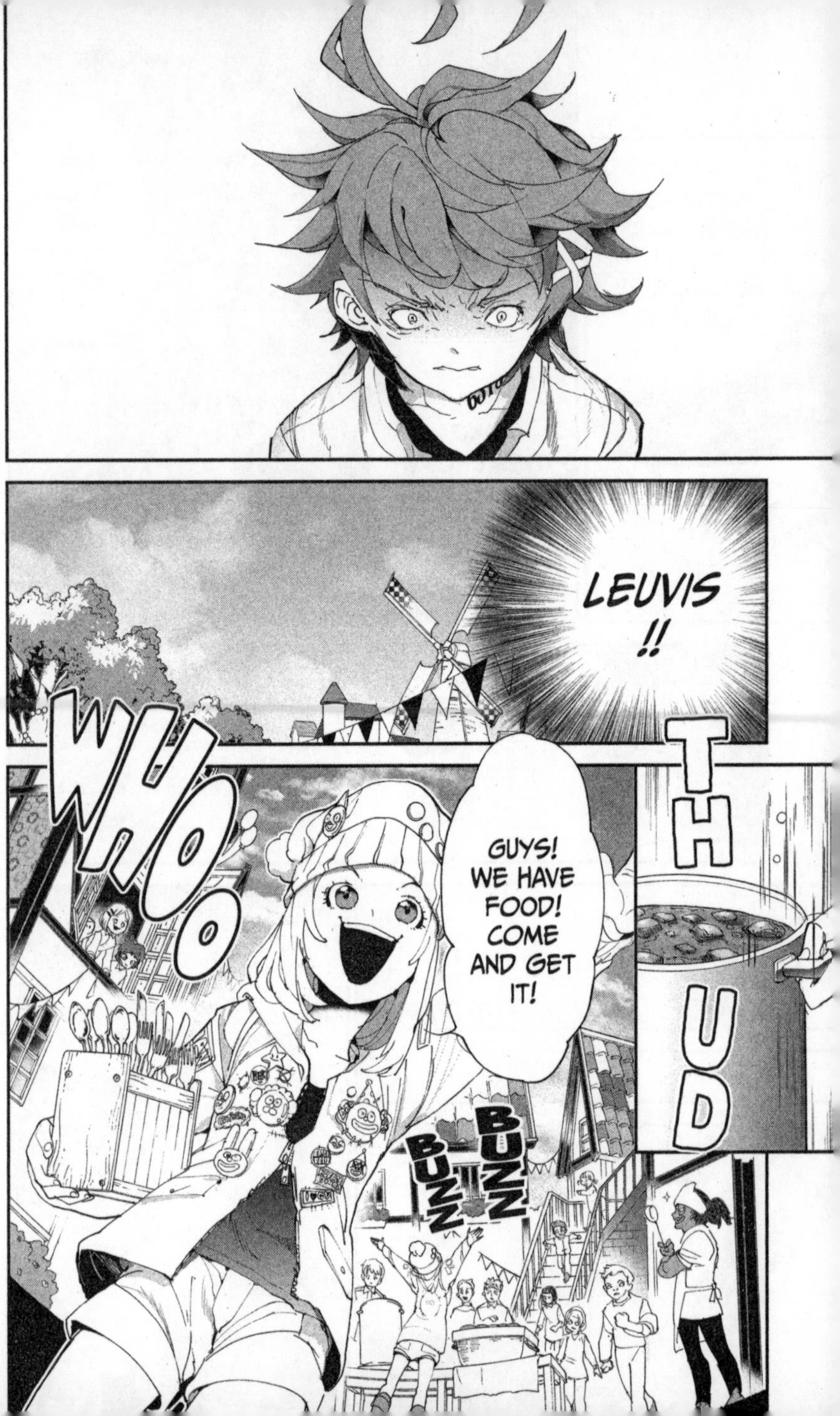
LEUVIS !!
THUD
WHOO
GUYS! WE HAVE FOOD! COME AND GET IT!
BUZZ BUZZ

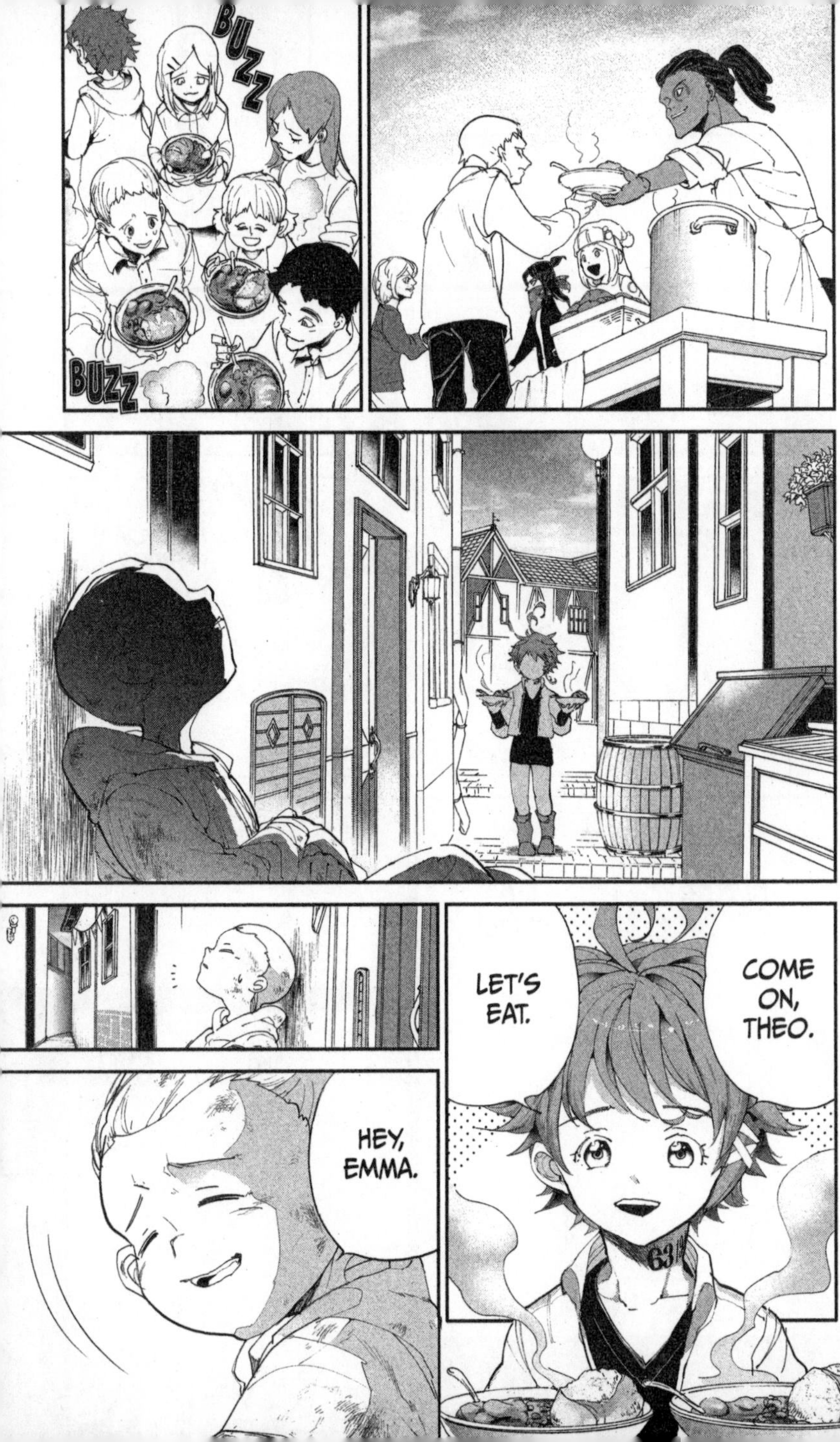
BUZZ
BUZZ
COME ON, THEO.
LET'S EAT.
HEY, EMMA.

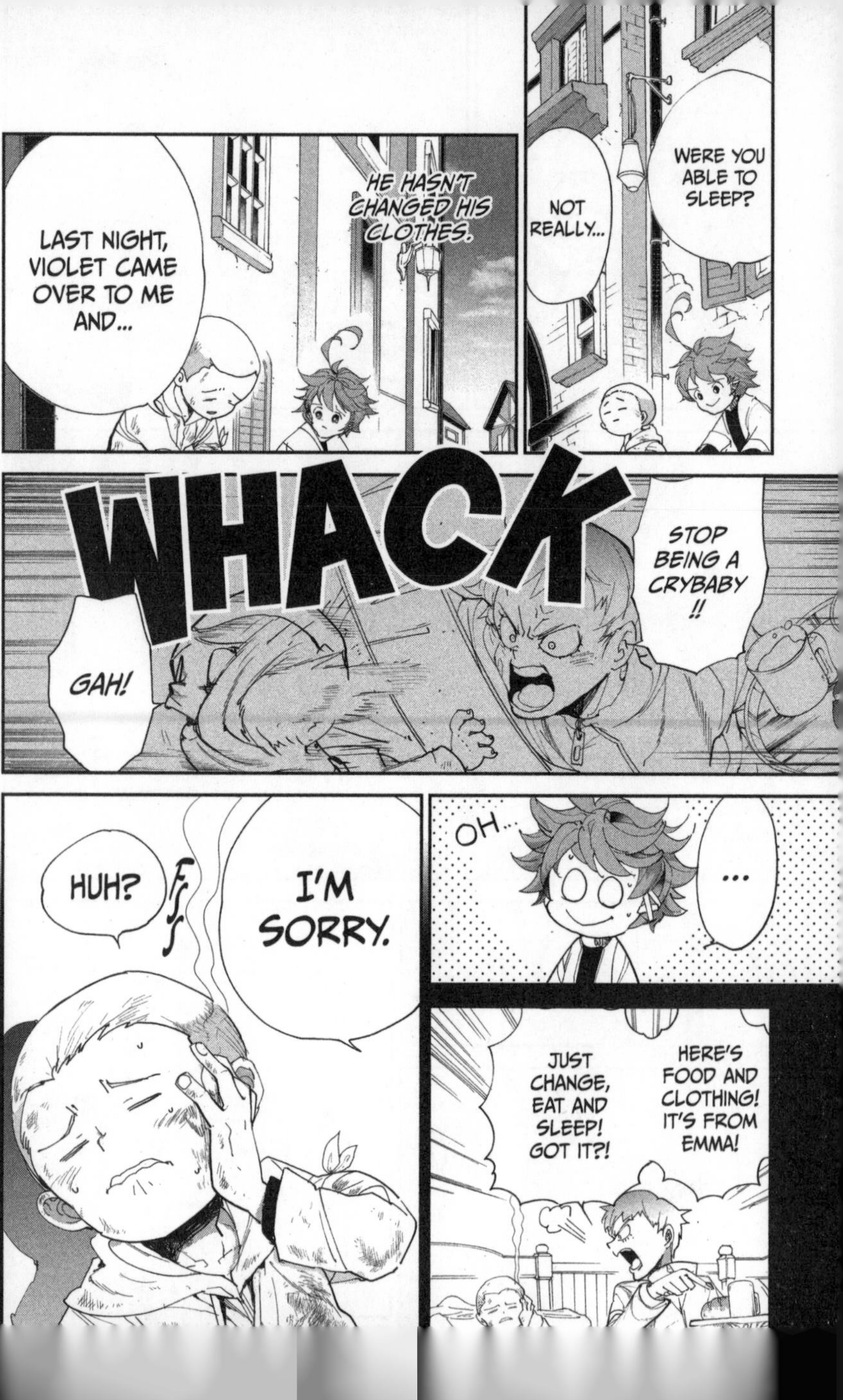
WERE YOU ABLE TO SLEEP?
NOT REALLY...
HE HASN'T CHANGED HIS CLOTHES.
LAST NIGHT, VIOLET CAME OVER TO ME AND...
STOP BEING A CRYBABY !!
WHACK
GAH!
...
OH...
HERE'S FOOD AND CLOTHING! IT'S FROM EMMA!
JUST CHANGE, EAT AND SLEEP! GOT IT?!
I'M SORRY.
FSS
HUH?

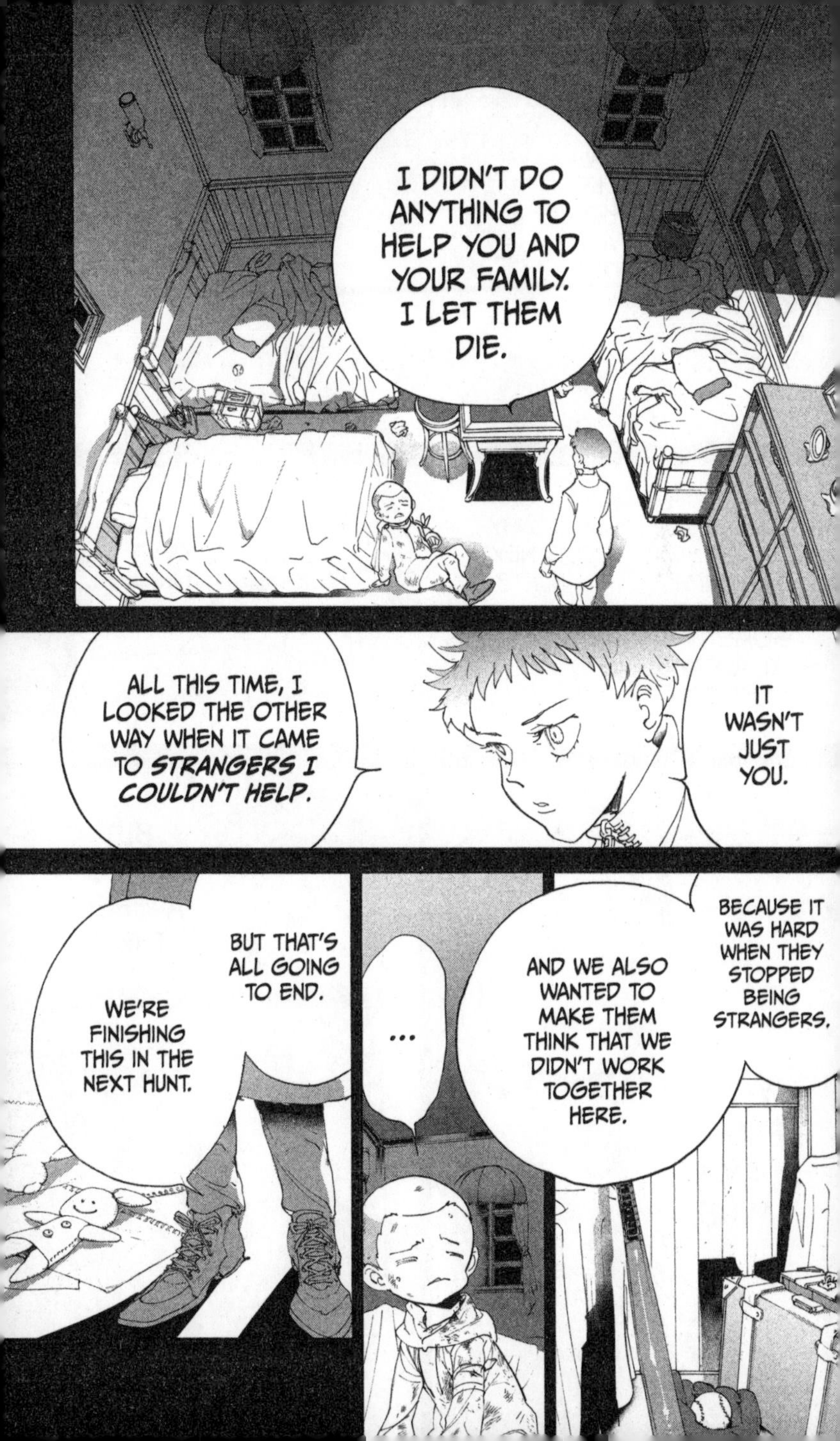
I DIDN'T DO ANYTHING TO HELP YOU AND YOUR FAMILY. I LET THEM DIE.
IT WASN'T JUST YOU.
ALL THIS TIME, I LOOKED THE OTHER WAY WHEN IT CAME TO *STRANGERS I COULDN'T HELP.*
BECAUSE IT WAS HARD WHEN THEY STOPPED BEING STRANGERS.
AND WE ALSO WANTED TO MAKE THEM THINK THAT WE DIDN'T WORK TOGETHER HERE.
...
BUT THAT'S ALL GOING TO END.
WE'RE FINISHING THIS IN THE NEXT HUNT.

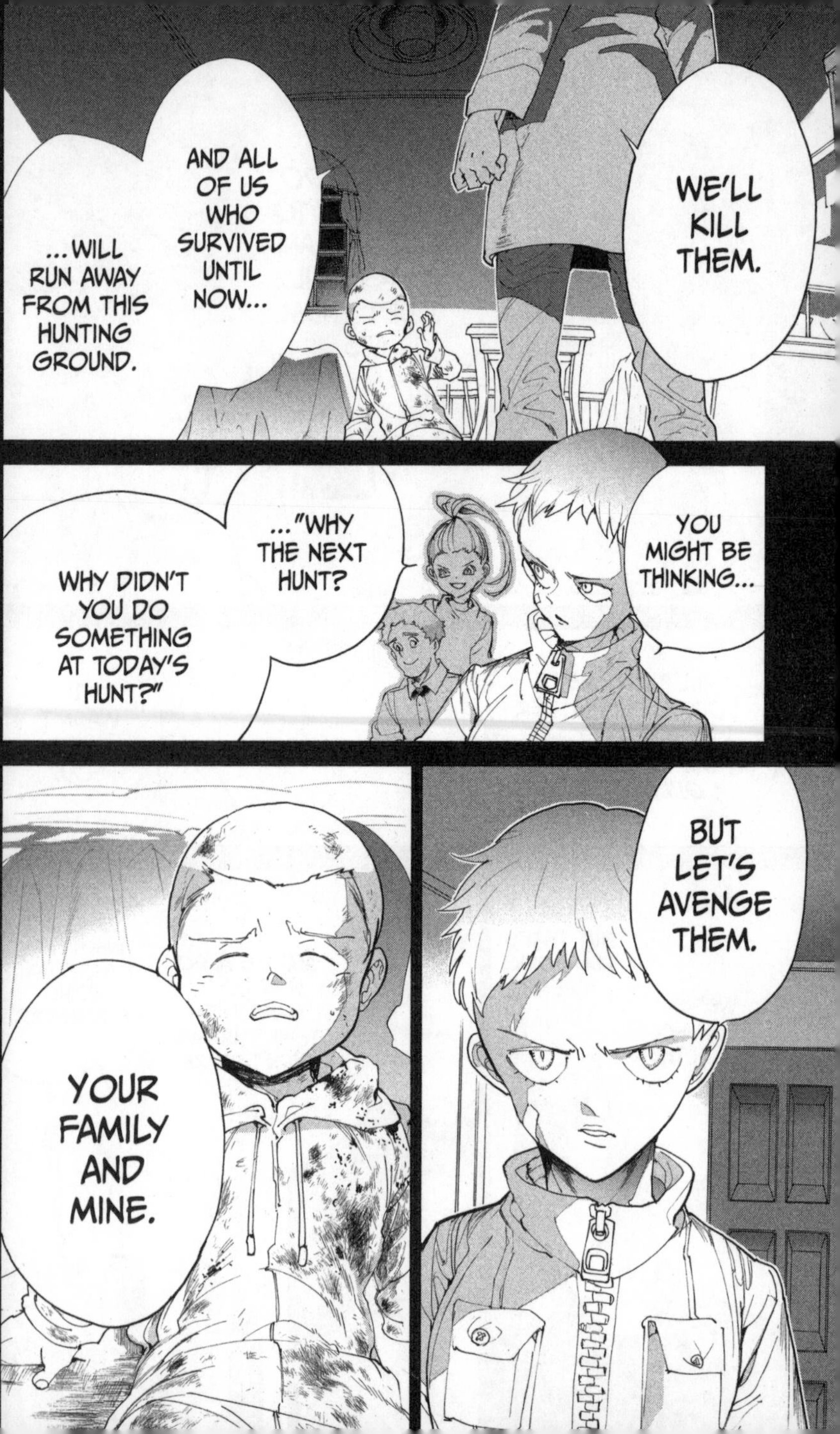
WE'LL KILL THEM.
AND ALL OF US WHO SURVIVED UNTIL NOW...
...WILL RUN AWAY FROM THIS HUNTING GROUND.
YOU MIGHT BE THINKING...
..."WHY THE NEXT HUNT?
WHY DIDN'T YOU DO SOMETHING AT TODAY'S HUNT?"
BUT LET'S AVENGE THEM.
YOUR FAMILY AND MINE.

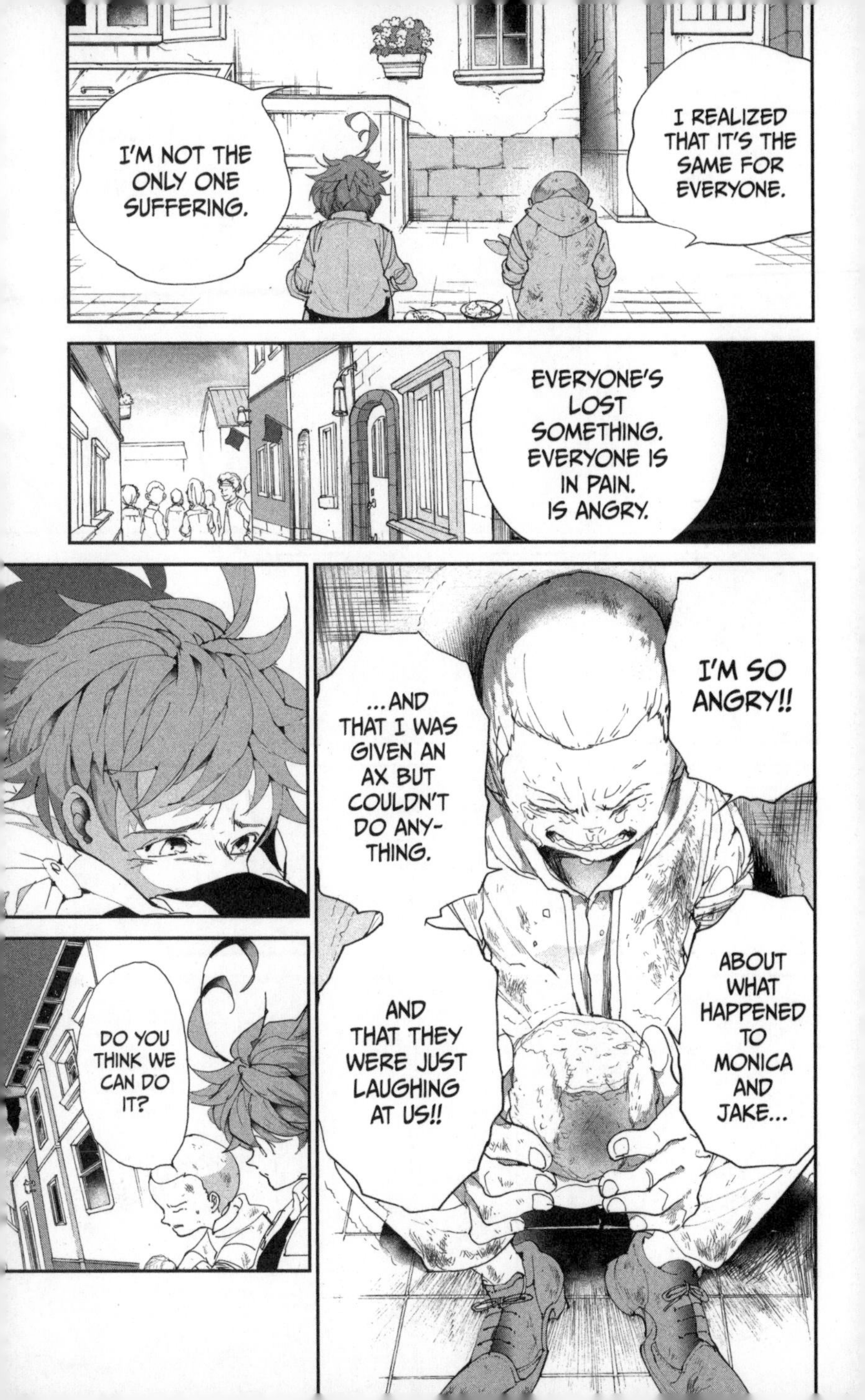
I REALIZED THAT IT'S THE SAME FOR EVERYONE.
I'M NOT THE ONLY ONE SUFFERING.
EVERYONE'S LOST SOMETHING. EVERYONE IS IN PAIN. IS ANGRY.
I'M SO ANGRY!!
ABOUT WHAT HAPPENED TO MONICA AND JAKE...
...AND THAT I WAS GIVEN AN AX BUT COULDN'T DO ANY-THING.
AND THAT THEY WERE JUST LAUGHING AT US!!
DO YOU THINK WE CAN DO IT?

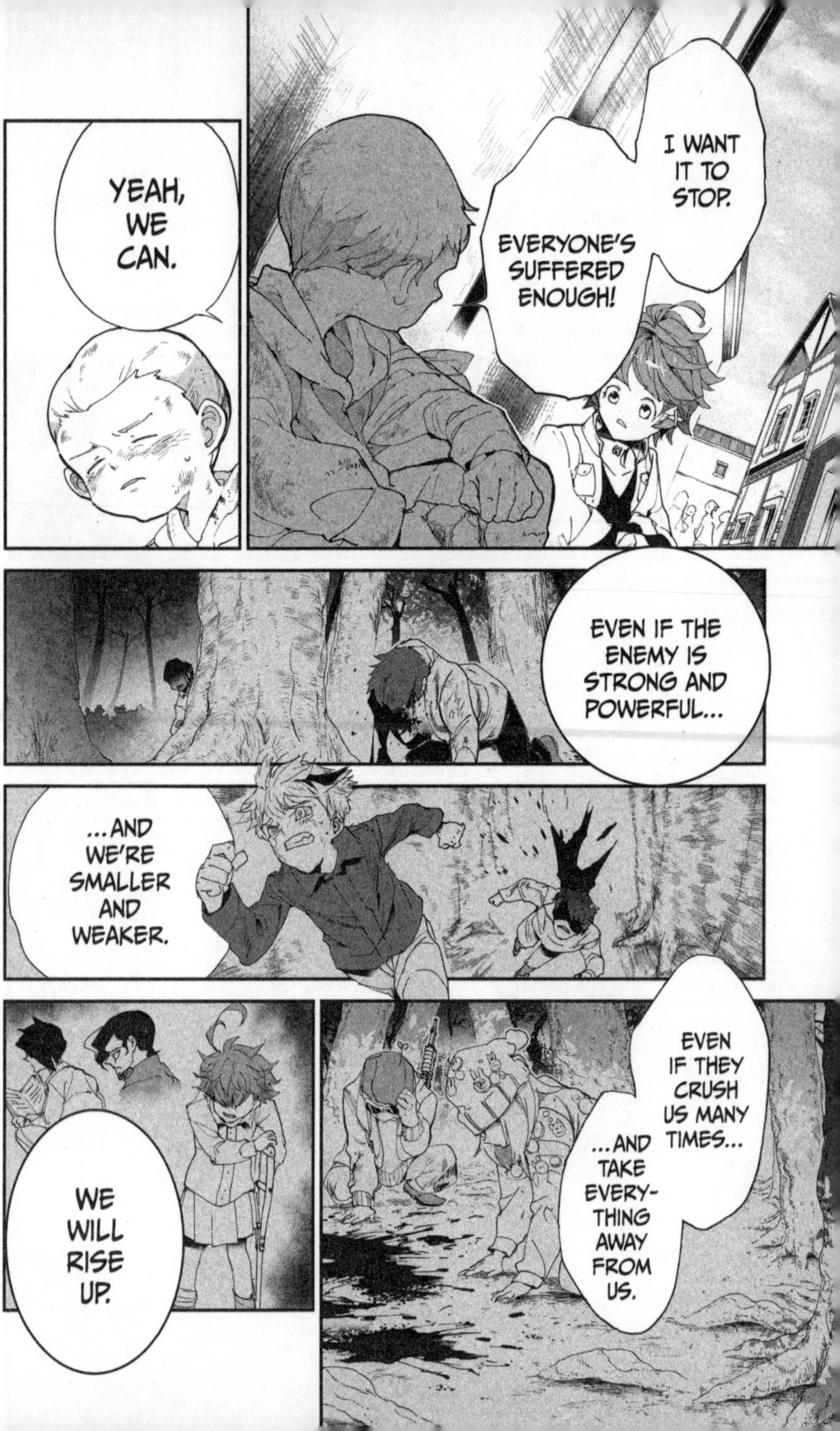
I WANT IT TO STOP.
EVERYONE'S SUFFERED ENOUGH!
YEAH, WE CAN.
EVEN IF THE ENEMY IS STRONG AND POWERFUL...
...AND WE'RE SMALLER AND WEAKER.
EVEN IF THEY CRUSH US MANY TIMES...
...AND TAKE EVERY-THING AWAY FROM US.
WE WILL RISE UP.

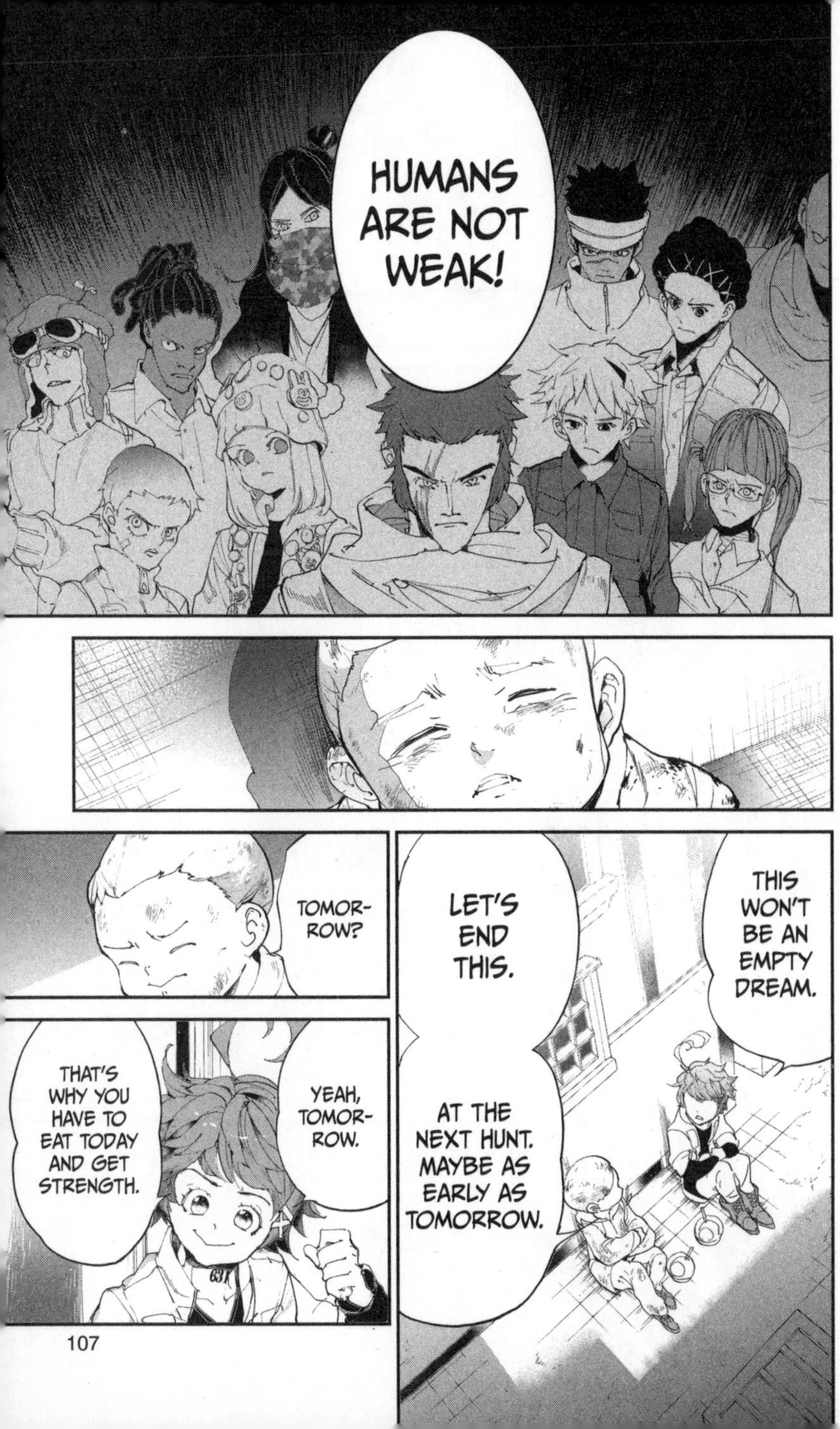
HUMANS ARE NOT WEAK!
THIS WON'T BE AN EMPTY DREAM.
LET'S END THIS.
AT THE NEXT HUNT. MAYBE AS EARLY AS TOMORROW.
TOMOR-ROW?
YEAH, TOMOR-ROW.
THAT'S WHY YOU HAVE TO EAT TODAY AND GET STRENGTH.

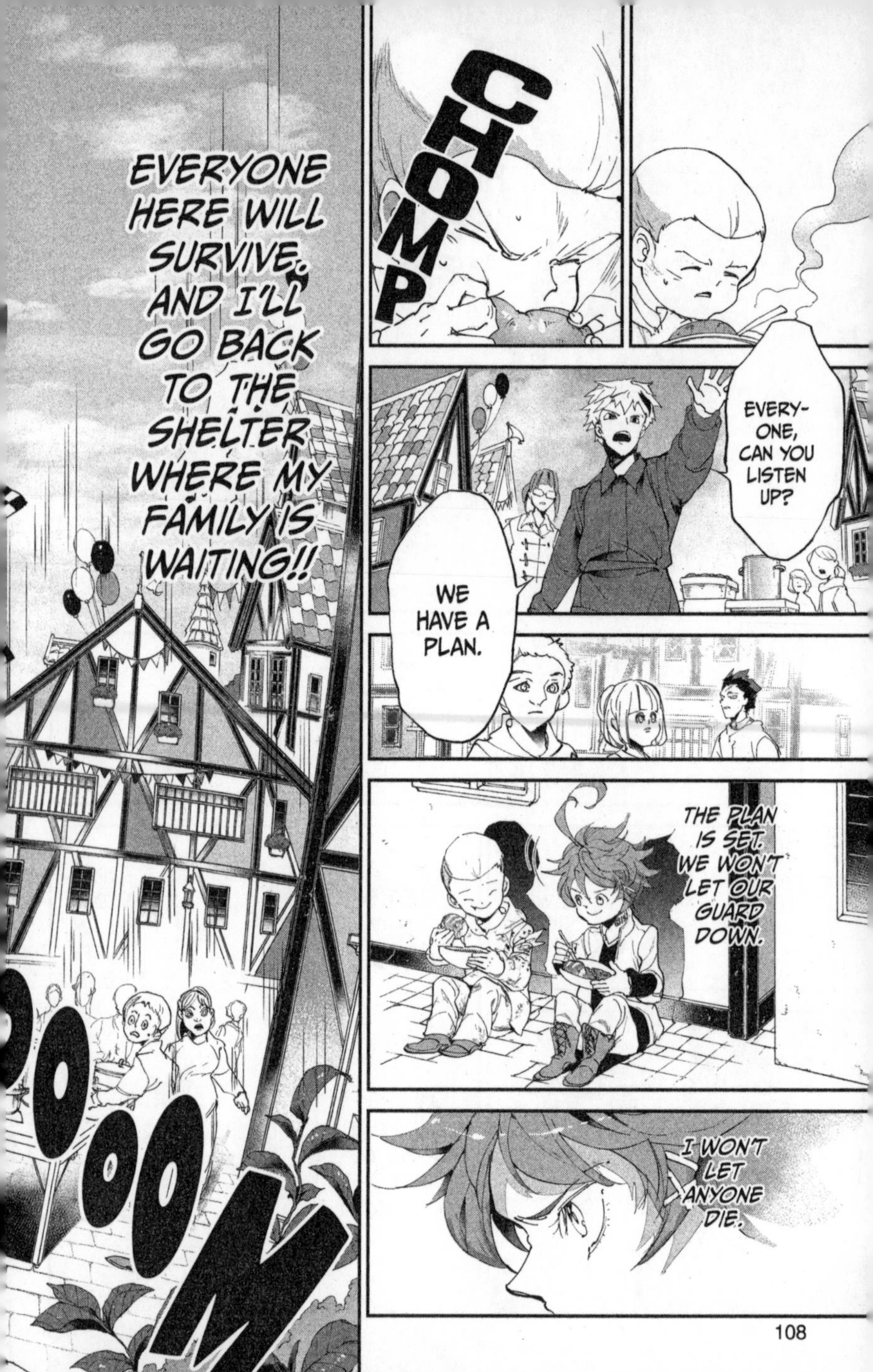
CHOMP
EVERYONE, CAN YOU LISTEN UP?
WE HAVE A PLAN.
THE PLAN IS SET. WE WON'T LET OUR GUARD DOWN.
I WON'T LET ANYONE DIE.
EVERYONE HERE WILL SURVIVE. AND I'LL GO BACK TO THE SHELTER WHERE MY FAMILY IS WAITING!!
OOOOM

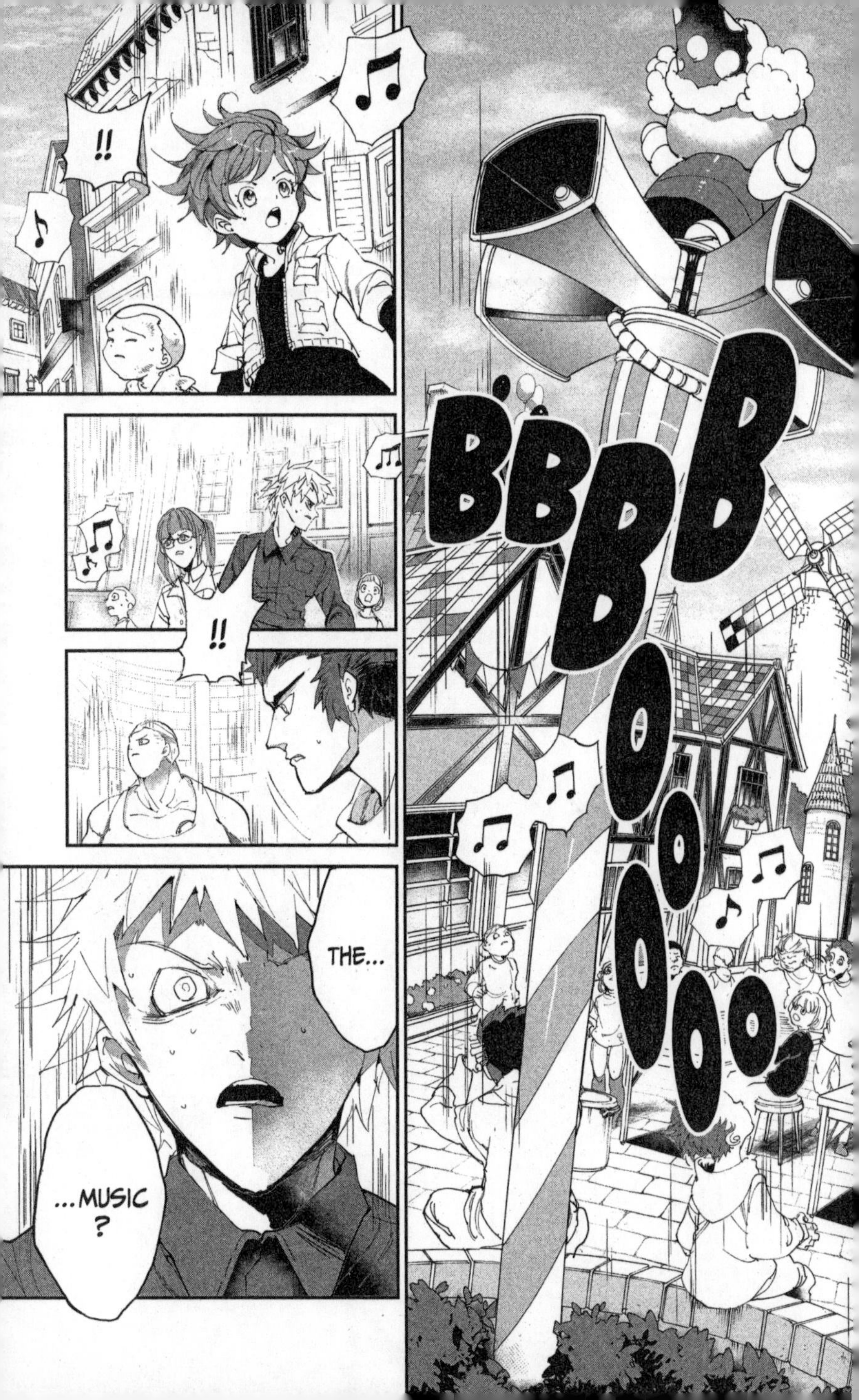
!!
!!
THE...
...MUSIC ?

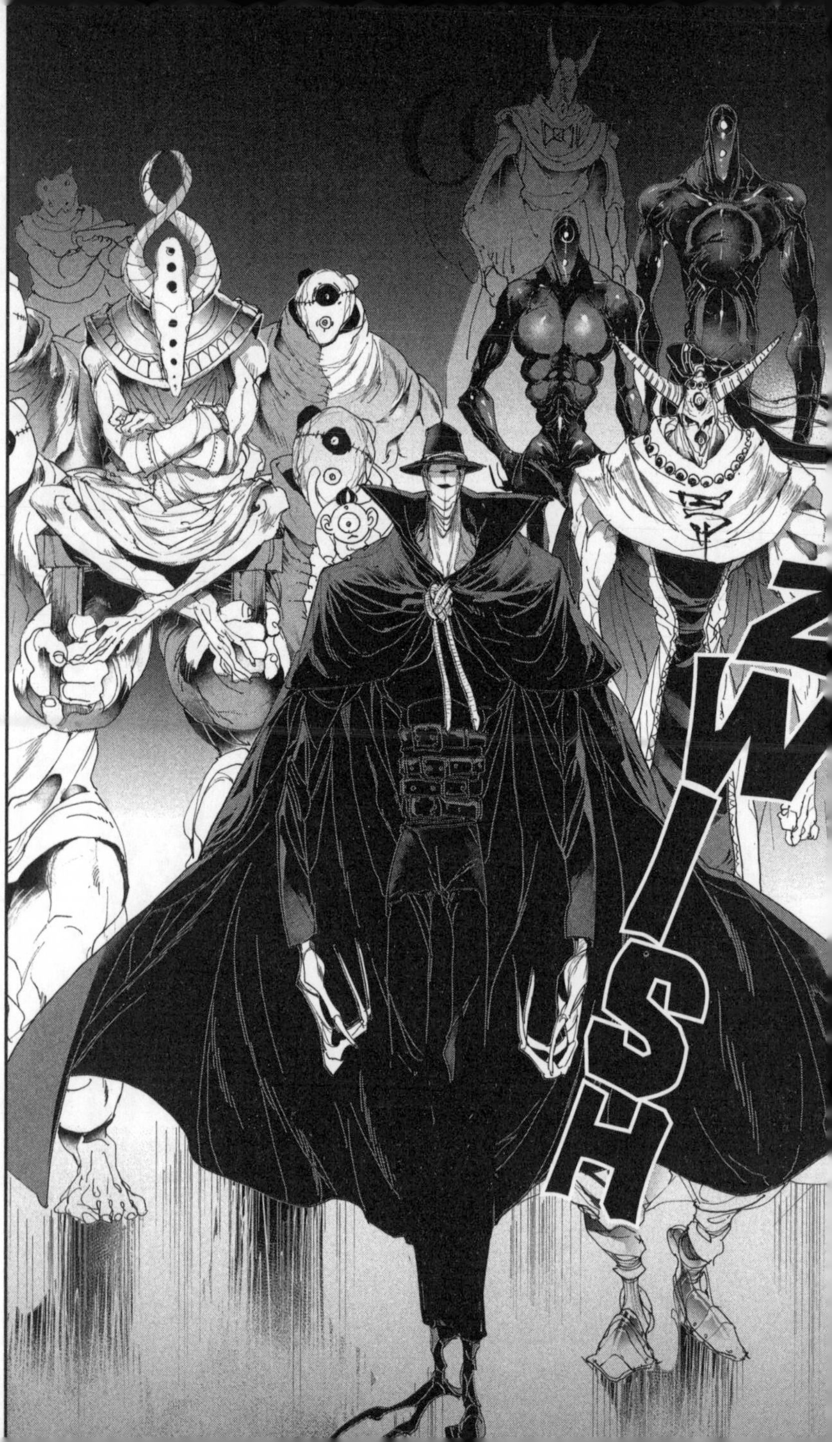
SWISH

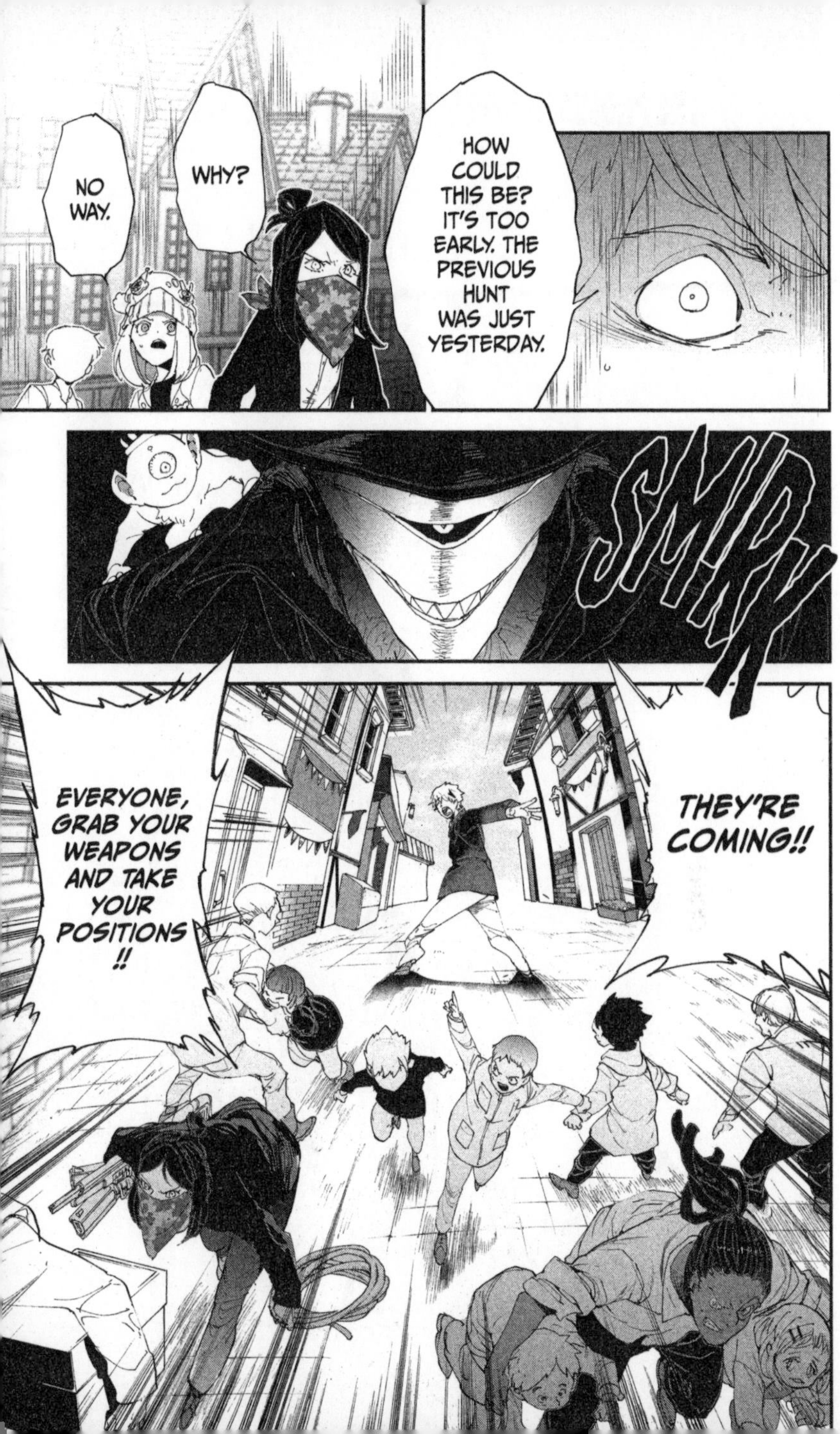
HOW COULD THIS BE? IT'S TOO EARLY. THE PREVIOUS HUNT WAS JUST YESTERDAY.
WHY?
NO WAY.
SMIRK
THEY'RE COMING!!
EVERYONE, GRAB YOUR WEAPONS AND TAKE YOUR POSITIONS!!

THE PROMISED NEVERLAND SIDE SCENE 016

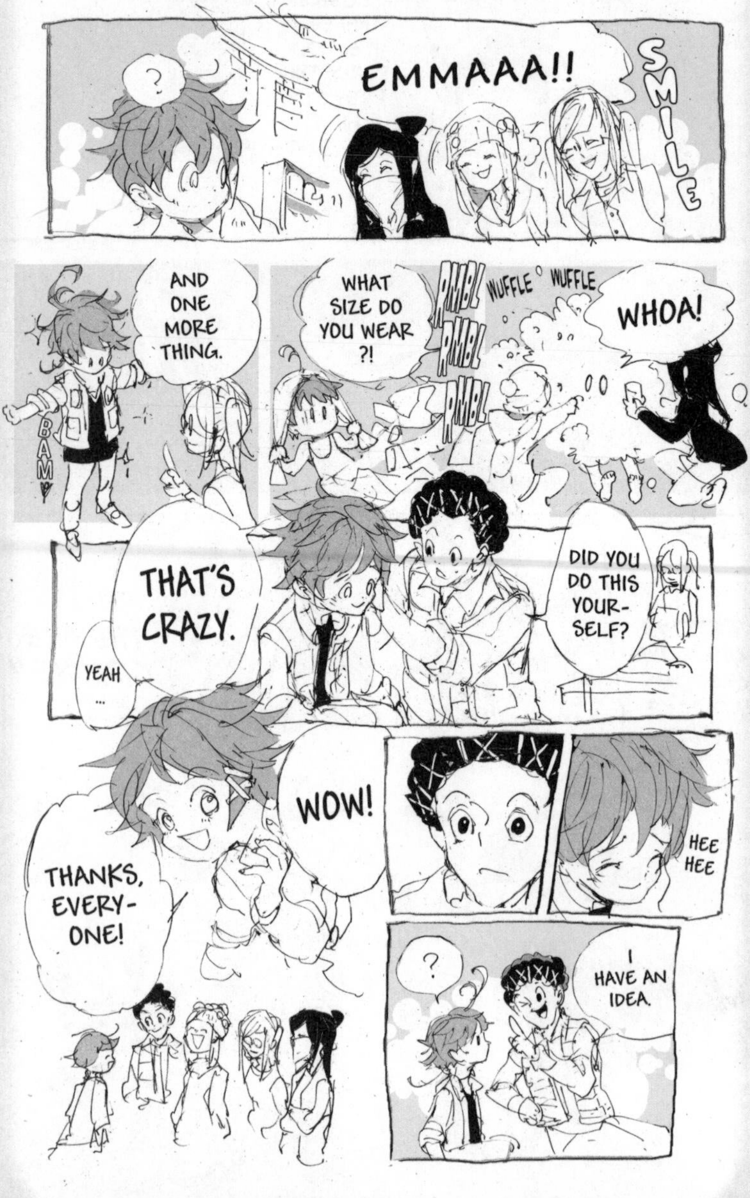
SMILE
EMMAAA!!
?
WHOA!
WUFFLE WUFFLE
RMBL RMBL RMBL
WHAT SIZE DO YOU WEAR?!
AND ONE MORE THING.
BAM
DID YOU DO THIS YOURSELF?
THAT'S CRAZY.
YEAH...
HEE HEE
WOW!
THANKS, EVERYONE!
I HAVE AN IDEA.
?

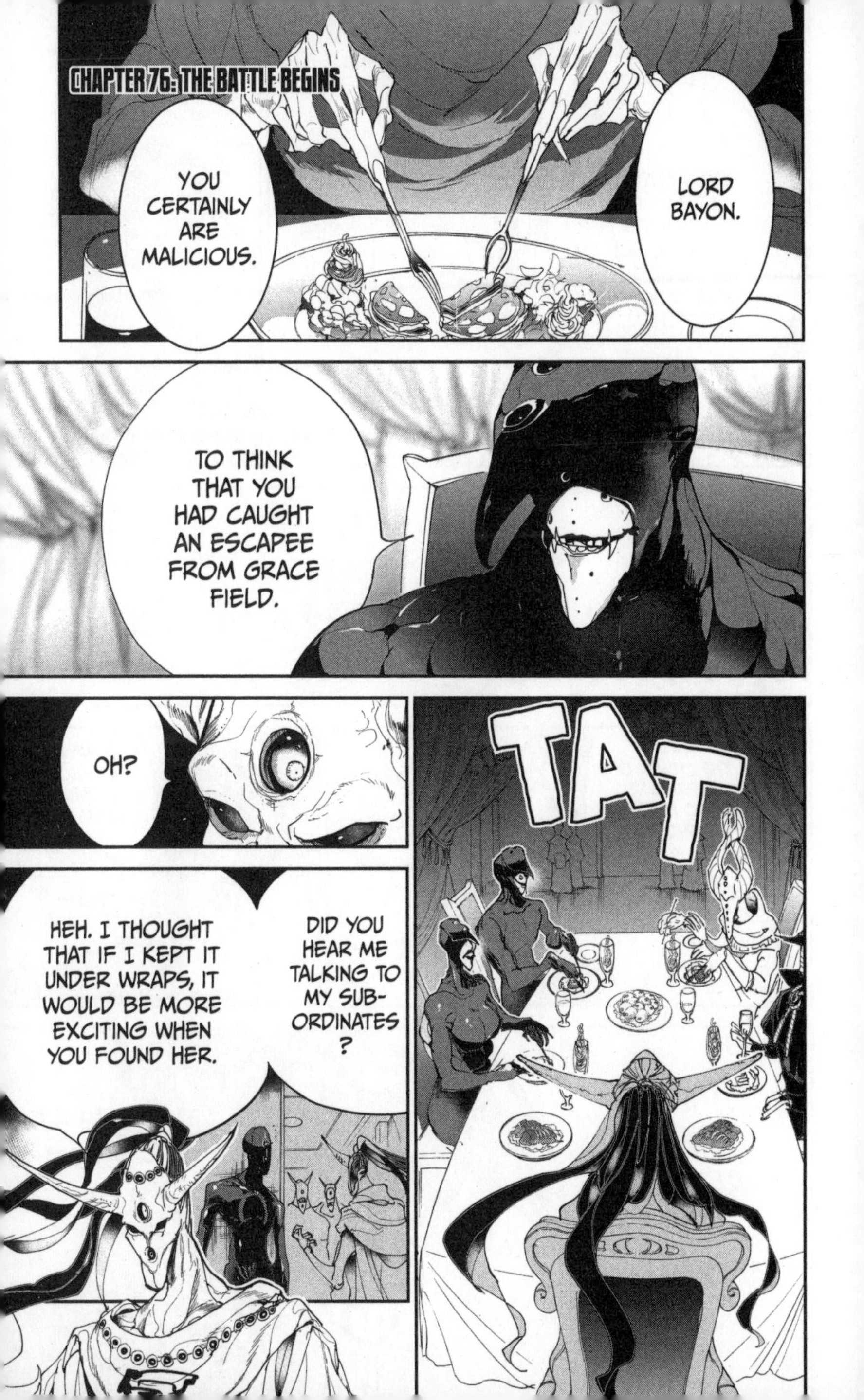
CHAPTER 76: THE BATTLE BEGINS
LORD BAYON.
YOU CERTAINLY ARE MALICIOUS.
TO THINK THAT YOU HAD CAUGHT AN ESCAPEE FROM GRACE FIELD.
TAT
OH?
DID YOU HEAR ME TALKING TO MY SUB-ORDINATES?
HEH. I THOUGHT THAT IF I KEPT IT UNDER WRAPS, IT WOULD BE MORE EXCITING WHEN YOU FOUND HER.

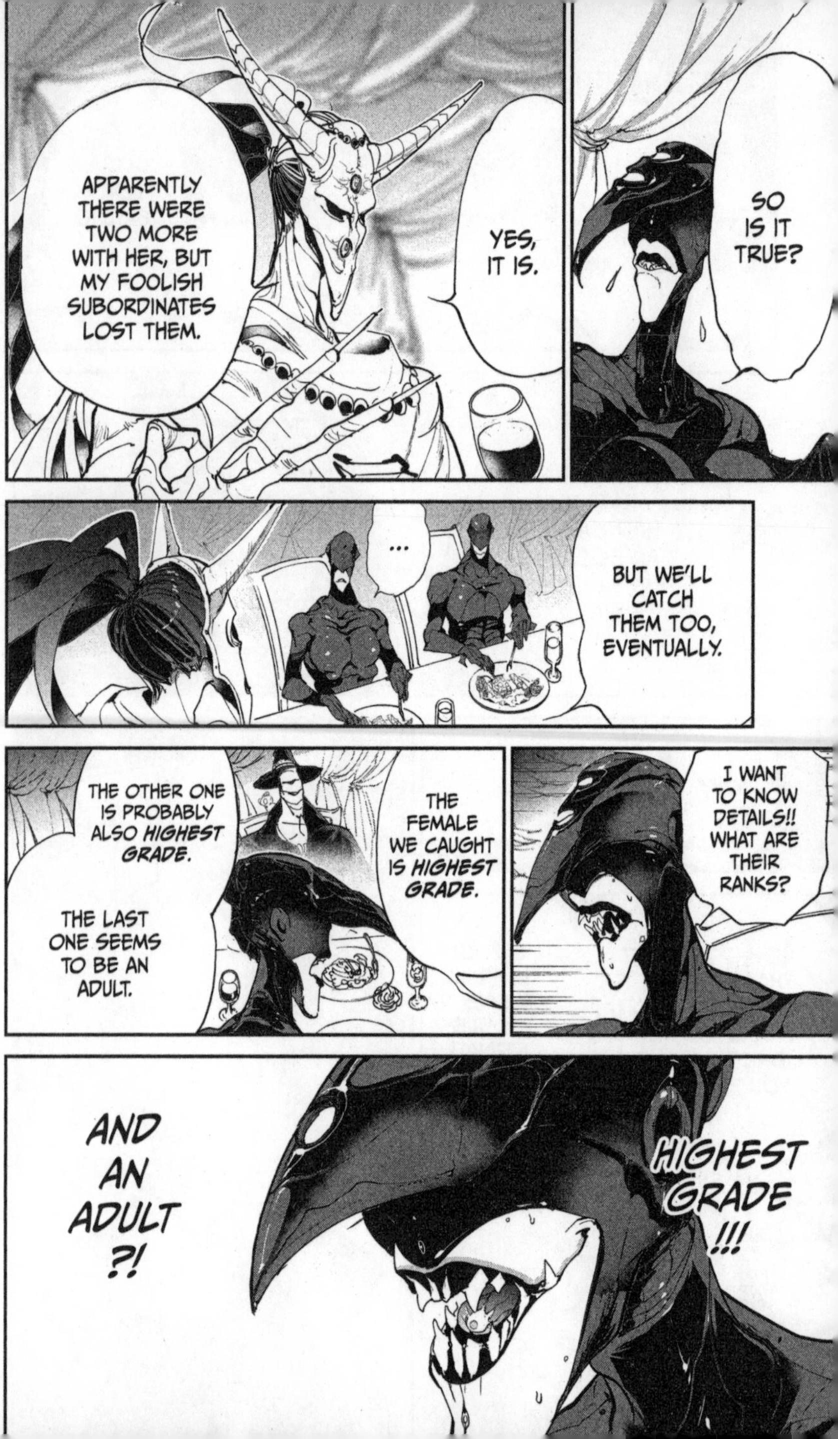
SO IS IT TRUE?
YES, IT IS.
APPARENTLY THERE WERE TWO MORE WITH HER, BUT MY FOOLISH SUBORDINATES LOST THEM.
BUT WE'LL CATCH THEM TOO, EVENTUALLY.
...
I WANT TO KNOW DETAILS!! WHAT ARE THEIR RANKS?
THE FEMALE WE CAUGHT IS *HIGHEST GRADE*.
THE OTHER ONE IS PROBABLY ALSO *HIGHEST GRADE*.
THE LAST ONE SEEMS TO BE AN ADULT.
HIGHEST GRADE!!!
AND AN ADULT?!

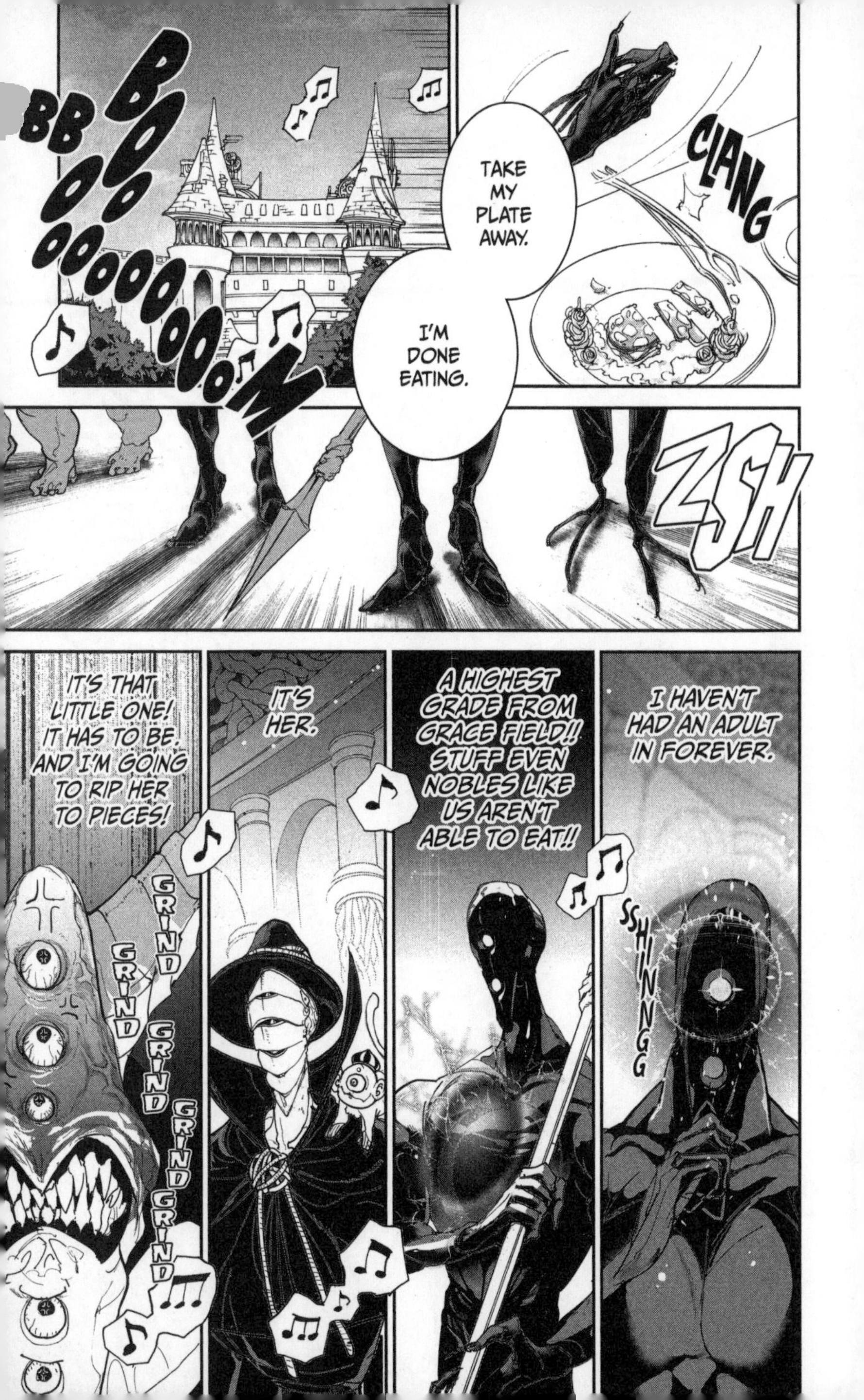
CLANG
TAKE MY PLATE AWAY.
I'M DONE EATING.
BBOOOOOOOOOOOOOOM
ZSH
I HAVEN'T HAD AN ADULT IN FOREVER.
SSHINNNGG
A HIGHEST GRADE FROM GRACE FIELD!! STUFF EVEN NOBLES LIKE US AREN'T ABLE TO EAT!!
IT'S HER.
IT'S THAT LITTLE ONE! IT HAS TO BE. AND I'M GOING TO RIP HER TO PIECES!
GRIND GRIND GRIND GRIND GRIND GRIND

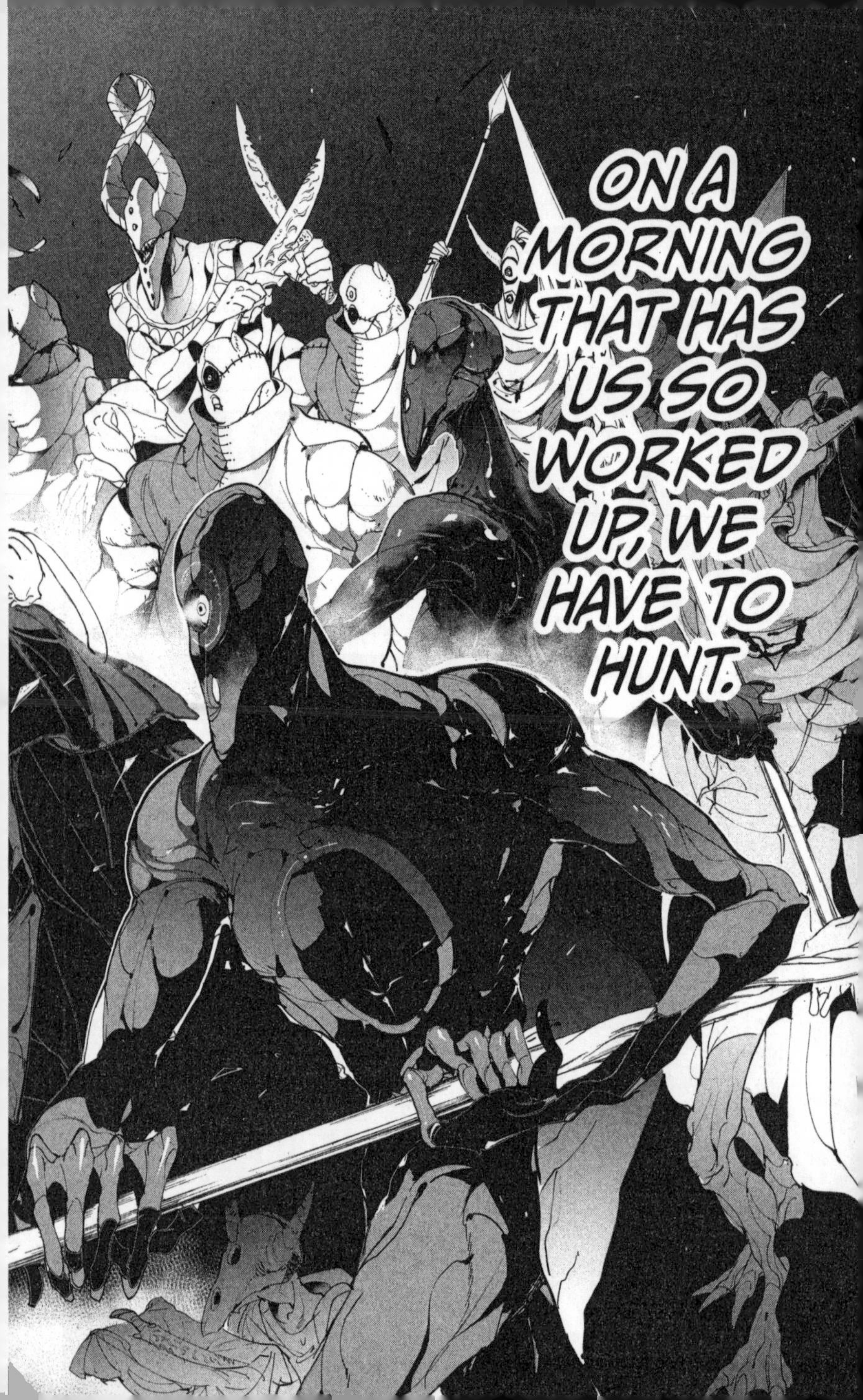
ON A MORNING THAT HAS US SO WORKED UP, WE HAVE TO HUNT.

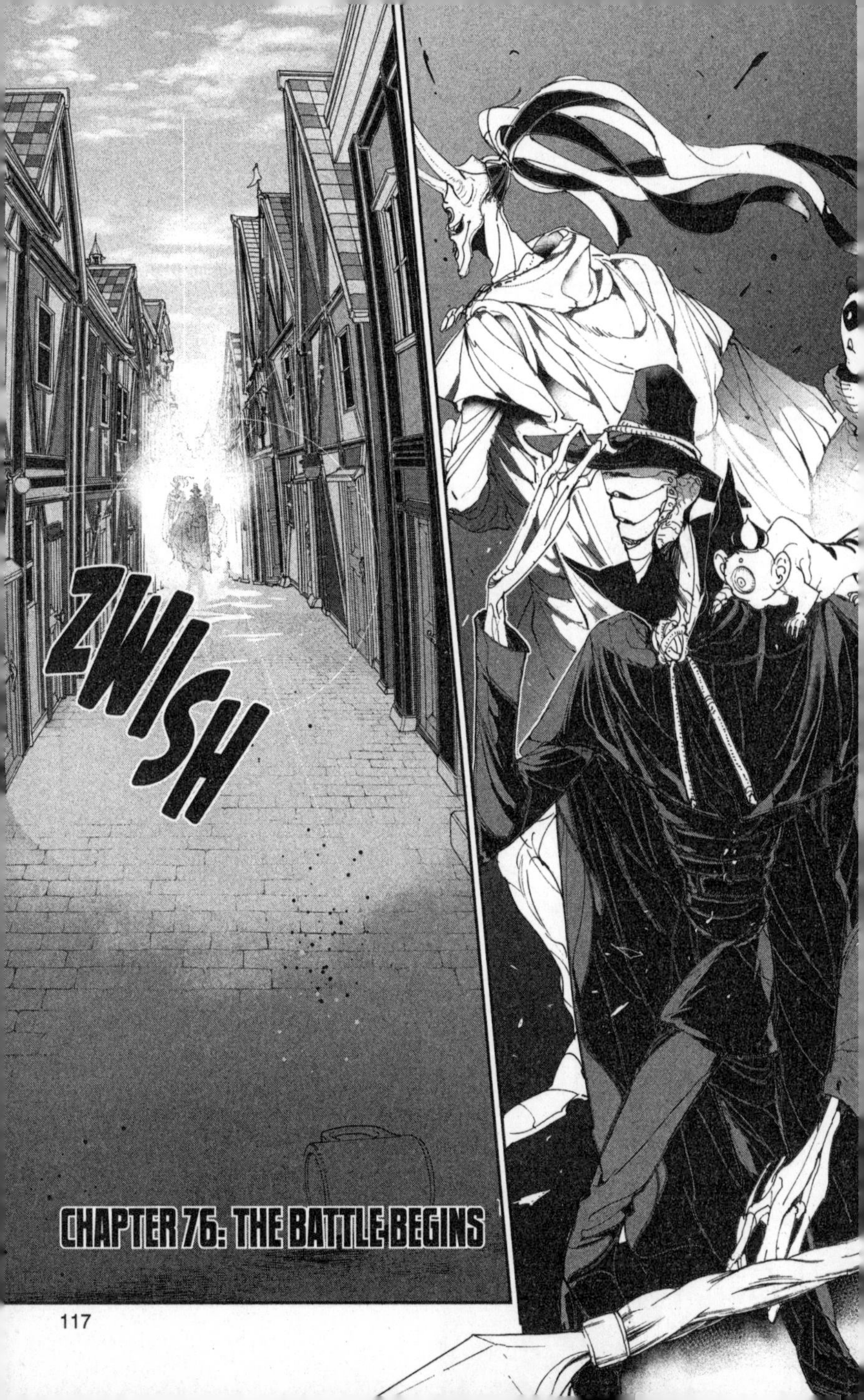
ZWISH
CHAPTER 76: THE BATTLE BEGINS

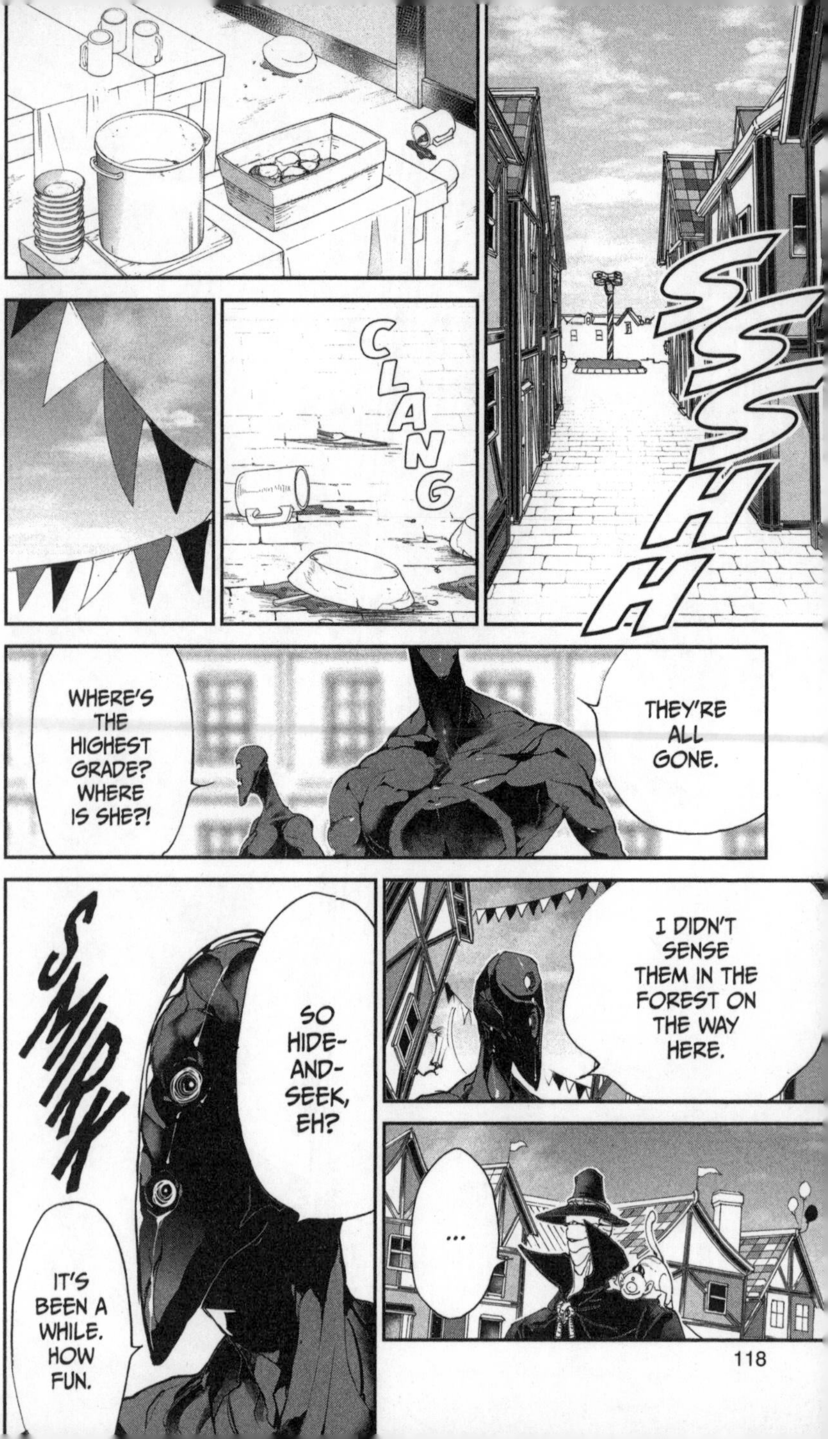
SSSHHH
CLANG
THEY'RE ALL GONE.
WHERE'S THE HIGHEST GRADE? WHERE IS SHE?!
I DIDN'T SENSE THEM IN THE FOREST ON THE WAY HERE.
...
SMIRK
SO HIDE-AND-SEEK, EH?
IT'S BEEN A WHILE. HOW FUN.

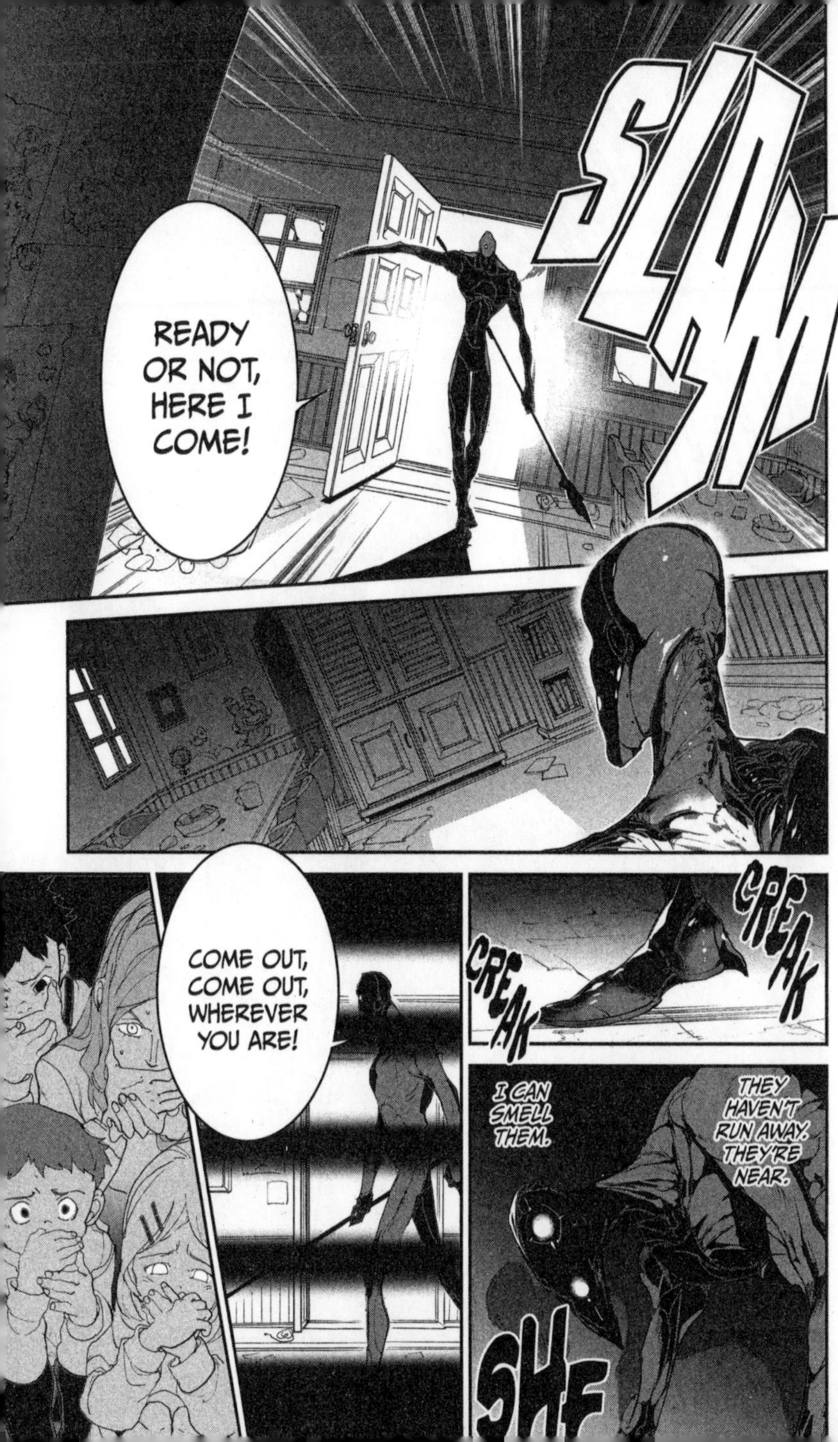
SLAM
READY OR NOT, HERE I COME!
CREAK
CREAK
THEY HAVEN'T RUN AWAY. THEY'RE NEAR.
I CAN SMELL THEM.
SHF
COME OUT, COME OUT, WHEREVER YOU ARE!

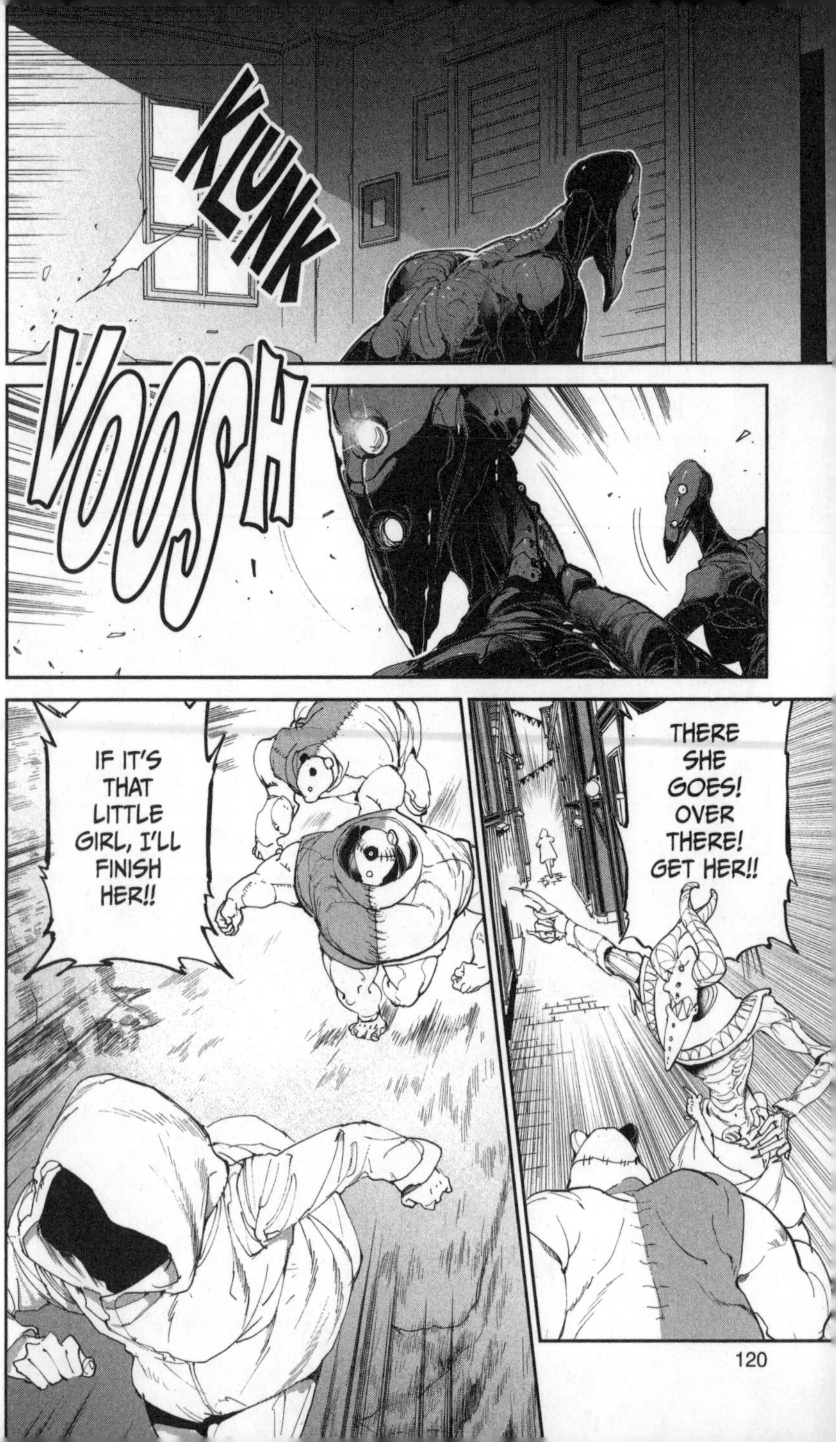
KLUNK
VOOSH
THERE SHE GOES! OVER THERE! GET HER!!
IF IT'S THAT LITTLE GIRL, I'LL FINISH HER!!

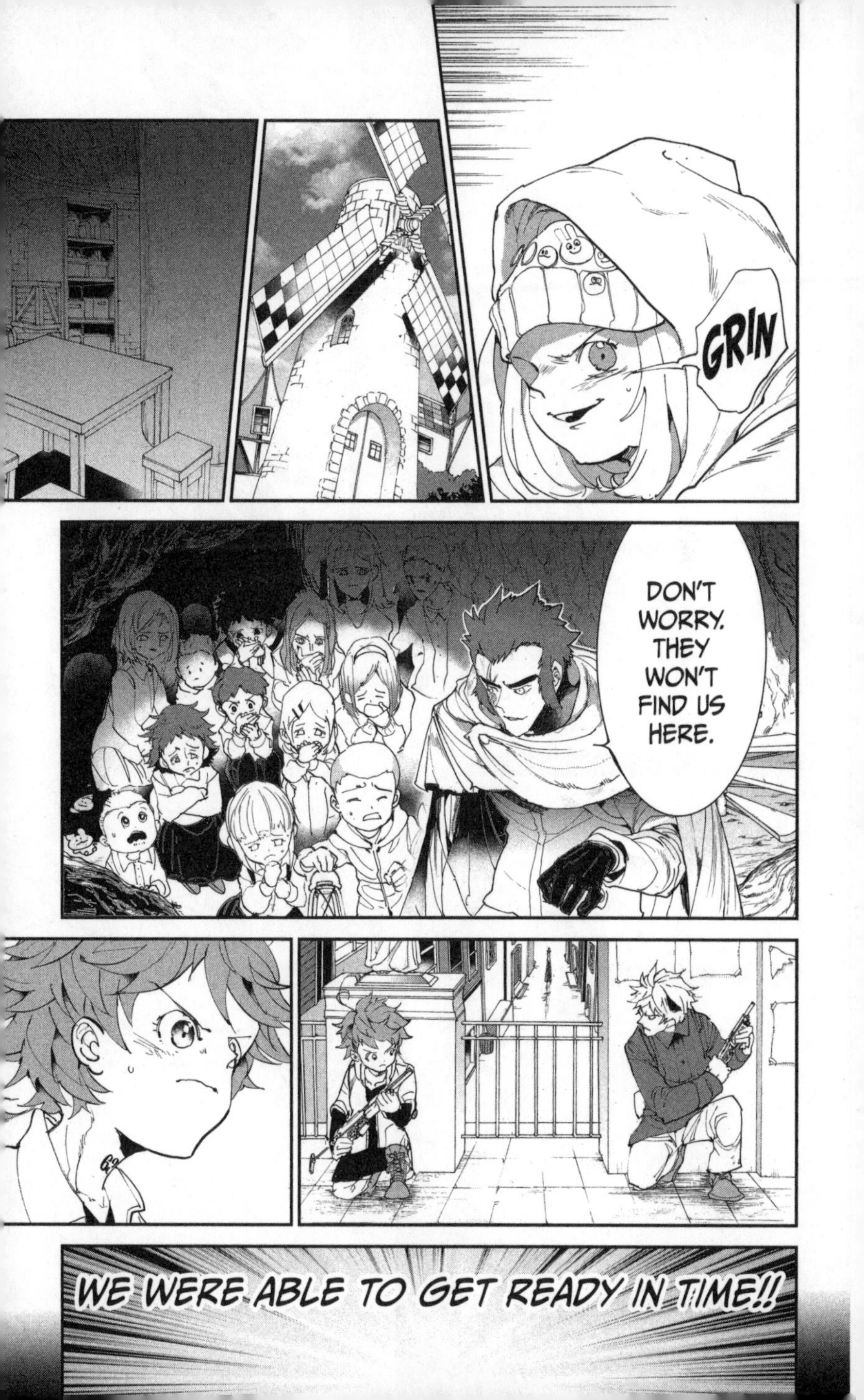
GRIN
DON'T WORRY. THEY WON'T FIND US HERE.
WE WERE ABLE TO GET READY IN TIME!!

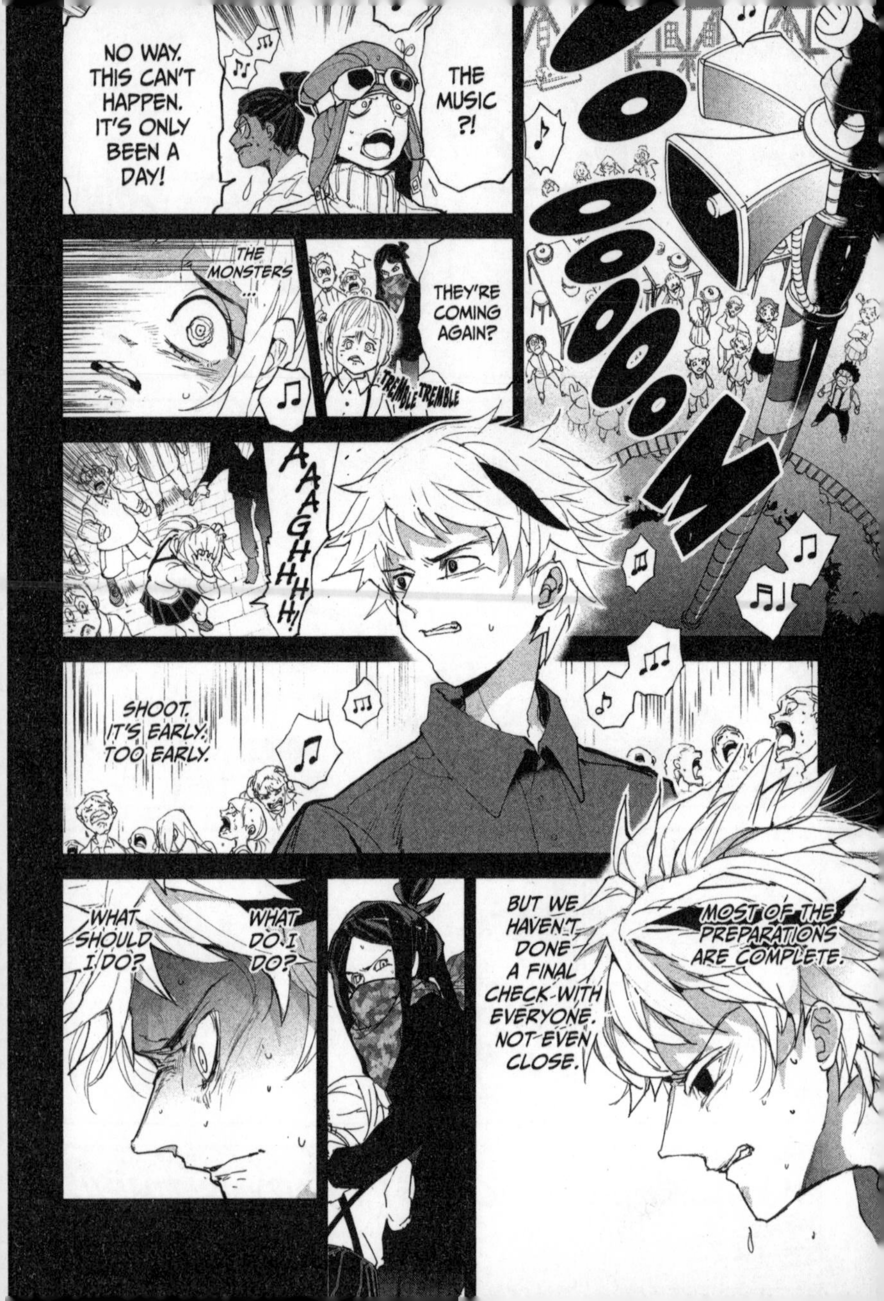
VOOOOOOM
THE MUSIC ?!
NO WAY. THIS CAN'T HAPPEN. IT'S ONLY BEEN A DAY!
THEY'RE COMING AGAIN?
TREMBLE TREMBLE
THE MONSTERS...
AAAGHHHH!
SHOOT. IT'S EARLY. TOO EARLY.
MOST OF THE PREPARATIONS ARE COMPLETE.
BUT WE HAVEN'T DONE A FINAL CHECK WITH EVERYONE. NOT EVEN CLOSE.
WHAT DO I DO?
WHAT SHOULD I DO?

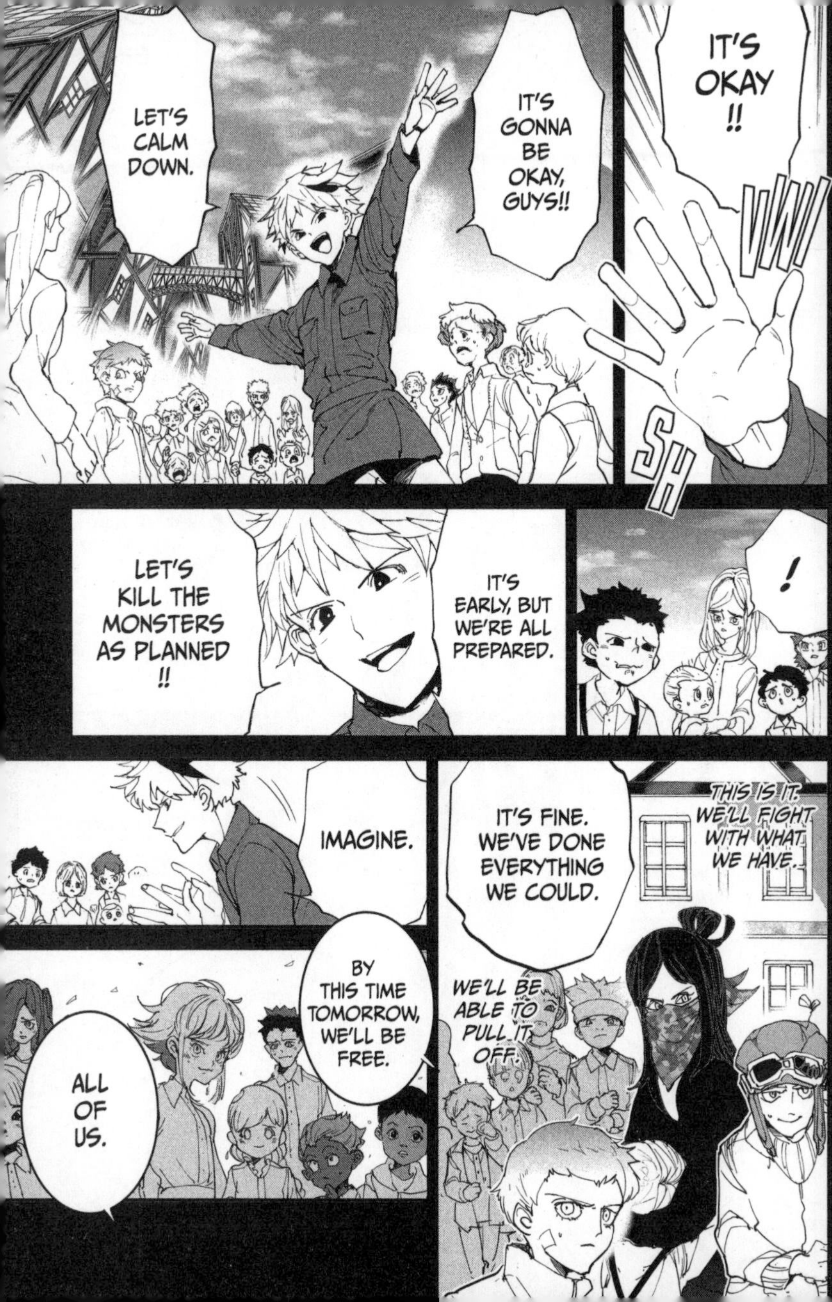
IT'S OKAY!!
VWI
SH
IT'S GONNA BE OKAY, GUYS!!
LET'S CALM DOWN.
!
IT'S EARLY, BUT WE'RE ALL PREPARED.
LET'S KILL THE MONSTERS AS PLANNED!!
IT'S FINE. WE'VE DONE EVERYTHING WE COULD.
THIS IS IT. WE'LL FIGHT WITH WHAT WE HAVE.
WE'LL BE ABLE TO PULL IT OFF.
IMAGINE.
BY THIS TIME TOMORROW, WE'LL BE FREE.
ALL OF US.

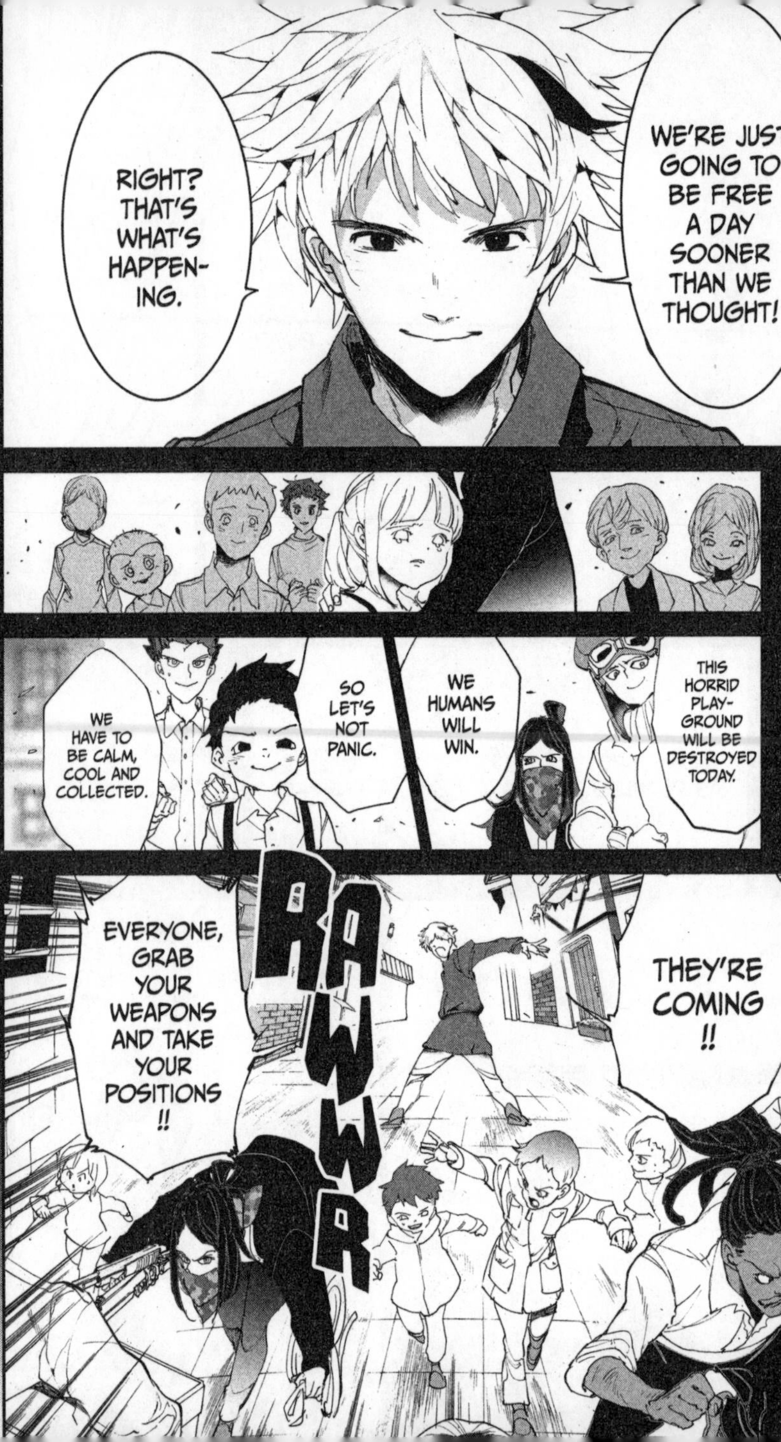
WE'RE JUST GOING TO BE FREE A DAY SOONER THAN WE THOUGHT!
RIGHT? THAT'S WHAT'S HAPPEN-ING.
THIS HORRID PLAY-GROUND WILL BE DESTROYED TODAY.
WE HUMANS WILL WIN.
SO LET'S NOT PANIC.
WE HAVE TO BE CALM, COOL AND COLLECTED.
THEY'RE COMING!!
RAWWR
EVERYONE, GRAB YOUR WEAPONS AND TAKE YOUR POSITIONS!!

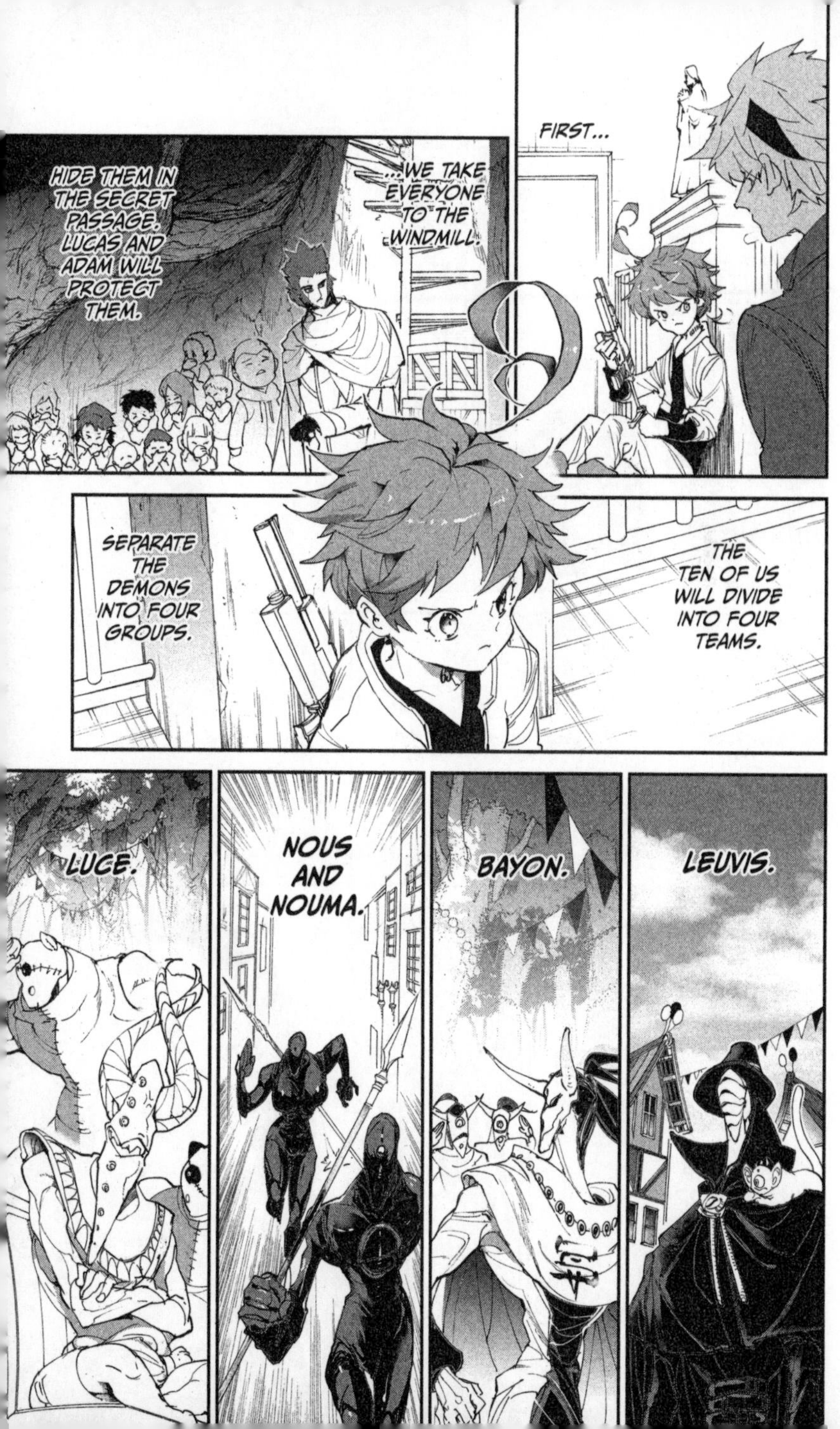
FIRST...
...WE TAKE EVERYONE TO THE WINDMILL.
HIDE THEM IN THE SECRET PASSAGE. LUCAS AND ADAM WILL PROTECT THEM.
THE TEN OF US WILL DIVIDE INTO FOUR TEAMS.
SEPARATE THE DEMONS INTO FOUR GROUPS.
LEUVIS.
BAYON.
NOUS AND NOUMA.
LUCE.

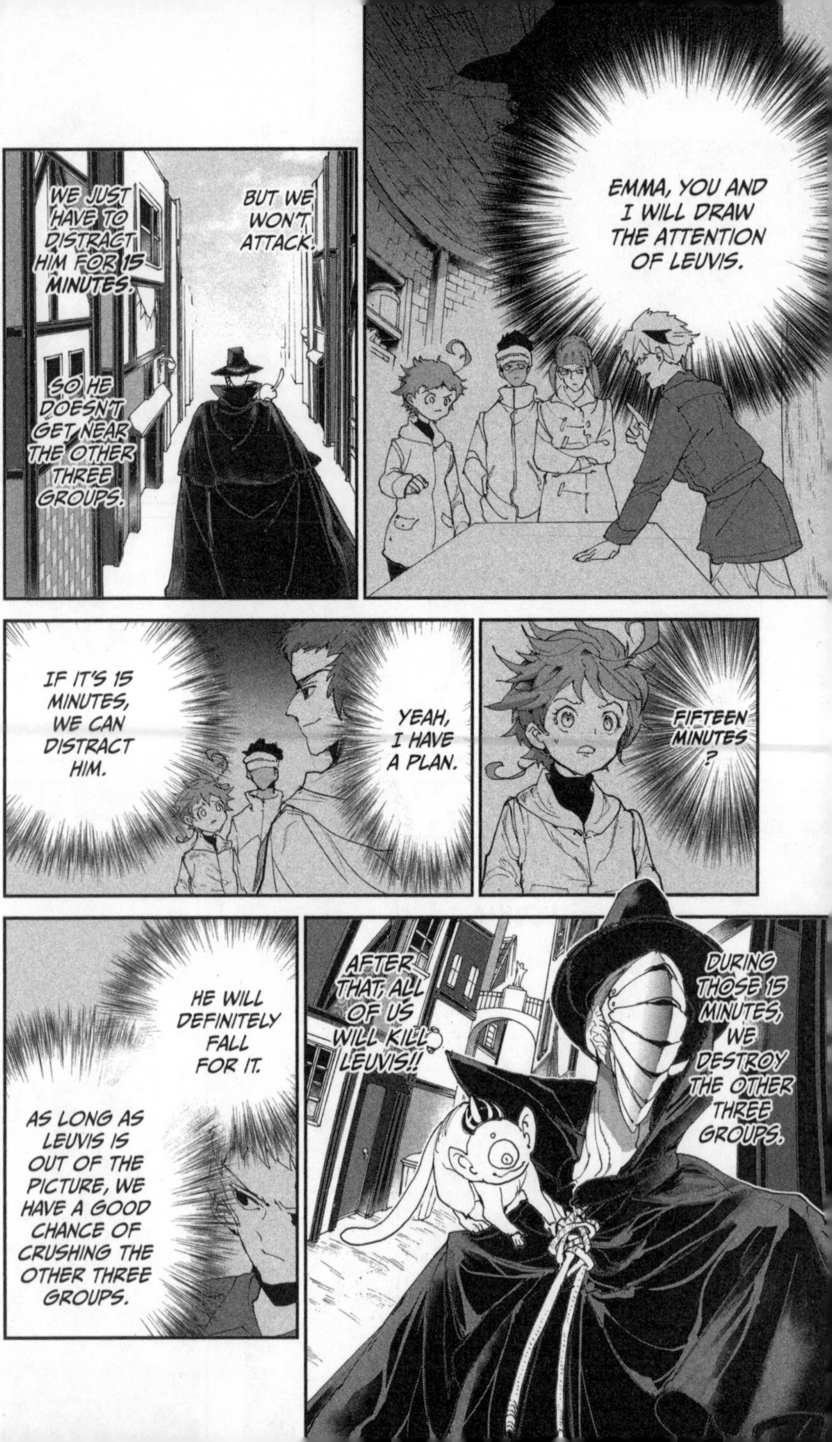
EMMA, YOU AND I WILL DRAW THE ATTENTION OF LEUVIS.
BUT WE WON'T ATTACK.
WE JUST HAVE TO DISTRACT HIM FOR 15 MINUTES.
SO HE DOESN'T GET NEAR THE OTHER THREE GROUPS.
FIFTEEN MINUTES?
YEAH, I HAVE A PLAN.
IF IT'S 15 MINUTES, WE CAN DISTRACT HIM.
DURING THOSE 15 MINUTES, WE DESTROY THE OTHER THREE GROUPS.
AFTER THAT, ALL OF US WILL KILL LEUVIS!!
HE WILL DEFINITELY FALL FOR IT.
AS LONG AS LEUVIS IS OUT OF THE PICTURE, WE HAVE A GOOD CHANCE OF CRUSHING THE OTHER THREE GROUPS.

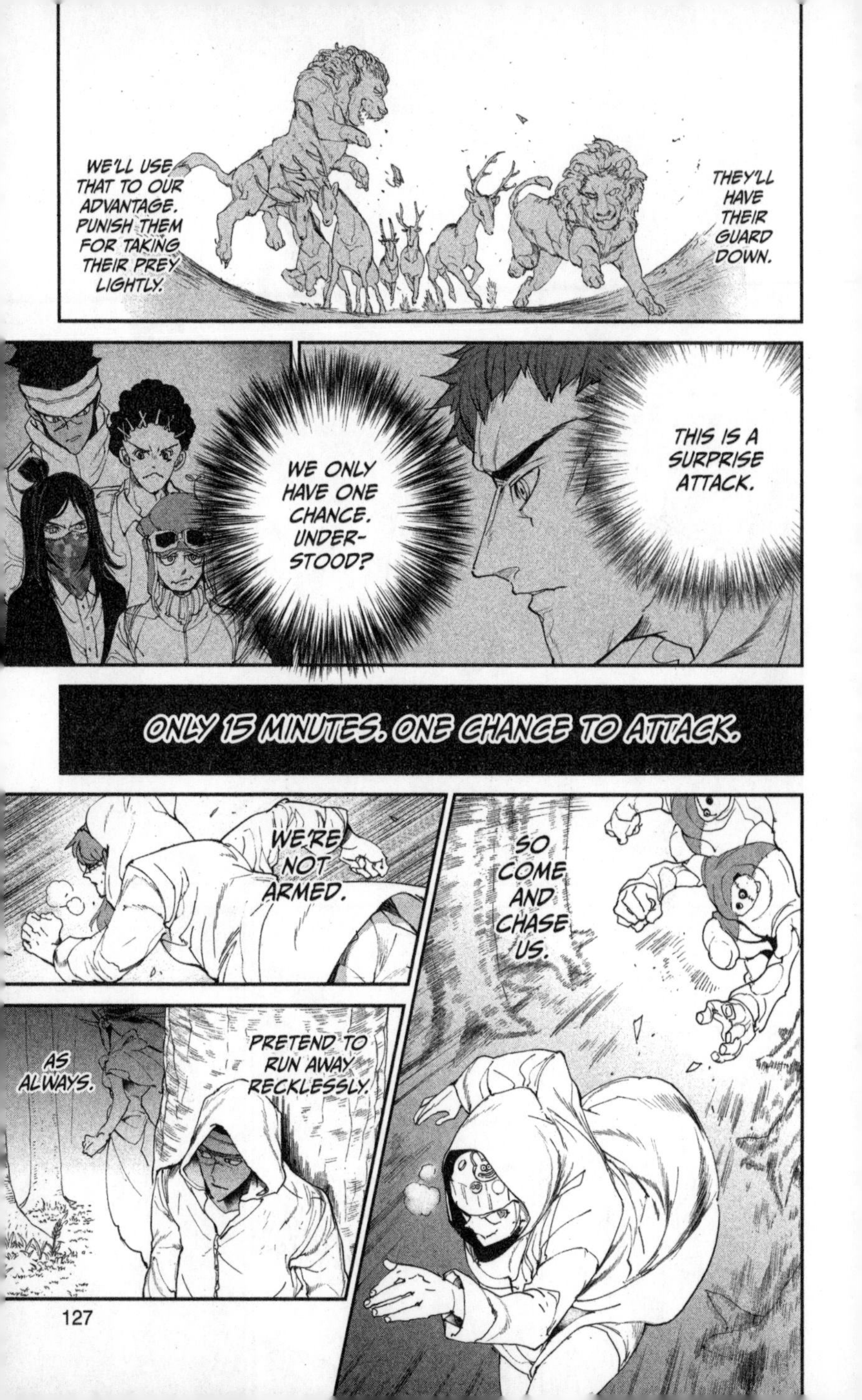
THEY'LL HAVE THEIR GUARD DOWN.
WE'LL USE THAT TO OUR ADVANTAGE. PUNISH THEM FOR TAKING THEIR PREY LIGHTLY.
THIS IS A SURPRISE ATTACK.
WE ONLY HAVE ONE CHANCE. UNDER-STOOD?
ONLY 15 MINUTES. ONE CHANCE TO ATTACK.
SO COME AND CHASE US.
WE'RE NOT ARMED.
PRETEND TO RUN AWAY RECKLESSLY.
AS ALWAYS.

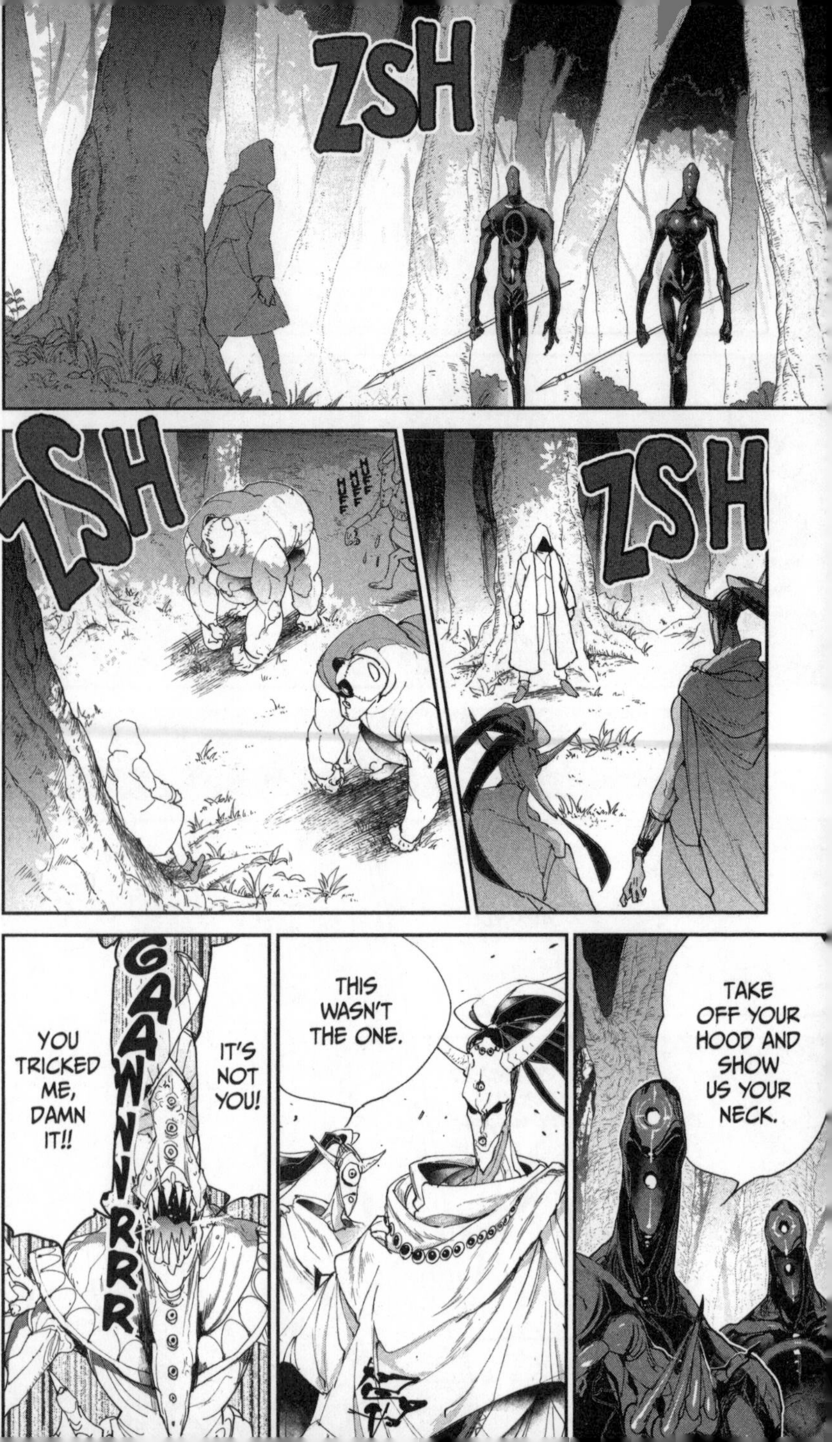
ZSH
ZSH
ZSH
TAKE OFF YOUR HOOD AND SHOW US YOUR NECK.
THIS WASN'T THE ONE.
IT'S NOT YOU!
YOU TRICKED ME, DAMN IT!!
GAAWNNRRR

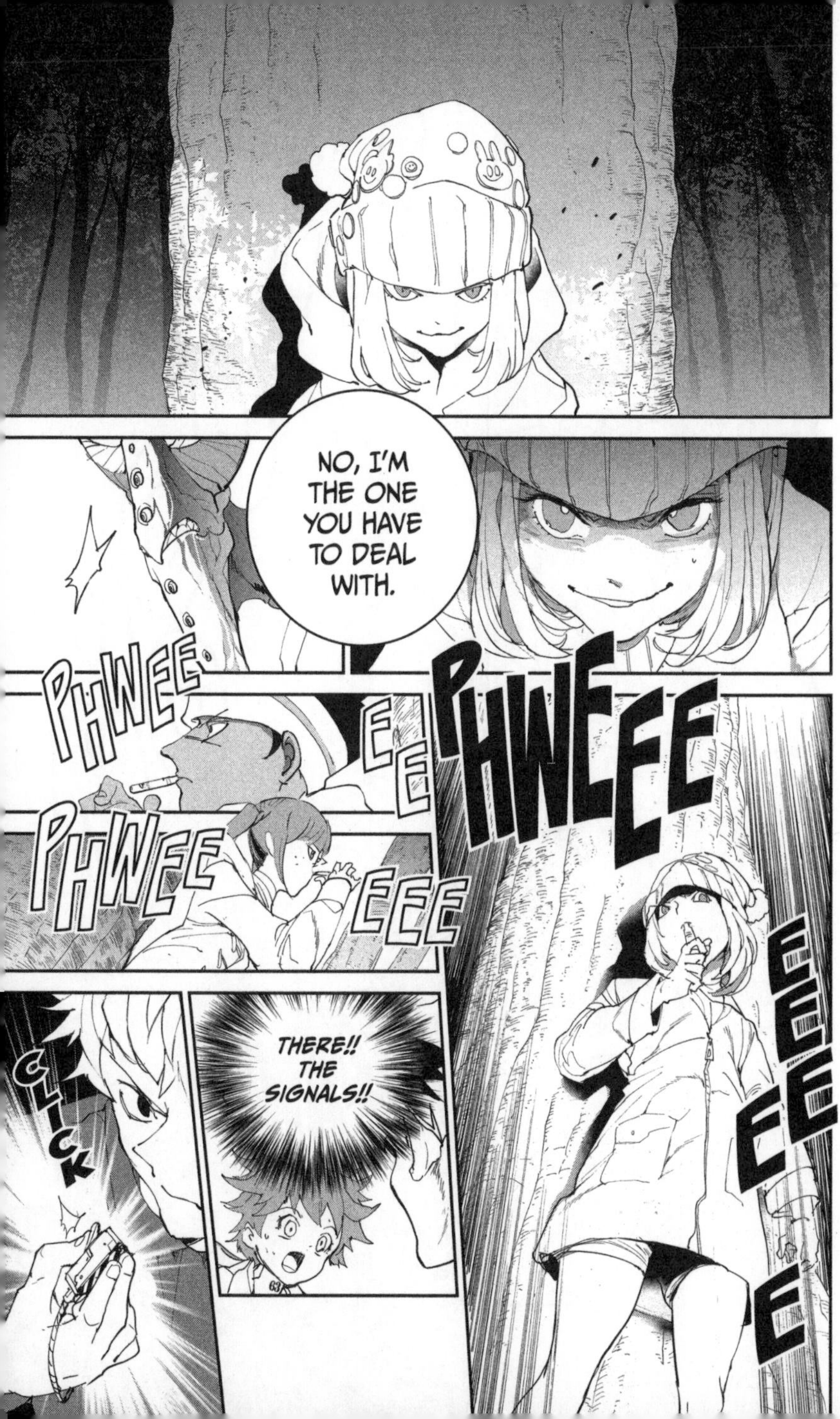

NO, I'M THE ONE YOU HAVE TO DEAL WITH.
PHWEE
EEEEE
PHWEE
EE
PHWEE
EEE
THERE!! THE SIGNALS!!
CLICK

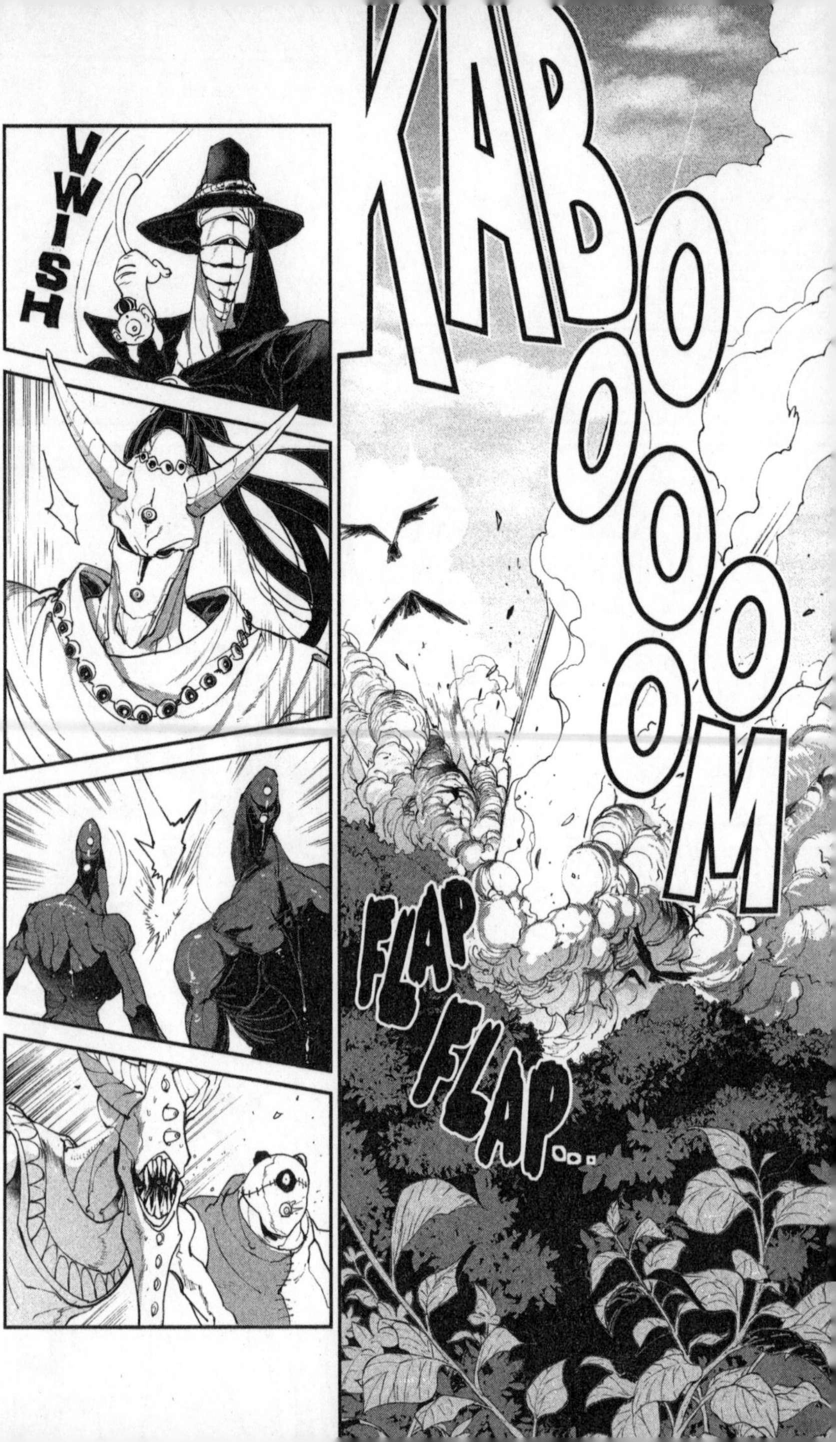
KABOOOOOOM
FLAP
FLAP
FLAP...
VWISH

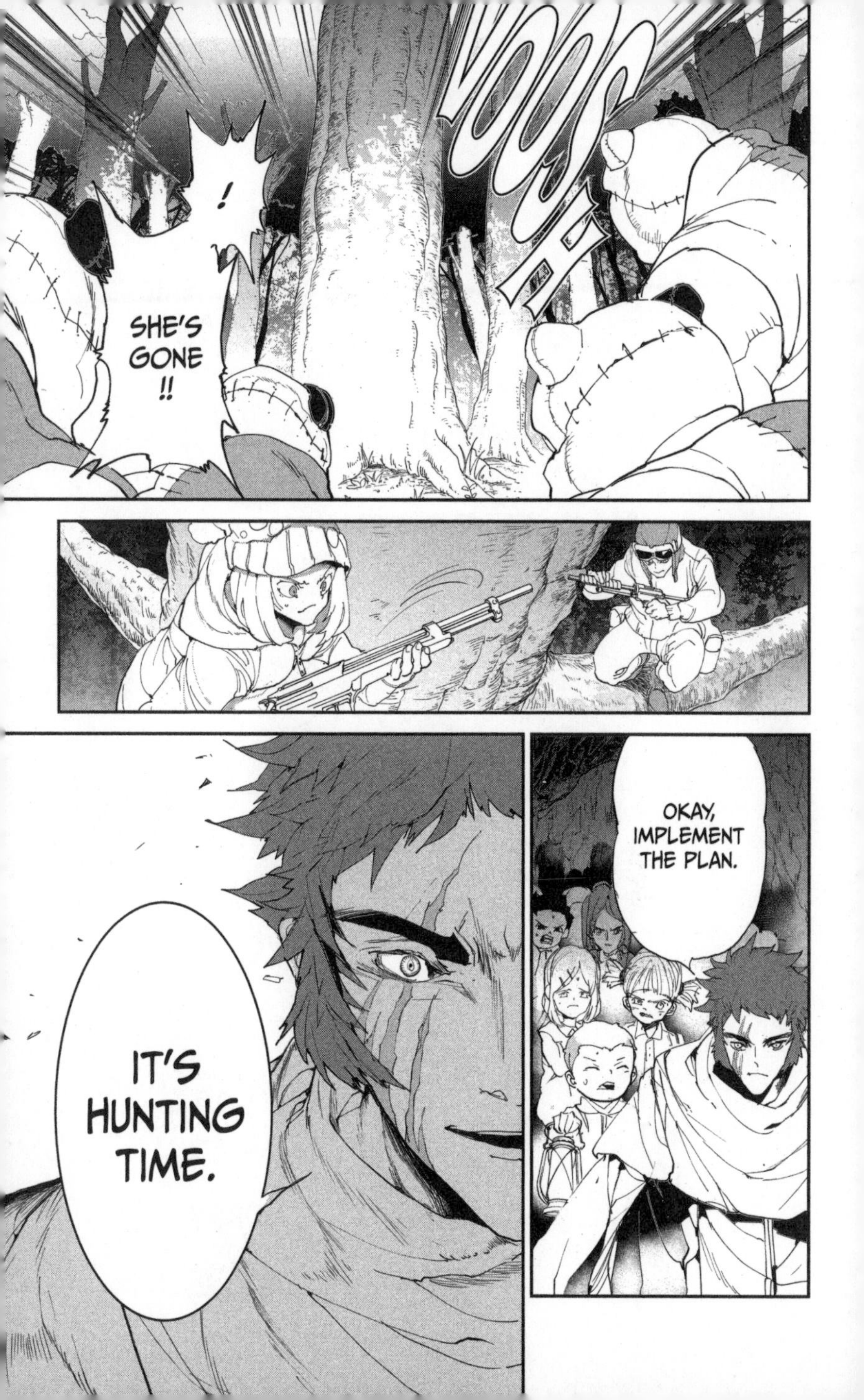

WOOSH
!
SHE'S GONE !!
OKAY, IMPLEMENT THE PLAN.
IT'S HUNTING TIME.

THE PROMISED NEVERLAND SIDE SCENE 017

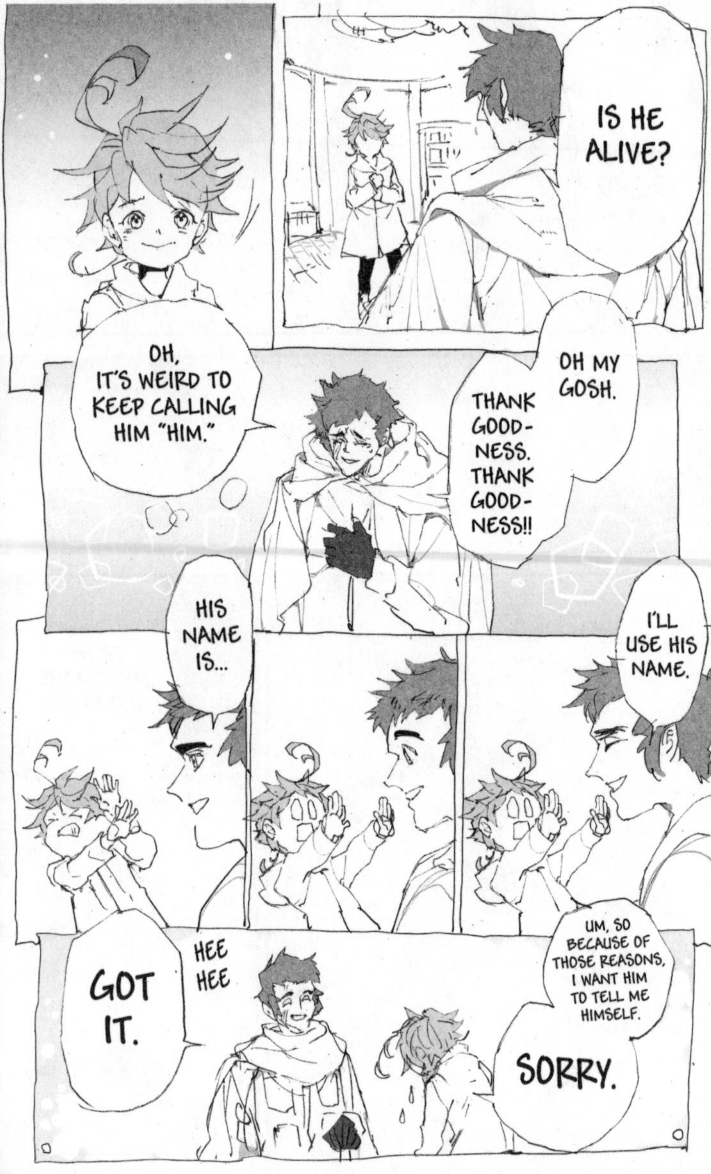
IS HE ALIVE?
OH MY GOSH.
THANK GOODNESS. THANK GOODNESS!!
OH, IT'S WEIRD TO KEEP CALLING HIM "HIM."
I'LL USE HIS NAME.
HIS NAME IS...
UM, SO BECAUSE OF THOSE REASONS, I WANT HIM TO TELL ME HIMSELF.
SORRY.
HEE HEE
GOT IT.

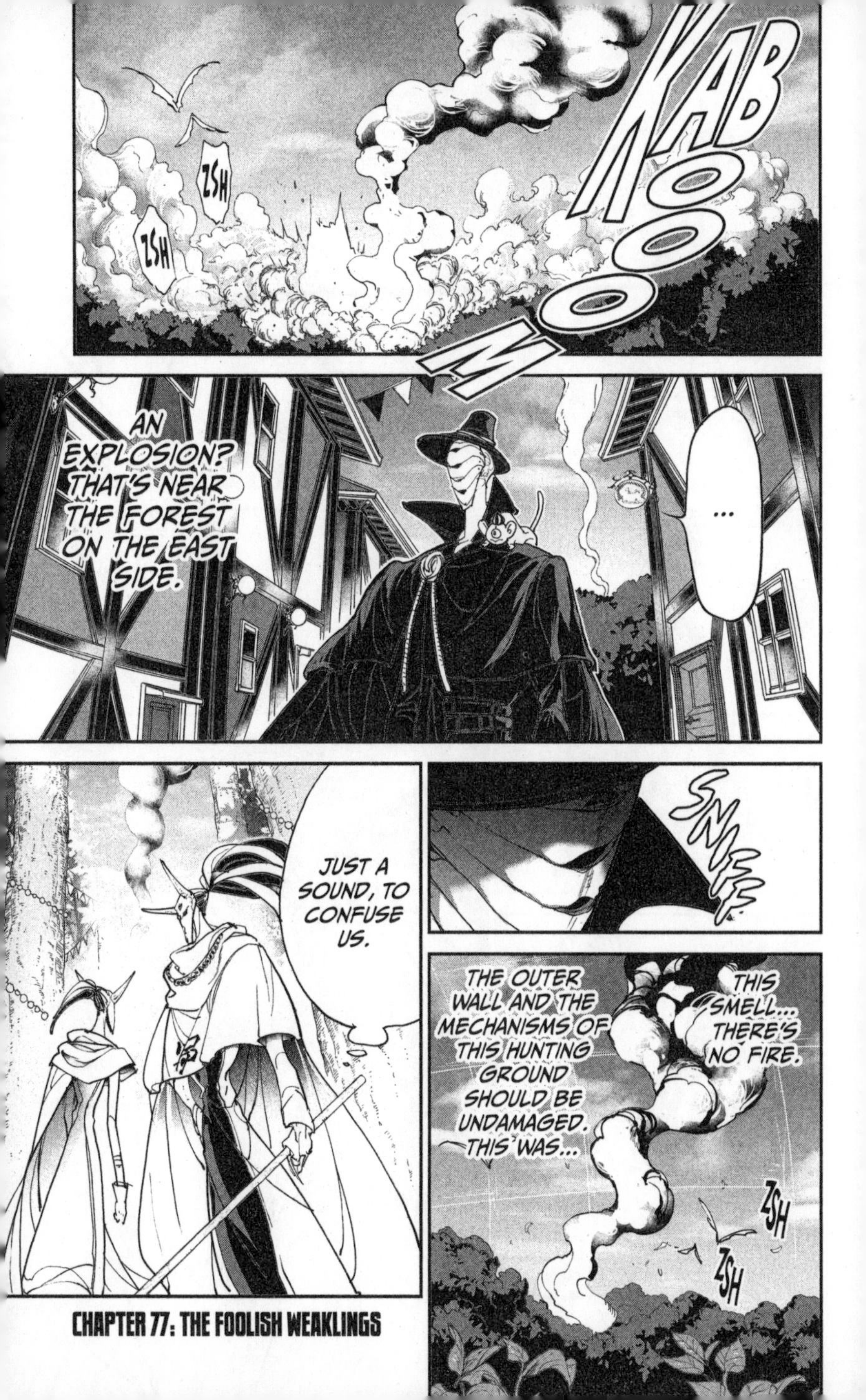
KABOOOOM
ZSH
ZSH
...
AN EXPLOSION? THAT'S NEAR THE FOREST ON THE EAST SIDE.
SNIFF
THIS SMELL... THERE'S NO FIRE.
THE OUTER WALL AND THE MECHANISMS OF THIS HUNTING GROUND SHOULD BE UNDAMAGED. THIS WAS...
ZSH
ZSH
JUST A SOUND, TO CONFUSE US.

CHAPTER 77: THE FOOLISH WEAKLINGS

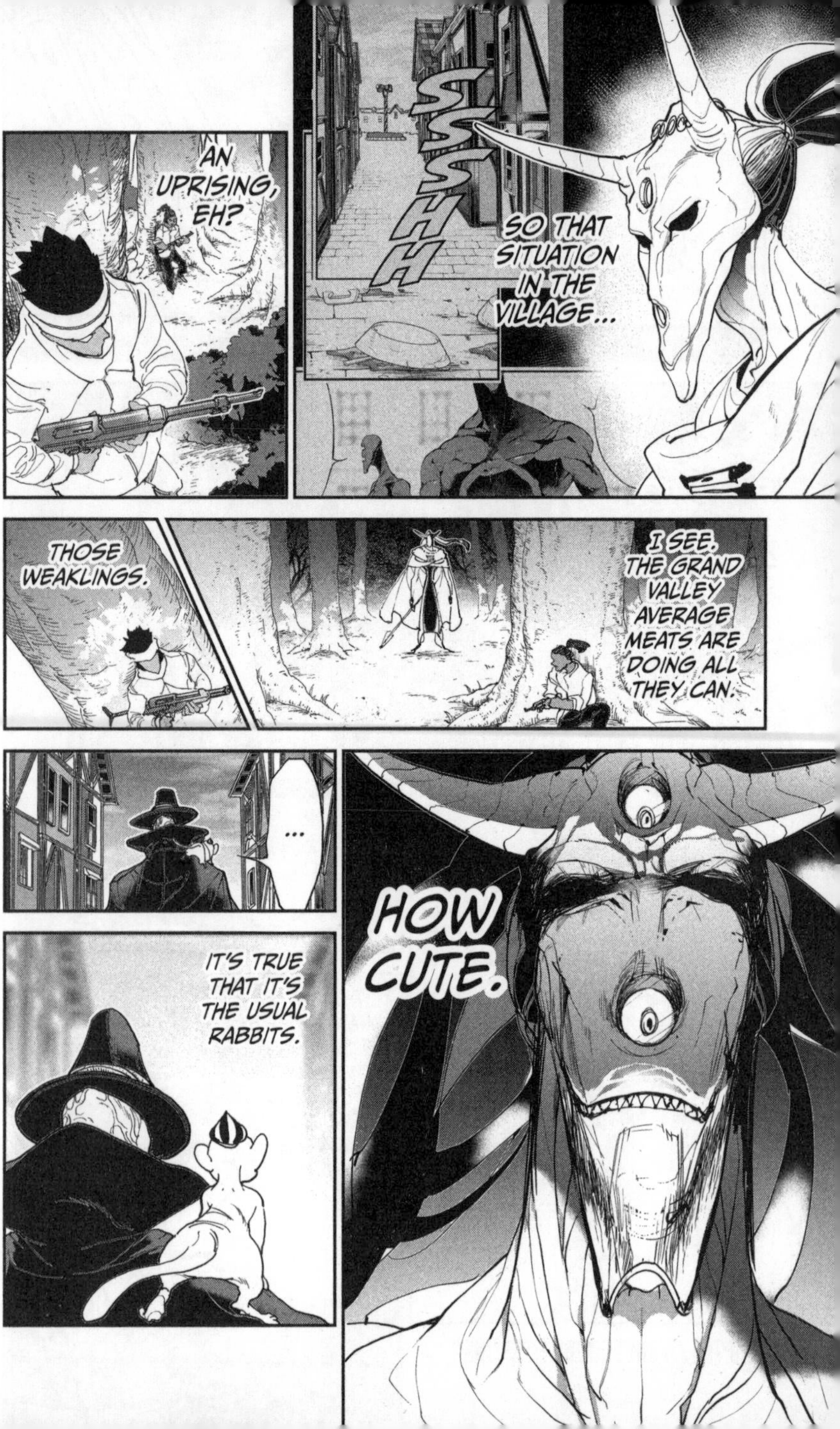
SO THAT SITUATION IN THE VILLAGE...
SSSHH
AN UPRISING, EH?
I SEE. THE GRAND VALLEY AVERAGE MEATS ARE DOING ALL THEY CAN.
THOSE WEAKLINGS.
HOW CUTE.
...
IT'S TRUE THAT IT'S THE USUAL RABBITS.

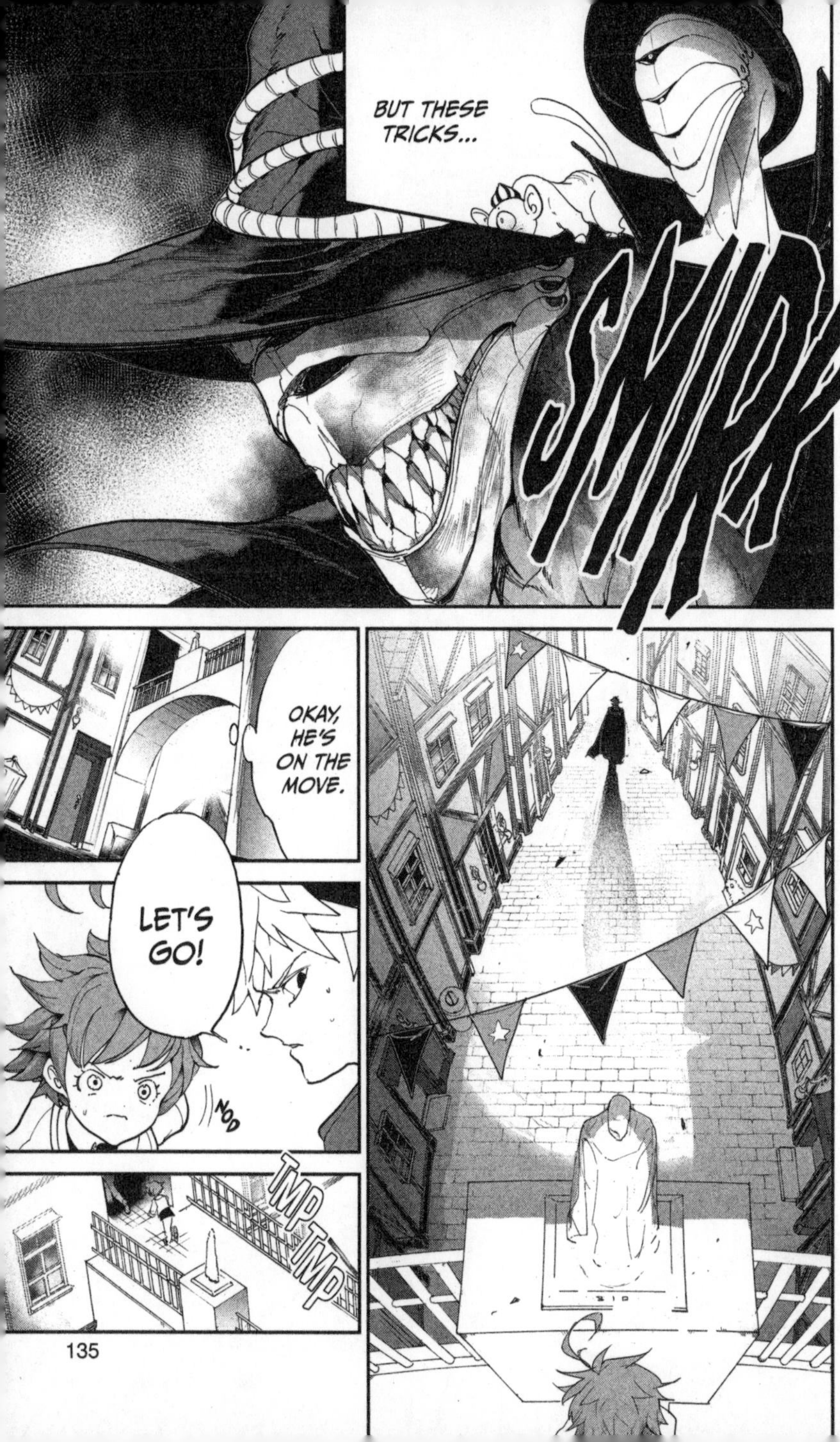
BUT THESE TRICKS...
SMIRK
OKAY, HE'S ON THE MOVE.
LET'S GO!
NOD
TMP TMP TMP

CHAPTER 77: THE FOOLISH WEAKLINGS

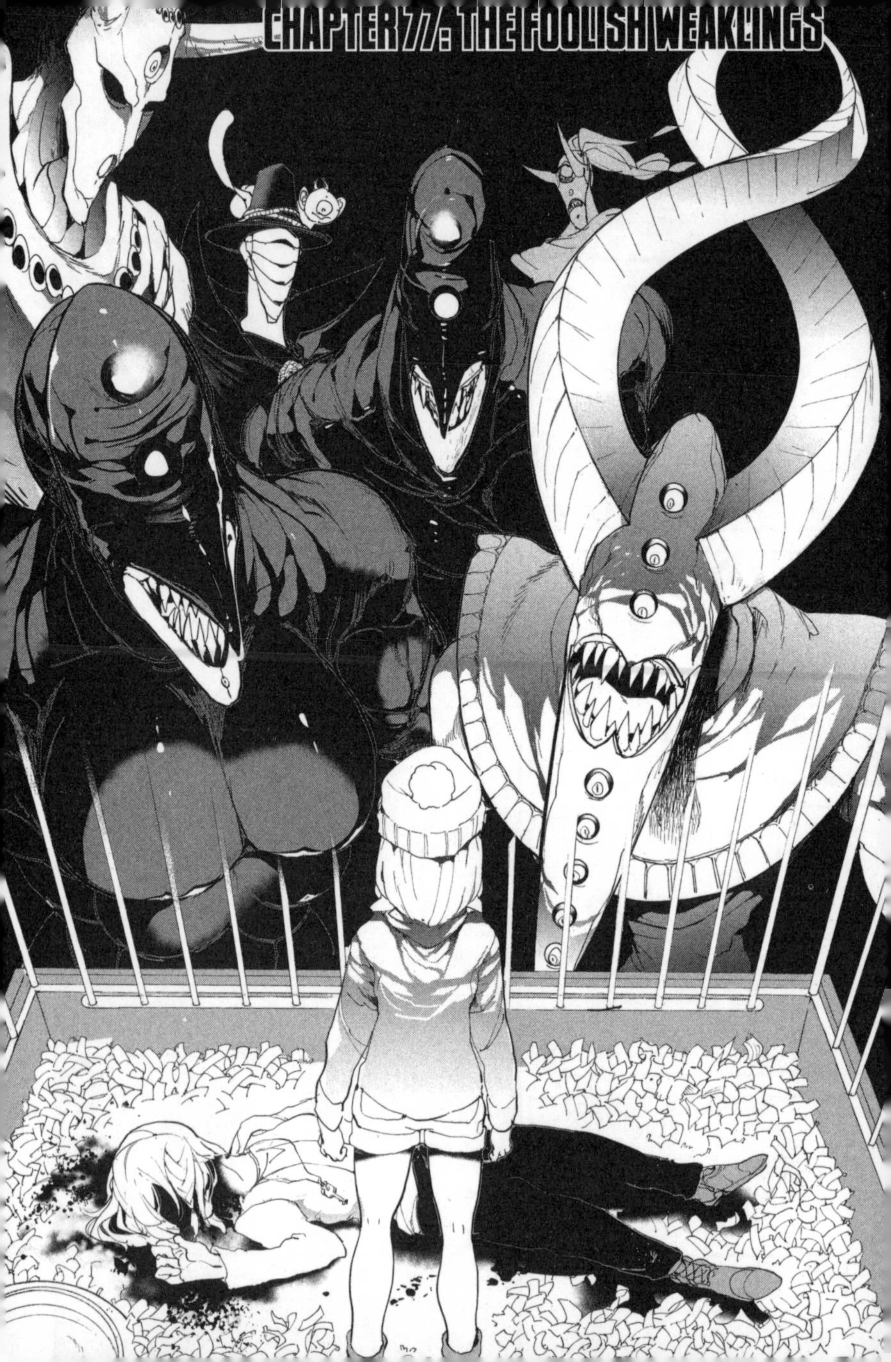

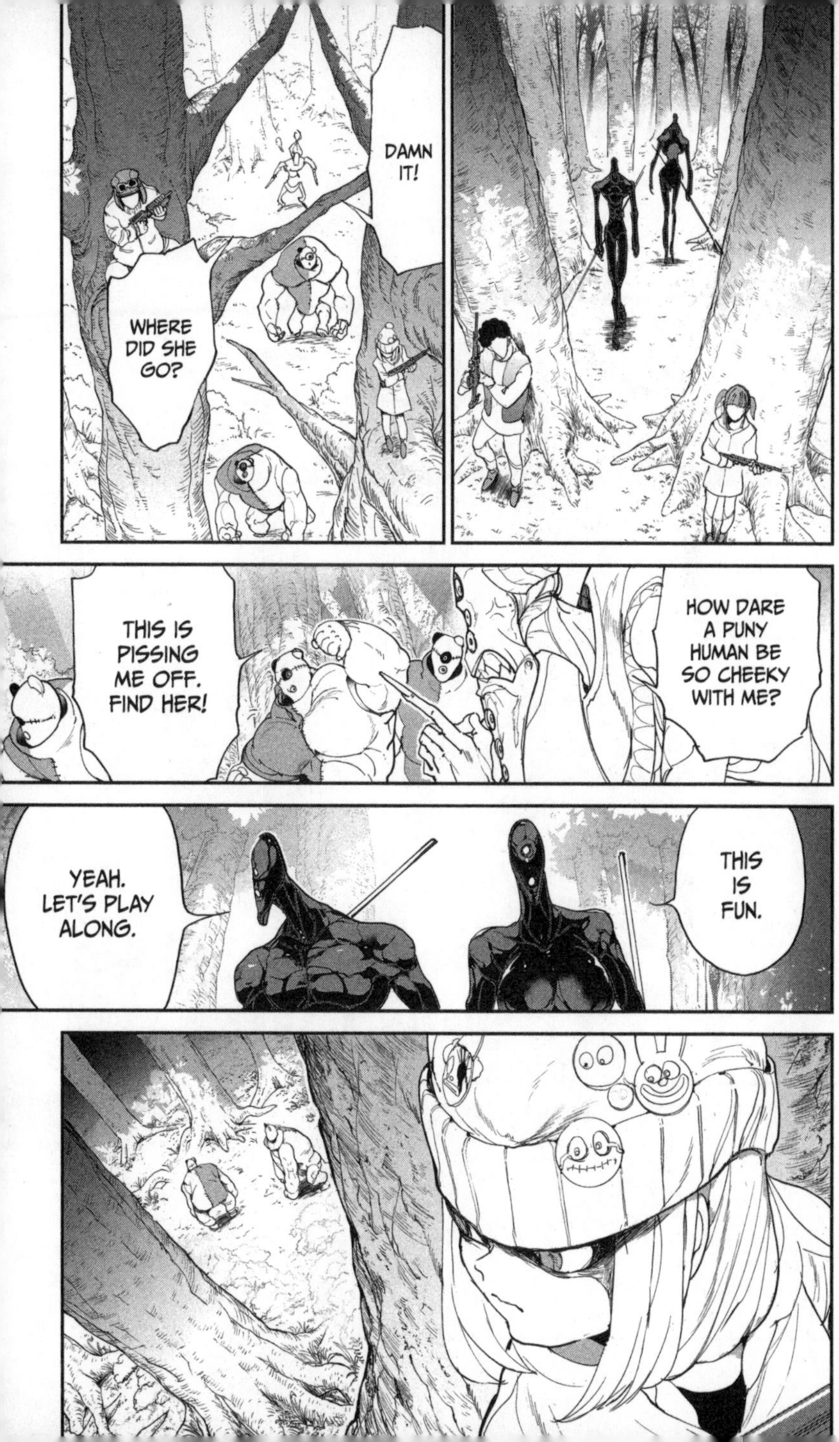
DAMN IT!
WHERE DID SHE GO?
HOW DARE A PUNY HUMAN BE SO CHEEKY WITH ME?
THIS IS PISSING ME OFF. FIND HER!
THIS IS FUN.
YEAH. LET'S PLAY ALONG.

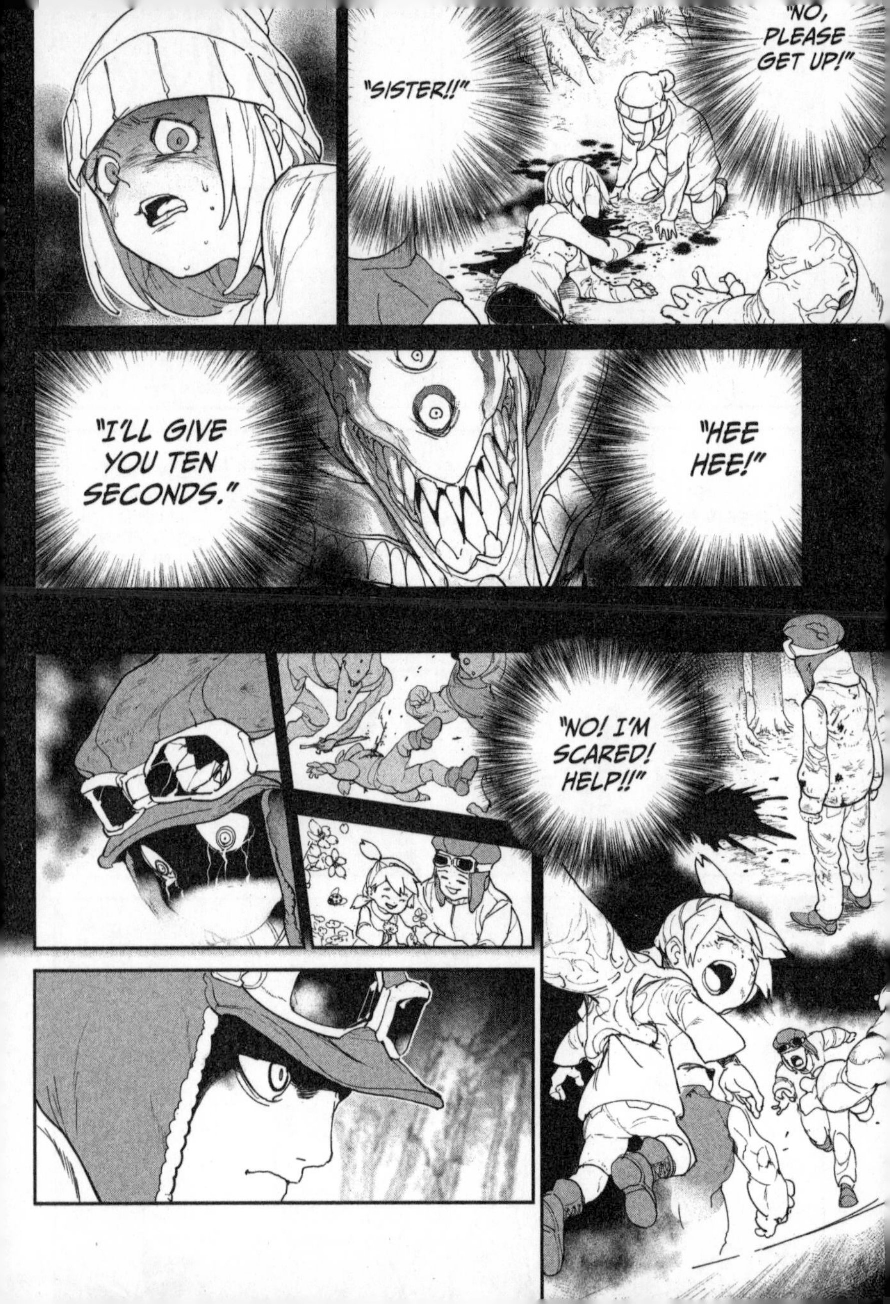
"NO, PLEASE GET UP!"
"SISTER!!"
"HEE HEE!"
"I'LL GIVE YOU TEN SECONDS."
"NO! I'M SCARED! HELP!!"

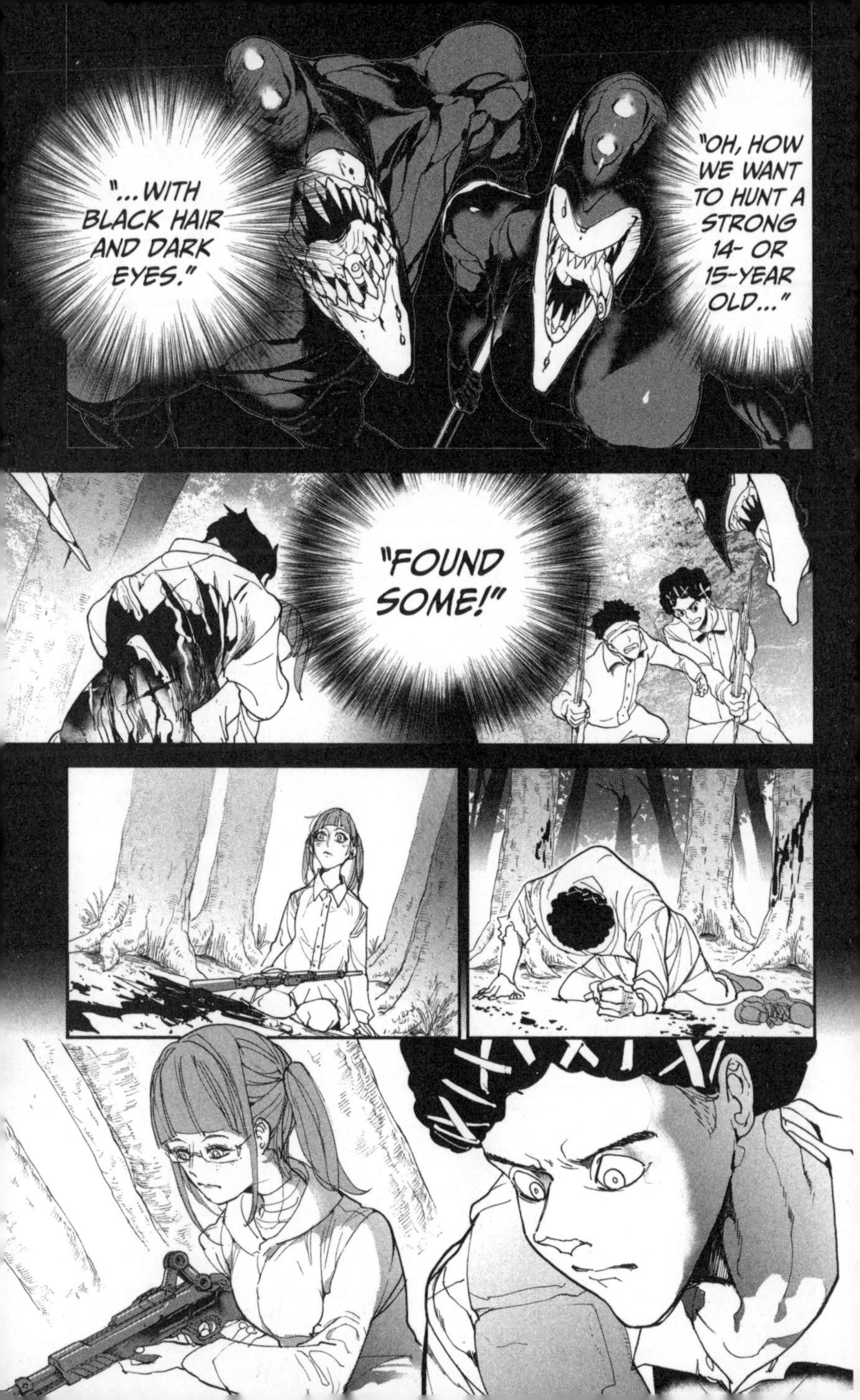
"OH, HOW WE WANT TO HUNT A STRONG 14- OR 15-YEAR OLD..."
"...WITH BLACK HAIR AND DARK EYES."
"FOUND SOME!"

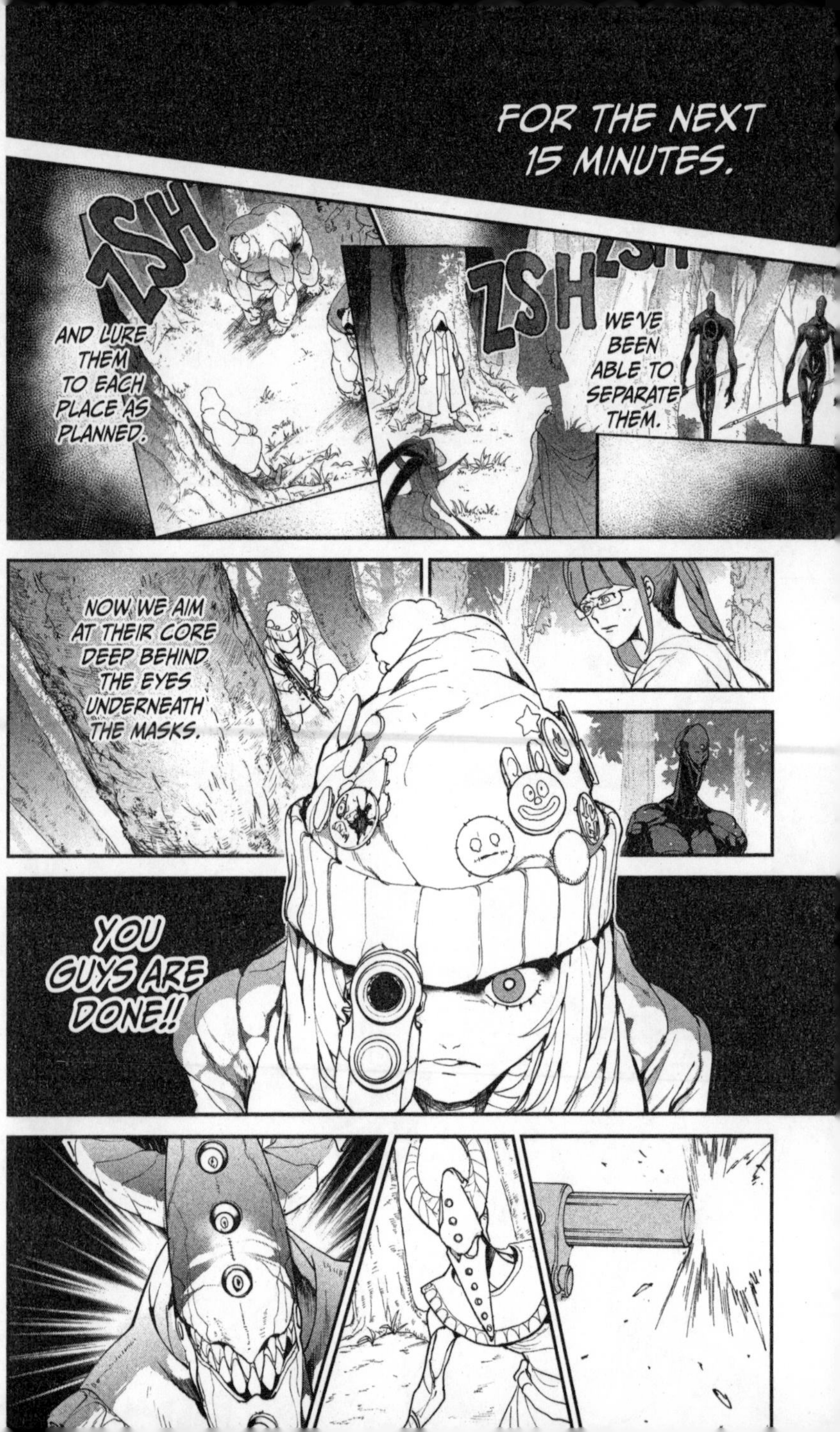
FOR THE NEXT 15 MINUTES.
ZSH ZSH
WE'VE BEEN ABLE TO SEPARATE THEM.
ZSH
AND LURE THEM TO EACH PLACE AS PLANNED.
NOW WE AIM AT THEIR CORE DEEP BEHIND THE EYES UNDERNEATH THE MASKS.
YOU GUYS ARE DONE!!

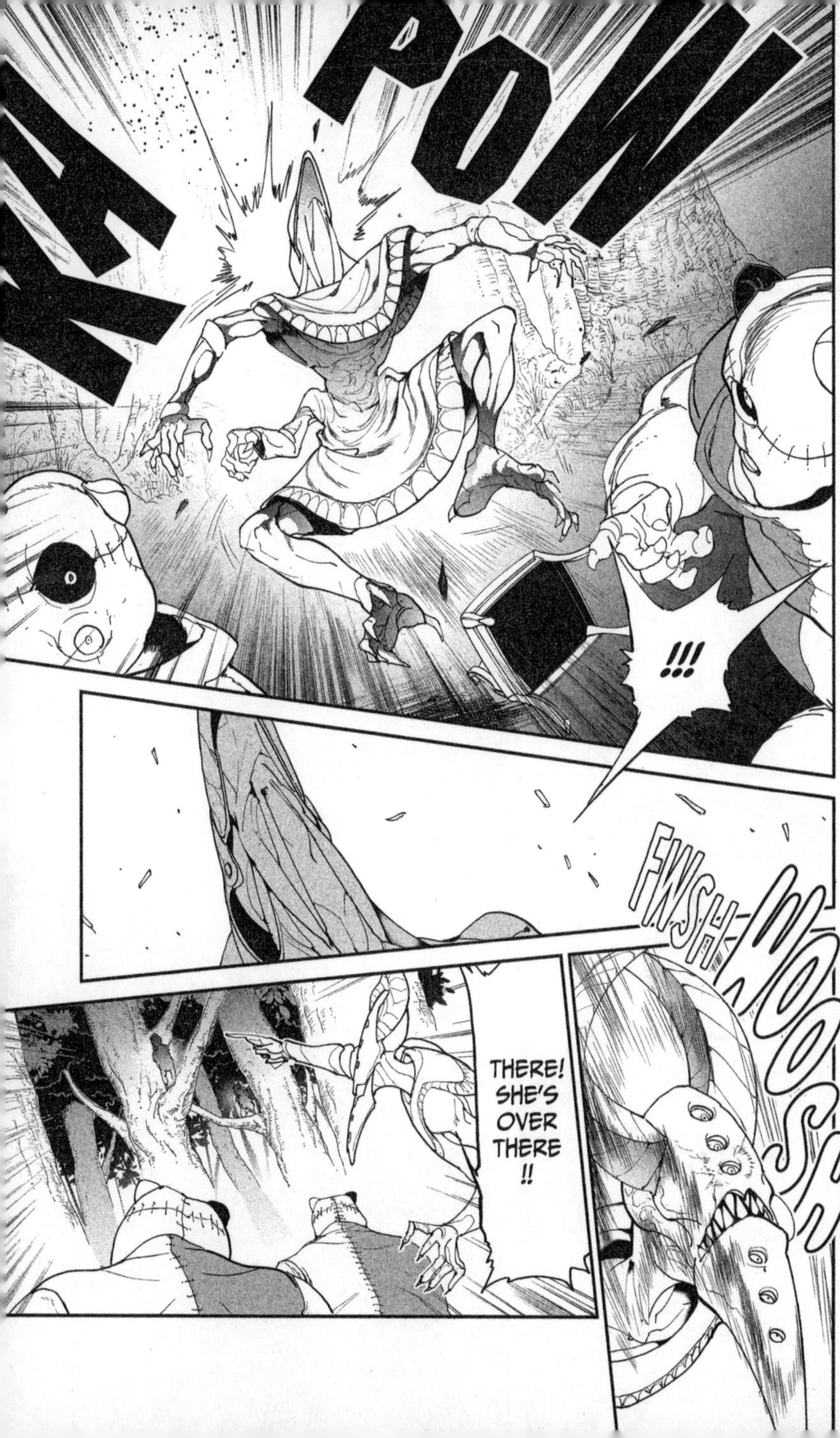
KA-POW!
!!!
FWSH
WOOOSH
THERE! SHE'S OVER THERE!!

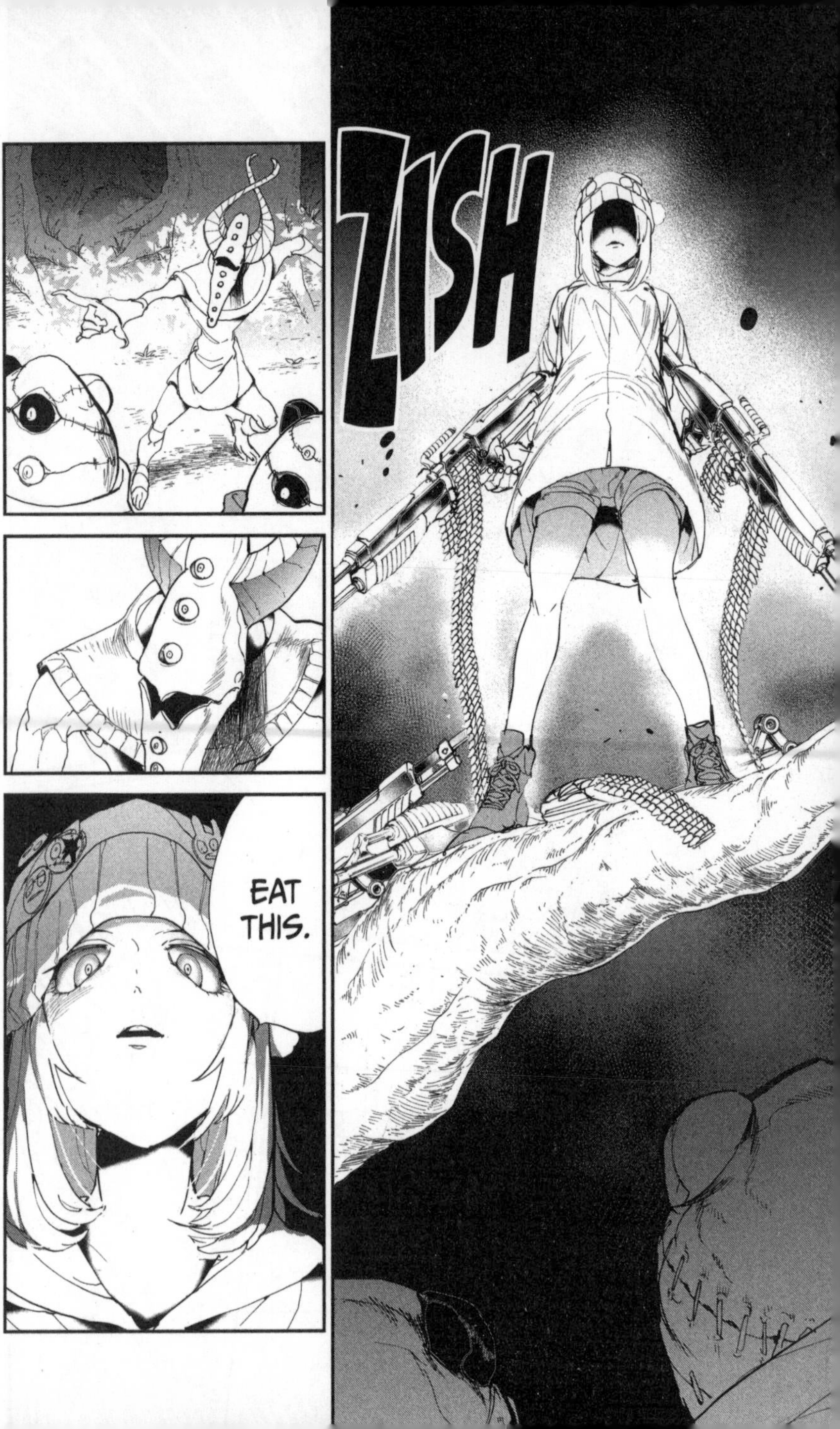
ZISH
EAT THIS.

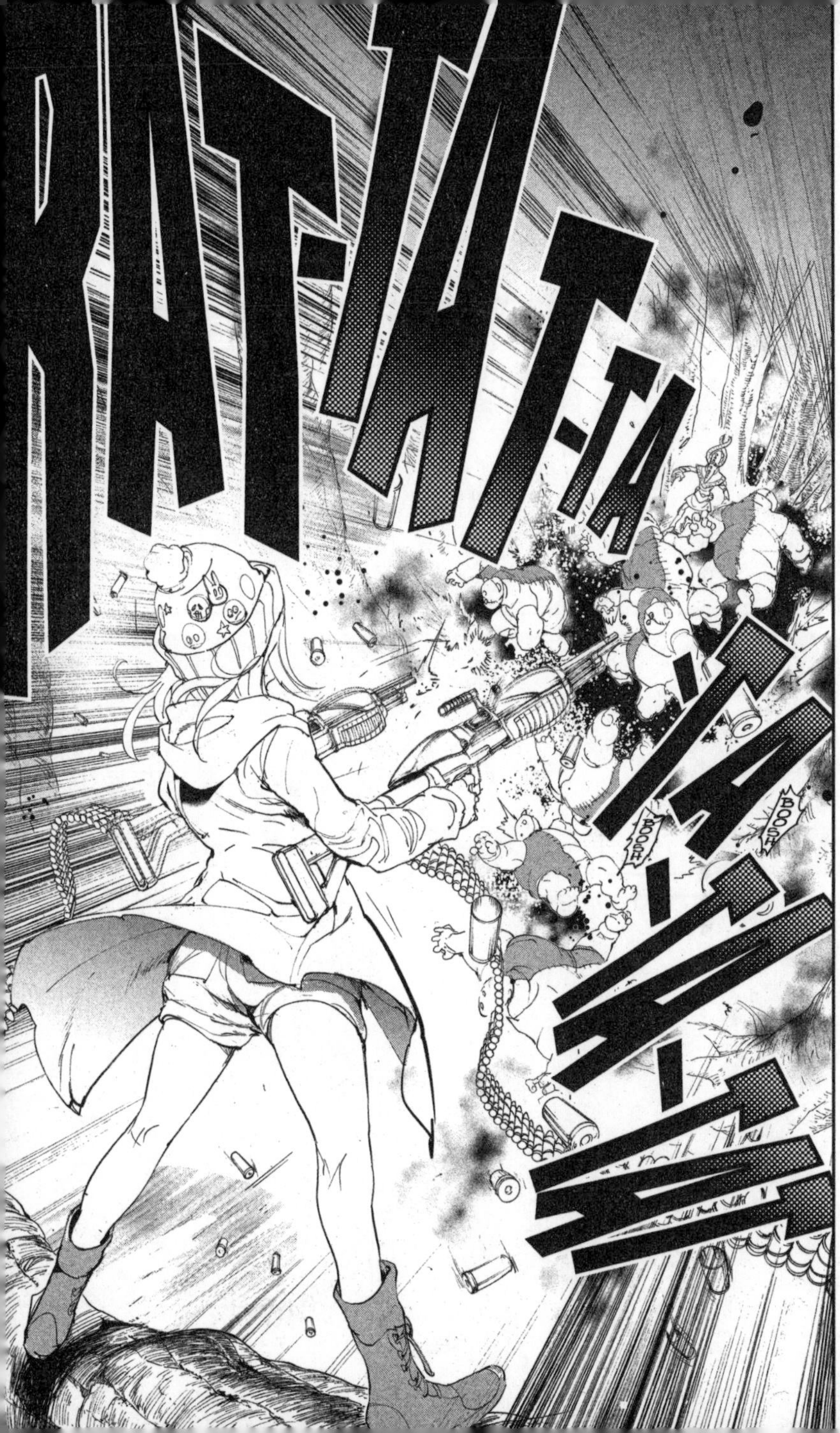
RAT-TAT-TA
BOOSH
BOOSH

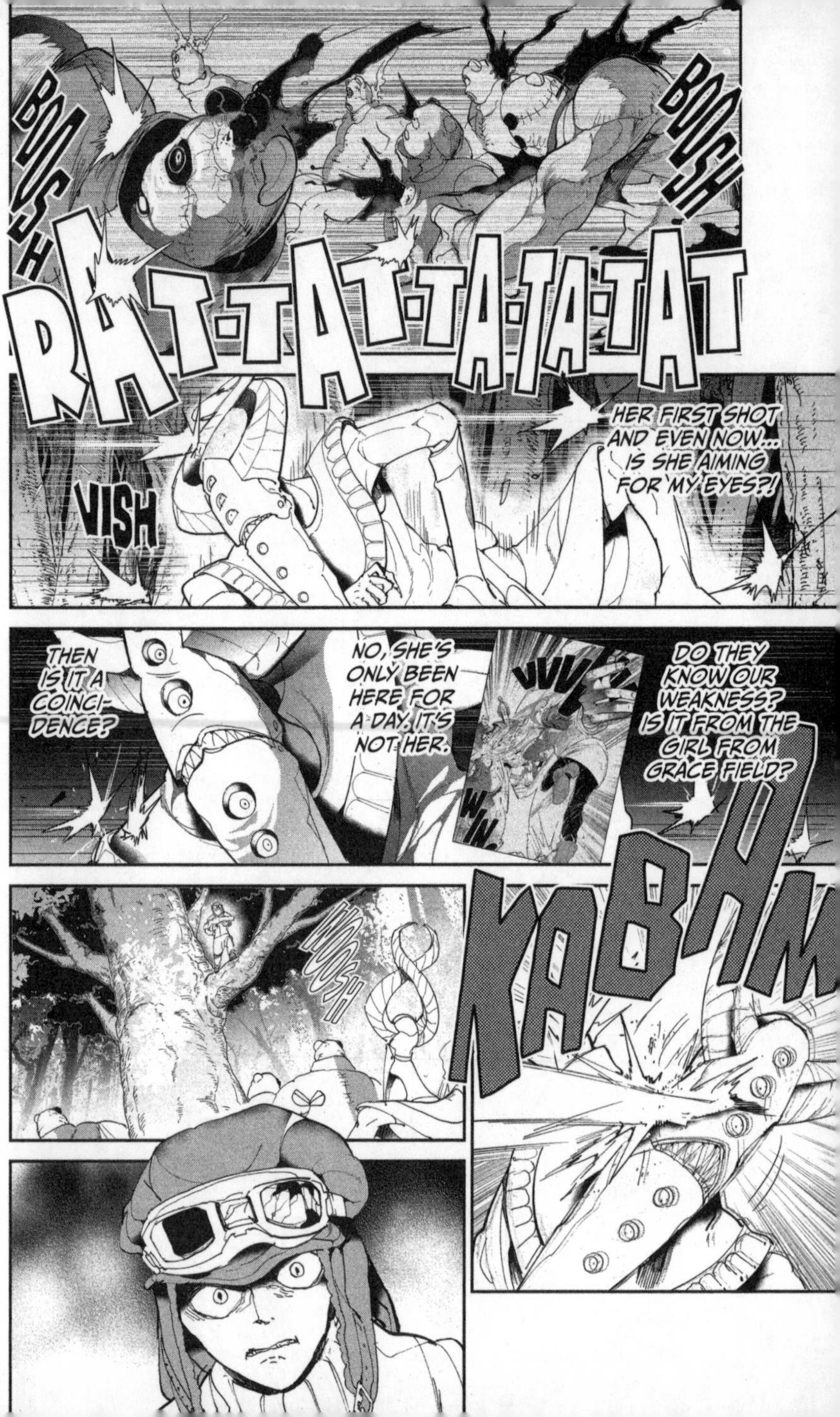
BOOSH
BOOSH
RAT-TAT-TAT-TA-TA-TAT
HER FIRST SHOT AND EVEN NOW... IS SHE AIMING FOR MY EYES?!
VISH
DO THEY KNOW OUR WEAKNESS? IS IT FROM THE GIRL FROM GRACE FIELD?
VVV
WIN
NO, SHE'S ONLY BEEN HERE FOR A DAY. IT'S NOT HER.
THEN IS IT A COINCI-DENCE?
KABHM
WOOSH

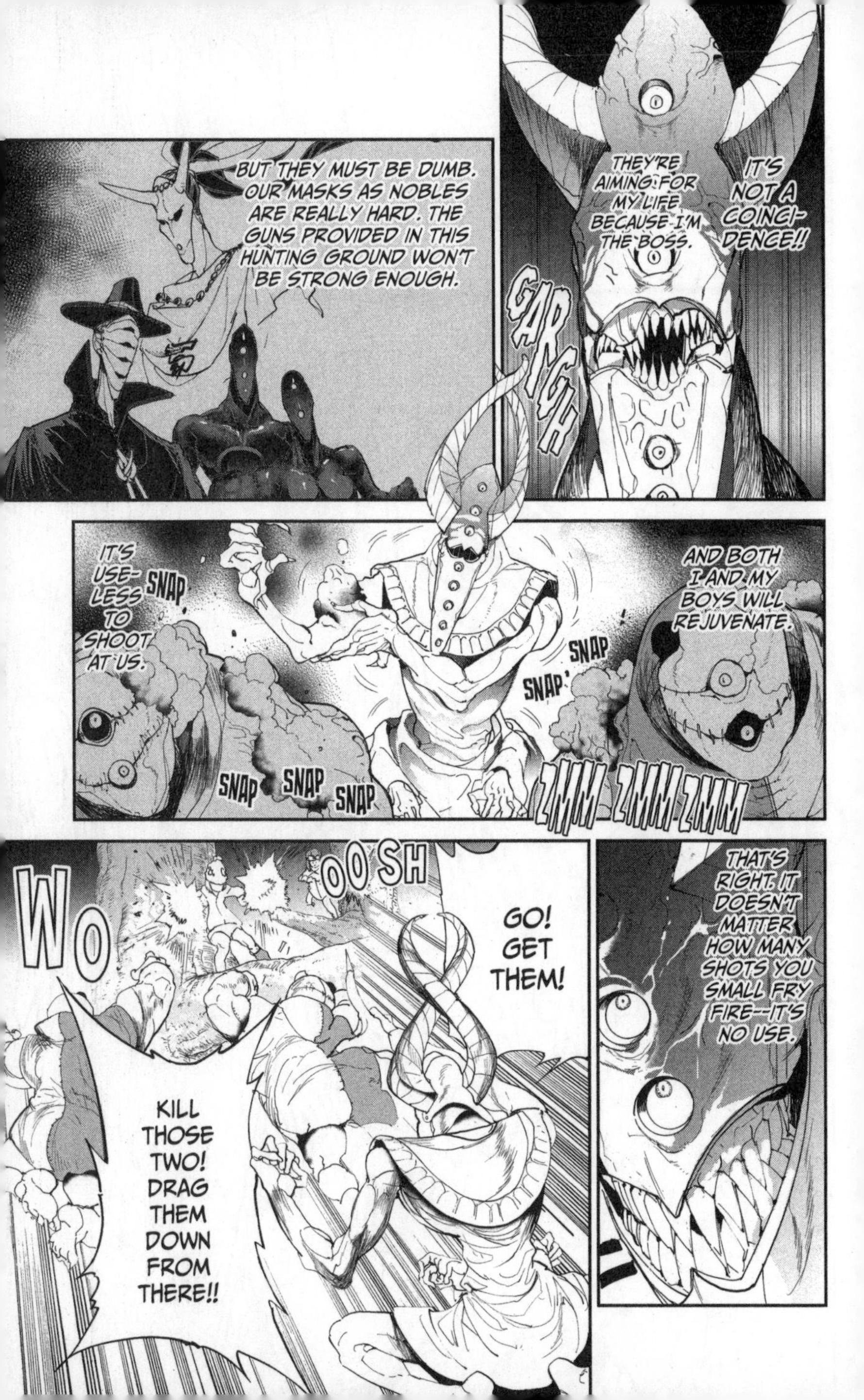
IT'S NOT A COINCIDENCE!!
THEY'RE AIMING FOR MY LIFE BECAUSE I'M THE BOSS.
GARGH
BUT THEY MUST BE DUMB. OUR MASKS AS NOBLES ARE REALLY HARD. THE GUNS PROVIDED IN THIS HUNTING GROUND WON'T BE STRONG ENOUGH.
AND BOTH I AND MY BOYS WILL REJUVENATE.
SNAP
SNAP
ZMM ZMM ZMM
IT'S USELESS TO SHOOT AT US.
SNAP
SNAP
SNAP
SNAP
THAT'S RIGHT. IT DOESN'T MATTER HOW MANY SHOTS YOU SMALL FRY FIRE--IT'S NO USE.
WOOSH
GO! GET THEM!
KILL THOSE TWO! DRAG THEM DOWN FROM THERE!!

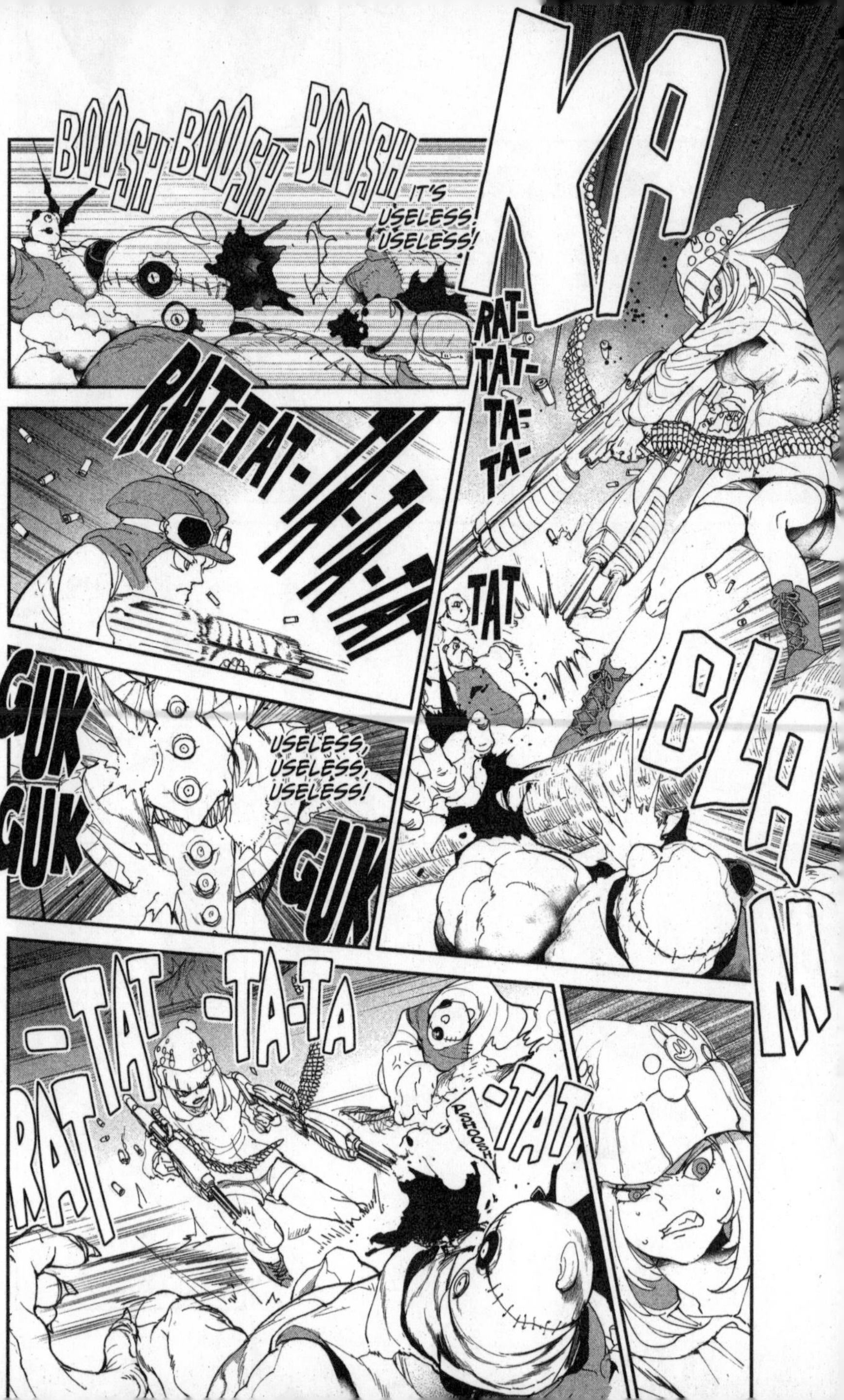
KA
RAT-TAT-TA-TA-
TAT
BLAM
BOOSH BOOSH BOOSH
IT'S USELESS! USELESS!
RAT-TAT-TA-TA-TA-TAT
GUK GUK
USELESS, USELESS, USELESS!
GUK
RAT-TAT-TA-TA-TAT
PSHOOOSH

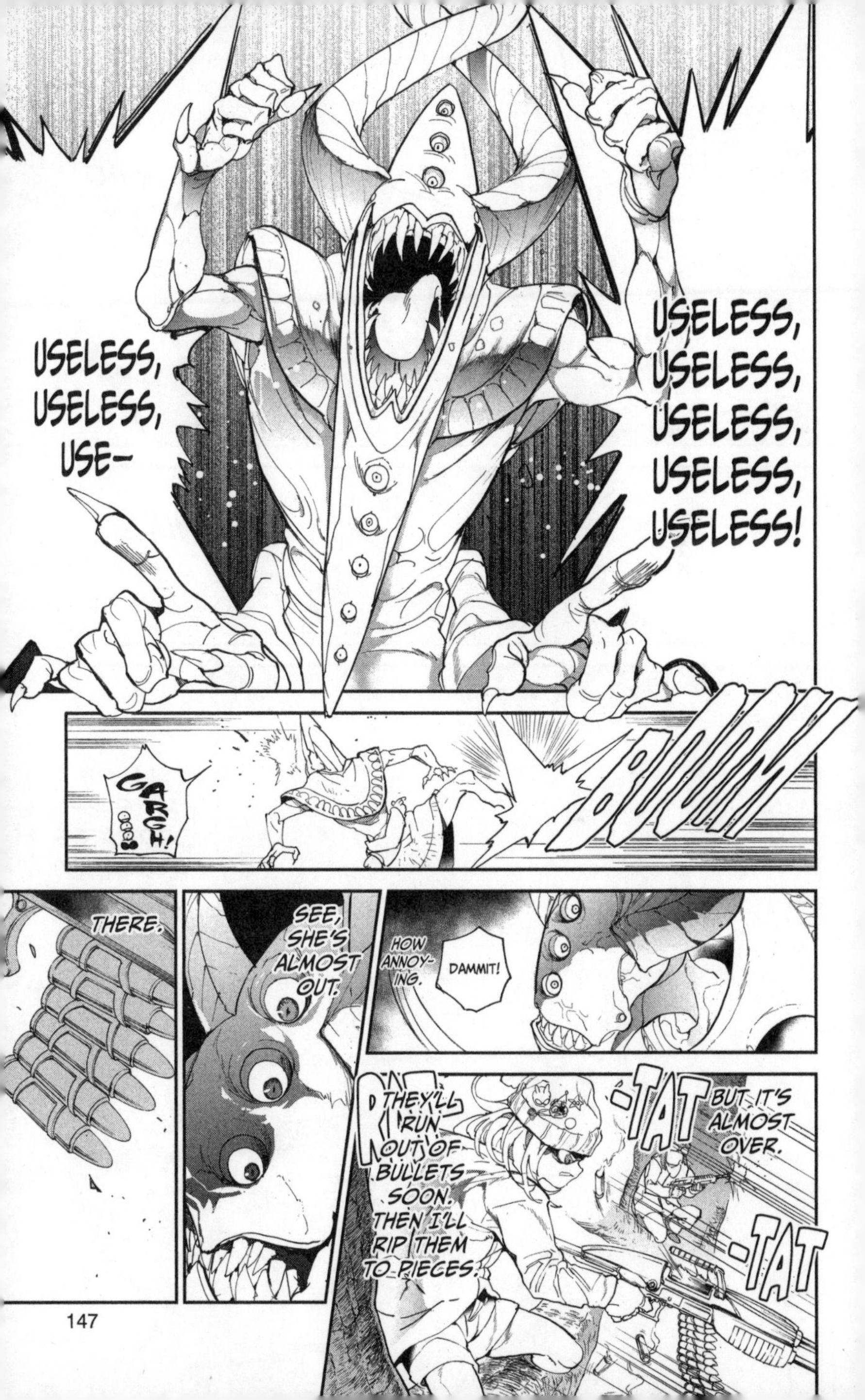
USELESS, USELESS, USELESS, USELESS, USELESS!
USELESS, USELESS, USE–
BOOOM
GARGH!!
DAMMIT!
HOW ANNOYING.
-TAT
BUT IT'S ALMOST OVER.
THEY'LL RUN OUT OF BULLETS SOON. THEN I'LL RIP THEM TO PIECES.
-TAT
SEE, SHE'S ALMOST OUT.
THERE.

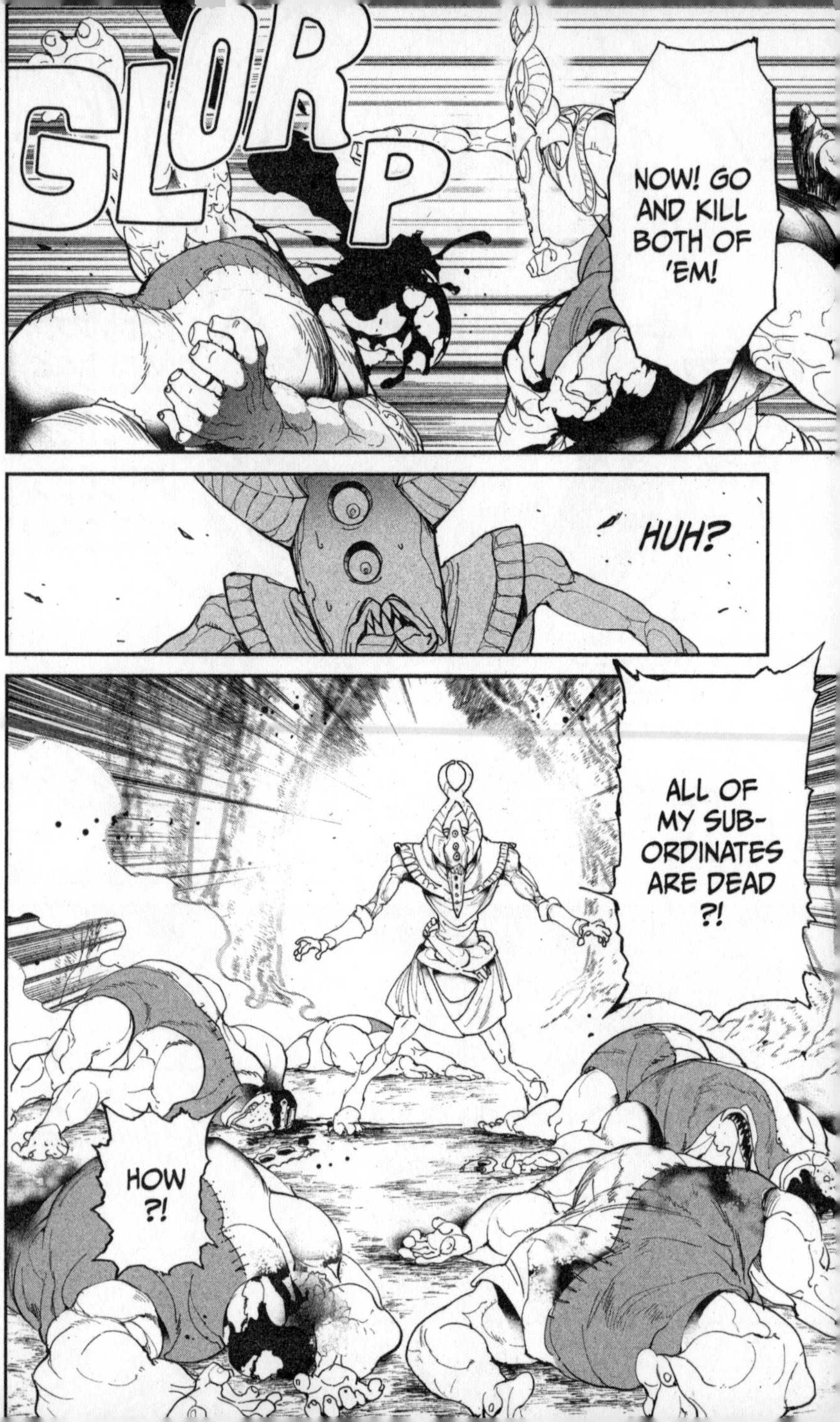
NOW! GO AND KILL BOTH OF 'EM!
GLORP
HUH?
ALL OF MY SUB-ORDINATES ARE DEAD?!
HOW?!

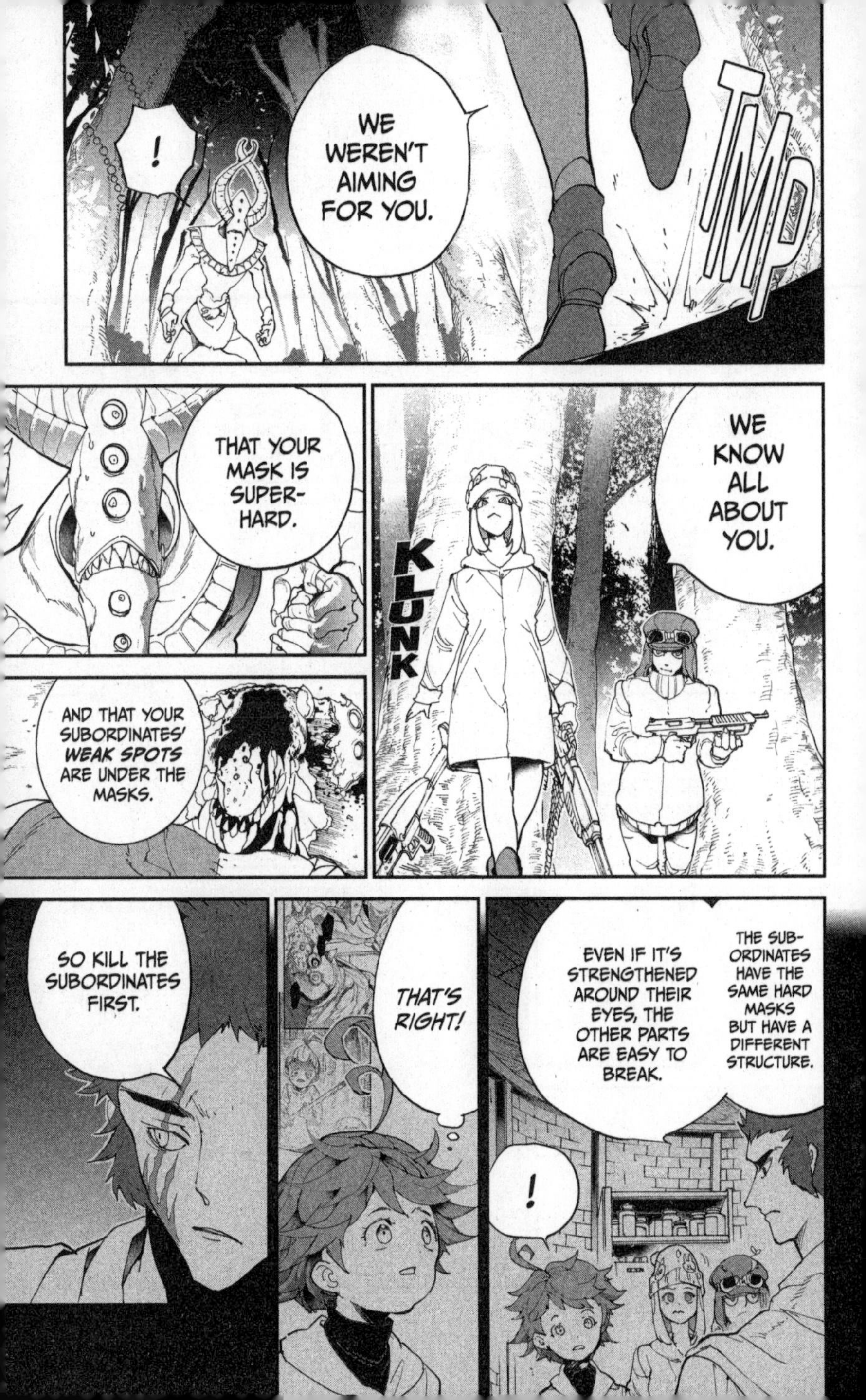
TMP
WE WEREN'T AIMING FOR YOU.
!
WE KNOW ALL ABOUT YOU.
KLUNK
THAT YOUR MASK IS SUPER-HARD.
AND THAT YOUR SUBORDINATES' *WEAK SPOTS* ARE UNDER THE MASKS.
THE SUB-ORDINATES HAVE THE SAME HARD MASKS BUT HAVE A DIFFERENT STRUCTURE.
EVEN IF IT'S STRENGTHENED AROUND THEIR EYES, THE OTHER PARTS ARE EASY TO BREAK.
!
THAT'S RIGHT!
SO KILL THE SUBORDINATES FIRST.

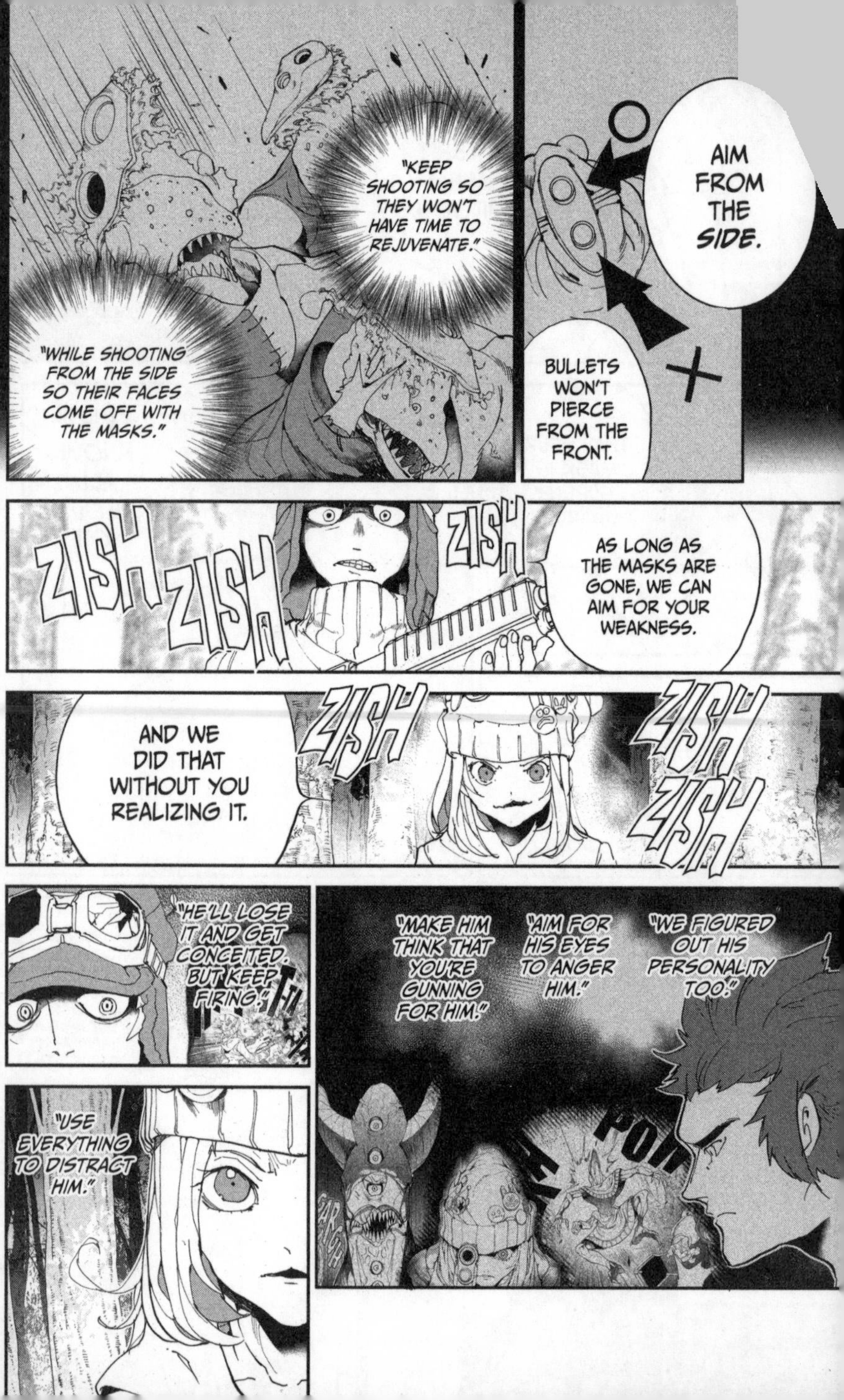
AIM FROM THE SIDE.
BULLETS WON'T PIERCE FROM THE FRONT.
"KEEP SHOOTING SO THEY WON'T HAVE TIME TO REJUVENATE."
"WHILE SHOOTING FROM THE SIDE SO THEIR FACES COME OFF WITH THE MASKS."
AS LONG AS THE MASKS ARE GONE, WE CAN AIM FOR YOUR WEAKNESS.
ZISH
ZISH
ZISH
ZISH
ZISH
ZISH
AND WE DID THAT WITHOUT YOU REALIZING IT.
"WE FIGURED OUT HIS PERSONALITY TOO."
"AIM FOR HIS EYES TO ANGER HIM."
"MAKE HIM THINK THAT YOU'RE GUNNING FOR HIM."
POW
"HE'LL LOSE IT AND GET CONCEITED. BUT KEEP FIRING."
"USE EVERYTHING TO DISTRACT HIM."

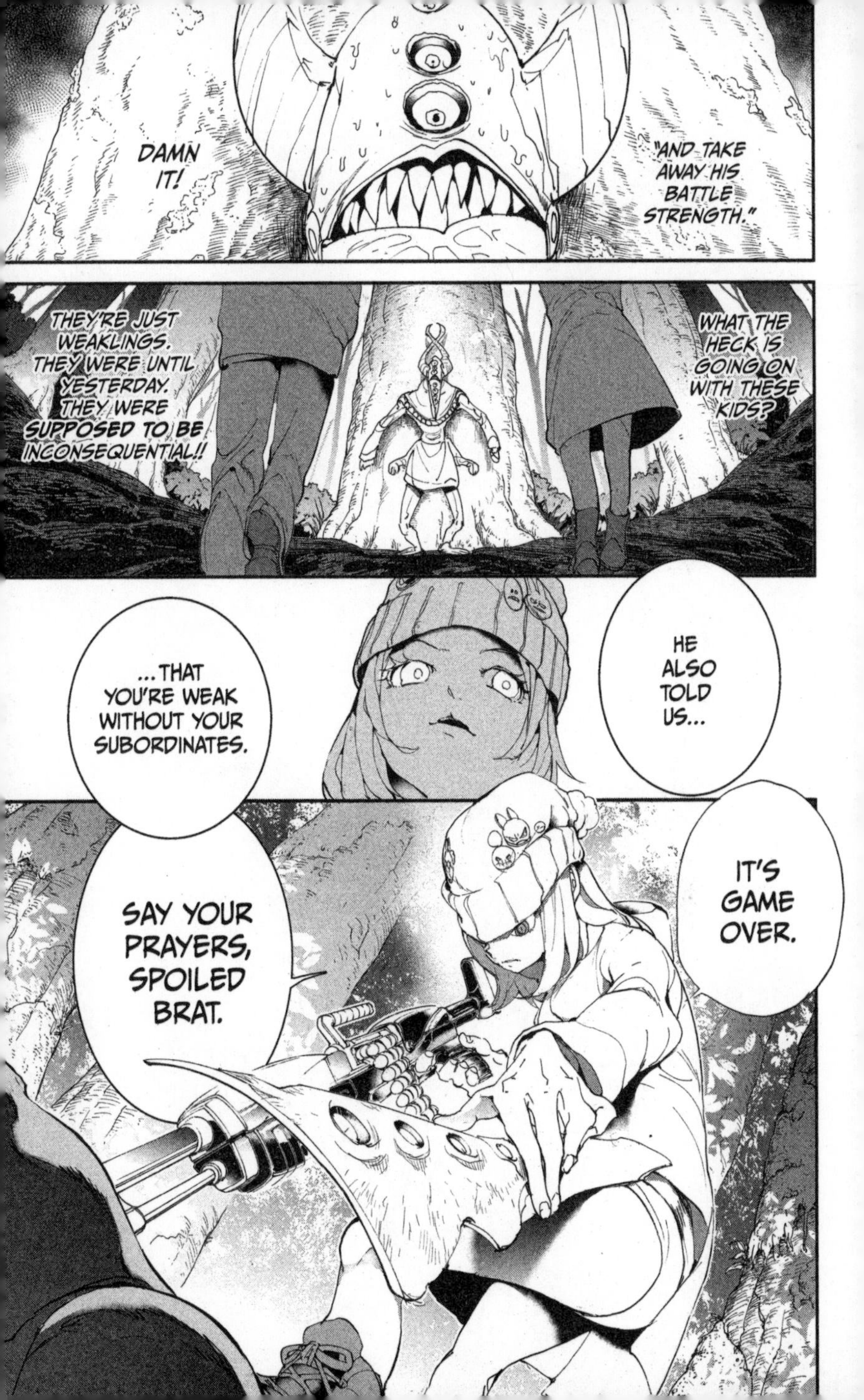
"AND TAKE AWAY HIS BATTLE STRENGTH."
DAMN IT!
WHAT THE HECK IS GOING ON WITH THESE KIDS?
THEY'RE JUST WEAKLINGS. THEY WERE UNTIL YESTERDAY. THEY WERE SUPPOSED TO BE INCONSEQUENTIAL!!
HE ALSO TOLD US...
...THAT YOU'RE WEAK WITHOUT YOUR SUBORDINATES.
IT'S GAME OVER.
SAY YOUR PRAYERS, SPOILED BRAT.

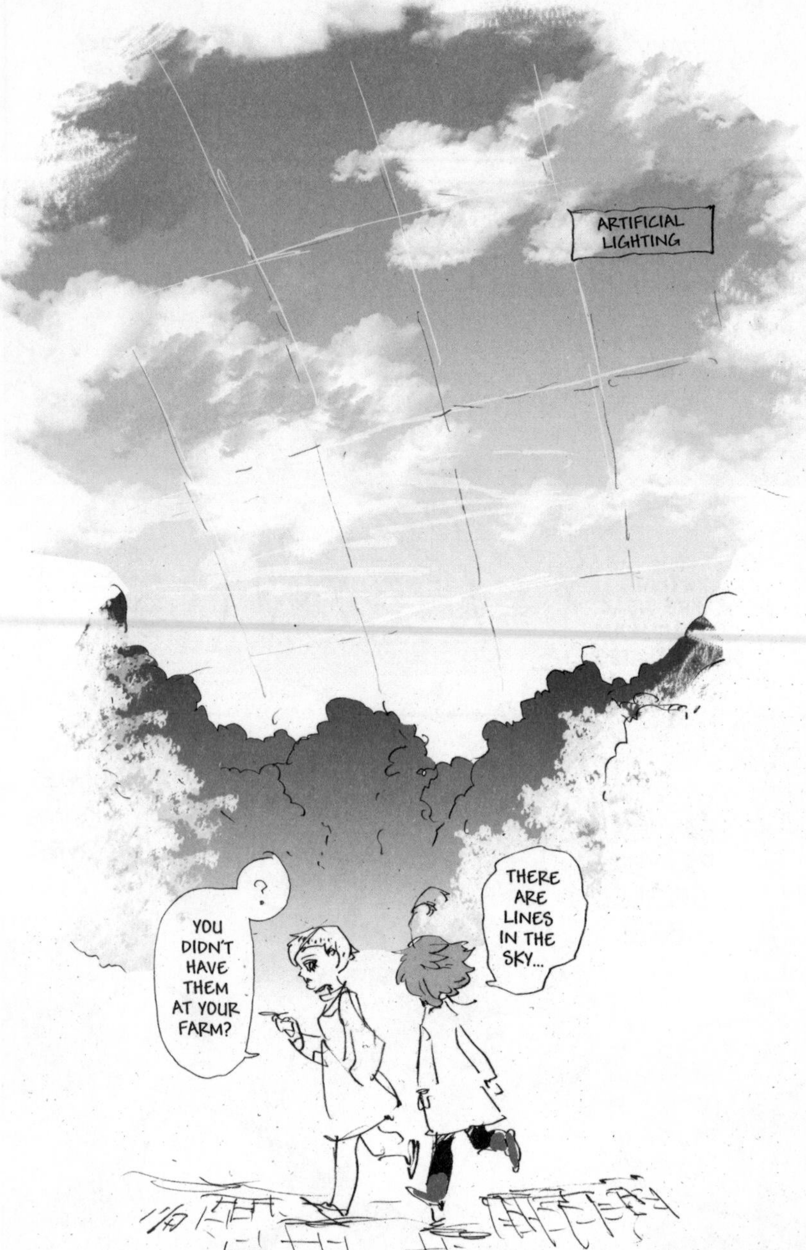
ARTIFICIAL LIGHTING
THERE ARE LINES IN THE SKY...
?
YOU DIDN'T HAVE THEM AT YOUR FARM?

CHAPTER 78: ONE DOWN

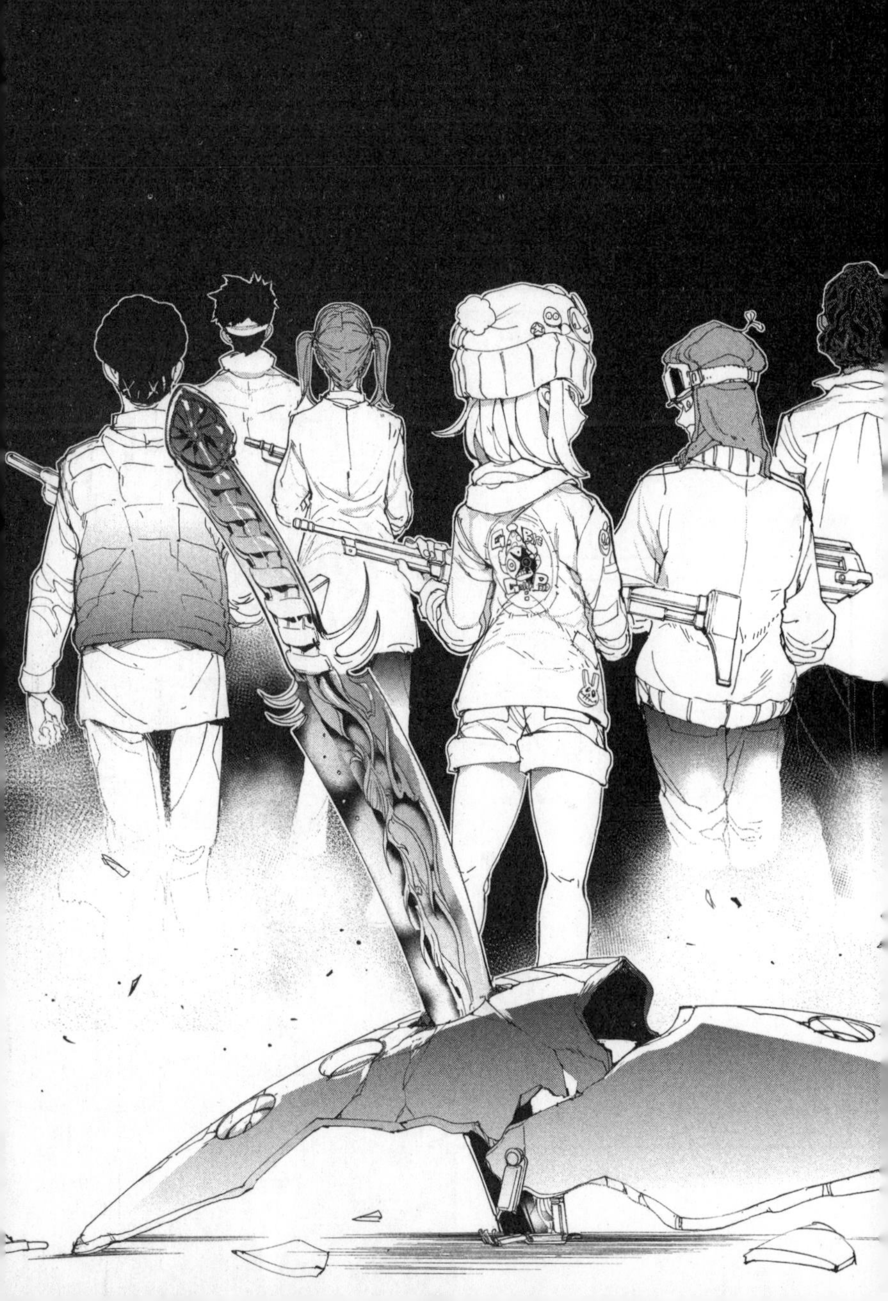

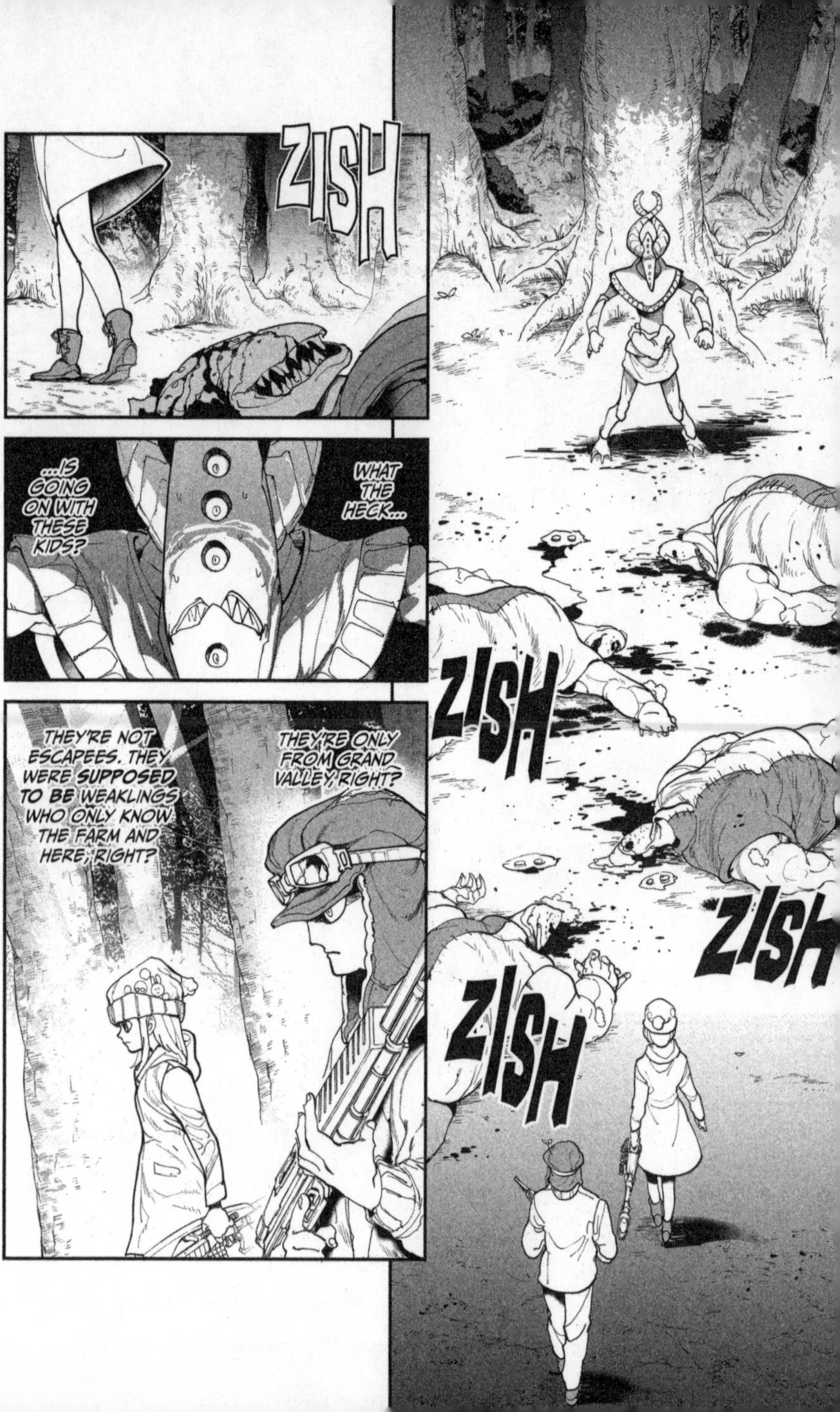
ZISH
ZISH
ZISH
ZISH
WHAT THE HECK...
...IS GOING ON WITH THESE KIDS?
THEY'RE ONLY FROM GRAND VALLEY, RIGHT?
THEY'RE NOT ESCAPEES. THEY WERE SUPPOSED TO BE WEAKLINGS WHO ONLY KNOW THE FARM AND HERE, RIGHT?

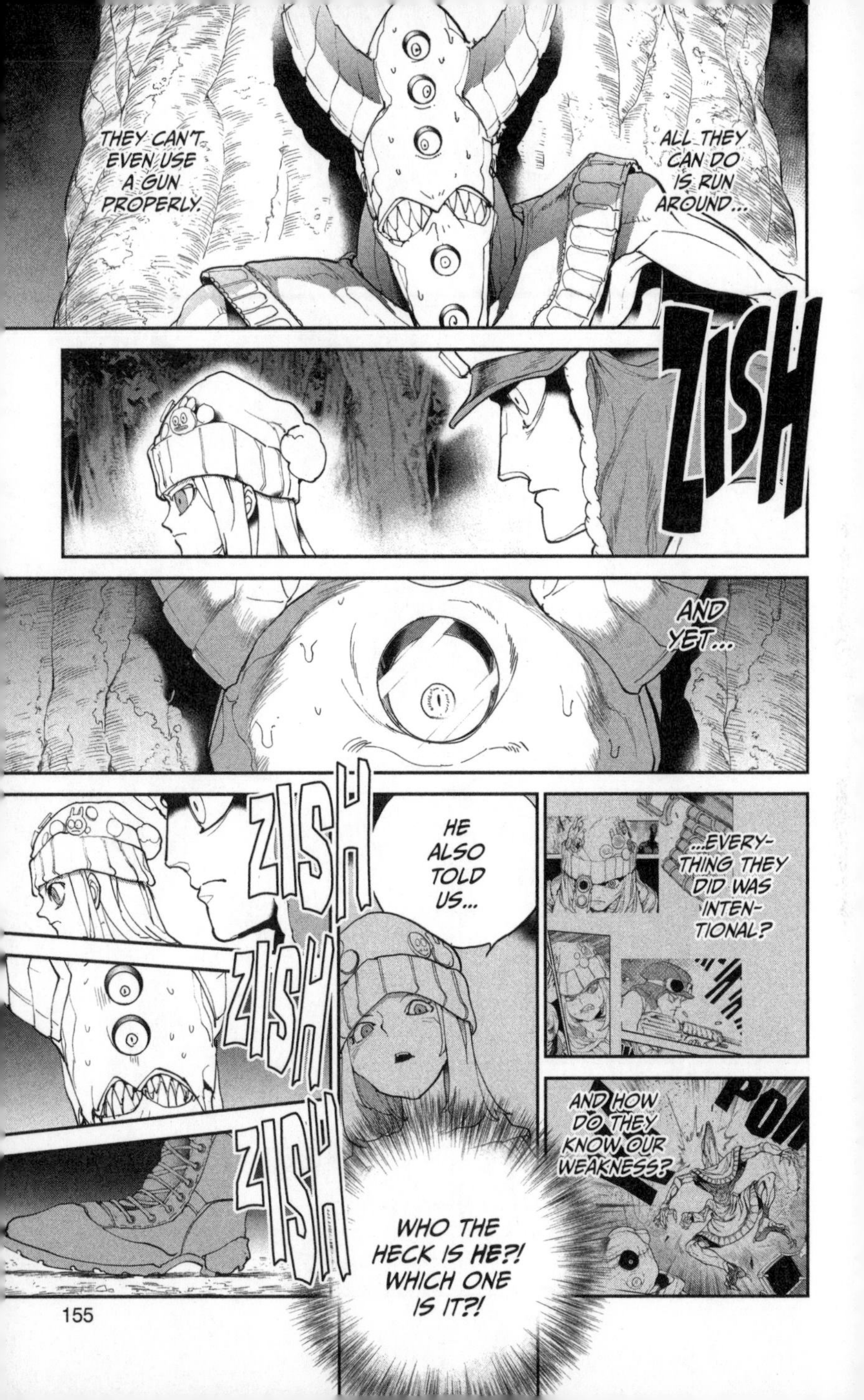
ALL THEY CAN DO IS RUN AROUND...
THEY CAN'T EVEN USE A GUN PROPERLY.
ZISH
AND YET...
...EVERYTHING THEY DID WAS INTENTIONAL?
AND HOW DO THEY KNOW OUR WEAKNESS?
POM
HE ALSO TOLD US...
ZISH
ZISH
ZISH
WHO THE HECK IS HE?! WHICH ONE IS IT?!

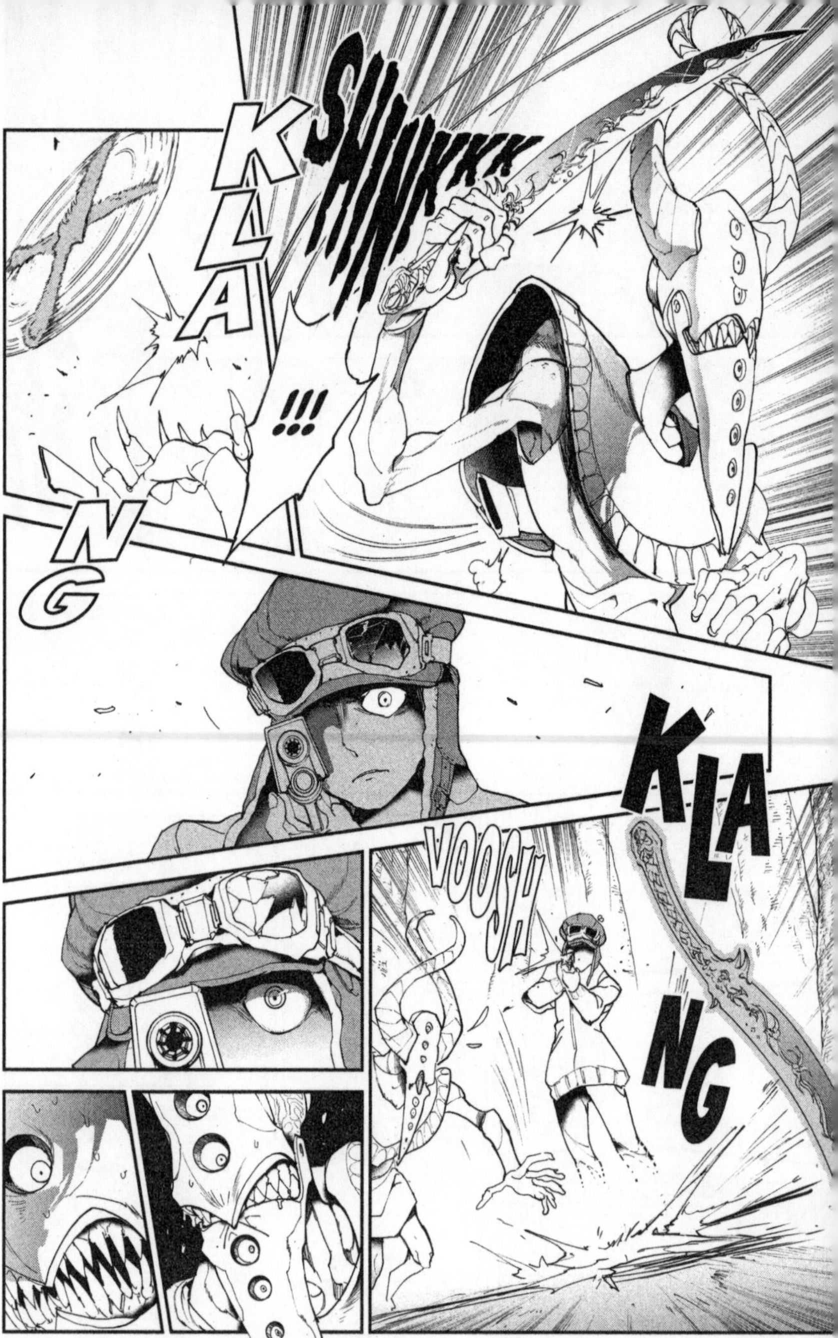
SHINKKK
KLANG
!!!
KLANG
VOOSH

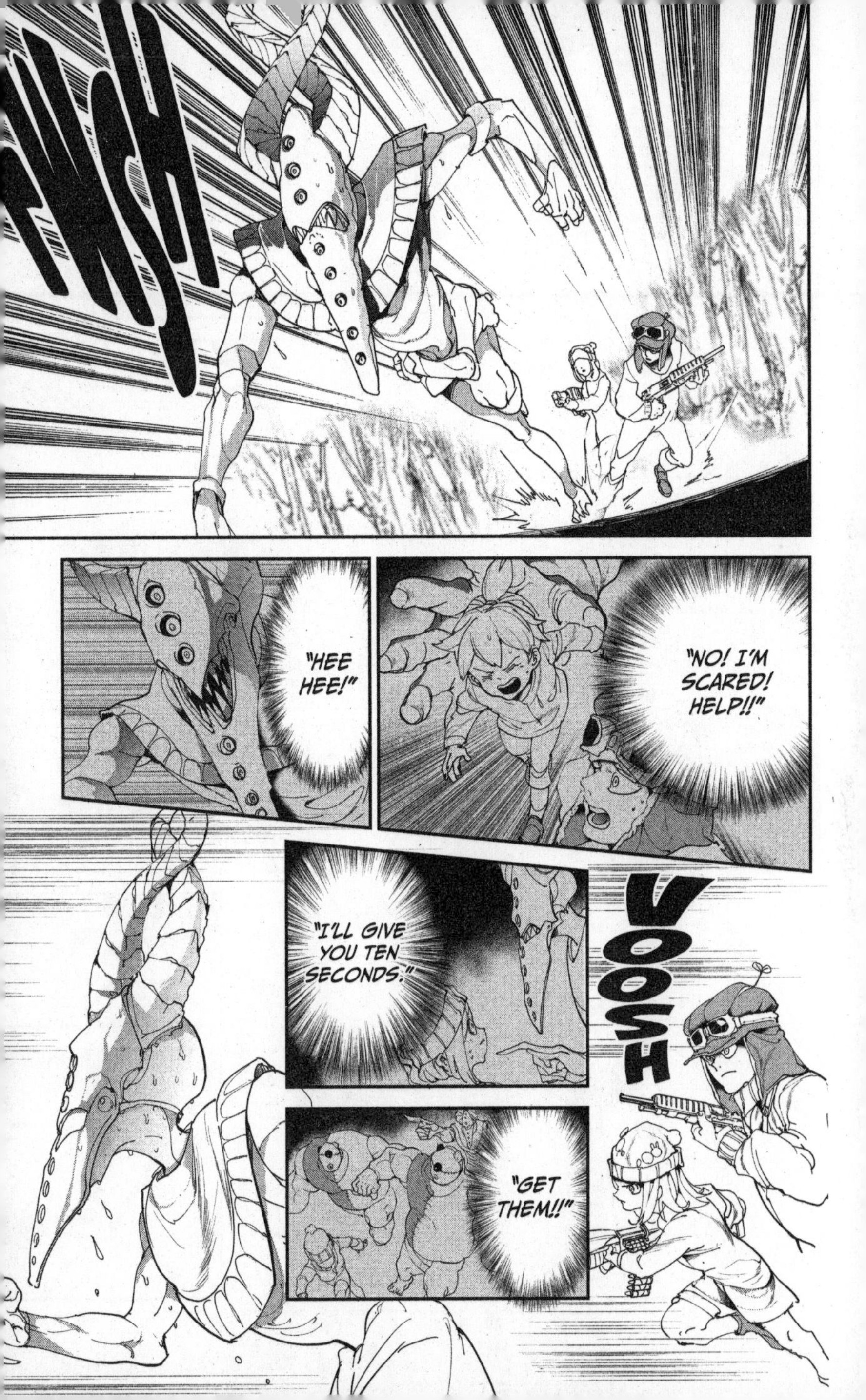
FWSH
"NO! I'M SCARED! HELP!!"
"HEE HEE!"
VOOSH
"I'LL GIVE YOU TEN SECONDS."
"GET THEM!!"

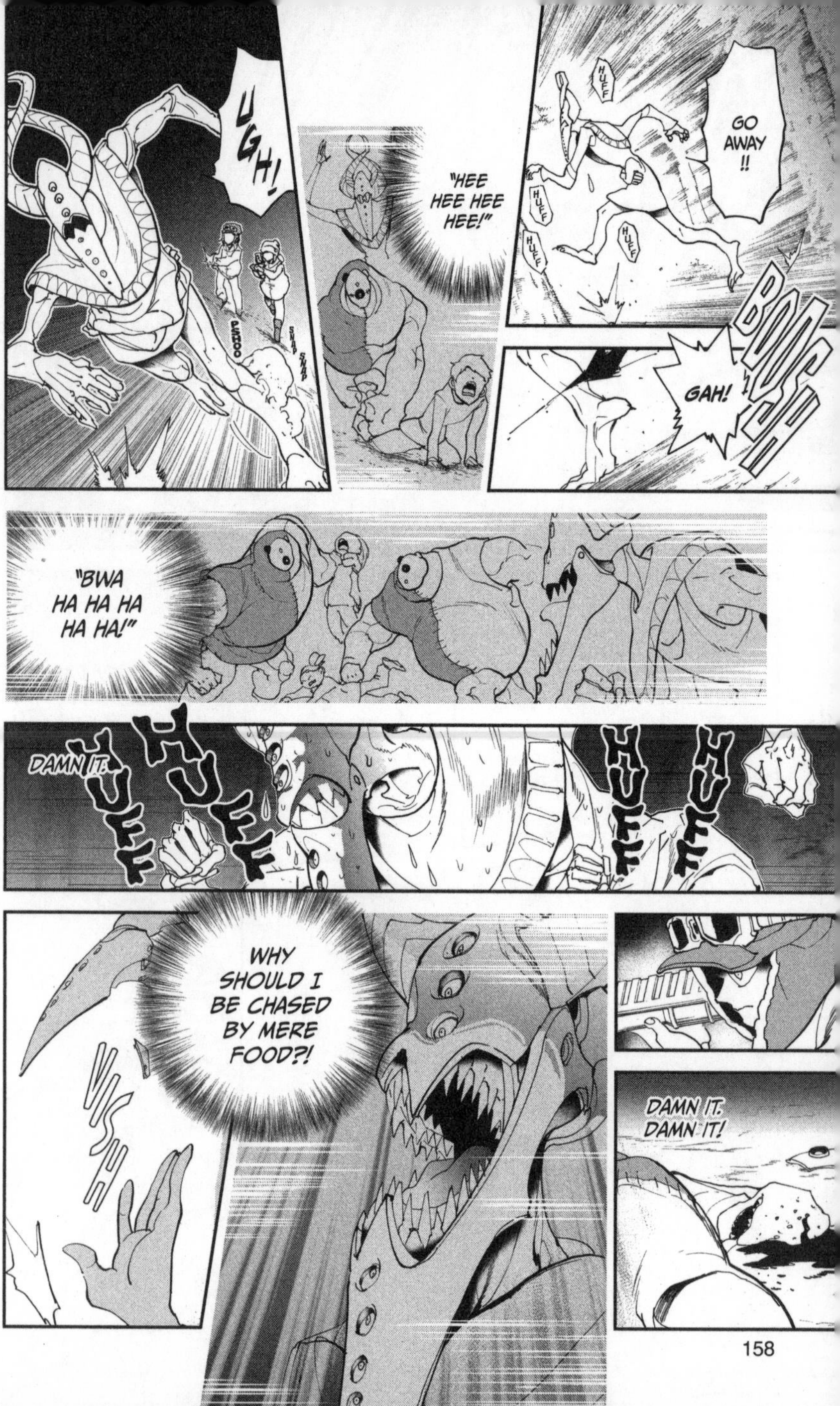
GO AWAY!!
HUFF
HUFF
HUFF
HUFF
HUFF
GAH!
BOOSH
"HEE HEE HEE HEE!"
UGH!
PSHOO
SNAP SNAP
"BWA HA HA HA HA!"
HUFF HUFF
HUFF HUFF
DAMN IT.
HUFF HUFF
DAMN IT. DAMN IT!
WHY SHOULD I BE CHASED BY MERE FOOD?!
VSHH

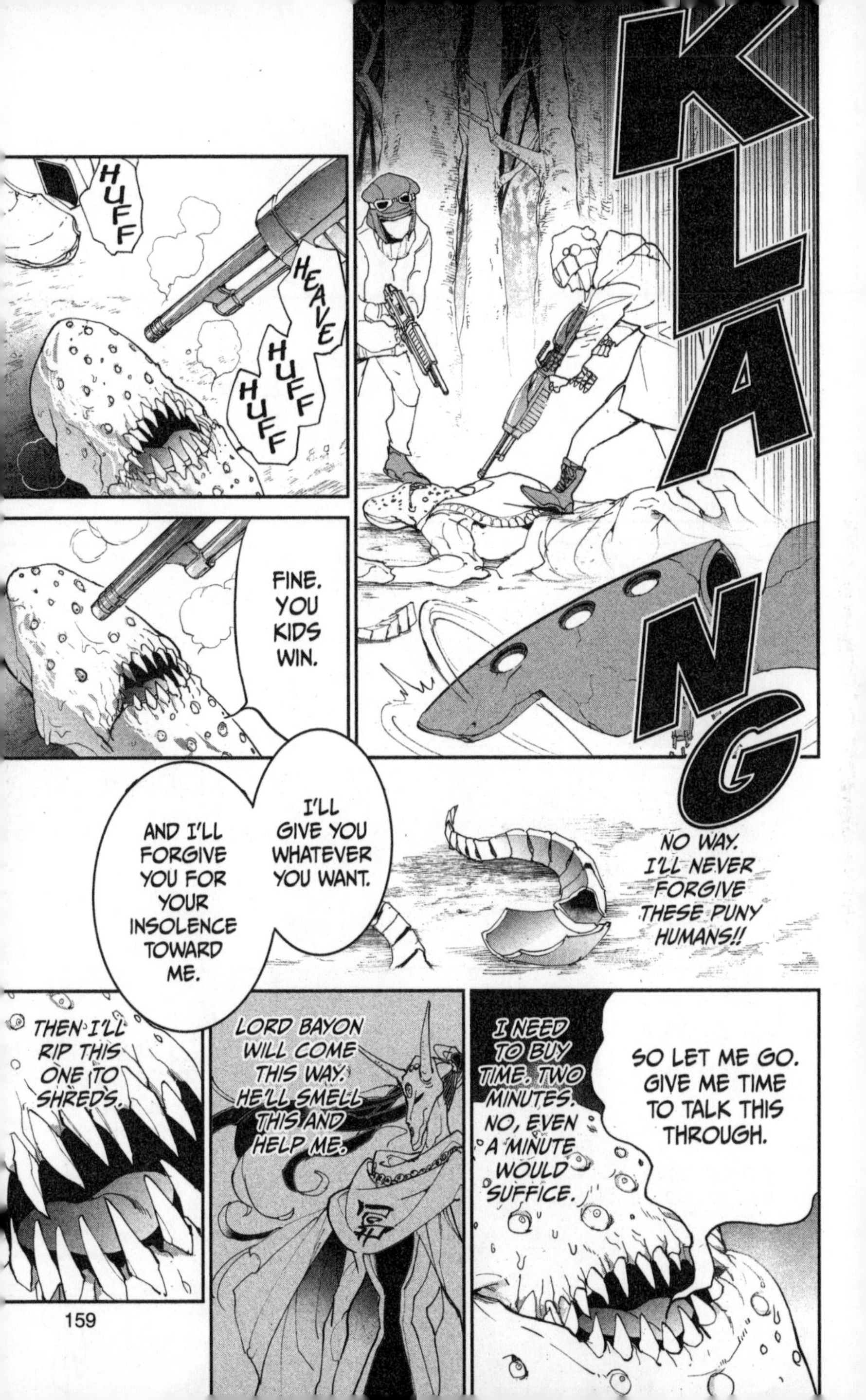
KLANG
HUFF
HEAVE
HUFF HUFF
FINE. YOU KIDS WIN.
I'LL GIVE YOU WHATEVER YOU WANT.
AND I'LL FORGIVE YOU FOR YOUR INSOLENCE TOWARD ME.
NO WAY. I'LL NEVER FORGIVE THESE PUNY HUMANS!!
SO LET ME GO. GIVE ME TIME TO TALK THIS THROUGH.
I NEED TO BUY TIME. TWO MINUTES. NO, EVEN A MINUTE WOULD SUFFICE.
LORD BAYON WILL COME THIS WAY. HE'LL SMELL THIS AND HELP ME.
THEN I'LL RIP THIS ONE TO SHREDS.

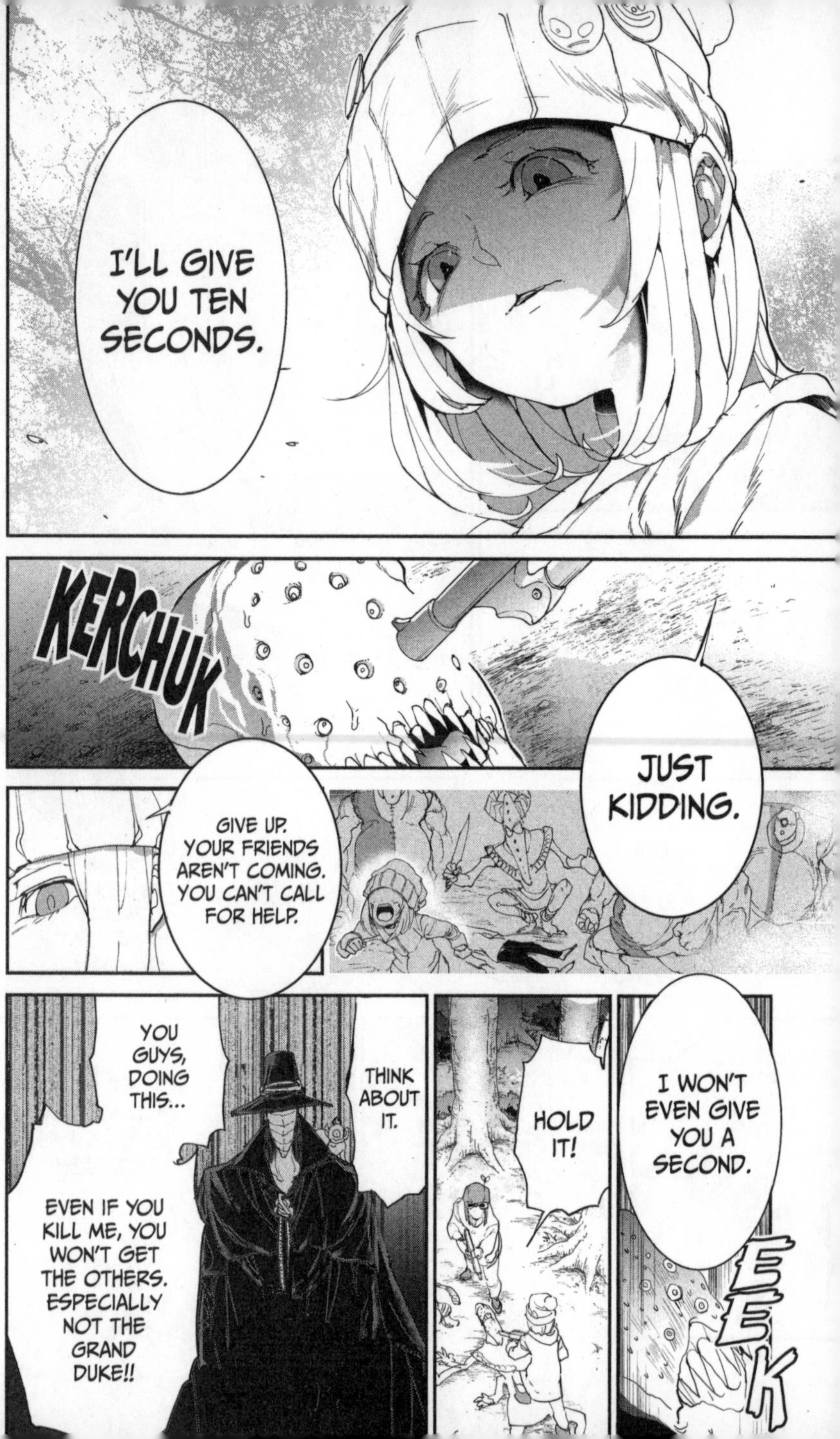
I'LL GIVE YOU TEN SECONDS.
JUST KIDDING.
KERCHUK
GIVE UP. YOUR FRIENDS AREN'T COMING. YOU CAN'T CALL FOR HELP.
I WON'T EVEN GIVE YOU A SECOND.
EEEK
HOLD IT!
YOU GUYS, DOING THIS...
THINK ABOUT IT.
EVEN IF YOU KILL ME, YOU WON'T GET THE OTHERS. ESPECIALLY NOT THE GRAND DUKE!!

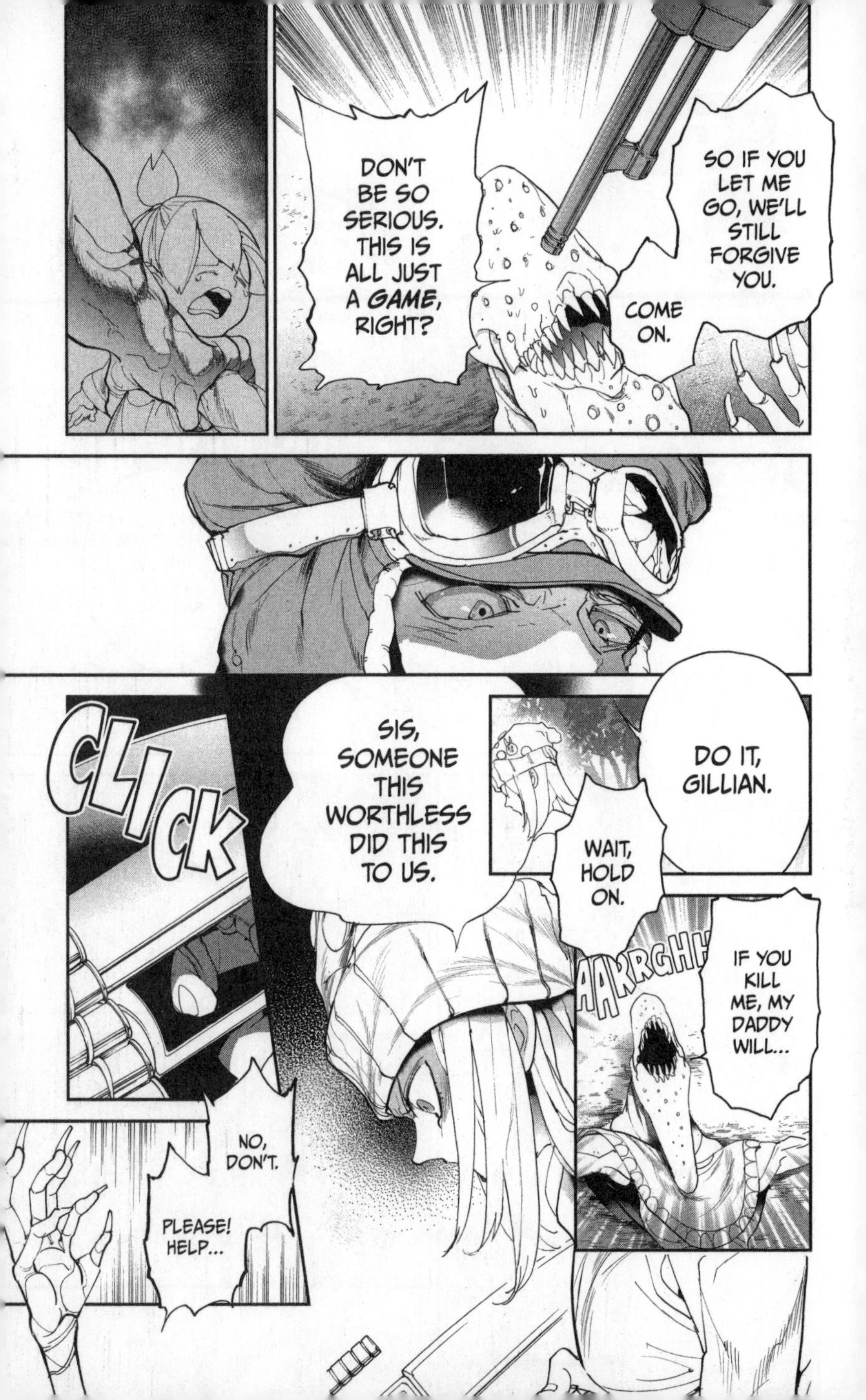
SO IF YOU LET ME GO, WE'LL STILL FORGIVE YOU.
COME ON.
DON'T BE SO SERIOUS. THIS IS ALL JUST A *GAME*, RIGHT?
DO IT, GILLIAN.
WAIT, HOLD ON.
SIS, SOMEONE THIS WORTHLESS DID THIS TO US.
CLICK
IF YOU KILL ME, MY DADDY WILL...
AARRGHH
NO, DON'T.
PLEASE! HELP...

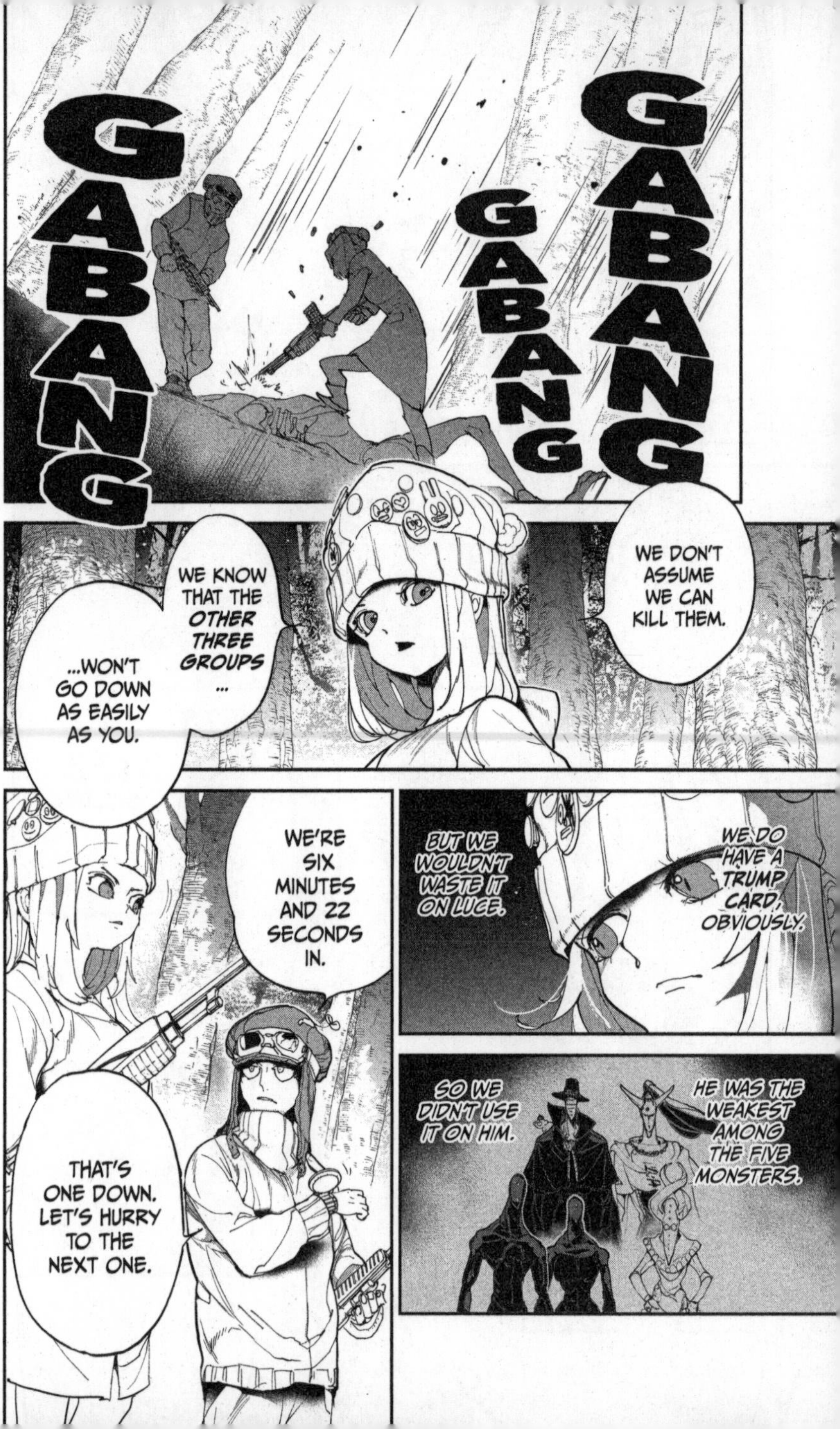
GABANG
GABANG
GABANG
WE DON'T ASSUME WE CAN KILL THEM.
WE KNOW THAT THE *OTHER THREE GROUPS* ...
...WON'T GO DOWN AS EASILY AS YOU.
WE DO HAVE A TRUMP CARD, OBVIOUSLY.
BUT WE WOULDN'T WASTE IT ON LUCE.
HE WAS THE WEAKEST AMONG THE FIVE MONSTERS.
SO WE DIDN'T USE IT ON HIM.
WE'RE SIX MINUTES AND 22 SECONDS IN.
THAT'S ONE DOWN. LET'S HURRY TO THE NEXT ONE.

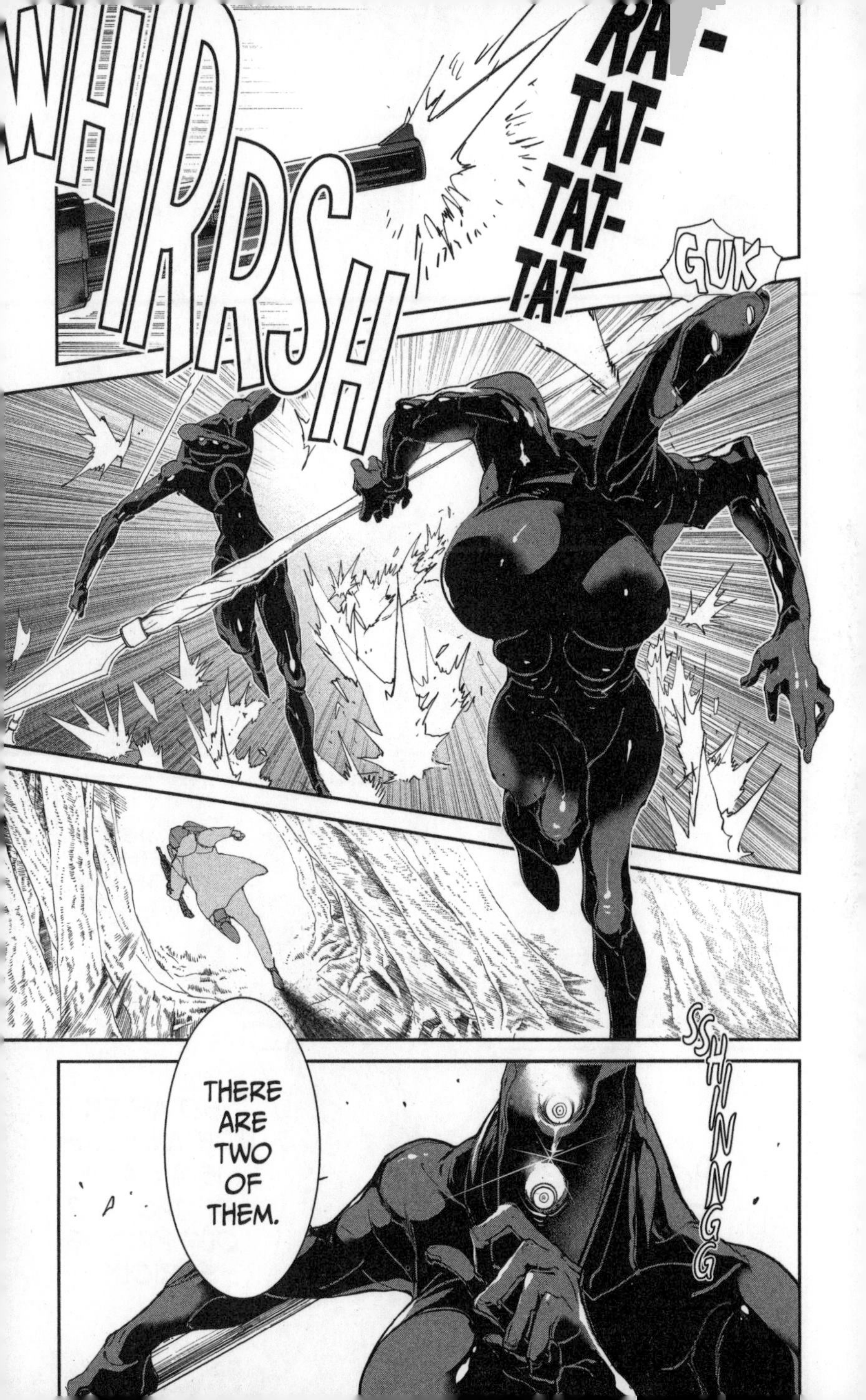
RA-TAT-TAT-TAT-TAT
GUK
WHIRRSH
SSHINNGG
THERE ARE TWO OF THEM.

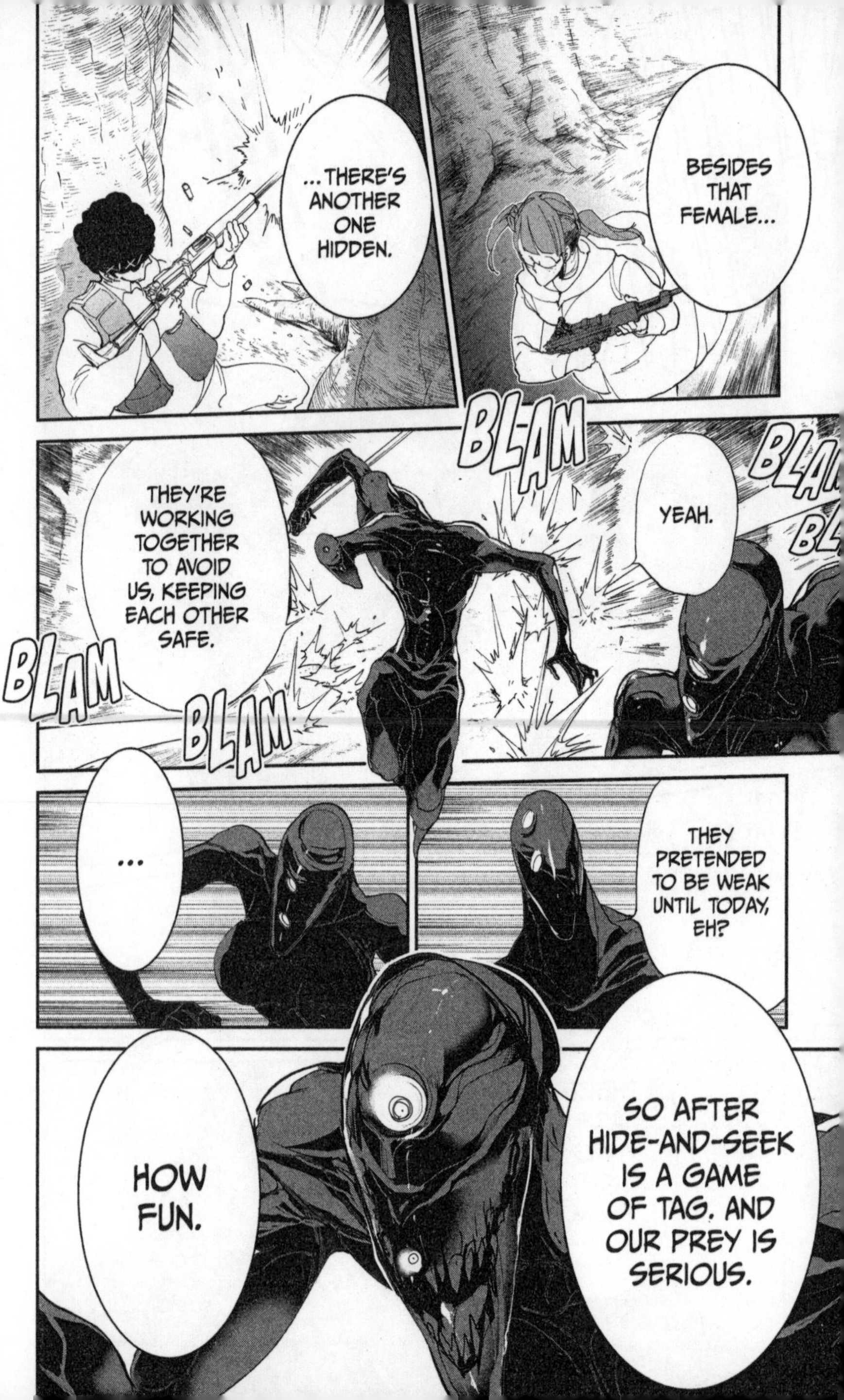
BESIDES THAT FEMALE...
...THERE'S ANOTHER ONE HIDDEN.
BLAM
YEAH.
THEY'RE WORKING TOGETHER TO AVOID US, KEEPING EACH OTHER SAFE.
BLAM
BLAM
THEY PRETENDED TO BE WEAK UNTIL TODAY, EH?
...
SO AFTER HIDE-AND-SEEK IS A GAME OF TAG. AND OUR PREY IS SERIOUS.
HOW FUN.

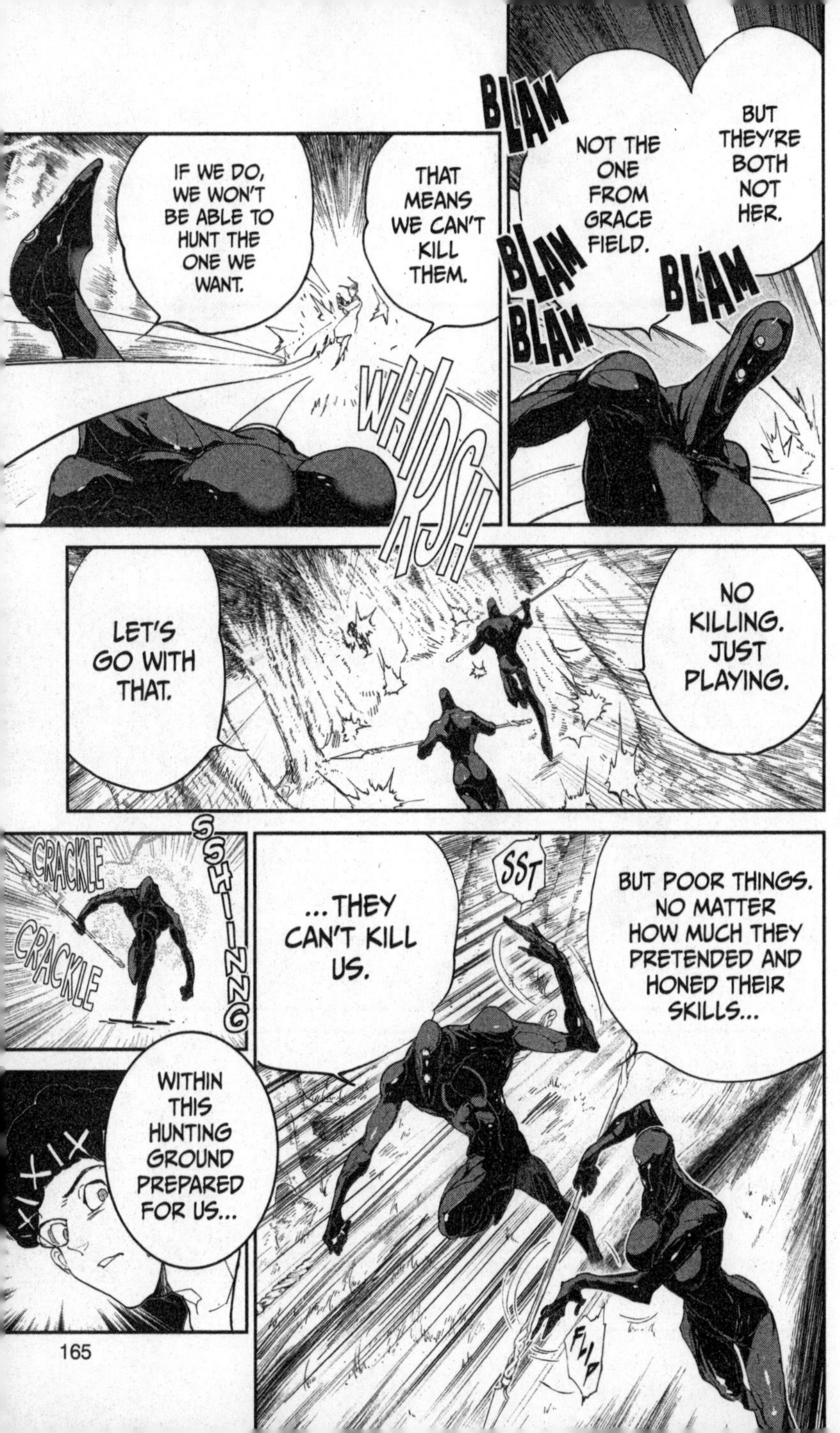
BLAM
NOT THE ONE FROM GRACE FIELD.
BUT THEY'RE BOTH NOT HER.
BLAM
BLAM
BLAM
THAT MEANS WE CAN'T KILL THEM.
IF WE DO, WE WON'T BE ABLE TO HUNT THE ONE WE WANT.
NO KILLING. JUST PLAYING.
LET'S GO WITH THAT.
BUT POOR THINGS. NO MATTER HOW MUCH THEY PRETENDED AND HONED THEIR SKILLS...
SST
...THEY CAN'T KILL US.
FLIP
SSHIIINNG
CRACKLE
CRACKLE
WITHIN THIS HUNTING GROUND PREPARED FOR US...

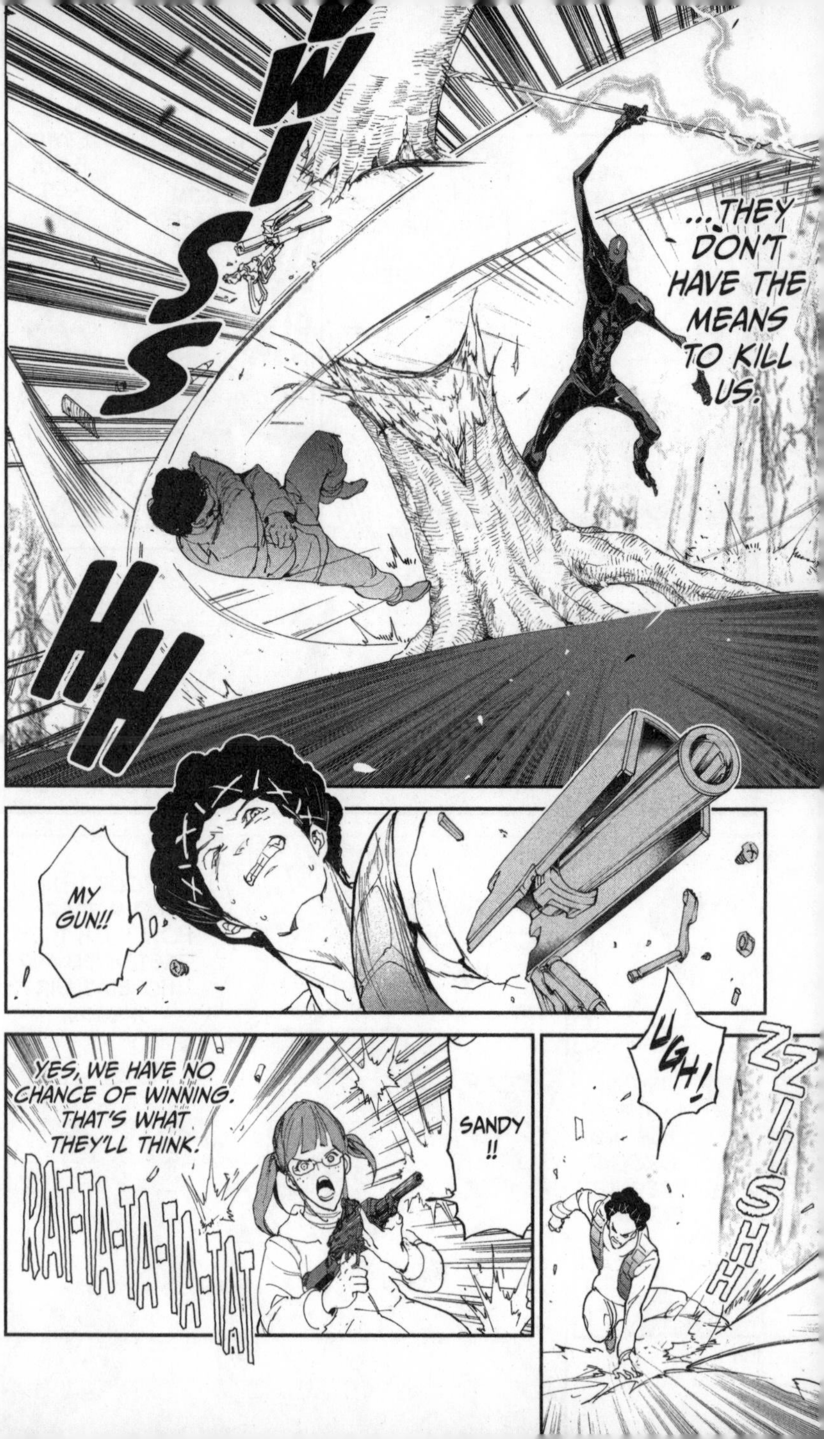
...THEY DON'T HAVE THE MEANS TO KILL US.
WHISSSHH
MY GUN!!
UGH!
ZZIIISHH
SANDY!!
YES, WE HAVE NO CHANCE OF WINNING. THAT'S WHAT THEY'LL THINK.
RAT-TA-TA-TA-TAT

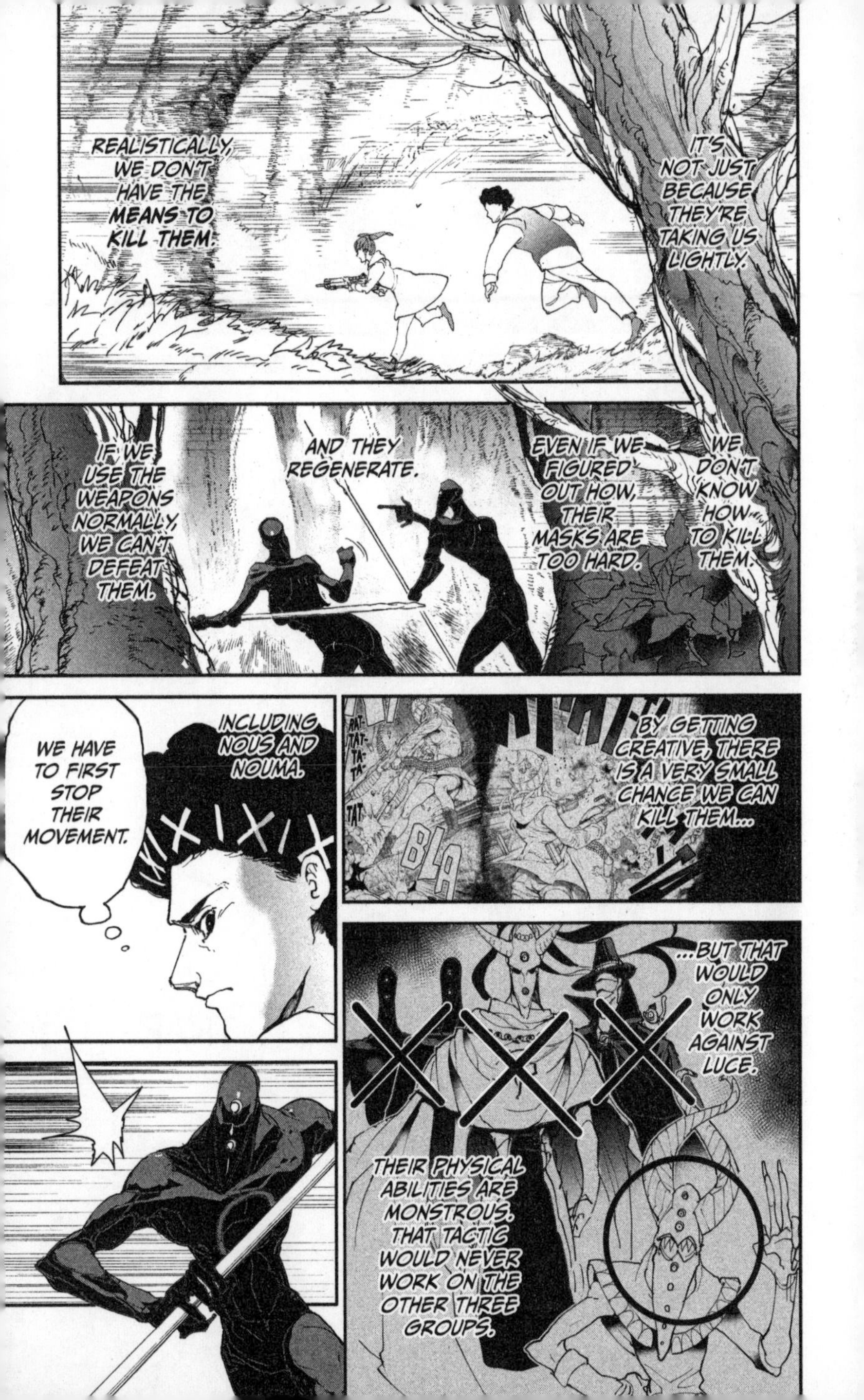
IT'S NOT JUST BECAUSE THEY'RE TAKING US LIGHTLY.
REALISTICALLY, WE DON'T HAVE THE MEANS TO KILL THEM.
WE DON'T KNOW HOW TO KILL THEM.
EVEN IF WE FIGURED OUT HOW, THEIR MASKS ARE TOO HARD.
AND THEY REGENERATE.
IF WE USE THE WEAPONS NORMALLY, WE CAN'T DEFEAT THEM.
BY GETTING CREATIVE, THERE IS A VERY SMALL CHANCE WE CAN KILL THEM...
RAT-TAT-TA-TA-TAT
BLA
...BUT THAT WOULD ONLY WORK AGAINST LUCE.
THEIR PHYSICAL ABILITIES ARE MONSTROUS. THAT TACTIC WOULD NEVER WORK ON THE OTHER THREE GROUPS.
INCLUDING NOUS AND NOUMA.
WE HAVE TO FIRST STOP THEIR MOVEMENT.

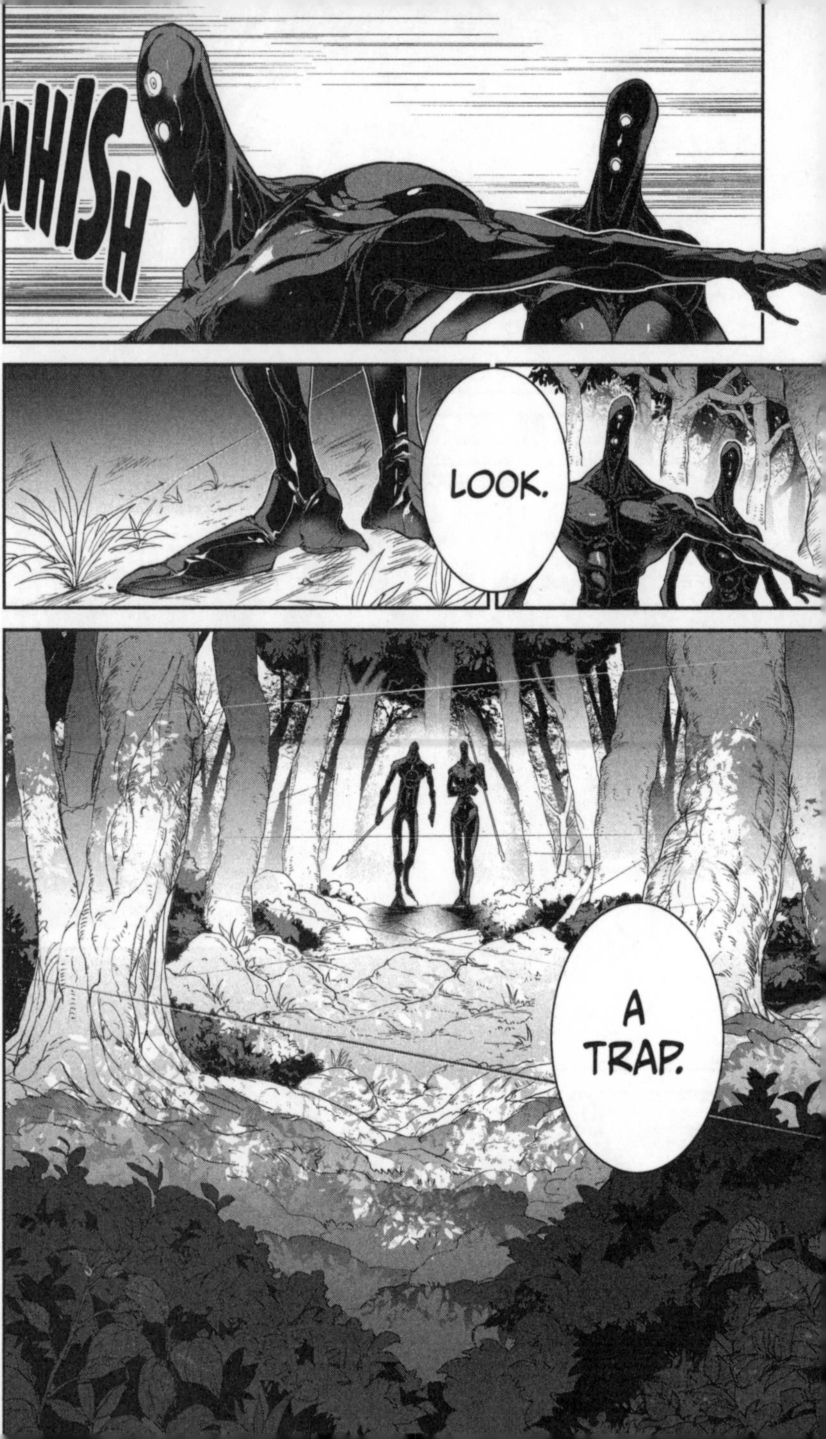
WHISH
LOOK.
A TRAP.

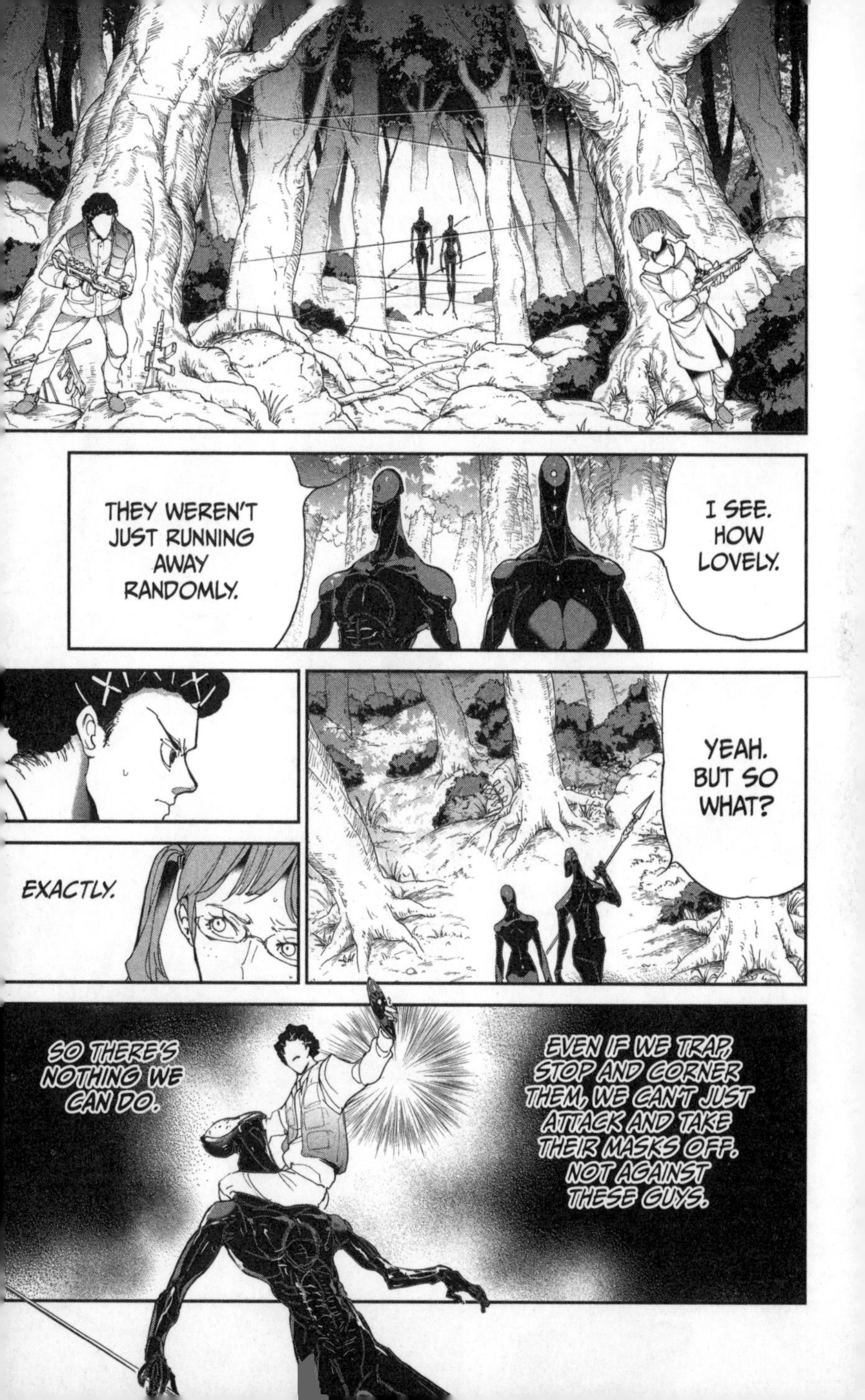
I SEE. HOW LOVELY.
THEY WEREN'T JUST RUNNING AWAY RANDOMLY.
YEAH. BUT SO WHAT?
EXACTLY.
EVEN IF WE TRAP, STOP AND CORNER THEM, WE CAN'T JUST ATTACK AND TAKE THEIR MASKS OFF. NOT AGAINST THESE GUYS.
SO THERE'S NOTHING WE CAN DO.

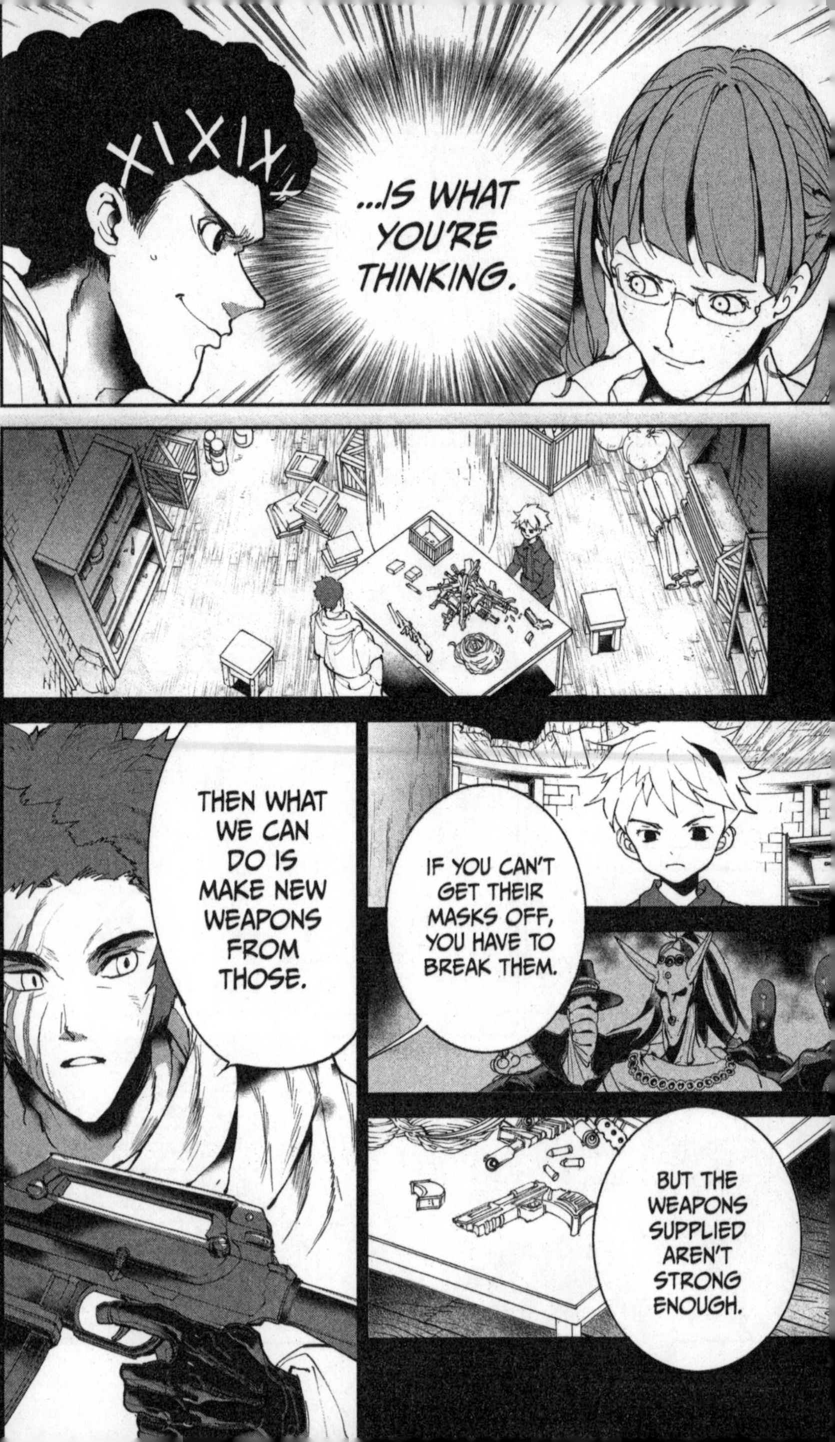
...IS WHAT YOU'RE THINKING.
IF YOU CAN'T GET THEIR MASKS OFF, YOU HAVE TO BREAK THEM.
BUT THE WEAPONS SUPPLIED AREN'T STRONG ENOUGH.
THEN WHAT WE CAN DO IS MAKE NEW WEAPONS FROM THOSE.

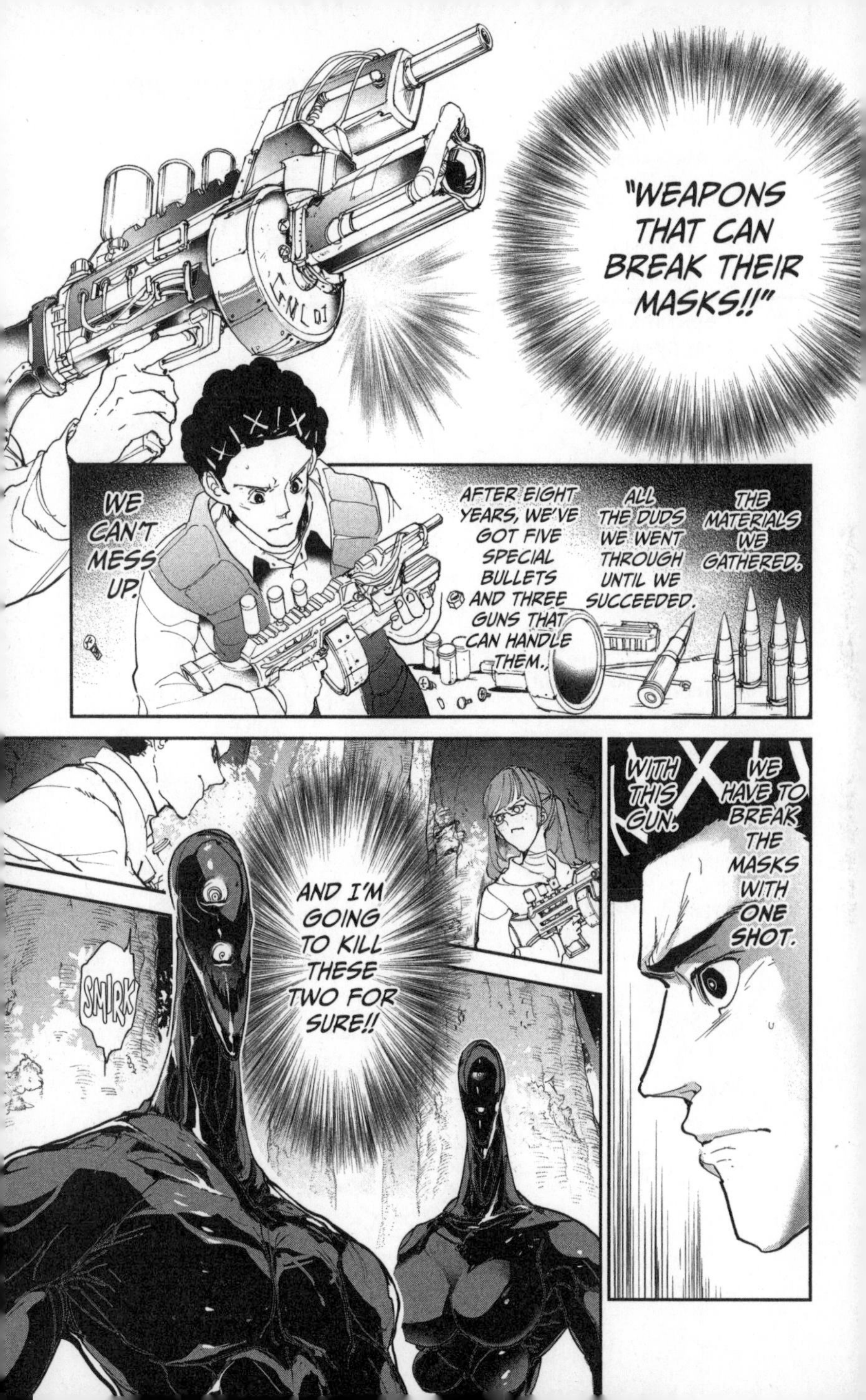
"WEAPONS THAT CAN BREAK THEIR MASKS!!"
THE MATERIALS WE GATHERED.
ALL THE DUDS WE WENT THROUGH UNTIL WE SUCCEEDED.
AFTER EIGHT YEARS, WE'VE GOT FIVE SPECIAL BULLETS AND THREE GUNS THAT CAN HANDLE THEM.
WE CAN'T MESS UP.
WE HAVE TO BREAK THE MASKS WITH ONE SHOT.
WITH THIS GUN.
AND I'M GOING TO KILL THESE TWO FOR SURE!!
SMIRK

A SPECIAL EXTRA CHAPTER 2

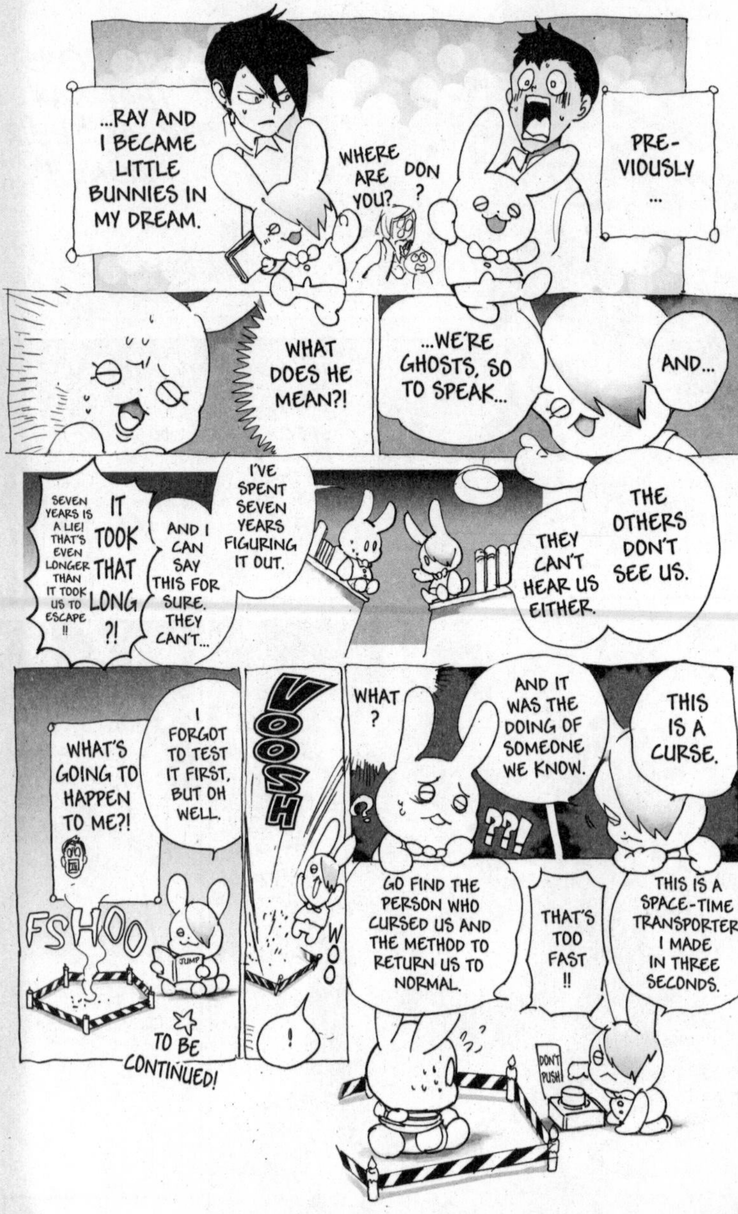

PRE-VIOUSLY ...
WHERE ARE YOU? DON?
...RAY AND I BECAME LITTLE BUNNIES IN MY DREAM.
AND...
...WE'RE GHOSTS, SO TO SPEAK...
WHAT DOES HE MEAN?!
THE OTHERS DON'T SEE US.
THEY CAN'T HEAR US EITHER.
I'VE SPENT SEVEN YEARS FIGURING IT OUT.
AND I CAN SAY THIS FOR SURE. THEY CAN'T...
IT TOOK THAT LONG?!
SEVEN YEARS IS A LIE! THAT'S EVEN LONGER THAN IT TOOK US TO ESCAPE!!
THIS IS A CURSE.
AND IT WAS THE DOING OF SOMEONE WE KNOW.
WHAT?
??!
THIS IS A SPACE-TIME TRANSPORTER I MADE IN THREE SECONDS.
THAT'S TOO FAST!!
GO FIND THE PERSON WHO CURSED US AND THE METHOD TO RETURN US TO NORMAL.
DON'T PUSH!
!
VOOSH
WOO
I FORGOT TO TEST IT FIRST, BUT OH WELL.
WHAT'S GOING TO HAPPEN TO ME?!
FSHOO
JUMP
TO BE CONTINUED!

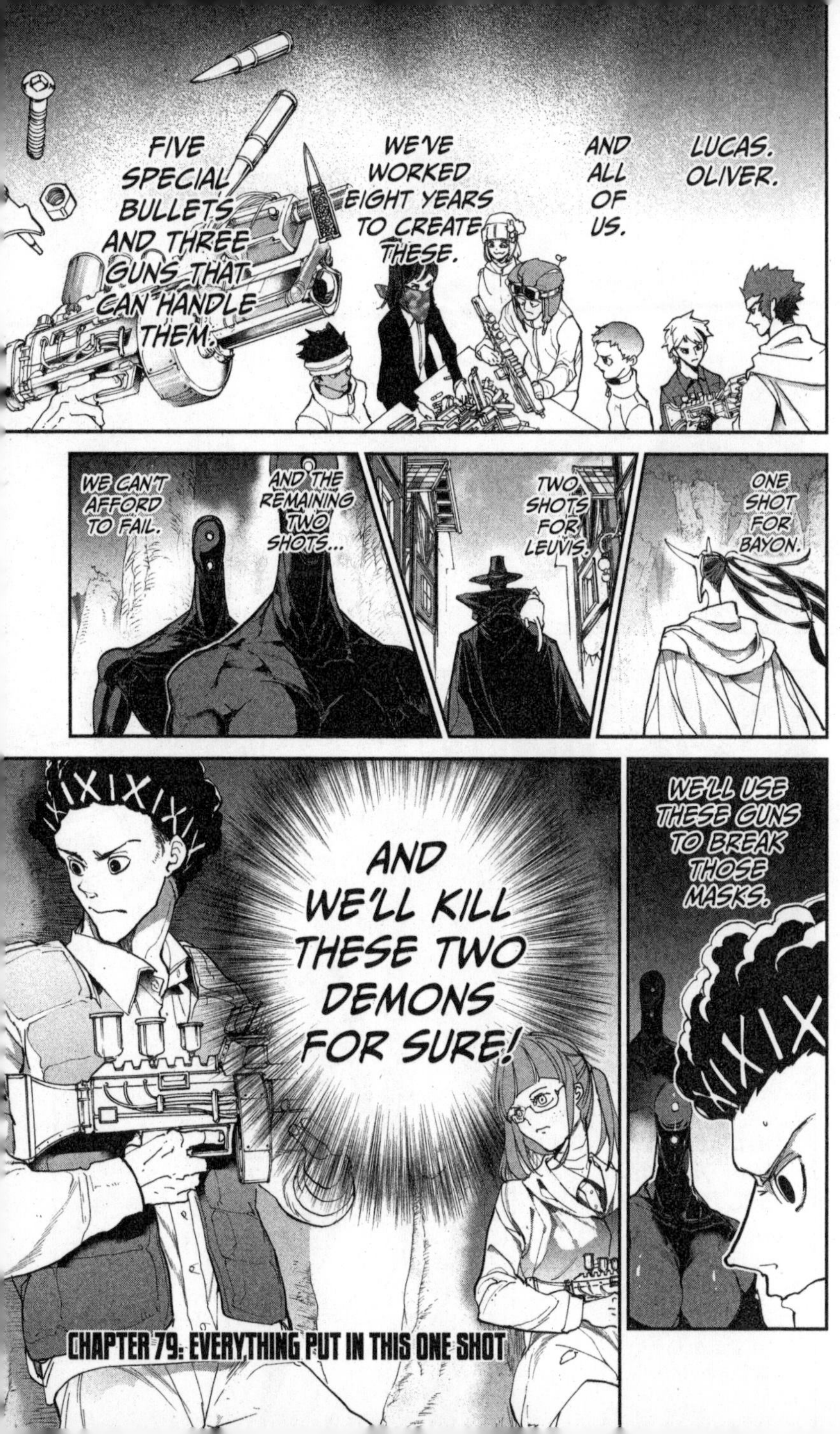
LUCAS. OLIVER.
AND ALL OF US.
WE'VE WORKED EIGHT YEARS TO CREATE THESE.
FIVE SPECIAL BULLETS AND THREE GUNS THAT CAN HANDLE THEM.
ONE SHOT FOR BAYON.
TWO SHOTS FOR LEUVIS.
AND THE REMAINING TWO SHOTS...
WE CAN'T AFFORD TO FAIL.
WE'LL USE THESE GUNS TO BREAK THOSE MASKS.
AND WE'LL KILL THESE TWO DEMONS FOR SURE!
CHAPTER 79: EVERYTHING PUT IN THIS ONE SHOT

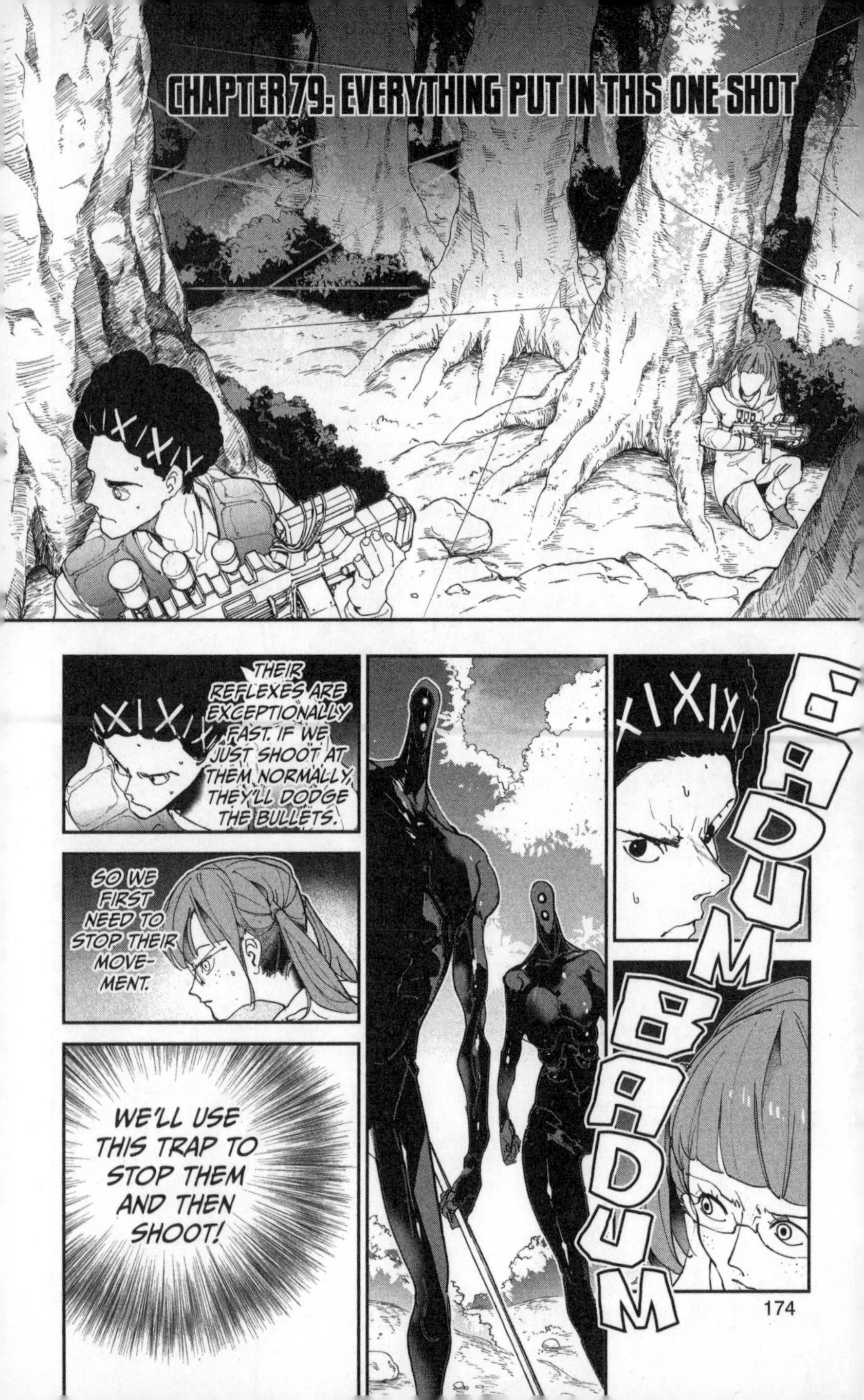
CHAPTER 79: EVERYTHING PUT IN THIS ONE SHOT
BADUM
BADUM
THEIR REFLEXES ARE EXCEPTIONALLY FAST. IF WE JUST SHOOT AT THEM NORMALLY, THEY'LL DODGE THE BULLETS.
SO WE FIRST NEED TO STOP THEIR MOVE-MENT.
WE'LL USE THIS TRAP TO STOP THEM AND THEN SHOOT!

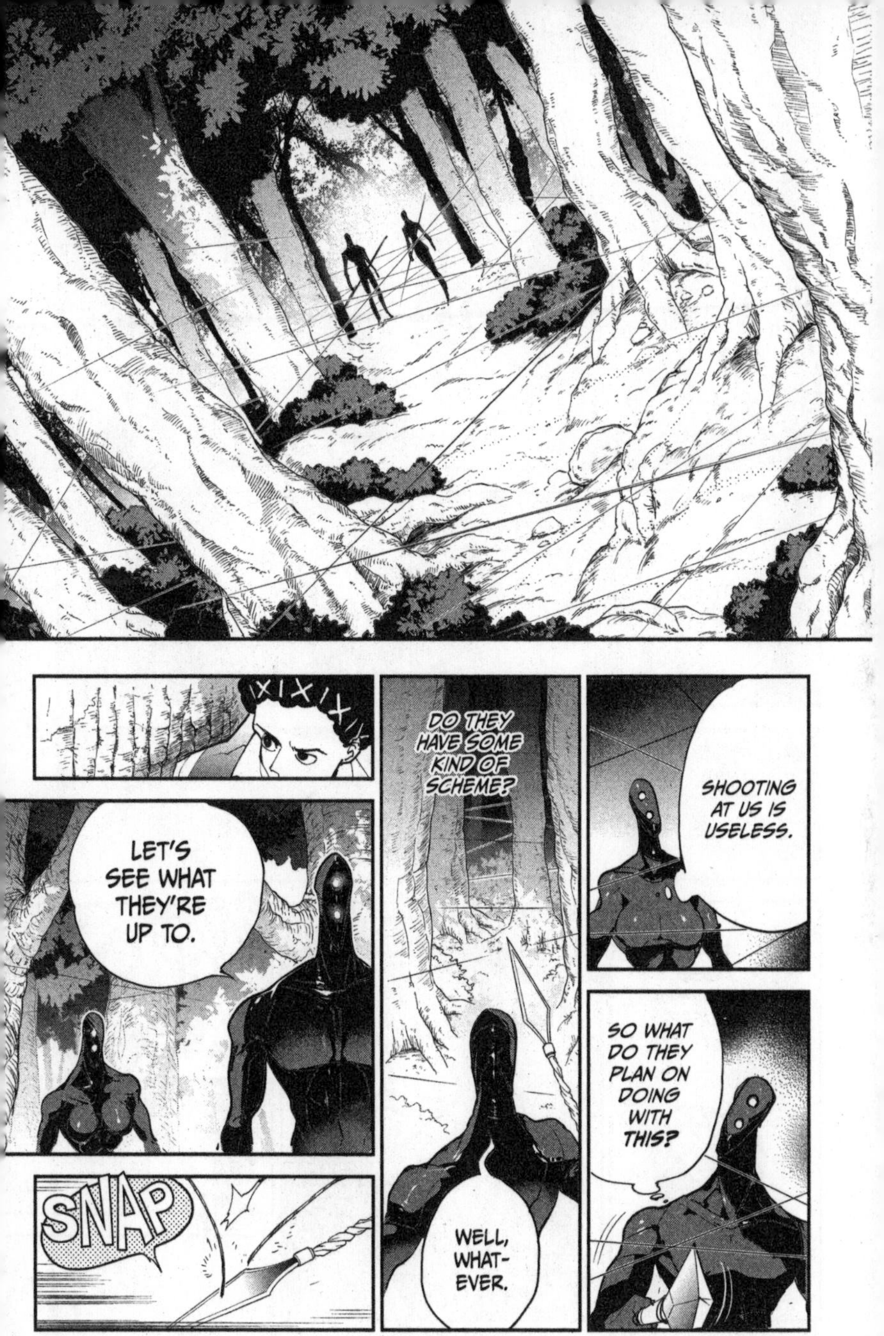
SHOOTING AT US IS USELESS.
SO WHAT DO THEY PLAN ON DOING WITH THIS?
DO THEY HAVE SOME KIND OF SCHEME?
WELL, WHATEVER.
LET'S SEE WHAT THEY'RE UP TO.
SNAP

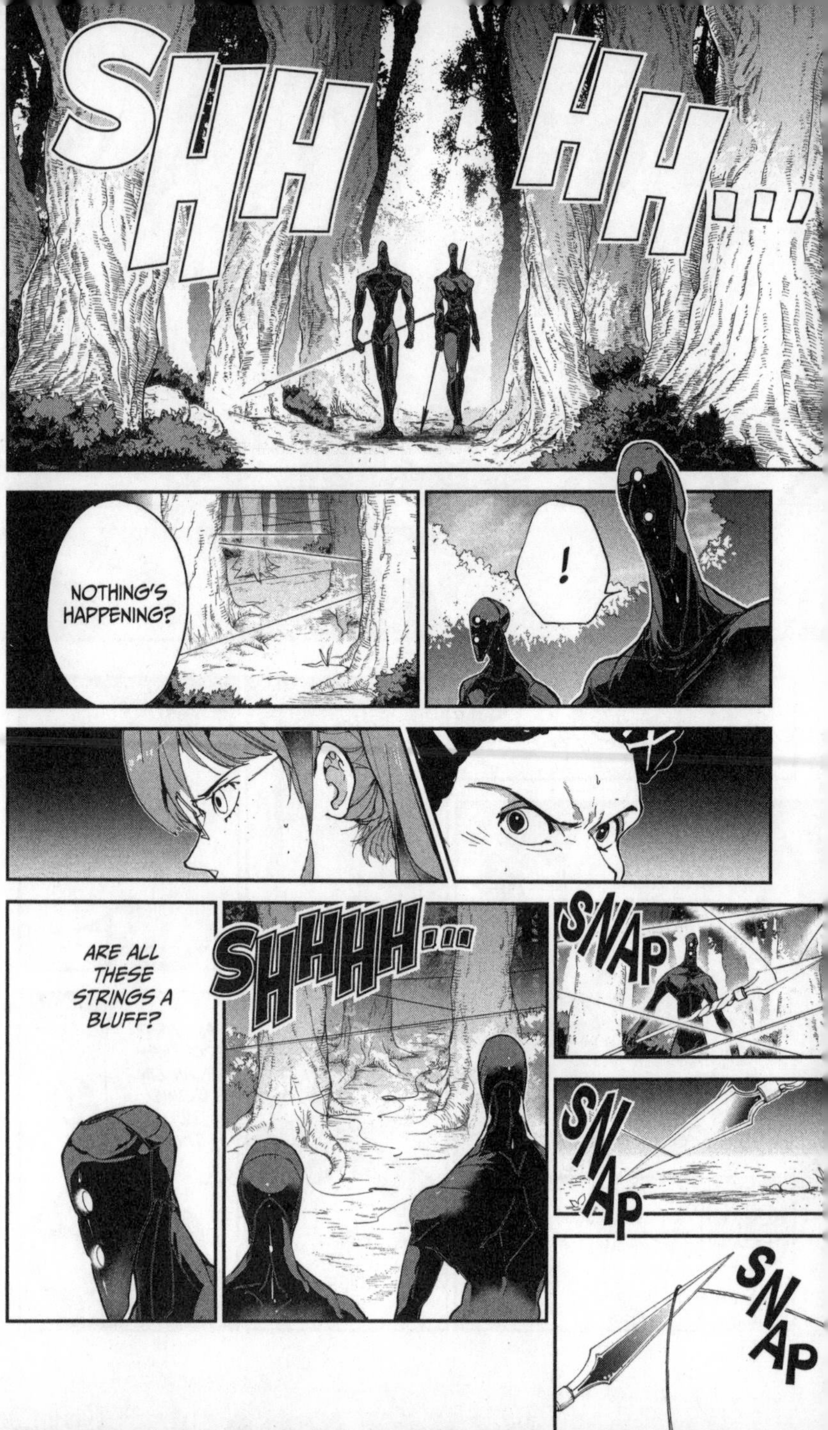
SHH HH...
!
NOTHING'S HAPPENING?
SNAP
SNAP
SNAP
SHHHH...
ARE ALL THESE STRINGS A BLUFF?

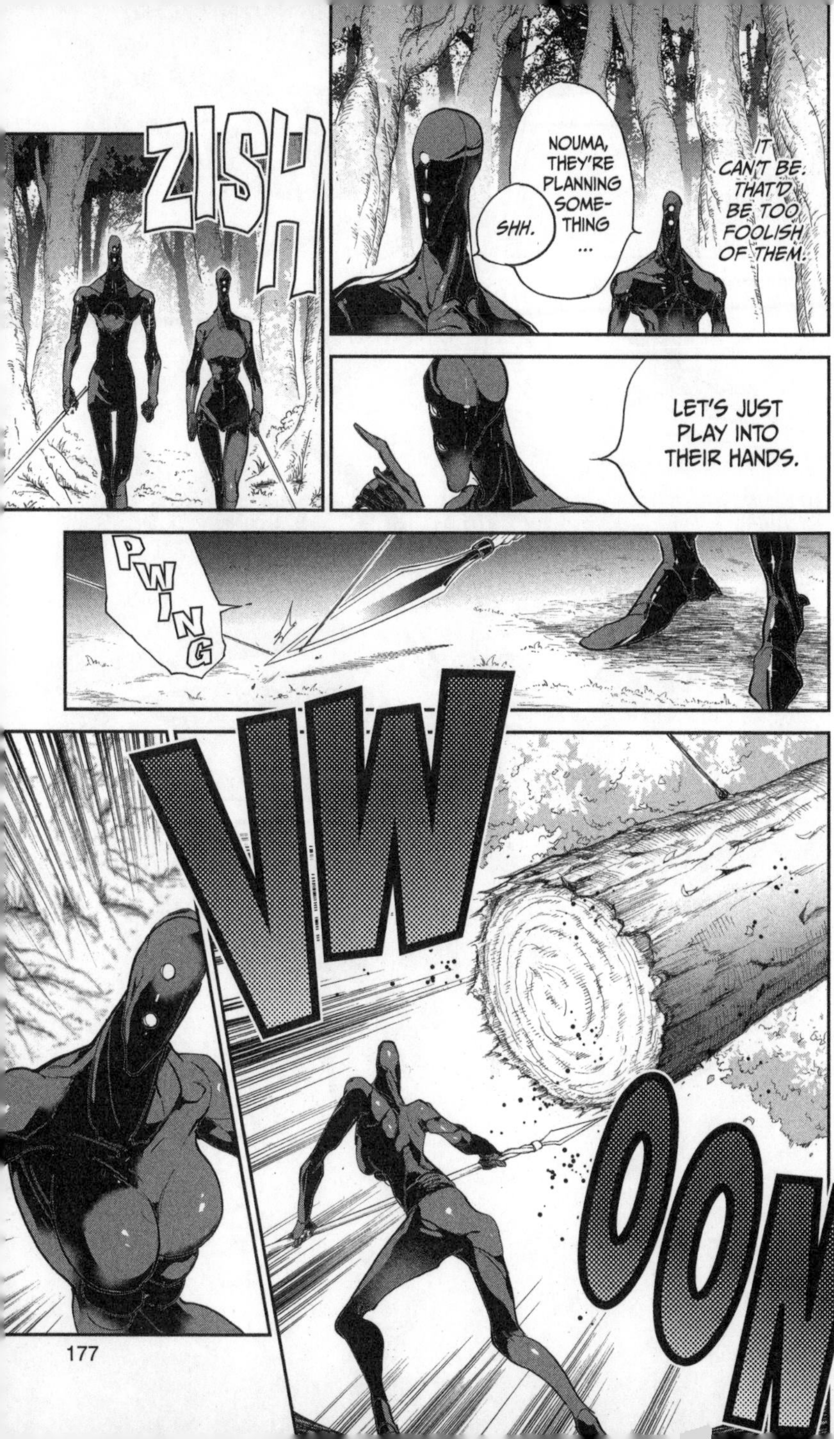
IT CAN'T BE. THAT'D BE TOO FOOLISH OF THEM.
NOUMA, THEY'RE PLANNING SOME-THING ...
SHH.
LET'S JUST PLAY INTO THEIR HANDS.
ZISH
PWING
VWOOON

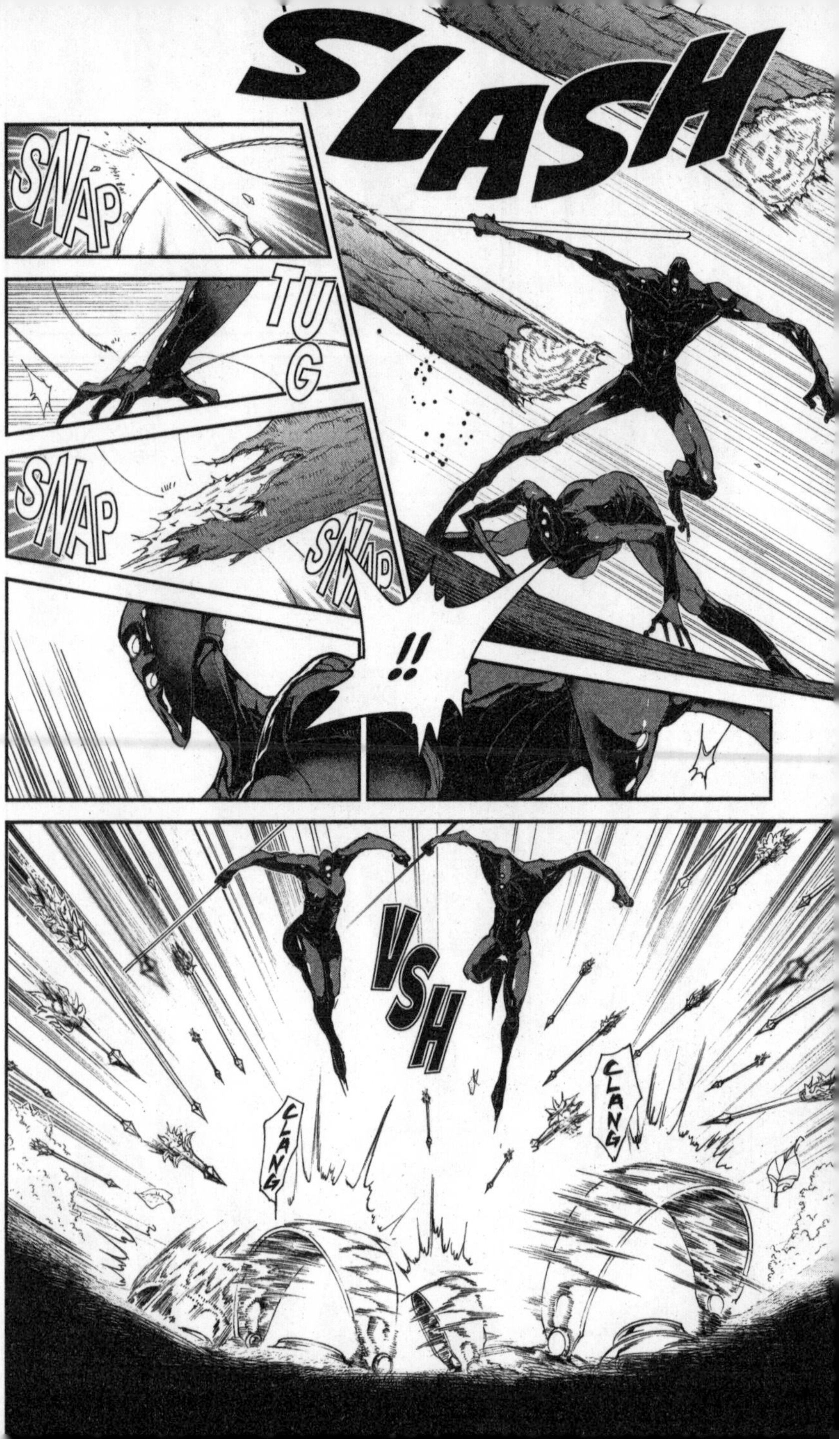
SLASH
SNAP
TUG
SNAP
SNAP
!!
VSH
CLANG
CLANG

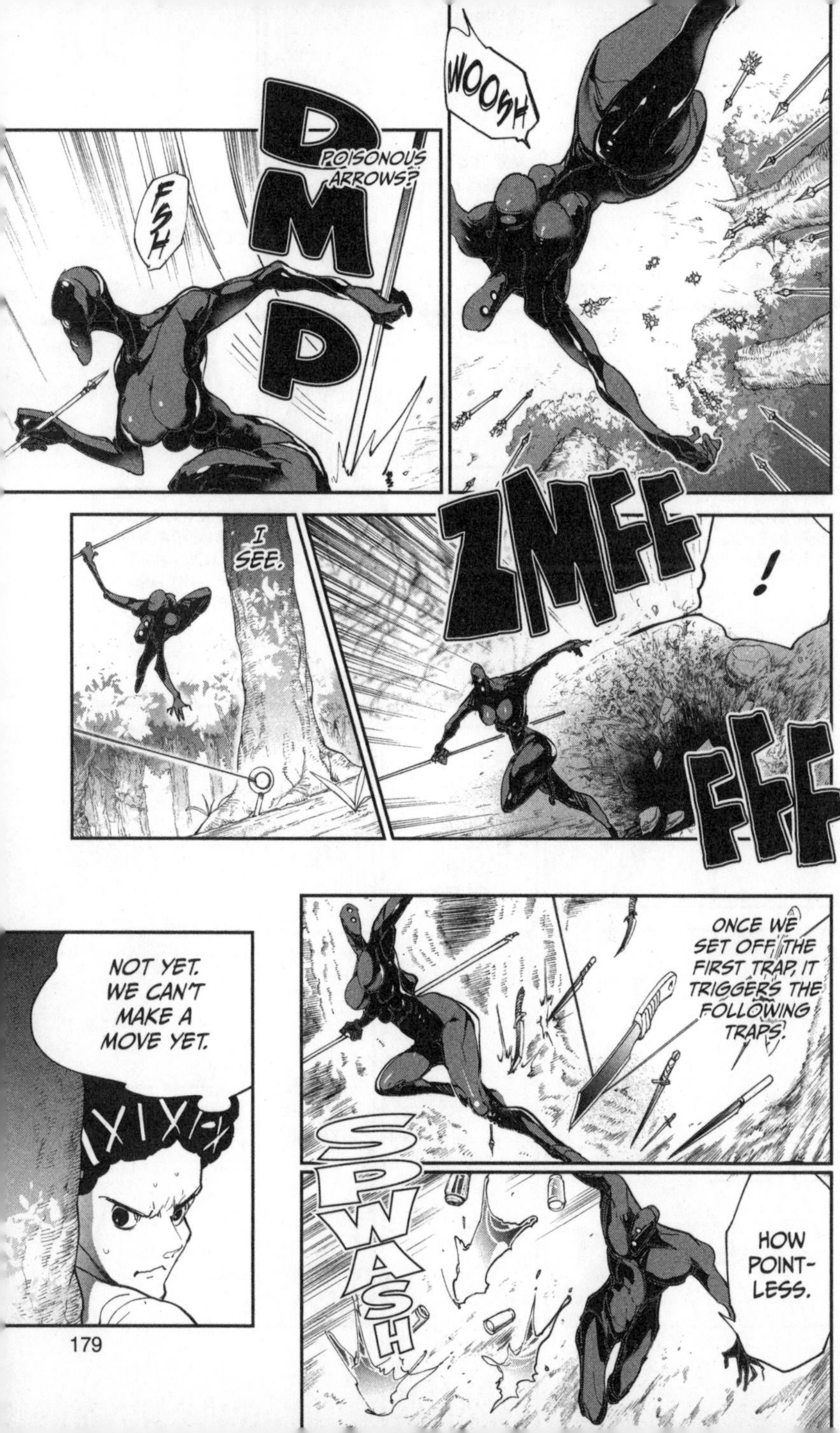
WOOSH
FSH
DMP
POISONOUS ARROWS?
ZMFF
!
FFF
I SEE.
ONCE WE SET OFF THE FIRST TRAP, IT TRIGGERS THE FOLLOWING TRAPS.
SPWASH
HOW POINT-LESS.
NOT YET. WE CAN'T MAKE A MOVE YET.

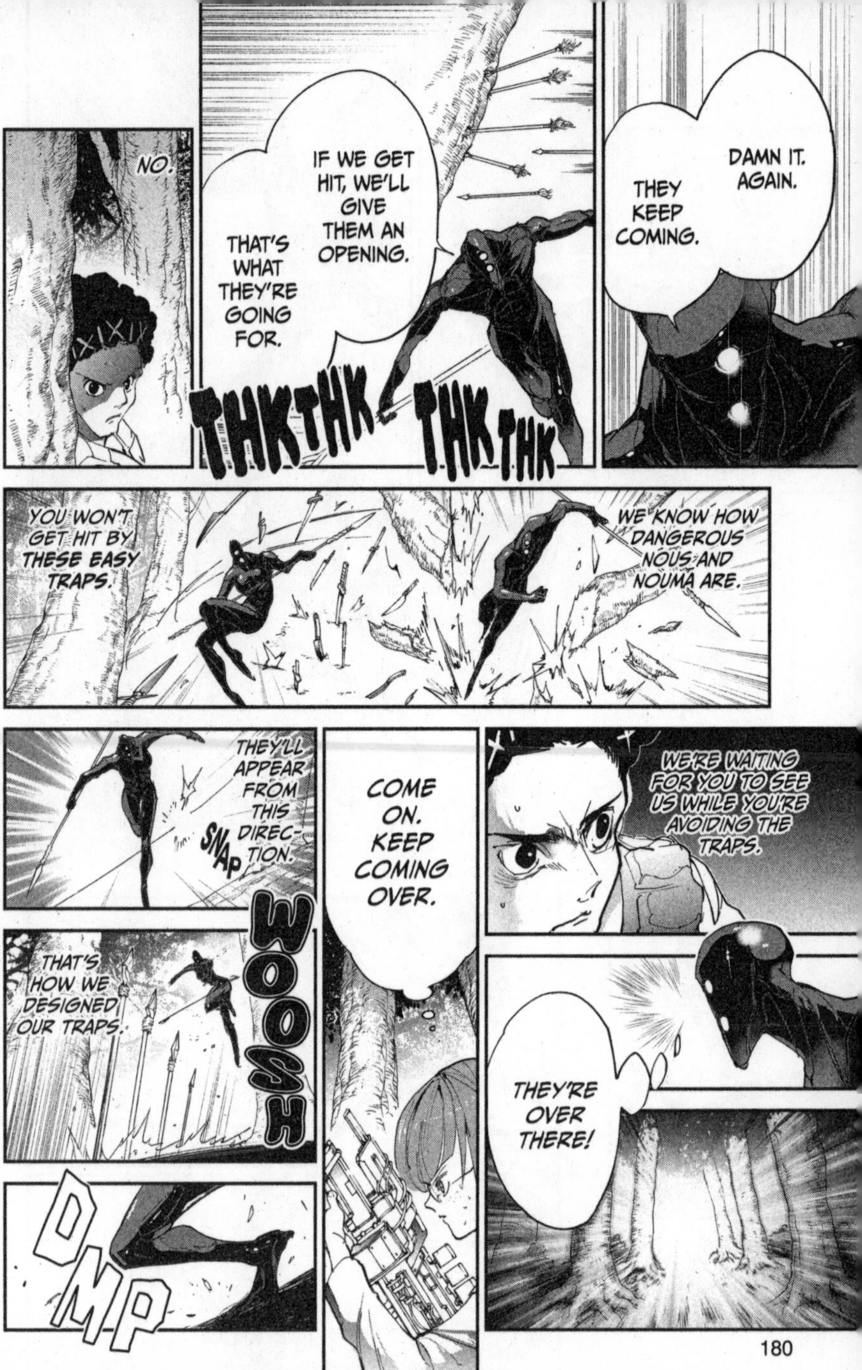
DAMN IT. AGAIN.
THEY KEEP COMING.
IF WE GET HIT, WE'LL GIVE THEM AN OPENING.
THAT'S WHAT THEY'RE GOING FOR.
THKTHK THK THK
NO.
WE KNOW HOW DANGEROUS NOUS AND NOUMA ARE.
YOU WON'T GET HIT BY THESE EASY TRAPS.
WE'RE WAITING FOR YOU TO SEE US WHILE YOU'RE AVOIDING THE TRAPS.
THEY'RE OVER THERE!
COME ON. KEEP COMING OVER.
THEY'LL APPEAR FROM THIS DIRECTION.
SNAP
WOOSH
THAT'S HOW WE DESIGNED OUR TRAPS.
DMP

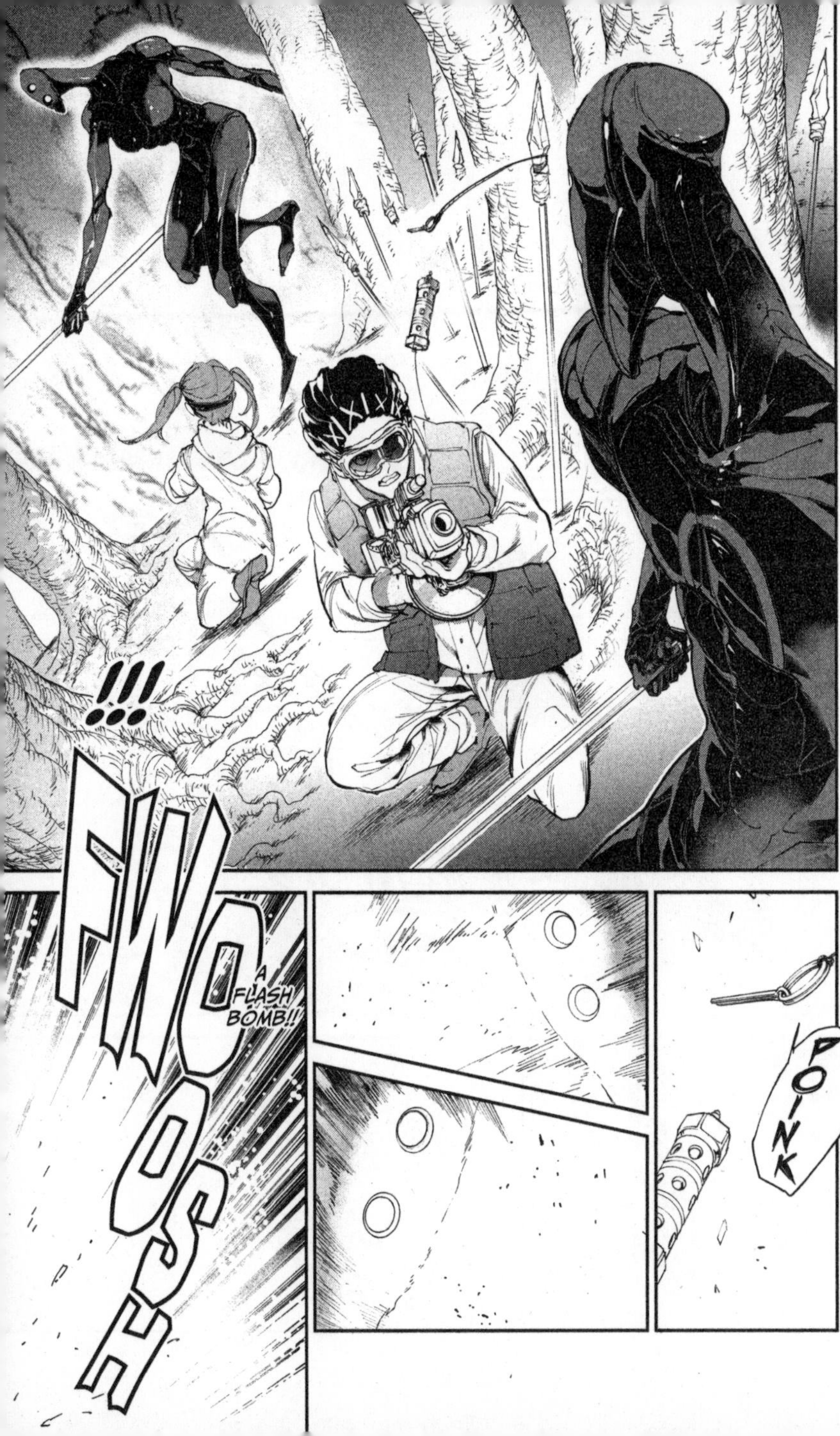
!!!
FWOOSH
A FLASH BOMB!!
POINK

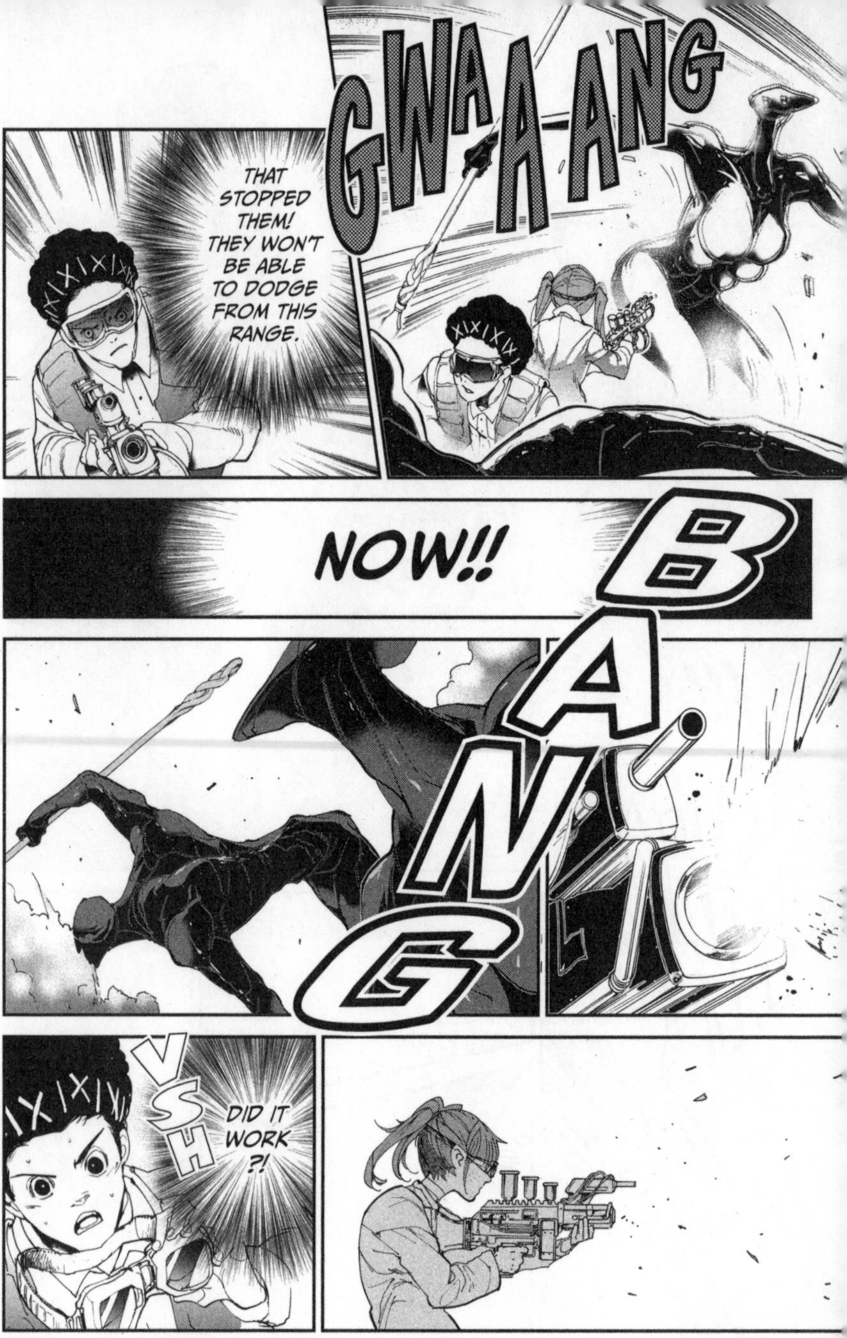
GWA-A-ANG
THAT STOPPED THEM! THEY WON'T BE ABLE TO DODGE FROM THIS RANGE.
NOW!!
BANG
VSH
DID IT WORK?!

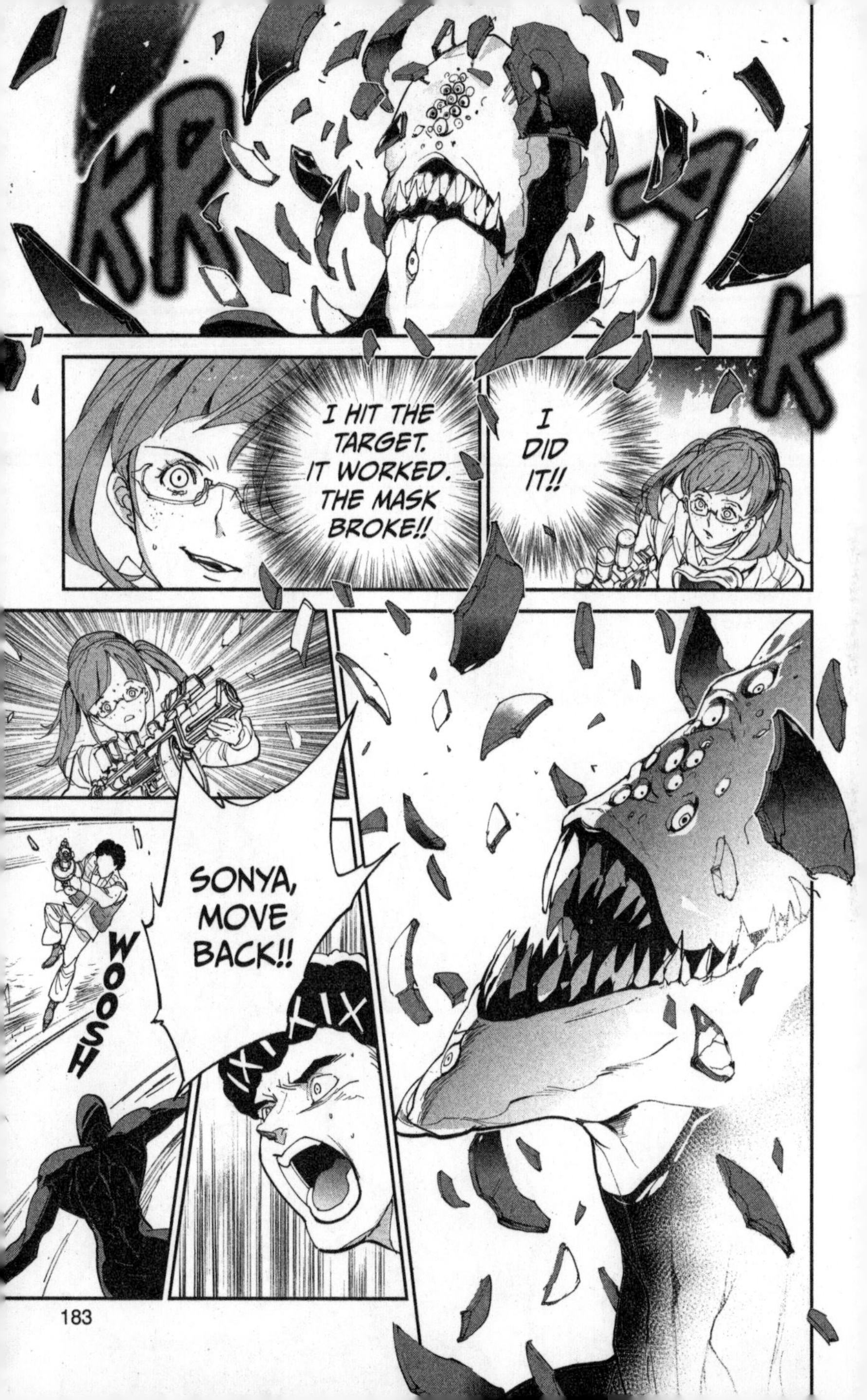
KRAK
I DID IT!!
I HIT THE TARGET. IT WORKED. THE MASK BROKE!!
SONYA, MOVE BACK!!
WOOSH

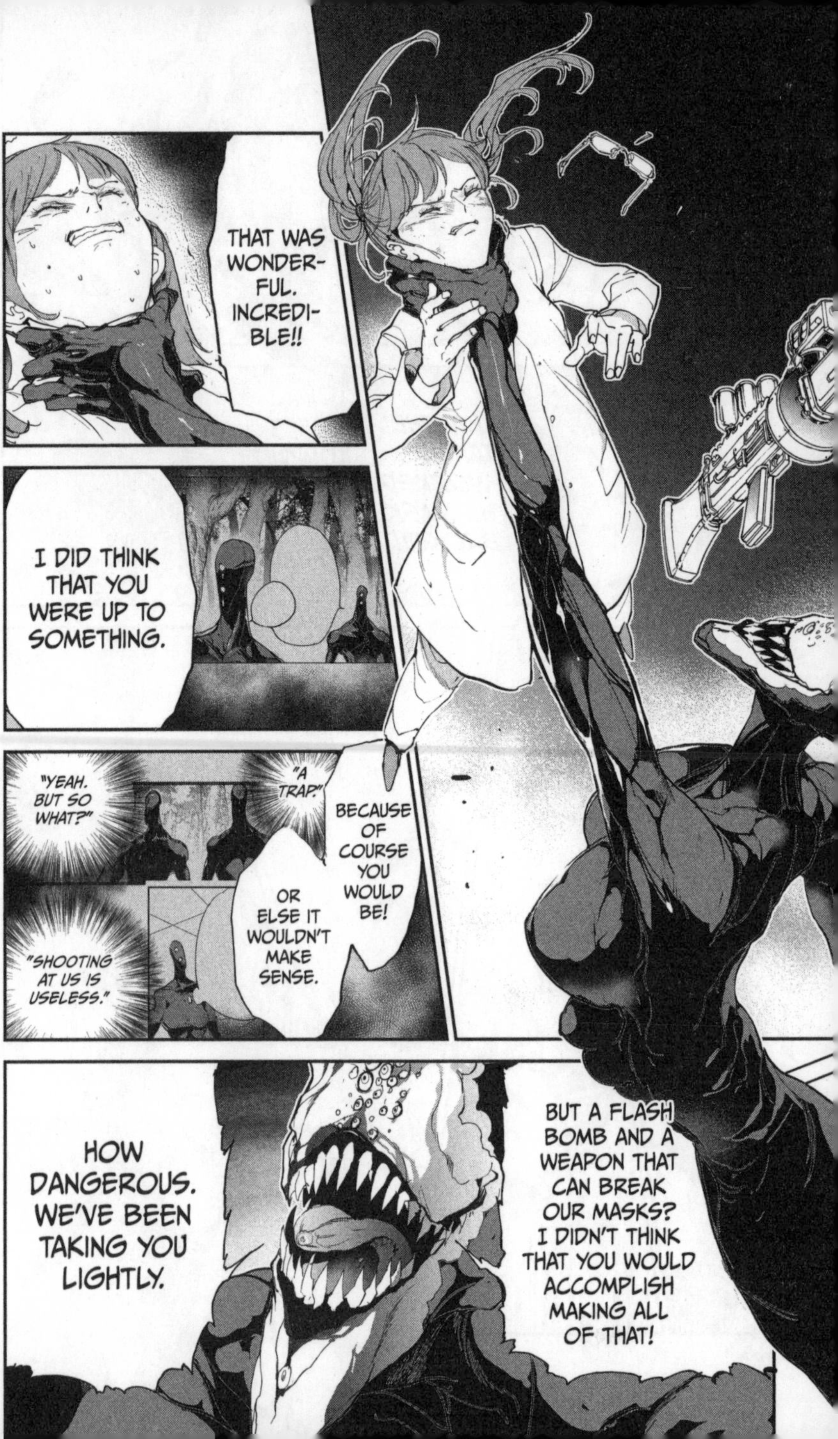
THAT WAS WONDERFUL. INCREDIBLE!!
I DID THINK THAT YOU WERE UP TO SOMETHING.
"A TRAP."
"YEAH. BUT SO WHAT?"
BECAUSE OF COURSE YOU WOULD BE!
OR ELSE IT WOULDN'T MAKE SENSE.
"SHOOTING AT US IS USELESS."
BUT A FLASH BOMB AND A WEAPON THAT CAN BREAK OUR MASKS? I DIDN'T THINK THAT YOU WOULD ACCOMPLISH MAKING ALL OF THAT!
HOW DANGEROUS. WE'VE BEEN TAKING YOU LIGHTLY.

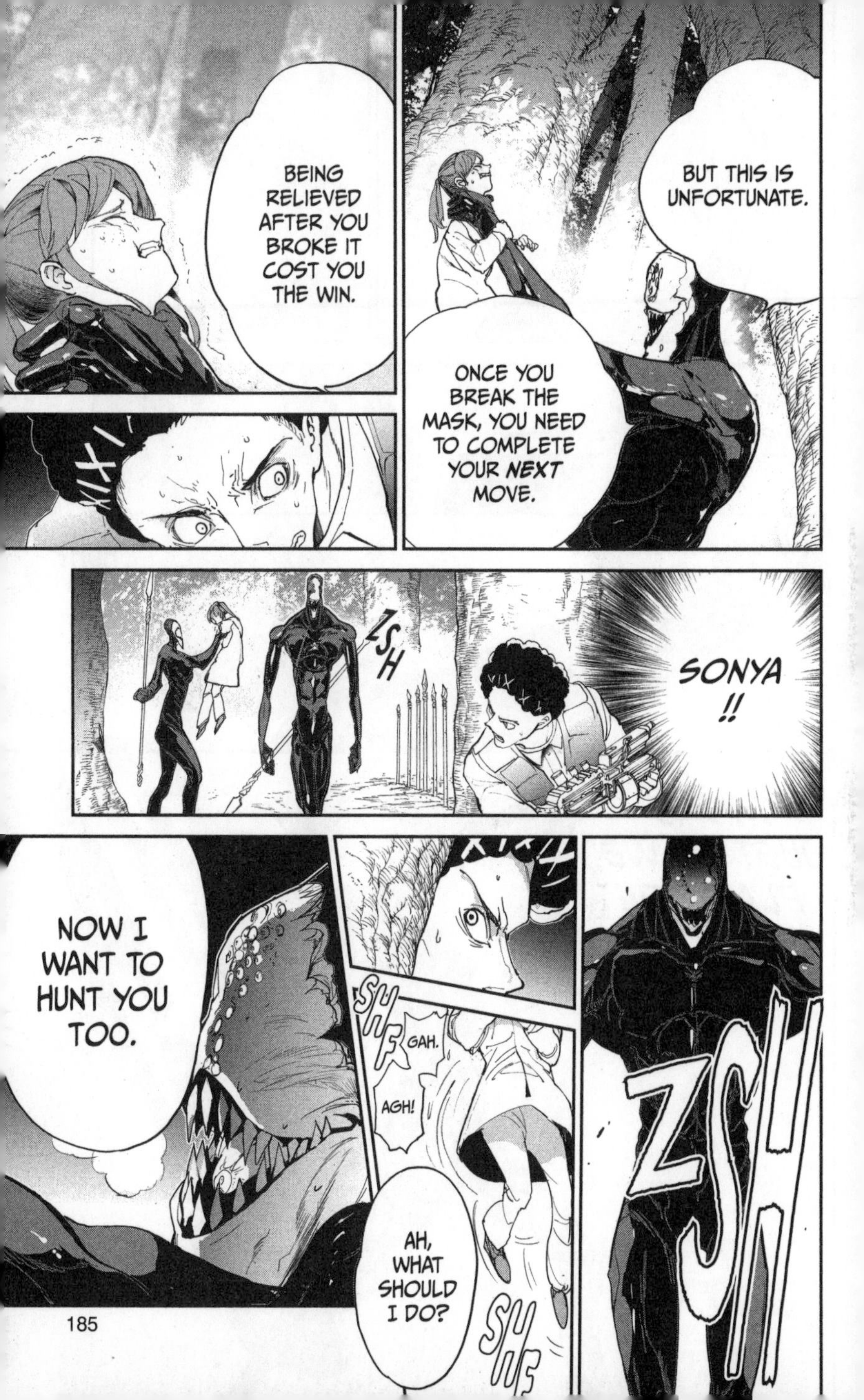
BUT THIS IS UNFORTUNATE.
ONCE YOU BREAK THE MASK, YOU NEED TO COMPLETE YOUR *NEXT* MOVE.
BEING RELIEVED AFTER YOU BROKE IT COST YOU THE WIN.
SONYA!!
ZSH
ZSH
SHF
GAH.
AGH!
AH, WHAT SHOULD I DO?
SHF
NOW I WANT TO HUNT YOU TOO.

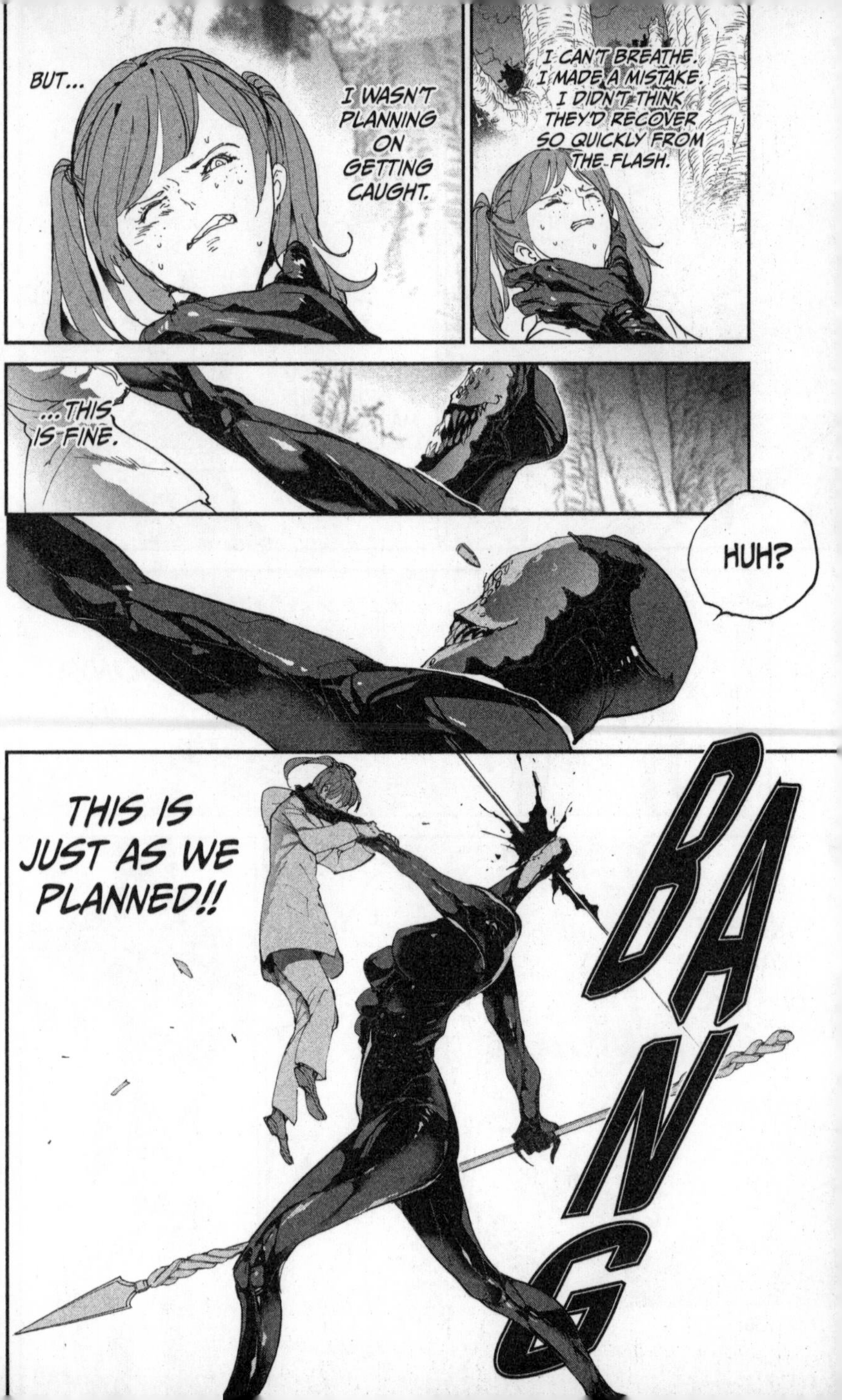
I CAN'T BREATHE. I MADE A MISTAKE. I DIDN'T THINK THEY'D RECOVER SO QUICKLY FROM THE FLASH.
I WASN'T PLANNING ON GETTING CAUGHT.
BUT...
...THIS IS FINE.
HUH?
BANG
THIS IS JUST AS WE PLANNED!!

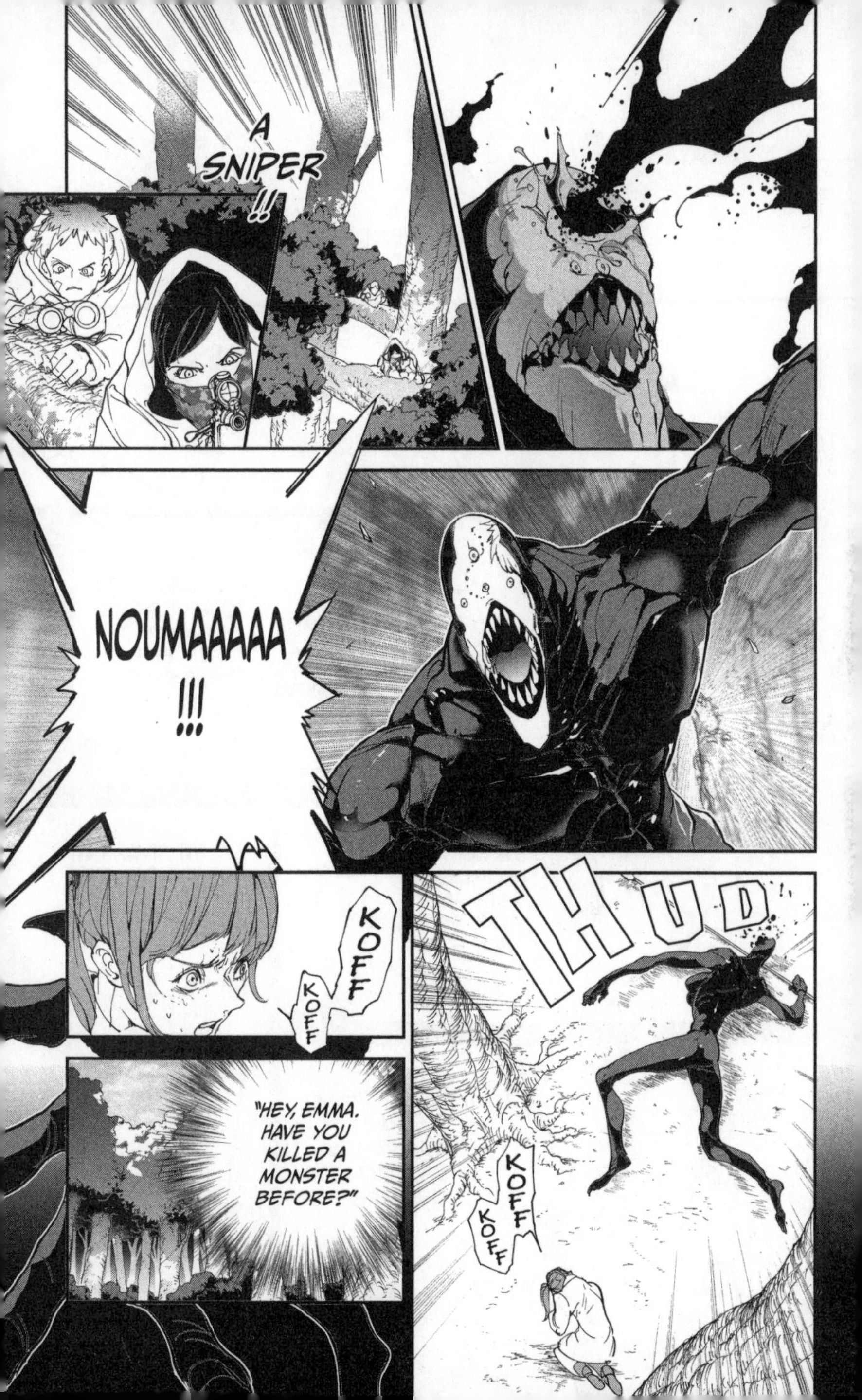
A SNIPER !!
NOUMAAAAA !!!
THUD
KOFF KOFF
KOFF KOFF
"HEY, EMMA. HAVE YOU KILLED A MONSTER BEFORE?"

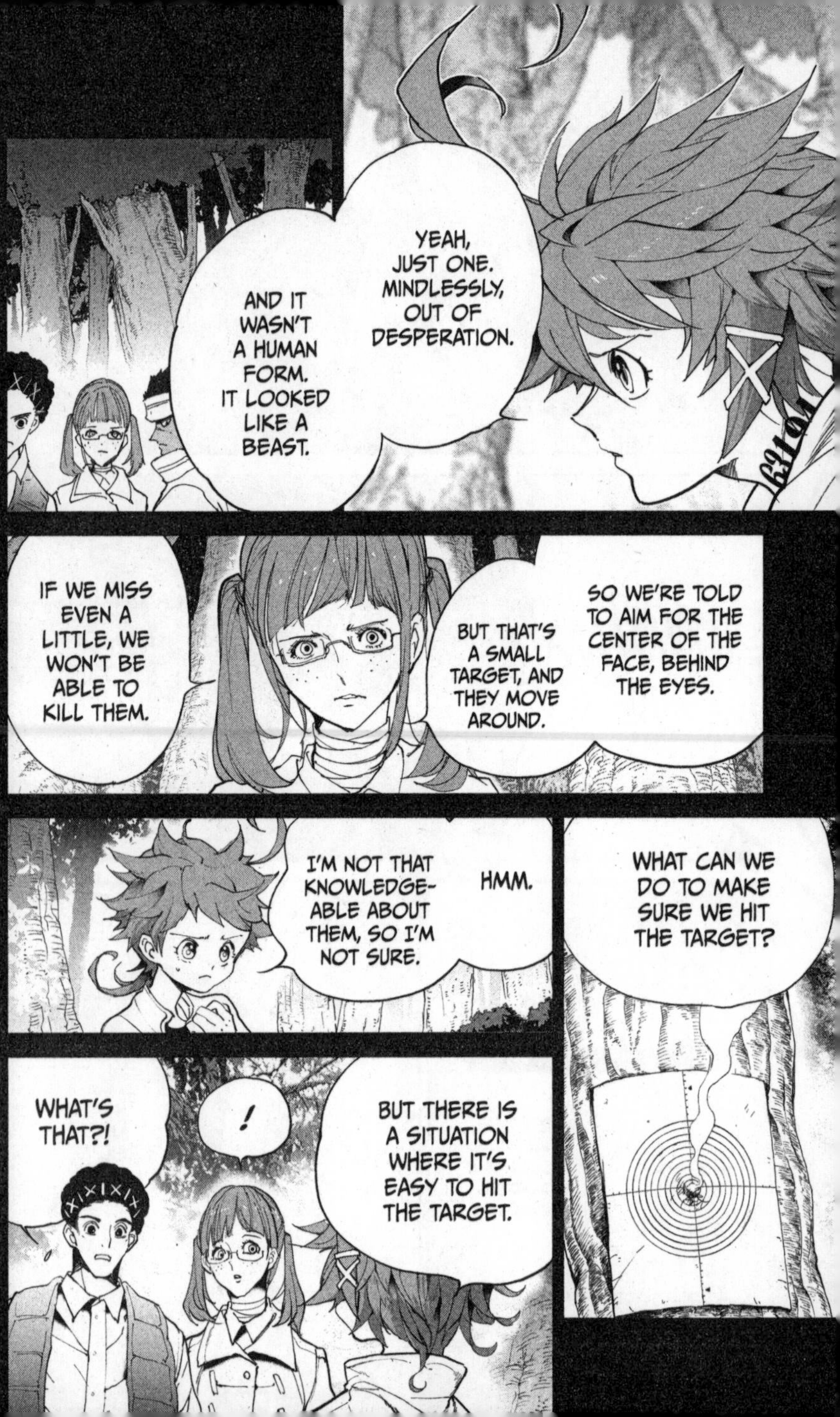
YEAH, JUST ONE. MINDLESSLY, OUT OF DESPERATION.
AND IT WASN'T A HUMAN FORM. IT LOOKED LIKE A BEAST.
SO WE'RE TOLD TO AIM FOR THE CENTER OF THE FACE, BEHIND THE EYES.
BUT THAT'S A SMALL TARGET, AND THEY MOVE AROUND.
IF WE MISS EVEN A LITTLE, WE WON'T BE ABLE TO KILL THEM.
WHAT CAN WE DO TO MAKE SURE WE HIT THE TARGET?
HMM.
I'M NOT THAT KNOWLEDGE-ABLE ABOUT THEM, SO I'M NOT SURE.
BUT THERE IS A SITUATION WHERE IT'S EASY TO HIT THE TARGET.
!
WHAT'S THAT?!

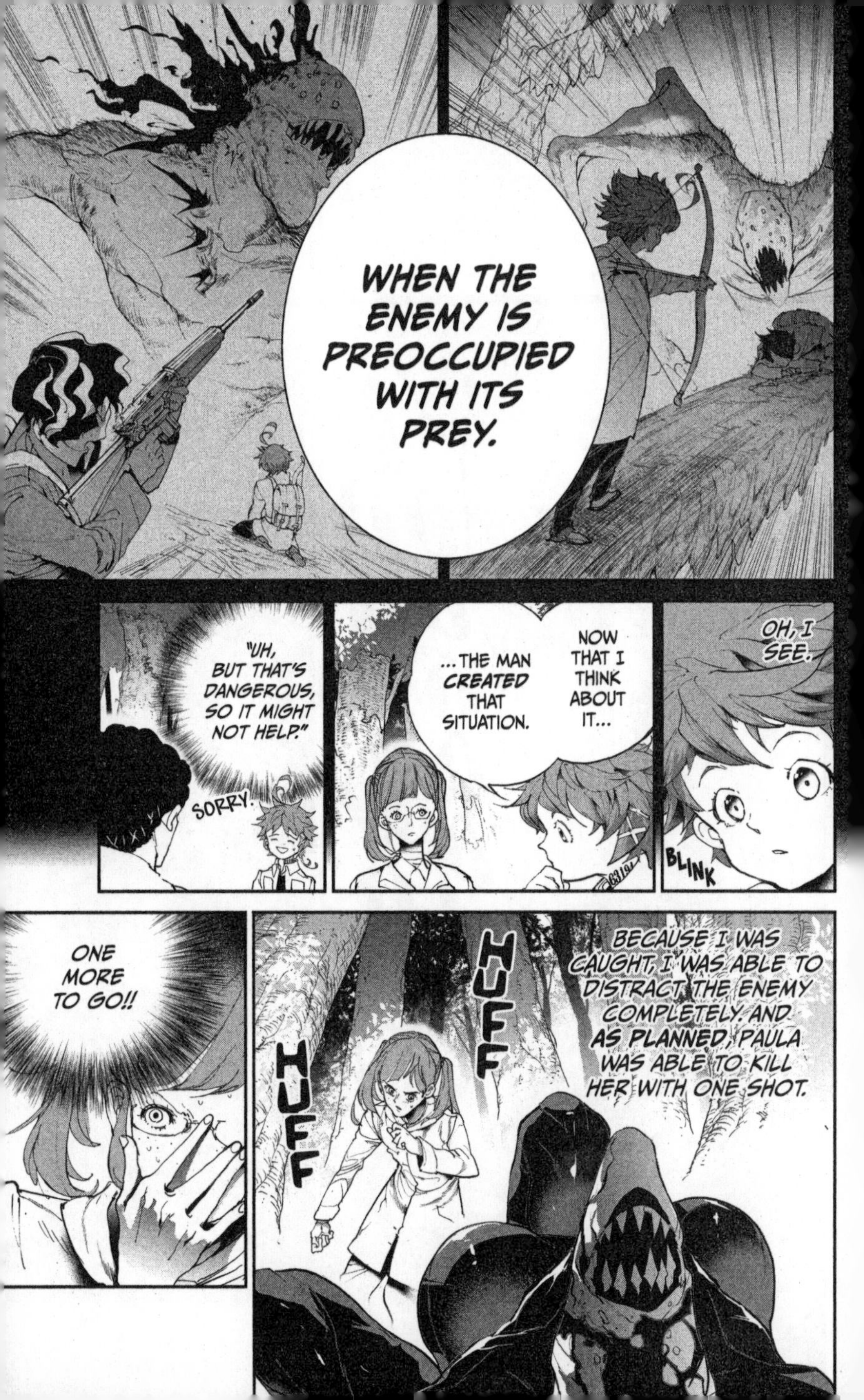
WHEN THE ENEMY IS PREOCCUPIED WITH ITS PREY.
OH, I SEE.
BLINK
NOW THAT I THINK ABOUT IT...
...THE MAN CREATED THAT SITUATION.
"UH, BUT THAT'S DANGEROUS, SO IT MIGHT NOT HELP."
SORRY.
BECAUSE I WAS CAUGHT, I WAS ABLE TO DISTRACT THE ENEMY COMPLETELY. AND AS PLANNED, PAULA WAS ABLE TO KILL HER WITH ONE SHOT.
HUFF
HUFF
ONE MORE TO GO!!

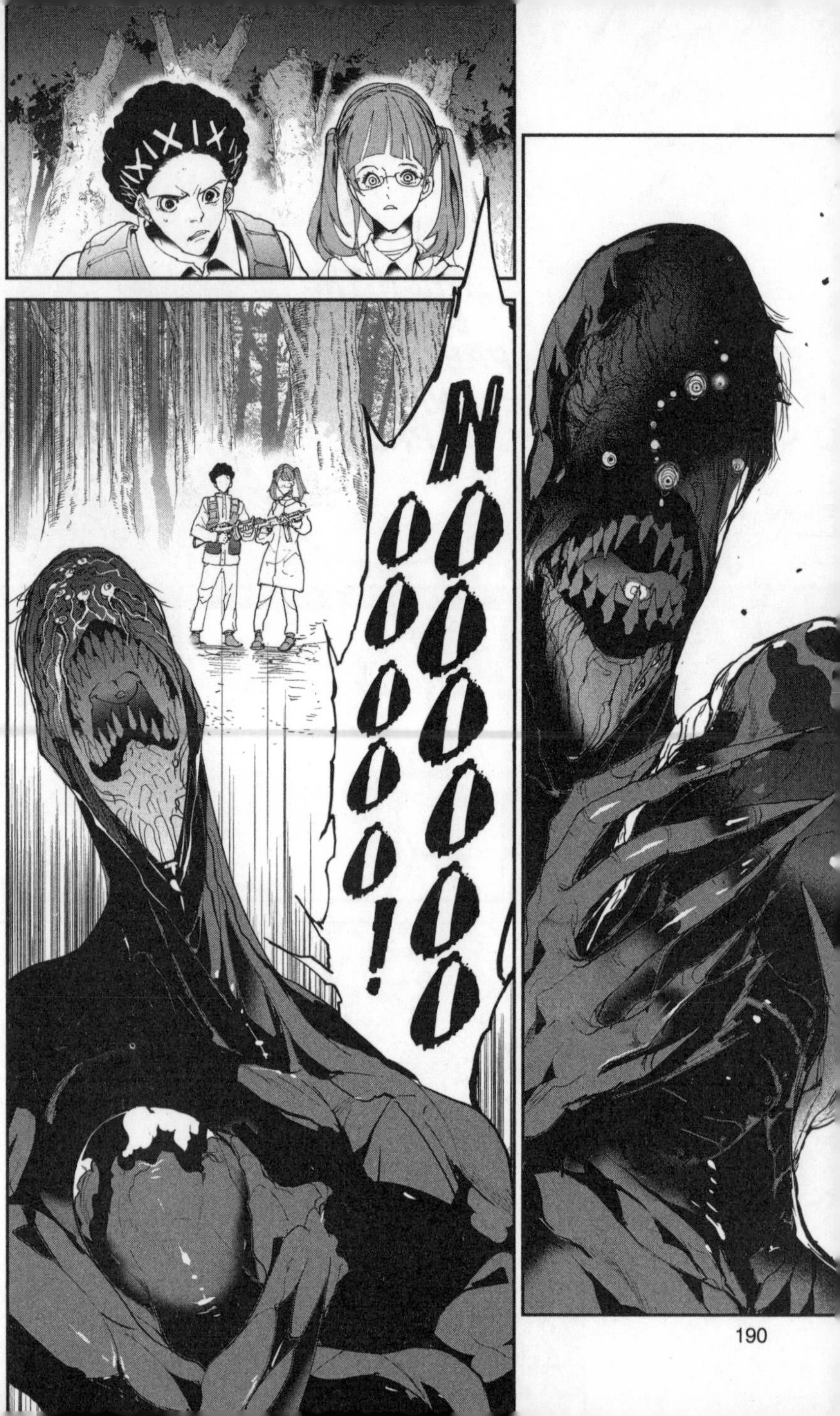
NOOOOOOOOOOO!

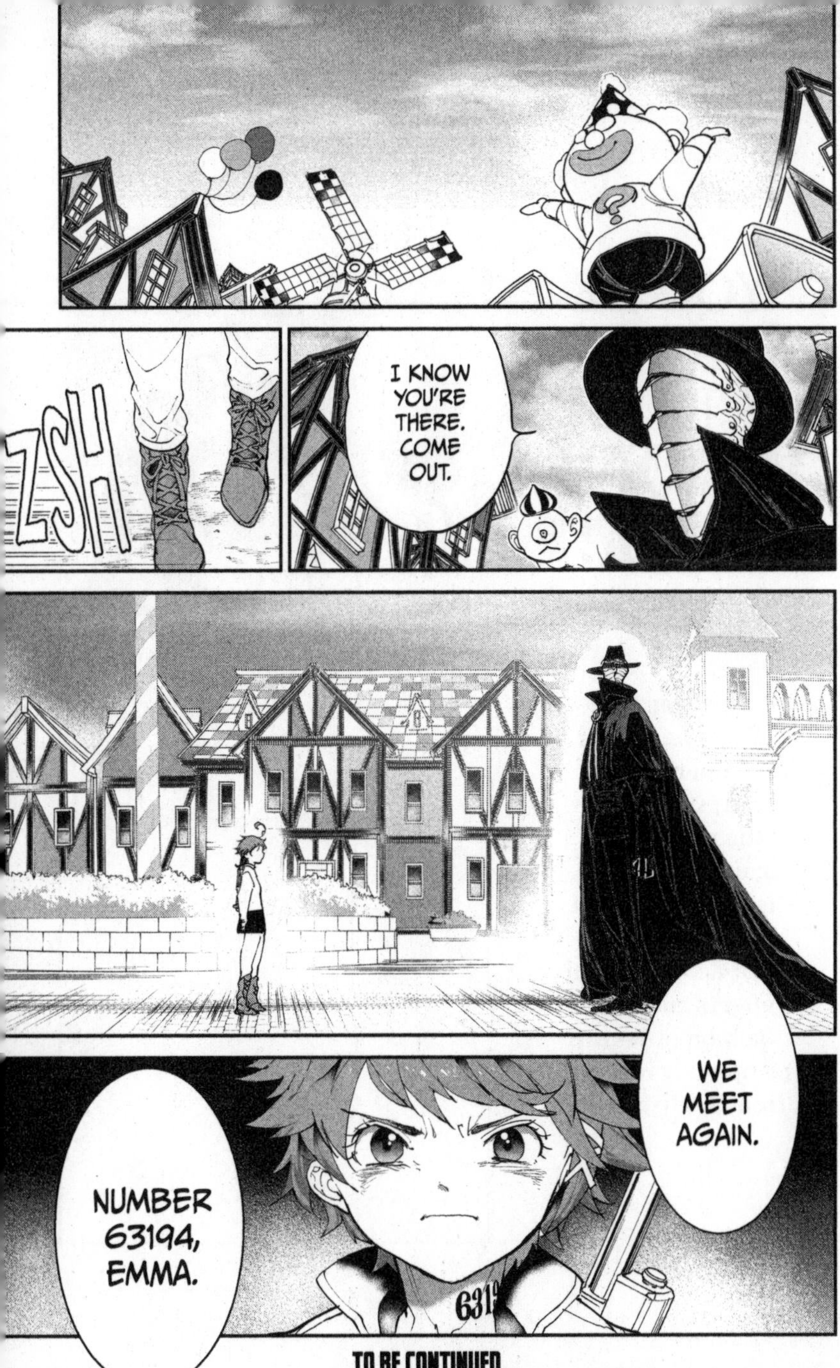
I KNOW YOU'RE THERE. COME OUT.
ZSH
WE MEET AGAIN.
NUMBER 63194, EMMA.

TO BE CONTINUED...

YOU'RE READING THE **WRONG WAY!**

The Promised Neverland reads from right to left, starting in the upper-right corner. Japanese is read from right to left, meaning that action, sound effects and word-balloon order are completely reversed from English order.

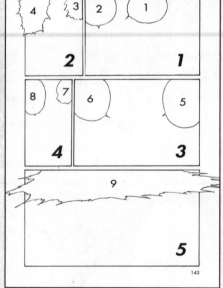